D0075828

Copyright © 1991 by Princeton University Press
Published by Princeton University Press, 41 William Street,
Princeton, New Jersey 08540
In the United Kingdom: Princeton University Press, Oxford

ALL RIGHTS RESERVED

Library of Congress Cataloging-in-Publication Data

Mendelssohn and his world / edited by R. Larry Todd.
p.   cm.
Includes bibliographical references and index.
ISBN 0-691-09143-9 (CL) — ISBN 0-691-02715-3 (PB)
1. Mendelssohn-Bartholdy, Felix, 1809–1847. I. Todd, R. Larry.
ML410.M5M47   1991   780'.92—dc20   [B]   91-16124

This book has been composed in Linotron Baskerville

Princeton University Press books are printed on acid-free paper,
and meet the guidelines for permanence and durability of the
Committee on Production Guidelines for Book Longevity of the
Council on Library Resources

Printed in the United States of America by Princeton University Press,
Princeton, New Jersey

10 9 8 7 6 5 4 3 2 1

10 9 8 7 6 5 4 3 2 1
(Pbk.)

Designed by Laury A. Egan

MENDELSSOHN
AND HIS WORLD

·

EDITED BY
R. LARRY TODD

PRINCETON UNIVERSITY PRESS

MENDELSSOHN

AND HIS WORLD

91005336

Contents

CONTENTS

CONTENTS

Preface

To speak of a twentieth-century Mendelssohn revival, Carl Dahlhaus observed as recently as 1974, would be a gross exaggeration.[1] At that time, Mendelssohn was still chiefly remembered as the youthful composer of the Octet and the *Midsummer Night's Dream* Overture, as a facile genius whose art neither plumbed the profound depths of Beethoven's music nor adequately anticipated the mythic-poetic dimensions of Wagner's music dramas. As we approach the 150th anniversary of Mendelssohn's death (1997), the broader view continues to encourage fresh reassessments of the composer's reception: to dismiss much of his music as superficial, as overly sentimental, is actually to reinforce and perpetuate a tangled part of the Mendelssohn critical reception that became established largely in the latter part of the nineteenth century and entrenched in the first part of the twentieth.

In 1850, of course, Richard Wagner had launched a scurrilous anti-Semitic attack on Mendelssohn in his "Das Judenthum in der Musik," which first appeared anonymously in the pages of the *Neue Zeitschrift für Musik*, the journal founded in 1834 and edited, until 1845, by Mendelssohn's friend and staunch admirer, Robert Schumann. By 1875, Friedrich Niecks took up his pen to defend Mendelssohn's music; but while he extolled the composer's elevation and mastery of the fanciful as an aesthetic category, Niecks had to admit that "the serene beauty of Mendelssohn's music has to most of us not the same charm as the rugged energy, the subtle thoughtfulness and morbid world-weariness of other composers."[2] During the 1880s, in a reaction against Victorian mores, George Bernard Shaw decried Mendelssohn's "kid-glove gentility, his conventional sentimentality, and his despicable oratorio mongering."[3] And, of course, Mendelssohn's place in history suffered a final blow during the 1930s, when the Nazis destroyed his statue in Leipzig and banned his music.[4]

This decline in Mendelssohn's stature contrasted sharply with the esteem he actually enjoyed during his lifetime. Indeed, during the 1830s and 1840s Mendelssohn arguably stood at the forefront of musical culture in Germany and England. What is more, after his death in 1847 at the age of thirty-eight, his memory was celebrated by a kind of hero worship that expressed itself probably most ardently in

Elizabeth Sheppard's fictional-historical romance *Charles Auchester*, which appeared in England in 1853 and offered a thinly veiled allusion to the idealized Mendelssohn in the character Seraphael. No doubt, too, the practice of devising fanciful titles and texts for Mendelssohn's textless *Lieder ohne Worte* (*Songs without Words*), a practice increasingly common after his death, added layer upon layer of that "conventional sentimentality" to which Shaw objected. To a large degree, this posthumous idealization of Mendelssohn encouraged a counterreaction, and so the view of Mendelssohn's music as overly sentimental—as, for example, of the *Songs without Words* as at best insipid, at worst saccharine creations, in contrast to Robert Schumann's view of them as exquisitely refined miniatures—took hold.

Now, in the closing years of the twentieth century, Mendelssohn scholarship shows healthy signs of revival. The "new image" of the composer proposed by Eric Werner in 1963 and the Mendelssohn "problem" articulated by Carl Dahlhaus in 1974 now engage the attention of numerous scholars approaching Mendelssohn's historical position from a variety of perspectives. The present volume, inspired by the Mendelssohn Music Festival held at Bard College, Annandale-on-Hudson, New York, in August 1991, seeks to explore various facets of the composer's life and work through several newly contributed essays, through a selection of primary sources, and through a sampling of nineteenth-century critical views.

In part I, eight essays address Mendelssohn's reception and his circle (Botstein, Little, and Reich), his critical approach to composition (Todd), and such works as the oratorio *Elijah*, the *Italian* Symphony and selected concert overtures, the anthem setting of Psalm 13, op. 96, and the music to Sophocles' *Antigone* (Staehelin, Spies, Brodbeck, and Steinberg). In part II, six relatively little known nineteenth-century memoirs of Mendelssohn provide enriched views of his activities as a composer, pianist, conductor, teacher, and man of letters. The authors include J. C. Lobe, who recorded notes of conversations he had with Mendelssohn in Leipzig; Adolf Bernhard Marx, the Berlin music critic and composer who was a close friend of Mendelssohn during the 1820s and 1830s; Julius Schubring, who prepared the librettos for Mendelssohn's oratorios *St. Paul* and *Elijah*; Charles Edward Horsley, an English musician who studied with Mendelssohn in Leipzig; F. Max Müller, the son of the poet Wilhelm Müller; and Ernst Rudorff, whose mother, Betty Pistor, was the secret dedicatée of Mendelssohn's String Quartet in E♭ major, op. 12. Of these memoirs, the pages from Ernst Rudorff's *Aus den Tagen der Romantik*, translated and edited by Nancy Reich, appear for the first time, while the Lobe and Marx memoirs appear here in translations by Susan Gillespie for the first time.

Mendelssohn was a prolific letter-writer whose correspondence began to be gathered into several volumes by his friends and relatives during the second part of the nineteenth century. (Regrettably, these early collections often employed uncritical editorial methods, so that they must be used with caution; a complete critical edition of Mendelssohn's letters remains a fundamental desideratum in Mendelssohn research.) Part III offers a selection of letters—here translated for the first time by Susan Gillespie—including portions of Mendelssohn's correspondence with Wilhelm von Boguslawski, who turned to Mendelssohn for advice about composition, and Aloys Fuchs, with whom Mendelssohn exchanged musical autographs. Finally, part IV contains several examples of nineteenth-century Mendelssohn criticism and reception from about 1840 to 1880, with viewpoints both pro and con. The selections from Heinrich Heine were chosen and prepared by Leon Botstein. The articles by Brendel, Jahn, and von Bülow, translated by Susan Gillespie, appear in English for the first time.

R.L.T.

MARCH 1991

NOTES

1. *Das Problem Mendelssohn*, ed. Carl Dahlhaus (Regensburg, 1974), "Vorwort."

2. See p. 386.

3. *London Music in 1888–1889 as Heard by Corno di Bassetto (Later Known as Bernard Shaw) with Some Further Autobiographical Particulars* (London, 1937; 3d ed., 1950), pp. 68ff.

4. For a consideration of "Mendelssohn and Posterity," see Eric Werner, *Mendelssohn: A New Image of the Composer and His Age* (New York, 1963), pp. 503–23.

Acknowledgments

Without the assistance of many individuals the present volume would not have come to full fruition. The idea for a Mendelssohn festival originated with Leon Botstein, who, with the support of the Andrew W. Mellon Foundation, founded the Bard Music Festival in 1990 as a means of exploring the music of major composers by placing it in the context of the work of their contemporaries. At Bard College, Susan Gillespie deserves a special acknowledgment: in remarkably short order, with unwavering attention to detail and characteristic stylistic grace, she rendered into English a sizeable amount of German prose. At Princeton University Press, Elizabeth Powers offered advice and encouragement at every turn and considerably smoothed the production process. I am grateful as well to members of the staff of the Press, including Lauren Oppenheim and Linda Truilo, for their expertise in the copy editing and related matters. At Duke University I owe a special debt to my research assistant, J. Michael Cooper, Mendelssohnian extraordinaire, who brought his remarkable energies to bear on the manuscript in any number of ways and diligently assisted in the often intractable editing of the nineteenth-century sources in parts II, III, and IV. Isabelle Bélance-Zank and Stephen Zank, also of Duke University, carefully proofread the volume in its later stages. Finally, we are indebted to Peter Ward Jones of the Bodleian Library, Oxford, and to the Rudorff-Archiv for permission to include illustrative material and to publish for the first time the deleted materials from Ernst Rudorff's *Aus den Tagen der Romantik,* and to Voggenreiter Verlag for permission to translate Martin Staehelin's article on *Elijah.*

R.L.T.

NOTE

As this volume went to press, word was received of the passing of Felix Gilbert, Emeritus Professor of History at Princeton, and a descendant of Felix Mendelssohn-Bartholdy. In 1975, Professor Gilbert edited a widely acclaimed volume of letters of the Mendelssohn family, *Bankiers, Künstler und Gelehrte: unveröffentlichte Briefe der Familie Mendelssohn aus dem 19. Jahrhundert* (Tübingen, 1975). This volume is dedicated to his memory.

MENDELSSOHN

AND HIS WORLD

PART

· I ·

ESSAYS

The Aesthetics of Assimilation and Affirmation: Reconstructing the Career of Felix Mendelssohn

LEON BOTSTEIN

The Mendelssohn Problem

Since the end of World War II, attempts to restore the stature of Felix Mendelssohn and bring more of his music onto the concert stage have become increasingly frequent. Among the reasons for this phenomenon is the postwar German guilt about the Nazis who sought to desecrate Mendelssohn's memory, suppress his music, and falsify his role in history in accordance with theories concerning race and art.[1] The postwar reaction to the Nazi campaign was significant, considering the extent of collusion by the musicological community in these efforts.[2] Interest in Mendelssohn since 1945 has spurred significant research and discoveries, which in turn have helped to strengthen Mendelssohn's reputation, particularly in view of the vitality and novelty of the early musical works that have entered the repertoire.

The Nazi interpretation of Mendelssohn was not exactly novel. It culminated a long history of antipathy, particularly in Germany. Even though some contemporaries, including Schumann and Berlioz, maintained certain doubts about much of Mendelssohn's output, the anti-Mendelssohn campaign began in earnest in 1850 with the publication of Wagner's essay "Judaism in Music."[3] The success of the contemptuous Wagnerian view of Mendelssohn the man, his music, and its social and cultural influence was profound. Wagner's aesthetics were framed in explicit opposition to Mendelssohn. Wagner even succeeded in obscuring the extent to which he, as a composer, was indebted to Mendelssohn's musical work.

The triumph of Wagnerianism by the end of the century created a barrier to wide-ranging appreciation of Mendelssohn's music. By the early twentieth century, much of the music had vanished from the repertory. Some—the piano music in particular—had been relegated to the category of well-written music adequate for amateur performance but lacking in profundity. The concert canon circa 1900 included a few overtures, the Third and Fourth Symphonies, the Octet, and the E-minor Violin Concerto. The programs conducted by Gustav Mahler in his career from 1870 to 1911 and performed by the Rosé Quartet in the years 1883–1932 exemplify this phenomenon.[4]

The transformation of aesthetic taste during the second half of the nineteenth century lent Mendelssohn's music an undeserved and pejorative symbolic meaning. After the 1880s, in England, Germany, and also America, the tenets of cultural modernism were linked to a generational revolt and a rejection of middle-class conceits of culture and art.[5] This triggered an aversion to Mendelssohn. His music, in part because of its affectionate refinement and the relative ease of performance and comprehension, had come to signify glib amateur music making—a facile consumption of an art of optimism by educated urban classes, an art that neither questioned nor resisted the presumed smugness of bourgeois aesthetic and moral values. *Elijah* and *St. Paul* and the *Songs without Words*, for example, were viewed as emblematic of a vacuous and affirmative tradition of music making, undertaken thoughtlessly within a hypocritical and exploitative world. George Bernard Shaw's 1889 denigration of Mendelssohn as "not in the foremost rank of composers" must be seen in the context of cultural politics of an era in which George Grove's enthusiasm can be placed at the opposite end of the spectrum. Shaw decried Mendelssohn's "kid-glove gentility, his conventional sentimentality, and his despicable oratorio mongering." At Mendelssohn's best, Shaw argued, his music was merely touching, tender, and refined. Even George Grove accepted the idea that cheerfulness and the absence of any hints of "misery and sorrow" characterized Mendelssohn's achievement. After all, Grove wrote, "surely there is enough of conflict and violence in life and in art. When we want to be unhappy we can turn to others. It is well in these agitated modern days to be able to point to one perfectly balanced nature . . . whose music . . . is at once manly and refined, clever and pure, brilliant and solid."[6]

The failure to penetrate the surface of Mendelssohn on the part of these notable English advocates and detractors can be compared with Nietzsche's oft-cited but misconstrued comment about Mendelssohn in the eighth section of *Beyond Good and Evil* (1886). With characteristic irony, Nietzsche mirrored dialectically why Mendelssohn "was so quickly forgotten," as well as why Mendelssohn's fate was undeserved. Nietzsche, himself an accomplished musical amateur, in his anti-Wagnerian phase recognized the dimensions of Mendelssohn's unique greatness within musical romanticism overlooked by most of Nietzsche's contemporaries. For Nietzsche, the lightness, elegance, and purity of Mendelssohn's music made him the beautiful "interlude" (*Zwischenfall*) in German music—better than Weber, early Wagner, Marschner, and others—which was why his music was so quickly honored and then so rapidly abandoned. In the same section, Nietzsche took care to link—in a positive sense—Mendelssohn with Beethoven, whom he declared had been a "passing occurrence" (*Zwischen-Begebniss*) in music history.[7]

Most of Mendelssohn's music, unlike that of his contemporaries (Schumann or Chopin), still fails to elicit loyalty from critics and listeners. Philip Radcliffe and Eric Werner published Mendelssohn biographies in 1954 and 1963 respectively. Although these books were overt attempts to make a new case for the composer, both writers were shockingly brutal in their criticism of much of the composer's music. They echoed the commonplace charge of sentimentality, superficiality, excessive regularity, weakness of invention, and sheer thinness. Their criticisms were applied even to such works as *St. Paul*, the D-minor Piano Concerto, and the *Lobgesang* Symphony-cantata (*Hymn of Praise*).[8]

It is as if the aesthetic of Wagnerian criticism, shorn of its evident political and racist content, still reigns. There is perhaps no composer in the nineteenth and twentieth centuries whose premortem reputation and popularity have undergone such difficulty in being restored postmortem.[9] A locus classicus of this overhang of Wagnerian and post-Wagnerian musical expectations—without a crude political agenda—are Ludwig Wittgenstein's comments on Mendelssohn. Wittgenstein's musical tastes, despite their somewhat rigid conservative antimodernisms, reflected a fine and discriminating training not untypical of the Viennese fin de siècle. In notes written during the 1930s, Wittgenstein remarked that for him Mendelssohn did "half rigorously" what Brahms did completely. Mendelssohn, just a "reproductive" artist, lacked the ability to write a "courageous melody." He produced no music "that is hard to understand." Mendelssohn was "like a man who is only jolly when the people he is with are jolly anyway, or like one who is only good when he is surrounded by good men; he does not have the integrity of a tree which stands firmly in its place whatever may be going on around it."[10] Wittgenstein concluded this observation with the confession "I too am like that and am attracted to being so."

Perhaps Wittgenstein (ironically, like Mendelssohn, the scion of a prominent, highly educated and wealthy family of Jewish origin) was right. If so, then an analogy between the two only heightens our need to locate Mendelssohn's greatness, as we already have that of Wittgenstein. Is the capacity to connect with one's proximate public necessarily a sign of superficiality? Perhaps the failures Wittgenstein attributed to Mendelssohn and himself are residues of Wagnerian notions, internalized by Wittgenstein and still broadly accepted as normative sixty years later.

The distinction between the individual with a fixed inner integrity (a rooted tree) and one who meets the expectations of those around him reflects the claim that in order to be great the artist is obliged to stand firmly and bravely apart from his audience somehow. Discordance between one's work and one's audience, a degree of difficulty in understanding on the part of the audience, and the derivation of inspiration from some original, individualistic source overtly out of step with the world in which one lives become, in this view, hallmarks of the creative genius.

These prejudices are in large measure the work of Wagner's self-image as expressed in his writings, particularly about himself, the public, and the significance of Beethoven in music history. That these Wagnerian views were in part hypocritical and dishonestly self-serving did not prevent their having an enormous influence on Wittgenstein's generation. The failure to grasp integrity, courage, and originality in Mendelssohn—in meanings understood perhaps in different terms from those shared by Wagner and even Brahms (who admired Mendelssohn greatly)—still represents the essence of the current obstacle to a broader and more admiring Mendelssohn reception.

Indeed, as the standard critique of Mendelssohn—echoed by Richard Hauser in his 1980 effort to show how, in *Die erste Walpurgisnacht*, Mendelssohn fell short of Goethe's text—makes plain, an overlay of musical and political interpretations that have developed since 1850, and still have not been understood adequately, must be taken apart.[11] This process should begin with another look at the Wagnerian critique. An analysis of the relationship of Mendelssohn's musical intentions to his Jewish identity and his social and economic position can generate new insights. Subsequent generations may have been so put off by the Biedermeier and (later) Victorian attributes of the many Mendelssohn enthusiasts that they were unable to penetrate to the power of the music. By reconstructing Mendelssohn's aesthetic, ethical, and musical ambitions—the cultural project centered on music that Mendelssohn assumed for himself—a fresh vantage point from which to hear and evaluate Mendelssohn's music may be created. The hypothesis of this essay, therefore, is that, freed of the quite arbitrary aesthetic and implicitly ideological (in the political sense) assumptions that have been applied to Mendelssohn's music since the middle of the nineteenth century, the audience at the end of our century might be able to recognize once again the invention, depth, significance, and emotional power of practically all of Mendelssohn's music.

The Wagnerian Critique

Richard Wagner's intense lifelong preoccupation with Felix Mendelssohn was more than the result of principled aesthetic misgivings on the part of a younger man. In her diaries, Cosima Wagner documented her husband's nearly obsessive engagement with Mendelssohn.[12] Until the last year of his life, Wagner regularly returned to playing Mendelssohn's works on the piano to his entourage only to demonstrate their "poverty of invention" or their "Semitic excitability."[13] Wagner repeatedly referred to *A Midsummer Night's Dream*, severely criticizing it. At the same time he remarked on the flawed but gifted painterly dimensions of some of Mendelssohn's overtures. In 1879 Wagner woke up and recounted a dream about Mendelssohn, whom "he addressed in the second person singular." As the dream progressed he found himself unable to guide a pontoon across a body of water. Cosima wrote, "no one could tell him how, and R. turned to General Moltke with a military salute; but he was a total simpleton and R. said to himself, 'What false ideas people have of him!'" A cursory analysis of this dream (much less a more ambitious psychoanalytic speculation) reveals the main themes of Wagner's obsession. Mendelssohn was the authority and the overt object of envy, with whom intimacy was sought. Help with a dangerous task (i.e., composing), however, was not forthcoming. In the dream, Wagner unmasks both his own fear of failure and his wish to reveal the fraud and illegitimacy of the reputation for excellence associated with the authority figure, who shifts from the Jew Mendelssohn to the quintessential German military hero, Moltke. Wagner's dreamwork mirrored Wagner's characteristic amalgam of musical and nationalist ambitions. As late as 1855, eight years after Mendelssohn's death, Wagner proudly described himself in a letter to Otto Wesendonck as having achieved the status of becoming Mendelssohn's "rival."[14]

Wagner's struggle at self-definition always possessed a link to the figure of Mendelssohn. In Wagner's first significant foray into polemics, his 1834 article "German Opera," he crudely tried to describe a new German national agenda for musical and dramatic art. Foreign influence needed to be fought. In writing this essay—as Glasenapp, his "official" biographer, noted—Wagner had already identified the enemy, the "other," as Felix Mendelssohn. From the start of his career, Wagner's conception of the new aesthetic agenda was measured, often artificially, against the example of Mendelssohn.[15]

Leipzig, Wagner's birthplace, which remained relatively resistant to his early attempts at recognition, was Mendelssohn's adopted home, the place where Mendelssohn created a conservatory, led the *Gewandhaus* concerts, and dominated much of the city's cultural life. In creating the narrative of his life, Wagner accused Mendelssohn alternately of slighting him and of being envious. Wagner recognized that Mendelssohn had been the most powerful man in German musical life. Wagner, one of the few who truly grasped the scale of Mendelssohn's ambitions, sought consciously to outdo Mendelssohn.

The family histories of the two men could not have been more different. Wagner lost his father early in life. Wagner's life and work reflected an ambivalent engagement with intimacy and family. In contrast, Mendelssohn was intensely close to his family, particularly to his father and his sister Fanny. Family framed his artistic and moral existence. If Wagner had little instinct for privacy and the intimate, Mendelssohn possessed it in excess. After marrying Cécile Jeanrenaud, his personal habits (externally at least) approached nearly the Biedermeier ideal: love of wife and children and a growing penchant for the pleasures of domesticity. As an adult, Mendelssohn sought to replicate the attachment to home life and the familial intimacy with which he had grown up. As many contemporary observers noted, both he in Leipzig and his father in Berlin achieved in their respective generations an enviable and widely admired model of domestic tranquility, graciousness, and bliss.[16] Although Wagner appeared externally to be the more complex personality, when compared to Mendelssohn, whose headaches, odd sleep patterns, and mood swings suggest a far more opaque psyche than is usually accounted for by biographers, Wagner may turn out to have been the more easily understood figure.

Mendelssohn, as all scholars have noted, was wealthy and well educated, privileged since childhood by money and all the access money could purchase. The residue of distinction accorded the Mendelssohn name since the time of his grandfather (enhanced in part by his aunt Dorothea Schlegel) combined with the family wealth to permit Felix to study with Zelter and Heyse and to enjoy direct contact with Schleiermacher, who attended the first performance of Mendelssohn's opera *Die Hochzeit des Camacho*, and Goethe. The letters of Mendelssohn are filled with hints of the ease and the conveniences of life and travel afforded by wealth and close contact with banking families and houses all around Europe.[17] The circumstances of Mendelssohn's youth stood in sharp contrast to the childhood experiences of all his professional musical contemporaries. It was a source of resentment and jealousy not only for detractors but also for Schumann, who counted himself among Mendelssohn's greatest admirers.

The musical careers of Wagner and Mendelssohn presented an even more striking study in contrasts. Mendelssohn, as Wagner knew, had been second only to Mozart in terms of his childhood success as player and composer. Wagner possessed no comparable early signs of talent, as either a performer or a composer. He lacked the depth of Mendelssohn's early musical and general education. Wagner succeeded in spinning these contrasts into a coherent social and political theory of culture and history that would explain his own difficulty in achieving recognition early in life and at the same time could undermine Mendelssohn's reputation.

Mendelssohn, despite periodic criticism, felt deeply attached to the idea of a distinctly German musical culture.[18] He was therefore eager to see Germany politically unified. In his correspondence with Moscheles, the differences between English and German musical life were constantly referred to. Despite gratitude for the warmth of the reception the English gave him, Mendelssohn's allegiance to what he perceived as the German tradition was clear. That cultural nationalism was even more pronounced when Mendelssohn compared the musical cultures of France and Italy to that of his native Germany. When comparing Wagner's nationalism with Mendelssohn's, one must recall a fact never lost on Wagner: that Mendelssohn and his contemporaries saw Mendelssohn as the leading force in the renewal of specifically German musical culture. The regeneration of the oratorio and the revival of Bach and Handel had catapulted Mendelssohn into prominence as a cultural leader of the nation. It is that role—as well as the more narrowly musical accomplishment—that Wagner coveted and envied.

Mendelssohn's career quickly became Wagner's model. As early as 1829 (the date of the *St. Matthew Passion* performance), Mendelssohn revealed his commitment to the idea of music as part of a national cultural project. Mendelssohn sought to assume the leadership of the Berlin Singakademie after Zelter's death. He wrote his monumental oratorios with an eye to their social use and ethical impact. Mendelssohn accepted the task of reforming Leipzig's concert life. He founded the conservatory in 1843 and, despite misgivings, accepted an appointment at the Prussian Court in order to help chart a new era in the musical culture of Berlin.

Wagner's awareness of all this was evident in the sarcasm of his references during the 1840s to "the musical religion of Felix Mendelssohn" to which Germany "gives its heart."[19] Despite his admiration for a performance of *St. Paul* in 1843, Wagner was consistent in his effort to distance himself from Mendelssohn's influence. Wagner heaped contempt on Mendelssohn's brand of historicism, the effort to restore the grandeur of the oratorio, and the use of baroque models, calling them "sexless opera-embryos." Wagner's competitive focus was pronounced in an 1849 sketch for the organization of a German National Theater in Dresden. Wagner suggested closing the Leipzig conservatory and folding it into his own project in Dresden.[20]

Wagner's own comparison of himself to Mendelssohn can also be seen in the extent to which he repeatedly made references to the inadequacies of Mendelssohn as a conductor.[21] As the essay "On Conducting" from 1869 revealed, Wagner's own self-definition as a conductor was cast partly in contrast to the fast and inflexible tempi and the presumed disregard for the spirit of Beethoven that Wagner associated with Mendelssohn. If Liszt presented a positive model, then Mendelssohn defined the negative.[22]

Wagner's obsession with Mendelssohn helps to explain his single-minded focus on the operatic form. In 1841, writing from Paris, Wagner noted that Mendelssohn was too intellectual and wanting in "passion" to write an opera. By succeeding in the theater and at the same time redefining it in a way that would undercut the aesthetic legitimacy of the genres in which Mendelssohn excelled, a double triumph could be achieved without inviting any direct comparison. By arguing a theory of artistic progress that undercut Mendelssohn's neoclassic historicism, Wagner's own failures in the traditional arenas of chamber music and choral and symphonic form could be explained.

Wagner took particular pleasure in the weakness of Mendelssohn's incidental music to the plays of Sophocles. Wagner's 1872 letter to Nietzsche contained much of the psychological and social undertone in Wagner's critique. Wagner noted that, despite Mendelssohn's superior education and knowledge of antiquity, he (Wagner) had demonstrated "more respect for the spirit of Antiquity."[23]

It was only in this context that Wagner could openly express any admiration (e.g., for the *Hebrides* Overture). In this oblique manner Wagner periodically alluded to the musical debt he owed to Mendelssohn. Too little work has been done to highlight how much Wagner took from Mendelssohn in terms of orchestration, choral writing, melodic figuration, length of line, dramatic gesture, and above all the rhetorical uses of the solo voice in his effort to fashion an alternative to the secular and religious impact of Mendelssohn's oratorio and choral music.

St. Paul, *Elijah*, and the *Lobgesang* Symphony are just three examples of works that Mendelssohn hoped would engender two related results: mass participation in music and a heightened ethical sensibility supportive of normative canons of beauty; receptivity to tradition; faith in God; tolerance; and a sense of community. Wagner's work, particularly *Lohengrin*, *Die Meistersinger*, and *Parsifal*, reflected an implicit dialogue with these objectives. Few works were as influential on the dramatic sound and rhetorical scale of early Wagner as *St. Paul*. Given the ethical and moral intent of Mendelssohn's activities, Wagner was determined to outdo Mendelssohn and replace him as the leading figure, not only of German musical culture but of the way in which music influenced the values of the German nation.

What differentiated Wagner's strategy from Mendelssohn's was the enthusiasm with which Wagner formulated the ideology of the modern, of the illusion that the new and the contemporary constituted a triumph over the dead hand of the past. Wagner's assumption of a prophetic stance on behalf of the present and future was an explicit rejection of Mendelssohn's aesthetic credo. As Mendelssohn wrote to Wilhelm Taubert, "the first obligation of any artist should be to have respect for the great men and to bow down before them . . . and not to try to extinguish the great flames, in order that his own small tallow candle can seem a little brighter."[24]

Schumann, Chopin, and later Brahms each shared some extramusical polemical agendas, but these agendas were relatively restricted. Mendelssohn and Wagner (and to a lesser extent Liszt and Berlioz) were convinced of the possibilities inherent in musical culture vis-à-vis society as a whole. They undertook grandiose plans as composers and performers to reform national standards and secure a place for music in the creation of a self-image for the nation. For Mendelssohn, the project was largely conservative and classicist, if not historicist, characterized by a benign and admiring focus on active music making in the home, in public, and in church.

In Wagner's case, the project became exclusive in racial and na-

tional terms, aestheticized and dependent on an audience of specta-
tors. He focused on the vicarious experience of art and the glorifica-
tion of the artist and dramatic hero as both surrogate and vehicle for
the conventional religious experience. The denial of the characterized self and the resistance to dramatic illusionism evident in Mendelssohn's large-scale works reflected Mendelssohn's faith in the vitality of the official institution and practices of Christian religion. Not
surprisingly, at the end of the 1880 essay "Religion and Art" Wagner
artificially inserted an anecdote about Mendelssohn, not as a composer but as a political figure. According to Wagner, Mendelssohn
pursued "barren aims" in the name of mankind. The barrenness was
the result of a sterile historicist theology. Wagner called on the artist
to base religion and art on morality and give them their proper place
in order to insure the "better state of future man."[25]

Wagner's most elaborate open attack (despite the pseudonym Wagner used in the first edition) was the 1850 essay "Judaism in Music."
Curiously, the other truly defamatory essay Wagner penned, directed
at Mendelssohn and his circle—the 1869 review of Devrient's memoirs about Mendelssohn—was also published under a pseudonym.[26]
Even at his worst, Wagner, in this display of cowardice, signaled some
ambivalent sign of critical self-recognition.

The crux of Wagner's criticism in the essay on Jews was that Mendelssohn's failure was not ultimately personal. Mendelssohn's music
failed to reach deep into the human heart and soul because of his
own Jewishness. By framing the critique in terms of a racial and social
theory, Wagner could at once praise Mendelssohn as the greatest of
the Jews, undercut his influence as a celebrated and widely played
composer of Protestant music in the nineteenth century, and deper-
sonalize his attack on Mendelssohn.

The 1850 Wagnerian argument became the primary source of the
claim that Mendelssohn's work was emotionally and dramatically superficial. Wagner described Mendelssohn's music as "vague" and
merely allusive, evoking neither objects nor emotional experiences
but mere shadows. Mendelssohn was a powerless artist. He was im-
potent. Only when he came close to expressing that impotence, Wagner argued, did the music begin to speak.[27]

The diagnosis of Mendelssohn's aesthetic impotence—linked directly to Mendelssohn's failure to write opera—became the center-
piece of Wagner's assessment of the place of the Jew in German culture. Mendelssohn, despite his assimilation, had not yet come to
terms with his own incapacity for real, "organic" rooted life. He, like
other Jews, could only reproduce and live as untrustworthy imitators,
as frauds who, in the midst of a healthy culture, sought merely to

exploit that culture. This contrast between the rootless but wealthy, powerful, assimilated Jew and the native, poor, but rooted son of the "people," blessed with an inner security and capacity to evoke deep sentiments among his people, frames exactly the core of the Mendelssohn-Wagner contrast. It can help to illuminate the origins and significance of the way the Parsifal-Amfortas dynamic unfolds and is resolved in *Parsifal*. In *Parsifal* the music at the end of Act 1 is decidedly Mendelssohnian in both thematic material and orchestration. The drama reflects the autobiographical. Wagner (Parsifal) is inspired to undertake the redemptive agenda through art on behalf of the community by curing sickness and restoring purity. It is indeed ironic that at the end of his life Wagner, in *Parsifal*, not only extended musical language but brilliantly demonstrated his own mastery of the Mendelssohnian musical rhetoric of *St. Paul* and *Elijah*. In his last work Wagner reveals, both ideologically and musically, the lingering power of the image of Mendelssohn, particularly Mendelssohn's ambition to render music an ethical, cultural, and religious force. The contrast between Parsifal, the innocent fool, and Amfortas, the privileged son of a king, and the redemption of the latter by the former are distillations of Wagner's career and ambition.

The image of Mendelssohn was never far from the surface of Wagner's consciousness. Beckmesser may have been a satire on Hanslick, but the music was a parody not of Brahms but of Mendelssohn. Further, Wagner tried to demolish the oft-made comparison between Mozart and Mendelssohn, a comparison of which Schumann was particularly fond. Early in "Opera and Drama" (1851), Wagner took care to point out that Mendelssohn could not be compared to Mozart, despite his precociousness. He was not the "naive" artist and could never have written a great opera or great dramatic music. He failed to grasp the essential relation between speech and music, between the poetic, the dramatic, and the musical.[28]

The focus on power as a musical attribute in Wagner's mind—on the link between creativity and potency—explained his ambition to create the modern dramatic equivalent of Beethoven's symphonies. The Wagnerian reinterpretation of Beethoven was tacitly another means to extend the contrast with Mendelssohn. Wagner regarded Mendelssohn's symphonies as weak imitations of Beethoven's example. Wagner, in the 1849 essay "The Artwork of the Future," derided Mendelssohn's *Lobgesang* Symphony precisely in this context.[29] Despite Mendelssohn's overt purpose—the praise of God—the real essence of human expressiveness implicit in nature expressed in Beethoven's Ninth Symphony eluded him. For Mendelssohn, decorative melody—to Wagner, Mendelssohn's primary vehicle—although ephemeral, seemed sufficient. Journalistic praise and financial reward in a corrupt present were forthcoming. In his own music Wagner sought to reconcile motivic coherence with a seamless extensive musical, dramatic narrative. He avoided the narrowly self-contained melodic form in which Mendelssohn excelled.

Wagner's progressive theory of art stood in stark contrast to Mendelssohn's more hesitant embrace of modernity. Yet Wagner's celebration of the future was the other side of a critique of the cultural present he shared with Mendelssohn. Mendelssohn's answer (which can be properly compared to Schumann's) to the philistine tastes he encountered during his lifetime was an aesthetic of creative restoration; a search for historic models; a backward glance tempered by a modern taste for the subjective, emotional, poetic voice of romanticism.

In 1879 Wagner published an essay in English, "The Work and Mission of My Life," in the American journal *North American Review*. As Ernest Newman suggested, Hans von Wolzogen may actually have written it.[30] But the essay certainly had Wagner's blessing. Wagner referred to Mendelssohn as "a member of that ubiquitous talented race." Warning Americans to be aware of their "taking the lead" in the New World, Wagner went on to recount the essential context against which his own agenda as an artist developed:

> Mendelssohn undertook with his delicate hand—his exquisite special talent for a kind of musical landscape-painting—to lead the educated classes of Germany as far away from the dreaded and misunderstood extravagances of a Beethoven, and from the sublime prospect opened to national art by his later works. . . . He was the savior of music in the *salon*—and with him the concert-room, and now and then even the church, did duty as a *salon* also. Amid all the tempests of revolution he gave to his art a delicate, smooth, quiet, cool, and agreeably tranquil form that excited nobody, and had no aim but to please the modern cultivated taste, and to give it occasionally, amid the shifting and turmoil of the times, the consolation of a little pleasing and elegant entertainment. A new idea in art was developed—the embodiment in it of a graceful, good-society element, quite foreign to the nation's character and social life.[31]

The Significance of Mendelssohn's Jewishness

The Wagner-Wolzogen 1879 argument was not new. Indeed, it represented an embarrassingly close paraphrase of the well-known analysis written by Wilhelm Heinrich Riehl (1823–1897) in the mid-1850s. Five years after Mendelssohn's death, Riehl had noted critically that Mendelssohn "often composed like a diplomat." Mendelssohn had been unparalleled in his success with the public and with publishers. According to Riehl he "centralized the direction of musical taste in Germany" and inspired hundreds of far lesser talents to write poor music in outdated forms. Only the lyricism of the short song struck Riehl as more than just influential. It was authentic and inspired. But the core of Riehl's criticism was that Mendelssohn, who possessed "a unique social position," wrote from within "his society." He was not

the gnarled, self-contained Burgher like Bach, but a many sided, socially adept, rich, well-brought-up man, known personally throughout Germany and sought out by all circles of outstanding people. What a contrast this was to the old musicians of the last century! Therefore Mendelssohn wrote in the spirit of this educated society, which now extends across all classes, moderating their differences and facilitating communication. He made the old disciplined forms of chamber music more elegant, cleaner and distinguished; he cleaned up and restrained the aesthetic slovenliness of modern salon pieces; he sought to enliven the doctrines of the church with a heightened subjective emotionalism. One can then say that Mendelssohn's chamber and concert music, his pieces for the salon and the church can be performed equally well before selected circles of society. This represents the collapse of standards (*Nivellment*) in modern education. Were one to perform a piece of Bach's at tea time, one would profane it. But a piece of Mendelssohn's church music would not be profaned since it actually evokes and lifts the mood of tea-time society.[32]

Both Riehl and Wagner's characterizations pointed directly to the identification of Mendelssohn with a particular stratum in society. Within the context of the politics of the mid-century, the group with which Mendelssohn was connected was the *Grossbürgertum*—Marx's bourgeoisie. Furthermore, this group was associated more with liberalism and less with the radical new direction of German nationalism in the 1850s. They were, in short, antirevolutionary defenders and beneficiaries of the pre-March social order who, in Riehl's and Wagner's eyes, sought to falsify the past (despite an explicit respect for the historical) and prettify their surroundings and thereby deny the deeper political and social realities and national possibilities.

But it was not merely this glib social historical link between Mendelssohn's music and its success during his lifetime that both Riehl and Wagner communicated. The underlying critique made a thinly veiled reference to Mendelssohn's status as Jew and to the Jew as exemplar of the salon bourgeois of the age. The interweaving of cultural criticism overtly based on class structure with anti-Semitic and nationalist polemic became a distinct pattern in the reception of Mendelssohn's music after his death. In Riehl's case, the framing of Mendelssohn as an apparent insider who was really foreign to the German spirit took two directions: the denial of Mendelssohn as legitimate heir (despite the historicist surface of his music) to the glorious German musical past; and the unmasking of Mendelssohn's claim to greatness as a Christian composer by stressing the nearly sinful superficiality of his religious music.

Wagner's reflections on the Jewish question and Riehl's cultural criticism from the 1840s and 1850s were contemporaneous with the writings of Bruno Bauer and Karl Marx on the same subject. The Jewish question had become a major part of the political discourse of German-speaking Europe since 1806, the date of the Prussian defeat at Jena. A new nationalism that sought to distinguish between the authentically German and the foreign began to take root. The link in the minds of many Germans between the dangers of French politics and culture and the Jewish presence was based in part on the identification of French liberalism with the emancipation of the Jews. The French Revolution and Napoleon were instrumental in the spread of religious tolerance. From 1806 to 1812, the granting of extensive civil liberties (beyond religious toleration) to Jews in German-speaking principalities was associated with French domination and influence.[33]

The resurgence of broad-based German anti-Semitism dates from 1806 and, later, 1819, when the "Hep Hep" riots took place in German-speaking lands. The irony in the anti-Semitism of the early nineteenth century was that it came on the heels of the promising first stage of emancipation within German-speaking regions—the golden era of Lessing, Kant, and Moses Mendelssohn. In the brief span of nearly thirty years—from the Habsburg emperor Joseph II's Edict of Toleration of 1781 to 1809, the year of Mendelssohn's birth—in most German principalities and monarchies Jews enjoyed new opportunities, and an elite of Jews achieved remarkable economic gains and social acceptance. The legendary salons of the high society of Berlin at the end of the century were one visible indication of the pace of assimilation (with and without conversion) and intermarriage.[34]

One consequence of the first phase of assimilation, which became apparent in the period 1806–1819, was the perception of social phenomena that ran parallel to emancipation. The transformation of the economic system coincided, it seemed, with the entrance into Gentile life by Jews. The process of exit from the ghetto and assimilation progressed concurrently with the liberalization of economic activity and the end of the vestiges of a restrictive feudal economic order. As early as the late eighteenth century, the economic impact of toleration and Jewish emancipation—in terms of tax revenue and economic activity and its benefits for the state—had been widely discussed, but in a largely positive vein. By the time Bauer, Marx, and Wagner came to write their tracts on Jews, a negative linkage between Jews and the evils of capitalism had become commonplace—a radical transformation of earlier images of the Jew as Shylock and court financier.

Furthermore, the late-eighteenth-century expectation that most Jews would convert after being emancipated had not been realized. Rather, Jews sought—as did Moses Mendelssohn's followers (but not all his children)—to modernize Judaism and turn it into a religion of reason and humanism, into an autonomous equivalent of Protestantism. The techniques included a new movement for modern Jewish education, the making of a German-language sermon central to the ritual, and other reforms of traditional liturgical practices.[35]

The inflammatory, widespread, and radical linkages that the young Wagner absorbed into his anti-Semitic rhetoric were tripartite: first, of Jews and an old-style French liberalism; second, of Jews with capitalism; and third, an unreasonable and irrational refusal of Jews to accept Christianity, despite emancipation. The Jew wanted to be, still as Jew, a member of society who practiced a different religion. What was new was that in the years after 1806 the prejudice against the Jews was not limited to the character of their religious beliefs. The new national consciousness, bolstered by romanticism and theories of history formulated after the Reign of Terror in France, cast the development of language and society (e.g., Herder) in a new light. It inspired a new form of race-based national solidarity in which the Jews seemed a historically distinct race and foreign, who, despite appearances, were deemed fundamentally incapable of integration.

Given the revolutionary energies that developed after 1815, owing in part to the rapid economic and social changes in Europe, an eminently plausible and progressive anti-Semitic ideology, one that seemed to contain the promise of a better world in the future—without Jews—became dominant. Riehl's and Wagner's idealized picture of the potential new national audience for art was therefore revolutionary. (One must discount the startling gap between rhetoric and action in Wagner's case; he sought the approval of Mendelssohn's public without restraint.) It was made up of the presumed victims of capitalism, the traditional peoples of the nation, and it excluded Jews and their cronies, the journalists.

Therefore, as Wagner recalled in 1879 (and Riehl in his characterization of Mendelssohn tacitly argued), the enemy was the assimilated Jew, not the evidently foreign ghetto Jew. The Jew who appeared to "pass" was the one who sought to prevent the development of a true and new national and social consciousness. This insidious outsider tried to camouflage himself as part of the society by assuming a place in (and ultimately controlling) the nation's cultural life. By insinuating themselves into the arts, the Jews undermined the national revolutionary potential of art through the medium of modern newspapers, and new fashion and trends.

The assimilated Jew was not only the most visible representative of capitalism. He assumed the leadership of a larger social class that sought to exploit the true historical "peoples." Jews fought to preserve political rights for themselves and all capitalists. The Jew became the symbol of both capitalism and liberalism, of possessive individualism and materialism. The cultural critique inherent in anti-Semitism—visible in Riehl—was the attack on the philistine, middle-class, self-conscious pursuit of refinement and culture. This consumption of art as entertainment sullied art and rendered it socially and morally irrelevant. The failure of the efforts, under the banner of liberalism, to unify Germany after the revolutions of 1848 only strengthened the strident critique of the 1850s. An alliance between liberalism and nationalism—which Mendelssohn himself hoped for in the late 1830s and early 1840s—was never realized.

To the new generation it seemed clear that the mission of art was to arouse the imminent possibilities for national and social regeneration evident in the "shifting" times of the 1830s and 1840s. In Wagner's view, no Jew could undertake such a task. No doubt he suspected that Mendelssohn had little use for the new nationalism. In the midst of growing antipathy between French and Germans in 1840, Mendelssohn, hardly a Francophile, refused to set patriotic verses to music: "I do not feel in the least disposed to this kind of 'patriotism,'" he wrote to Fanny.

How Jewish was Felix Mendelssohn? Doubtless, as his father wrote to him, no one with the name Mendelssohn would ever pass as anything other than a Jew. Abraham Mendelssohn, unlike his father, Moses, confronted the logic of the new anti-Semitism. The major disappointment of Abraham's generation was in 1806, when, in the heat of national fervor, an ugly anti-Semitic sentiment was expressed within the very circles of educated individuals who had embraced earlier the ethics and politics of emancipation. Mendelssohn's father and uncle, Bartholdy, unlike Moses Mendelssohn, believed that only by disappearing as a Jew over time, through conversion, intermarriage, and name change, could anti-Semitism possibly be avoided.[36]

However, Mendelssohn experienced his early childhood, before the conversion in his seventh year in 1816, as a Jew. Mendelssohn's parents converted six years later. Two years thereafter, while on vacation in 1824, Mendelssohn and his sister, as Jews, were roughed up by a roving gang. Jews were visibly identifiable as Jews to many non-Jews (or so they thought) at sight. Even Zelter, Mendelssohn's beloved teacher, noted to Goethe in 1821 that it would be exceptional for the son of a Jew to become a real artist. When the Goethe-Zelter letters were published in the 1830s, Mendelssohn was hurt by this evidence of Zelter's anti-Semitism.[37]

Being a Jew was not something that could easily be eradicated by a name change and the adoption of a new religion, particularly when anti-Semitism was as significant a force in daily life as it was during Felix Mendelssohn's lifetime. From the vantage point of late-twentieth-century standards, Mendelssohn's behavior on the Jewish question was exemplary. He never displayed the satirical discomfort of Heine. Nor did he waver in his religious ideas and allegiances as Heine did. Heine's sardonic attitude toward Mendelssohn and his music and Heine's mockery of its religious content and refined surface prefigured much of the tone and content of later criticism, including Wagner's. Heine's critique, however, was much more about the ironies and self-deceptions of Jewish behavior than about music. His mistrust of Mendelssohn's Christian faith, his ambitions, and self-image as Jew may, however, have been misplaced.[38] Mendelssohn insisted, contrary to his father's wishes, on using the Mendelssohn name together with the new name Bartholdy, a clear signal of identification with his Jewish past and of his resistance to the feelings of self-doubt, shame, confusion, and embarrassment shared by many contemporary Jews. He did not seem to share his father's definition of Judaism as "antiquated, distorted, and self-defeating." He took special interest in colleagues who were Jews with whom he felt particularly comfortable, such as Moscheles and later Joachim. When he wrote home expressing his delight at the successful passage in Parliament in England of legislation extending rights to Jews, he referred to the object of the legislation as "us."[39] The presence of anti-Semitism—from traumatic childhood incidents,[40] through the prejudiced selection process in the Singakademie, to Mendelssohn's profound regret in 1834 at having to encounter anti-Semitism in the Goethe-Zelter correspondence—was never far removed from Mendelssohn's daily life.

Mendelssohn's prominent and public commitment to and interest in the theology of Christianity and his reverent use of music to evoke Christian faith and religious sentiment reflected a quality and depth of conviction that rivaled that of J. S. Bach. However, the residue of commitments to what Mendelssohn knew to be the heritage of his forebears is evident in his music. The texts Mendelssohn selected, the prominence played by the issues of conversion and graven images (in *St. Paul*), and the attraction to the figure of Elijah are markers of the extent to which Mendelssohn devoted his artistic energy to finding bridges between Judaism and Christianity, between his childhood and his adult life. Mendelssohn may have shared his father's view that Christianity was a "purified" form of Judaism. Mendelssohn's intense attraction to older models of vocal sacred music, to the organ and the historical tradition, may well have been, as Heine suspected, the result of Mendelssohn's strength to sustain psychological certainty about his status as a Christian. However, the letters and evidence point rather to the depth of Mendelssohn's theological convictions and his faith in the rituals of common Christian worship.

The most remarkable example of Mendelssohn's residual psychological loyalty to his Jewish heritage was the secular cantata *Die erste Walpurgisnacht*. The first version was completed in 1832; the work was subsequently revised in 1843. Mendelssohn wrote to Goethe: "the more I became occupied with the task, the more important it seemed to me . . . when the old Druid offers up his sacrifice . . . there is no need of inventing music; it is already there."[41] As was often the case with Mendelssohn, who was among the most self-critical composers in music history, this work underwent serious revision. It was overtly a tribute to Goethe's poetry. In its final form it became one of Mendelssohn's favorite works, and it remains one of Mendelssohn's finest achievements.

As Heinz Klaus Metzger has argued, Mendelssohn transformed Goethe's Druids and pagans into Jews who refuse to convert (as did some of Mendelssohn's extended family). The final scene of the pagans defending their faith against Christian soldiers while musing on the extent to which Christians perverted the meaning of their religious ideas—although taken straight from Goethe—can be understood, in terms of its emotional lure for Mendelssohn, by its obvious analogy to the historical and contemporary plight of Jewry, particularly in the context of the new anti-Semitism of the 1830s and 1840s.

The *Allvater* of Goethe was a metaphor for Mendelssohn of the Jewish God, which Arnold Schoenberg termed a century later, in the first line of *Moses und Aron*, the "single, eternal, all present, invisible and unrepresentable God." Mendelssohn extended the ending of the Goethe poem by placing enormous stress, and a C-major grand choral finale, on the phrase "your light, who can steal it from you?"[42]

This ending provides one clue to Mendelssohn's religious philosophy. If one compares this stress on the power of faith as the light of God to the Lutheran text Mendelssohn used in a work that may have been his favorite large choral composition, the B♭-major symphony of 1840, the *Lobgesang* (also subjected to revision), one realizes that there, too, the stress is on the contrast between darkness and light, on the transformation by God's grace and man's faith of night into day. Music was pivotal to the public celebration of faith in the divine work of enlightenment.

The high point of the symphony occurs before the soprano-tenor duet and final chorus. The praise of the Lord expressed in those two closing sections is a direct response to the changing of night into day. The dramatic center of the work occurs in the two preceding sections, during the soprano-tenor exchange about the coming of the day and the great chorus that ensues. It highlights the departure of night and God's "armor of light." For Mendelssohn the advent of Protestant Christianity was itself a sign of human progress, for through it the historic religious divisions between Jew and Christian could be reconciled.

Mendelssohn was syncretic, not sectarian. His Christian faith focused on the extent to which Christianity was a universalization of Judaism. Like his father, who argued that conversion implied no essential contradiction to the essence of Judaism, Mendelssohn believed in Christian religion as the proper route to human solidarity. The claim to universalism in Christianity appealed to Mendelssohn. Faith in and the acceptance of Christ were logical fulfillments of Judaism. Christian faith, given its universalist premise, if genuinely stirred in the soul of individuals, would permit them to see God's light: brotherly love, tolerance, and reason. Reason, for Mendelssohn, meant a resistance to superstition, which he and his father identified as characteristic of traditional Judaism.

The themes of reconciliation and brotherhood are mirrored in Mendelssohn's attraction to two musical forms—the chorale (whose use by Mendelssohn in the oratorio form was controversial) and majestic major-key choralelike finales in his large instrumental works designed for public use (the First, Third, and Fifth Symphonies, for example). Both imply human unity—one through common singing, simplicity, emotional power, directness, comprehensibility, and shared recognition; and the other through melodic lines and instrumental timbres that lend a discursive musical form, a clear and affirmative resolution comprehensible to even the least sophisticated listener. Mendelssohn, writing to Pastor Bauer in 1835, compared his own ambitions to the "edification" generated by Bach's Passion music. Mendelssohn sought to renew the relationship among human beings through the merger of music and faith.[43]

Mendelssohn's definition of the theatrical in public music making was therefore didactic and participatory. The fact that his music for *Antigone* (arguably, for Mendelssohn, a quasi-Christian heroine) could be performed by schools pleased him. The theatrical impact of the *Lobgesang* Symphony and *St. Paul* was defined by the extent to which the singers and the audience, through the perception of the music, shared in the ethical sensibility of community. After the completion of *St. Paul*, in his search for a text for an oratorio, Mendelssohn asked Julius Schubring in 1837 whether the subject of St. Peter could "become something equally important and deeply intimate for every member of the community."[44]

Mendelssohn's use of so-called folk material in the Third and Fourth Symphonies was executed so as to transform the local into the universal. Comparison with later examples of musical symbols of locality—Dvořák, Tchaikovsky, and Sibelius—highlights the extent to which a realistic musical particularism in Mendelssohn is subordinated to an idealized and novel conception of the formal and universal language of instrumental musical discourse.[45]

These ideas and ambitions hark back to Felix Mendelssohn's grandfather, particularly the vision outlined in the 1783 tract *Jerusalem*. Felix Mendelssohn's conversion was not, as Heine might have implied, taken cynically by Felix. Rather, he embraced it as a logical extension of the reform and modernization of Judaism begun by his grandfather. Inherent in Mendelssohn's extension of Judaic notions through Christianity was, of course, faith in the rational character of Christian doctrine and the possibilities of realizing freedom and faith in this world through reason. Mendelssohn's negative reaction to the authoritarian tendencies among the followers of Saint Simon in Paris in the early 1830s did not prevent him from observing that "from time to time certain ideas appear—e.g., ideas of universal brotherly love, of disbelief in hell, the devil and damnation, of the annihilation of egoism—all ideas which in our country spring from nature, and which prevail in every part of Christendom, ideas without which I would not wish to live, but which they regard as a new invention and discovery."[46]

In this letter Mendelssohn brought together the varied strands of his ethical and aesthetic credo: national pride framed by a respect for universalism, brotherhood, and reason, as well as some skepticism with respect to the claims of the moderns over the ancients. As with the relationship of Judaism to Christianity and the relationship of modern music to the classical past (Bach and Handel), the task was to find new effective expression for old truths. Historicist neoclassicism in the musical aesthetics of romanticism paralleled the belief in the essential humanistic link between Judaism and Christianity.

Mendelssohn's persistent dissatisfaction with the operatic librettos he asked for and was sent was not merely the result of perceived inadequacies in diction and the musicality of subject and language. Rather, subjects such as his friend Devrient's *Hans Heiling* seemed not to offer a framework in which music could exert a moral force.[47] In order to do that the true musical subject had to reflect not subjective individuality but generalizable truths whose ethical and aesthetic meaning was coincident with universal applicability. Mendelssohn wrote to Devrient in 1831, "If you can come to the point of not thinking about singers, decorations and situations but rather about presenting men, nature and life, I am convinced that you will write the best opera texts that we possess."[48] Mendelssohn, after all, was not an admirer of Meyerbeer and French grand opera.[49] It was precisely this paradox, perceived by Mendelssohn, about how alluring theatrical spectacles and the higher purposes of art could be reconciled on the operatic stage that Wagner took upon himself to solve. The theater could transcend the role of providing mere fantasy and entertainment and become a moral, emotional, and political force.

Mendelssohn's ambition to achieve in music more than personal success and originality—which he termed the "depressing, flighty and evanescent" aspects of musical life—and to further a humanistic cause was expressed in a letter to his brother Paul in 1837: "So little remains after performances and festivals, and of all which surrounds the personality; people certainly shout and applaud, but it disappears again so quickly, without any trace; and still it absorbs as much of life and strength as the *better* aims, if not more. . . . I dare not withdraw, not even once, lest the cause for which I stand suffer. Yet how much I would prefer to see that the cause be seen not merely as personal, but rather as one of the good as such, or of universality itself!"[50]

Language and Music:
The Mendelssohnian Aesthetic

Crucial to Mendelssohn's religious convictions and musical aesthetics was his conception of the relationship between words and music. What distinguished Felix Mendelssohn's credo from that of his grandfather was Felix's confidence in the ultimate coherence of Christianity and Judaism and the logic of conversion. Felix Mendelssohn, who admired literary romanticism—Jean Paul Richter and Ossian, in particular—and grew up under the spell of Goethe, sensed that human insight and communication were not limited to linguistic exchanges. Visual aesthetic perception rivaled the power and influence of the word.

Mendelssohn was strikingly gifted in the visual arts. He was among the most visual of composers. Drawing and painting came second only to making music. The letters from Mendelssohn's youth are filled with both drawings and vivid descriptions of nature, architecture, and people. In this sense, one can compare Mendelssohn's use of the visual in his extensive correspondence, with Goethe, for whom visual perception was even more crucial to the act of knowing and understanding. Mendelssohn formed pictures in his mind and frequently retained ideas as images. As with Goethe, the process of seeing was transformative. It carried with it insights and sensibilities for which the young Mendelssohn found adequate expression only through music. His 1831 descriptions of the Roman liturgy reveal the reciprocal workings of what was seen and heard in his mental processes.

As R. Larry Todd has argued, the genesis of the *Hebrides* Overture began with Mendelssohn's making a pen-and-ink drawing. A musical sketch of the basic thematic idea bears the same date. The elaboration of the music in ways that related to Macpherson's *Fingal*—to Ossianic poetry—was itself related to the visual impetus. The poetic was mediated through the visual into the musical.[51] Writing Fanny in 1840 in order to query her about the "Nibelungen" as a possible opera subject, Mendelssohn asked her particularly to evaluate its visual dimensions, its "colors and characteristics."[52]

Wagner's characterization of Mendelssohn as a painterly composer of landscapes was well earned. However, Wagner's perception that the *Hebrides* called for a program is striking evidence of the profound divergence in the views of the two men with respect to the relation between words and music. Music, for Mendelssohn, was never written to follow closely the structure of narration implied by a picture or determined by either prose or poetry. In the *Calm Sea and Prosperous Voyage* Overture, a setting of a Goethe text, the visual imagery again frames the musical form. Mendelssohn was able to depict the sense of distance, color, light, and three-dimensional space through orchestration. The sections of the work follow as would a series of sequential paintings, which do more than chronicle action. Mendelssohn's evocation of mood in orchestral works (e.g., *A Midsummer Night's Dream*) mirrored the autonomous impact of a scene visualized. Likewise in *Die schöne Melusine* Overture, the visual imagery, even of the key characters of the drama, dominates. Mendelssohn's attachment to literary romanticism was in part a measure of the extent to which such literature spurred the imagination to make mental pictures.[53]

Mendelssohn's engagement with visual perception influenced his approach to musical expression. His stress on the recognizability of melodic line in his instrumental work can be understood as a response to the criterion of visual recognition in painting. The nineteenth-century painter relied on the capacity to confirm, deepen, and alter the viewer's independent experience and recognition of external reality and nature. For instrumental music to achieve the same end it had to contain a comparable surface that could create, with some immediacy, the evident trust that existed between artist and viewer derived from the shared perception—even in the case of visual depictions of psychological moods—of the external world. As Mendelssohn wrote after meeting the Danish sculptor Thorwaldsen, "One knows at once that he must be a wonderful artist; one sees so clearly through his eyes, as if everything takes on within him the aspects of form and image."[54] A better evocation of the aesthetics of Mendelssohn's own paintings and drawings could hardly be found.

Moses Mendelssohn believed that enlightenment would be the consequence of the spread of culture and *Bildung*.[55] For him culture and education were contingent on the word. Reason and universality were conceived of in terms of language use. As he wrote in 1783, "thought and speech" were the "inalienable heritage" and "immutable right" granted all men by God. Through a common language extended into rational philosophical, literary, and ordinary communication—in German—tolerance and enlightenment could be spread, consistent with the "diversity" that was the "plan and purpose of Providence."[56] The shattered optimism over emancipation and enlightenment that Moses Mendelssohn's children experienced occasioned the start of a long process of critical reflection throughout the nineteenth century, particularly within the community of assimilated German-speaking Jewry, about the character of reason, language, and communication. The first fifty years of emancipation had shown the weakness of language alone as an instrument of assimilation and tolerance.

It may be no accident or matter of aesthetic engagement, then, that a mistrust of the power of words, as Carl Dahlhaus observed, became a central element in Mendelssohn's musical strategy as a composer.[57] In taking up the cause of enlightenment and universal tolerance, the young Mendelssohn turned to forms of expression foreign to his grandfather: musical sound and visual images. However, among assimilated Jews of the early nineteenth century, these forms fit into Moses Mendelssohn's categories of culture and *Bildung*.

Therefore, when Felix claimed in 1832 that "nature" was the source of brotherly love in Germany, he expressed a faith in the ethical consequences of the visual experience and perception of landscape. The painter and sculptor, through the imitation of nature, evoked a psychologically essential and compelling recognition of what is implicit in nature: the shared existential framework given by God, upon which the experience of subjectivity and the realization of individuality are contingent. The musician's task was to deepen through music that ethical awareness.

The visual image of a scene or perspective influenced Mendelssohn's model of musical form insofar as it led him to focus on the capacity for the whole of a composition to be grasped, even superficially, at the time of performance. In other words, the cognitive process on the part of the player and listener demanded that the structure be evident and clearly outlined, much the way it needed to be in a mural or painting. Transformation of musical material, in which the links between moments—the dynamic dimension of musical form—created secondary levels of impressions. These required the listener's capacity to follow extensive elaboration. In Mendelssohn's aesthetic these transformations needed always to be contained by audible formal requirements—such as symmetry, balance, and clarity, which had clear visual analogues. Hence Mendelssohn's penchant for the strophic song.

Mendelssohn made a determined effort to make a piece appear to listeners as a unified entity without an undue stress on underlying levels of extensive elaboration, which could obscure the focus on the outline of the foreground object. Therefore, many lyric slow movements in Mendelssohn lack, in comparison with Beethoven or even Schumann, extensive development. They have, however, subtly extended melodic statements. Variation is built into exposition itself. One thinks of the slow movements of the two piano concerti. Mendelssohn was attracted to short choral forms and the distinct sections of the oratorio format because they mirror the visual model of a discrete painting (or series of paintings), whose surface logic remains undisturbed by the existence of depth and detail, shading and perspective. The idea of a focal point (despite a complex background-foreground tension) within the music as central to the aesthetic experience is never far from Mendelssohn's music. Counterpoint in Mendelssohn is handled traditionally in the sense that the clarity of lines is underscored. The fugue, for example, appealed to him in part because grandeur and drama were consistent with the clarity and imitative character of the form. Mendelssohnian narrative is not unified by free discursive variation but by a depth created within the fixed frame defined by the clear musical subject line and structure.

The stress on sequential, coincident perception within the forms of his instrumental music led Mendelssohn to truncate recapitulations. For him, the experience of statement, memory, and recall had to be integrated, to be rendered associative at the moment of aural perception. The impact on the hearer needed to be accessible and direct, much the way a painting or a scene from nature might have an initial impact and then be recalled as a unit, as an object of later reflection. Therefore, in the *Lobgesang*, the thematic material that binds the work is announced at the start and periodically restated—relatively untransformed. The three initial, purely instrumental movements were designed to create a sequence of experiences that the choral finale could underscore as the final grand tableau. Structure in a work was designed along clear units and sections. Each unit would have a function that was made evident through repetition of thematic material. The deepening of recognition and response through the process of hearing depended on the clarity of a formal compositional frame. Therefore Mendelssohn experimented with ways to unify large forms made up of discrete units. Mendelssohn, like Wagner, utilized extensively untransformed units of thematic repetition.

That the temporal encounter with music should permit a deeper reflection through subsequent memory was equally clear. But for Mendelssohn listening to music was not analogous to reading, in which stopping and thinking and penetrating a complex surface in an often solitary act, controlled by the individual, were integral elements. Music was an object of contemplation organized in time, through which meaning could be transmitted without demanding the sort of analytic experience that one associates with reading. The listener needed to walk away with a sufficiently large unit of musical recollection upon which to muse. The unity of perception and experience, as a piece of music went on, facilitated the sharing of the aesthetic moment with others. Therefore, retrospective referential association, for example, to the start of a work during the hearing was designed not to disturb the capacity, at the end, to recall the frame of the whole and the sequence of even highly contrasting events.

This conception of the musical experience, which was closely related to the experience of the visual, was highlighted by Mendelssohn in his favorable comments to his sister Rebecka on the *tableaux vivants*, which accompanied a performance of Handel's *Israel in Egypt* in 1833 in Düsseldorf.[58] The model of the visual tableau can be applied as well to the evaluation of the dramatic sequence of events in the two oratorios. It also can explain the use of three distinct themes in the first movement of the *Scottish* Symphony and the return of the introduction. Mendelssohn's devotion to an inherited formal structure, however, stands in sharp contrast to Wagner. In Wagner the literary and dramatic complexities—with all the attendant emotions, sentiments, and thoughts—were woven into an interrelated, seamless, and dynamically designed musical narrative that organically evolved toward an end that mirrored a process of internal transformation despite the use of motivic repetition. Drama and prose fiction found their musical equivalent. Wagner explicitly rejected a seemingly static symmetry and antidramatic ideal found in Mendelssohn.

Mendelssohn's view of language in relation to music was best expressed in two letters—one to Friedrich Kistner in 1835, rejecting the offer to write and teach music; and the other to Marc André Souchay in 1842, in which Mendelssohn tried to explain the idea behind the "song without words." Mendelssohn explained to Kistner that he was unable to "speak on music" properly for more than half an hour. Nor was he able to follow someone talking about music. Listening to such verbal discourse made him come away "being more unmusical than I was when I went in."[59]

The gap between music and words did not mean that words and music could not be related. But that task proved difficult for Mendelssohn. Despite the many songs he wrote, it was primarily religious texts that satisfied him most as a basis for music. The very nature of traditional religious texts limits highly subjective interpretation on the part of the auditor. The intent of religious texts was, after all, to unify faith, a task that Mendelssohn regarded as appropriate to music.

But Mendelssohn articulated the essence of his misgivings about language as an instrument for creating a common ground among human beings in his letter to Souchay:

> So much is spoken about music and so little is said. For my part I do not believe that words suffice for such a task, and if they did I would no longer make any music. People usually complain that music is too many-sided in meanings; it is so ambiguous about what they should think when they hear it, whereas everyone understands words. For me it is exactly the reverse. And not only with whole speeches, but also with single words. They too seem so ambiguous, so vague, so subject to misunderstanding when compared with true music, which fills the soul with a thousand better things than words. The thoughts that are expressed to me by the music I love are not too indefinite to put into words, but on the contrary, too definite. And I find every effort to express [in words] such thoughts legitimate, but all in all inadequate. . . . this however is not your fault, but the fault of words, which cannot do better . . . because the same word never means the same thing to different people. Only melody can say the same thing, can arouse the same feelings in one person as in another, a feeling which may not be expressed, however, by the same words.[60]

Mendelssohn, after citing Goethe in defense of his argument, concluded with an example of how resignation, the praise of God, melancholy, and a hunting song could be confused for one another in certain circumstances. In the case of an individual who had mistaken the meaning of one of these, he said, "however long we might discuss it with him, we should never get any farther. The word retains many meanings, but music we can both understand correctly." The essential aspects of this view (which represent his mature position) are that, in a counterintuitive sense, music is precise in terms of human communication, an idea with which Wittgenstein toyed much later. Despite its apparent abstract nature, music could remain clear.

But here Mendelssohn switched the focus from a language-based notion of descriptive or explanatory meaning to the idea of "filling the human soul" with feelings and states of mind through music—complexes of meaning and sensibilities. It is these, then, that exceed, in depth and precision, ordinary language. What music does is arouse sympathetically the same feelings in different people. Music becomes, through the capacity for emotion, the best language for communication with fellow human beings. The evocation and expression of a recognizable commonality within humanity in response to nature and to faith in the divine were best achieved through music. Music avoids misunderstanding and can therefore triumph over the confusion of meanings engendered by verbal exchange. In doing this, music certainly does not function merely by illustrating verbal propositions.

This view further illuminates Mendelssohn's compositional strategy. It helps to explain—along with the visual impetus in Mendelssohn's music—the premium on surface, the stress on formal clarity and coherence, the long line, and the avoidance of developmental complexity and a sense of asymmetry.[61] Mendelssohn's commitment constituted an ethical response to his concern for the failures of ordinary language to transmit truth and engender harmony.

Music and the Public: The Mendelssohnian Project

The primacy of music as a means of human communication in Mendelssohn's mind had little to do with the notion of absolute music associated with Eduard Hanslick and the opponents of Wagner that became widespread after the publication of Hanslick's tract (*On the Beautiful in Music*) in 1854. Mendelssohn was convinced that, through music, ideas and feelings could be exactly communicated and recognized in purely musical terms. Therefore, the music of Mendelssohn can be understood to have meaning in the ordinary sense, and also to be "absolute music" (rather than "programmatic music," in the sense of requiring something to be tacked on as a literary analogue or having been derived, at the expense of the musical, from nonmusical sources).

The relationship between the literary texts and Mendelssohn's music, therefore, cannot be regarded as an example of translation from one medium to another. Perhaps a visual image was generated, whose musical analogue then clarified and deepened the essence of the image. Or the meaning and emotions associated with an image in combination with words found a musical means for essential significance to be unambiguously transmitted. Or the sentiment expressed in words alone found a parallel musical form, whose integrity, precision, and power exceed the verbal.[62] Meaning—content of a nonmusical nature—was not therefore extramusical. In fact Mendelssohn, in contrast to Wagner, rarely made an effort to use musical patterns to illustrate or augment the linguistic, nor did speech patterns influence his musical line in instrumental works.

Quite to the contrary; for Mendelssohn, music unleashed the central core of meaning, often obscured by words or the necessarily fixed and static character of imagery in literary and visual materials. The presence of the immanently musical within language and painting—or the capacity to express linguistic or painterly meanings in music—vindicated the ethical significance of those visual and linguistic forms. But in music resided the ultimate sources and mechanisms of the ethical in human discourse. The criteria for musical discourse were "purely" musical, however, since for Mendelssohn they derived from historical models of musical greatness, whose imaginative emulation helped to preserve normative aesthetic values. As Mendelssohn wrote in 1841, commenting on the text of Sophocles' *Antigone*, "I worked with sincere pleasure. It astonished me how much immutable there is in art; the moods of all these choruses are still today so musical, and yet so varied that no person could wish for something more beautiful to compose."[63]

The sign of the successful communication of ethical meaning through music was the "filling" of the soul with precise and deep feeling. Any evaluation of Mendelssohn's music must take this conception into account. The application of Wagnerian, Brahmsian, Schumannesque, or, for that matter, Beethovenian models to Mendelssohn's music is inappropriate in that it fails to confront Mendelssohn's explicit objective: the stimulation of subjective emotions with precise and universal meaning. And this lack of a proper understanding of Mendelssohn's intentions—even among contemporaries—should not justify aesthetic expectations that condemn the music as lacking in dramatic depth and as being merely refined.[64]

This aesthetics of emotion and feeling with which Mendelssohn associated himself was akin to the aesthetics and theology of Schleiermacher. It is in Schleiermacher's aesthetics, rather than in Hegel's, that one can locate the connection Mendelssohn made between the musical and the ethical.[65] For Schleiermacher, all subjective self-consciousness mirrored the presence of God. Feeling was the moment of self-recognition. Love of God was expressed by emotion and feeling. Music, and art in general, had the task of stimulating feeling and intensifying emotion in the service of religious faith.[66] Art could be judged by its impact on sensibility, by its influence on emotion. This theology and aesthetics of emotion corresponded to Mendelssohn's own aesthetic project.[67] Mendelssohn employed clarity and formal structure to intensify the emotional power of music over his contemporaries. In fact, rarely has such an intensity of emotion—often bittersweet—been written into musical material. Operating under the objectives of the theology of feeling, Mendelssohn sought, through his aesthetic procedures, to drive clearly and deeply into the listener and elicit not merely affirmation but introspection—both the pain and the pleasure of feeling. This was hardly a sentimental objective.

As Eric Werner noted, the church choir was for both Mendelssohn and Schleiermacher "the artistic representation of the congregation." Either by participation or by identification, Mendelssohn's choral music was designed to generate love of God among the worshipers.[68] Schleiermacher and Mendelssohn understood clearly that the gift for music was unevenly distributed among humans. Yet passive appreciation could achieve the desired end among the less musical, thereby preserving the unique emotional power and impact of music. But the music had to be clear, as evident as the principles of faith. The task was to generate, through music, an affectionate association in the listener between two normative principles: beauty and truth. It is in this context that Mendelssohn's claim that his goal was to "purify and restore the public taste" needs to be understood. Writing to Pastor Bauer in 1833, Mendelssohn, after admitting that aesthetic discourse made him "silent and dejected," noted that

> there is no such thing as too much sensibility, and what is called "too much" is always rather "too little." The soaring and elevation of emotion which people gladly associate with music constitute no excess; since the individual who is capable of feeling should feel emotions to the utmost—and whenever, even more so, if possible. . . . A plant never blossoms so much as to cause it to become sick; except when one forces it and then to the extreme. And such sickness is no more a real blossoming than sentimentality can be regarded as sentiment.[69]

It is precisely the ability to respond spontaneously and spiritually to the clear beauty and power of sentiment in Mendelssohn's music, and not to perceive mere sentimentality, that has been so hard for subsequent audiences. The ease of comprehension that Wittgenstein denigrated may be uniquely a mark of the greatness of Mendelssohn's music. Mendelssohn found a way to communicate widely but with rare immediacy and intensity—without descending into triviality.

Once one penetrates the theological and aesthetic drive toward collective communication at the moment of hearing in Mendelssohn's works, one recognizes the uniqueness of Mendelssohn's position. He did not wish to create a distance between himself and his listeners. But that did not mean he accepted their values or mirrored them. Rather, he used affection, lightness, refinement, and clarity to achieve trust and empathy, as a prelude to a deeper and more emotional engagement.

Consistent with this strategy, Mendelssohn celebrated the idea of music making as amateur and a family activity. Great musicians were obligated to set standards within a wide public so that musical activity could engender the sort of universal sensibility he sought. For that sensibility to have wide significance, he believed every musician needed to have a humanistic education in order to become a great artist.[70]

As Lothar Gall observed, Mendelssohn's towering place in the center of the social structure of his age was widely observed, particularly within the expanding public life characterized by the many middle-class musical societies that flourished during his lifetime.[71] Mendelssohn viewed his fame increasingly as an indispensable burden, since music making was a civic virtue that formed community. When Mendelssohn wrote music for Shakespeare and Sophocles or sought to improve on Conradin Kreutzer's musical response to Grillparzer's *Melusina,* he employed a language and rhetoric of music that played off the specific dramatic or historical material by using the musical language of the day. Universality was expressed in a musical style that balanced normative criteria and historical standards with a contemporary aesthetic sensibility. The subjective and objective were reconciled through the medium of music. In this sense the verbal and visual were always time-bound and particular. Music, however, was an objective language that could transcend specificity without abandoning shifts in style and taste. But these shifts required historical grounding. Therefore, serious music demanded education, which in turn helped music to elicit the emotional response envisaged by Schleiermacher. A critical didactic intent was always present. The music Mendelssohn wrote was designed to be judged normatively, to last through time in its emotional power just as Bach's had. Mendelssohn sought to edify normative standards applied to contemporary taste, to deepen true faith in one's own time through true art—that is, music.

Given Mendelssohn's self-conscious concern to reach and influence his audience, it is no wonder that the apex of Mendelssohn's popularity was in his lifetime. But was he successful in his terms? With the revolution of 1848 and the changes in European life and culture, the spiritual ambition of Mendelssohn's social and ethical project became rapidly incomprehensible; the receptivity within the culture had vanished.

Mendelssohn's confidence in the power of music as a peaceful instrument of human solidarity and love of God and nature—the cultural project to which he committed himself—justified his efforts at regenerating the historical repertoire and developing institutions of musical education.[72] He sought to counter the failures of a strategy of assimilation among Jews that relied entirely on language and philosophical argument. His belief in the link between musical aesthetics and theology helped convince him of the truth and universality of Christianity. But Felix Mendelssohn also embraced anew the cause of Moses Mendelssohn—to bring religions and their adherents under a common societal framework marked by respect, love of truth, and reason. "Render unto God what is God's! Love truth! Love peace!" admonished Moses Mendelssohn.[73] His grandson, by the use of music, sought to solve what rational philosophy employed by his grandfather could not—to end, by the spread of music, the "deception" Moses Mendelssohn believed humans too often engaged in daily with one another through the use of "delusive words."

The poignancy of the Mendelssohnian project rests not merely in its peculiar merger of the aesthetic ideals of romanticism and the ethical claims of the Enlightenment, but also in the manner in which the scope and ambition of it were sharply inverted by Richard Wagner. It was, finally, Wagner's capacity to communicate philosophical and political sensibilities to a broad audience, not merely an elite—using words and drama—that transformed not only the aesthetics of music, but the cultural politics of art in nineteenth-century Europe. It is this context that lends Jiri Weil's fictional anecdote its irony: an SS Officer who seeks to take down a bust of Mendelssohn from among a group of statues in Prague does not know what Mendelssohn looked like; assuming that the one with the longest nose must be the right one, he destroys the bust of Richard Wagner.[74]

In 1929 Wittgenstein remarked that "tragedy is something un-Jewish" and that "Mendelssohn is, I suppose, the most untragic of composers."[75] Perhaps Wittgenstein was too influenced by Wagner, for the tragic is evident in Mendelssohn. It is audible (in the Wagnerian sense) not only in key works, such as the String Quartet, op. 80, and moments such as the "Jerusalem" aria from *St. Paul*, but in the contrast between what the music is—the authorial conceit and intention—and the way it has been understood subsequently.

Mendelssohn sought to seize what he realized might be the last moment in European history to further the project of assimilation, enlightenment, and the universal love of God. Our ability once again to appreciate the emotional depth, sentiment, and transcendent beauty of Mendelssohn's music may depend to some degree on our capacity to identify with Mendelssohn's goals of affirmation through the art and practice of music, with the creation of a language of communication that can bind humans together through the recognition of a divine presence that does not pit human against human. Can a common love of and response to musical beauty engender a more tolerant world? One is reminded of the admonition of J. W. Davison, the nineteenth-century English critic. In 1842 he wrote that Mendelssohn's music was intended for those who

> love music for more than its jingle . . . who look upon it as one of the most intense mediums of poetic expression; who perceive in it a world and many worlds; whose souls are moved by it to deep and passionate thought; to abstruse and metaphysical reverie; whose senses are anointed by it . . . whose minds are instructed by it, as by the words of a philosopher; whose enthusiasm is kindled by it, as by the voice of the loved one; whose emotions are fed by it as the flame by fuel; whose minds are ennobled by it as by the song of the poet.[76]

NOTES

1. Among the scandalous pseudo-scholarly Nazi efforts were Karl Blessinger, *Judentum und Musik* (Berlin, 1944), pp. 47–74, and the entry on Mendelssohn by Ernst Bücken, then a professor at the University of Cologne, in his *Wörterbuch der Musik* (Leipzig, 1940), pp. 272–73.

2. See, for example, the introduction to Hans Christoph Worbs, *Felix Mendelssohn-Bartholdy* (Hamburg, 1974).

3. See Leon Plantinga's "Schumann's Critical Reaction to Mendelssohn," in Jon W. Finson and R. Larry Todd, eds., *Mendelssohn and Schumann: Essays on Their Music and Its Context* (Durham, 1984), pp. 12–19; one thinks of Berlioz's portrait of Mendelssohn in his memoirs.

4. Knud Martner, *Gustav Mahler im Konzertsaal. Eine Dokumentation seiner Konzerttätigkeit: 1870–1911* (Copenhagen, 1985); and *Das Rosé Quartett: Fünfzig Jahre Kammermusik in Wien. Sämtliche Programme* (Vienna, 1932). A relatively unexplored but important area of investigation is the role Mendelssohn's music had on the development of the music of Gustav Mahler. One thinks immediately of a comparison of their respective second symphonies and of the influence of *St. Paul*, which Mahler knew and conducted, on works such as the latter's Eighth Symphony. Donald Mitchell has made some tantalizing observations on this matter. See Donald Mitchell, *Gustav Mahler: The Wunderhorn Years* (Berkeley, 1975), pp. 294–95; idem, *Gustav Mahler: Songs and Symphonies of Life and Death* (Berkeley, 1985), p. 595; and Norman Lebrecht, *Mahler Remembered* (New York, 1988), p. 252.

5. It is, for example, striking how few references to Mendelssohn there are in the writings of Arnold Schoenberg. With the exception of the young Richard Strauss and Max Reger, the absence of a Mendelssohn influence (as opposed to that of Brahms, Schumann, or Wagner) in twentieth-century musical modernism is marked. It can be ascribed to the critical reaction after 1850.

6. See Grove's article "Mendelssohn" in *Grove's Dictionary*, ed. J. A. Fuller Maitland (Philadelphia, 1904), vol. 3, pp. 110–77; and Bernard Shaw, *Shaw's Music. The Complete Music Criticism*, ed. D. Laurence (New York, 1981), vol. 1, p. 565.

7. Nietzsche was also poking fun at German musical tastes and Wagner's view of Beethoven (and Wagner's attempt to assume for himself the legacy of Beethoven). In Friedrich Nietzsche, *Jenseits von Gut und Böse*, in *Nietzsches Werke. Kritische Gesamtausgabe* 6/2 (Berlin, 1968), pp. 193–94. See also section 157 in the second part of Nietzsche's *Human, All Too Human* (1886).

8. Eric Werner, *Mendelssohn: A New Image of the Composer and His Age*, trans. Dika Newlin (Glencoe, 1963), p. 358. Werner relies exclusively on a negative comment by Mendelssohn about the D-minor Piano Concerto and seems not to account for Mendelssohn's self-critical habits. See also pp. 352–54 and 287–96; and Philip Radcliffe, *Mendelssohn*, rev. ed. (London, 1990), pp. 101, 113–31.

9. See Carl Dahlhaus, "Vorwort," in *Das Problem Mendelssohn* (Regensburg, 1974), hereafter cited as *DPM*, pp. 7–9.

10. Ludwig Wittgenstein, *Culture and Value*, ed. G. H. von Wright, trans. Peter Winch (Chicago, 1980), p. 2; see also pp. 16, 21, 23, 35, 38.

11. Richard Hauser, "In rührend feierlichen Tönen: Mendelssohns Kantate *Die erste Walpurgisnacht*," in *Felix Mendelssohn-Bartholdy*, ed. Heinz Klaus Metzger and Rainer Riehn (Munich, 1980), pp. 75–93.

12. The references in this section are from *Cosima Wagner's Diaries*, 2 vols., ed. M. Gregor-Dellin, trans. G. Skelton (New York, 1977), cited hereafter as *CW*, vol. 1 or 2; and from Richard Wagner, *Gesammelte Schriften und Dichtungen* (Leipzig, 1907), cited hereafter as *GW*, with volume number. *CW*, vol. 2, p. 138.

13. *CW*, vol. 2, p. 959.

14. *Selected Letters of Richard Wagner*, ed. and trans. S. Spencer and B. Millington (New York, 1988), p. 334.

15. Carl F. Glasenapp, *Das Leben Richard Wagners*, 5th ed. (Leipzig, 1923), vol. 1, pp. 202–4; and vol. 2, pp. 23–24; also Robert W. Gutman, *Richard Wagner the Man, His Mind and His Music* (New York, 1968), p. 45. Glasenapp's anti-Semitism more than rivaled that of his idol Wagner.

16. See Friedhelm Kemp, "Mendelssohns Berliner Umwelt," in *DPM*, pp. 11–21.

17. See, for example, the recollection of Caroline Pichler, who recalled meeting Mendelssohn in Baden in the context of the elite of the wealthy com-

mercial "second society" of Vienna. In Caroline Pichler, *Denkwürdigkeiten aus meinem Leben*, vol. 2 (Munich, 1914), pp. 158–59.

18. See the letter to Zelter from Paris, dated 15 February 1832; and to his father on 21 February, in *Briefe aus den Jahren 1830 bis 1847* (Leipzig, 1882), vol. 1, p. 247; and vol. 4, p. 149. The citations from Mendelssohn's letters are taken from this work, the two-volume set (Leipzig, 1863); *Briefe aus Leipziger Archiven*, ed. H.-J. Rothe and R. Szeskus (Leipzig, 1972); and *Briefe*, ed. R. Elvers (Frankfurt, 1984), cited hereafter as *MB*, vol. 1, 2, 3, or 4.

19. *GW*, vol. 1, p. 187.

20. The Wagnerian criticism from the 1840s, particularly from Paris, bears an unflatteringly close resemblance to Heine's; see *GW*, vol. 2, pp. 267–68, and the Heine selections in this volume.

21. Richard Wagner, *My Life*, ed. A. Gray, trans. M. Whittal (Cambridge, 1983), pp. 272, 319.

22. *GW*, vol. 8, pp. 276–77.

23. Letter dated 12 June 1872, in W. A. Ellis, *Richard Wagner's Prose Works*, vol. 5 (New York, 1966), p. 293.

24. Letter from Lucerne, dated 27 August 1831, in *MB*, vol. 2, p. 256.

25. *GW*, vol. 10, pp. 251–52.

26. Ibid., vol. 8, pp. 226–38.

27. Ibid., vol. 5, pp. 66–85, especially pp. 81–82.

28. Ibid., vol. 3, pp. 228ff.

29. Ibid., p. 98.

30. Ernest Newman, *The Life of Richard Wagner*, vol. 4 (Cambridge, 1973), p. 600.

31. Richard Wagner, "The Work and Mission of My Life," in *North American Review* 273 (August 1879): 120–21.

32. W. H. Riehl, "Bach und Mendelssohn aus dem socialen Gesichtspunkte," in *Musikalische Charakterköpfe* (Stuttgart, 1857), p. 101; see also pp. 94–100.

33. The literature on this subject is immense. See, however, three newer works, Paul Lawrence Rose, *Revolutionary Antisemitism in Germany from Kant to Wagner* (Princeton, 1990); Leon Botstein, *Judentum und Modernität: 1848–1938* (Vienna 1990); and Jacob Katz, *The Darker Side of Genius* (Hanover, N.H.,1986).

34. See Deborah Hertz, *Jewish High Society in Old-Regime Berlin* (New Haven, 1988).

35. See David Sorkin, *The Transformation of German Jewry 1780–1840* (New York, 1987).

36. Werner, pp. 28–44; see also Wilfrid Blunt, *On Wings of Song: A Biography of Felix Mendelssohn* (New York, 1974), pp. 23–24.

37. An interesting question remains: Was Mendelssohn circumcised? Zelter sarcastically noted to Goethe that Abraham had made the supreme sacrifice of *not* circumcising his sons. But given that Felix was converted at age seven and the parents only later, there is reason to believe that he, like all Jews, had

been circumcised on the eighth day after birth. Among assimilated Reform German-Jews, the anticircumcision movement began only in the 1840s. Circumcision was not only an indelible mark of Jewishness; in nineteenth-century Germany it was exclusively a sign of Jewishness. Every day, and particularly in the conduct of his routine and intimate life, Mendelssohn, if circumcised, would have been reminded of the difference in his birth. See Wulf Konold, *Felix Mendelssohn-Bartholdy und seine Zeit* (Regensburg, 1984), p. 77. Konold uses an older edition of the Goethe-Zelter correspondence that deletes the reference to circumcision. In the newer critical edition, from 1913, the reference by Zelter to Mendelssohn's Jewishness reads "[Felix] is a good, handsome boy, happy and obedient. He may be certainly the son of a Jew, but no Jew. The father, with significant sacrifice, has not circumcised his sons and brings them up properly as it should be done. It would really be a rare thing [in Yiddish] if an artist came out of the son of a Jew." Konold's text, from 1834, was made more respectable and replaced "not circumcised" with "educated correctly." See Max Hecker, ed., *Briefwechsel zwischen Goethe und Zelter* (Frankfurt, 1987), vol. 2, p. 158. The question remains as to which text is right and, if the later version is accurate, whether Zelter was being metaphoric (as with, for example, today's use of "kosher") or literal.

38. See the Heine selections in this volume from *Lutezia* and the letters.

39. Letter of 23 July 1833; cited in Konold, p. 75.

40. Werner, p. 39. Varnhagen von Ense recounted an incident in 1819, when Mendelssohn, who was ten years old, was spat upon by a member of the Prussian court. See Varnhagen von Ense, *Denkwürdigkeiten und vermischte Schriften*, vol. 9 (Leipzig, 1859), p. 615. There is no other confirmation of this incident.

41. Letter to Goethe, 28 August 1831; in *Letters*, ed. G. Selden-Goth (New York, 1972), p. 172.

42. Heinz-Klaus Metzger, "Noch einmal: 'Die erste Walpurgisnacht,' Versuch einer anderen Allegorese," in Metzger and Riehn, pp. 93–97.

43. Letter of 12 January 1835, in *MB*, vol. 2, pp. 75–77.

44. Letter of 14 July 1837, in ibid., p. 148.

45. See Martin Witte, "Zur Programmgebundenheit der Sinfonien Mendelssohns," in *DPM*, pp. 119–28.

46. Cited in Ralph P. Locke, *Music, Musicians and the Saint-Simonians* (Chicago, 1986), p. 109.

47. See Devrient's account in Eduard Devrient, *My Recollections of Felix Mendelssohn-Bartholdy* (New York, 1972), pp. 40–42.

48. Letter to Devrient dated 27 August 1831, in *MB*, vol. 1, pp. 200–201.

49. Werner, p. 186.

50. Letter of 29 October 1837, in *MB*, vol. 2, pp. 155–57.

51. See R. Larry Todd, "Of Sea Gulls and Counterpoint: The Early Versions of Mendelssohn's *Hebrides* Overture," in *19th-Century Music* 2 (1979): 197–213.

52. Letter of 14 November 1840, in *MB*, vol. 2, p. 241.

53. This speculative analysis differs somewhat from that of R. Larry Todd, who identified the concern for an "organic" unity in the *Scottish* Symphony as deriving from literary rather than visual sources. See R. Larry Todd, "Mendelssohn's Ossianic Manner, with a New Source," in Jon W. Finson and R. Larry Todd, eds., *Mendelssohn and Schumann*, pp. 137–60. See also the discussion of the relation of text and music in Mendelssohn's *Midsummer Night's Dream* by Friedhelm Krummacher in *DPM*, pp. 89–118.

54. Letter from Rome, dated 10 December 1830, in *MB*, vol. 2, p. 74.

55. Moses Mendelssohn, "Über die Frage: Was heisst Aufklären?" in Moritz Brasch, ed., *Moses Mendelssohn's Schriften zur Philosophie, Aesthetik und Apologetik* (Leipzig, 1880), vol. 2, pp. 246–50.

56. Moses Mendelssohn, *Jerusalem*, trans. A. Arkush (Waltham, 1983), p. 138.

57. See Carl Dahlhaus, *Klassische und romantische Musikaesthetik* (Regensburg, 1988), pp. 140–49.

58. Letter to Rebecka of 26 October 1833, in *MB*, vol. 1, pp. 6–11.

59. Letter of 3 January 1835, in *MB*, vol. 4, pp. 175–76.

60. Letter from Berlin, dated 15 October 1842, in *MB*, vol. 2, p. 337–38.

61. Friedhelm Krummacher has suggested that late in his life Mendelssohn's compositional ambitions and procedure changed. Mendelssohn, Krummacher argues, using the late chamber music, was moving from "homogeneity and unity" to "divergence and dissolution." I believe that the String Quartet, op. 80, and the 1845 Quintet, op. 87, can still easily fall within this argument. See F. Krummacher, "Mendelssohn's Late Chamber Music," in Todd and Finson, p. 84.

62. This notion is strikingly similar to Arnold Schoenberg's articulation of the proper relationship between text and music. See his "The Relationship to the Text," in *The Blaue Reiter Almanac*, ed. Wassily Kandinsky and Franz Marc (New York, 1989), pp. 90–103.

63. Letter from Berlin to Ferdinand David, 21 October 1841, in *MB*, vol. 3, p. 168.

64. In this regard see Arno Forchert's discussion of the texts and dramatic character of *Elijah* in *DPM*, particularly pp. 70–77.

65. Adolf Nowak, *Hegels Musikaesthetik* (Regensburg, 1971), pp. 58–66.

66. See F.D.E. Schleiermacher, *Aesthetik* (1819), ed. Thomas Lehnerer (Hamburg, 1984), pp. ix, 69–81.

67. See, for example, Mendelssohn's letters from Rome in 1831, particularly the ones dated 4 April and 16 June 1831.

68. Werner, p. 451.

69. Letter from Berlin, dated 4 March 1833, in *MB*, vol. 2, p. 2.

70. Letter from Leipzig, dated 19 September 1839, in *MB*, vol. 2, pp. 208–11.

71. Lothar Gall, *Bürgertum in Deutschland* (Berlin, 1989), pp. 212–13.

72. On Mendelssohn's lifelong engagement with the educational signifi-

cance of historical repertoire, see Susanna Grossmann-Vendrey, *Felix Mendelssohn und die Musik der Vergangenheit* (Regensburg, 1969).

73. Moses Mendelssohn, *Jerusalem*, p. 139.

74. From Weil's 1960 novel, *Mendelssohn is on the Roof*, recounted by Philip Roth in his preface to Jiri Weil's *Life with a Star* (New York, 1989), p. vii.

75. Wittgenstein, *Culture and Value*, p. 1.

76. J. W. Davison, "Mendelssohn's 'Temperaments,'" in Henry Davison, ed., *From Mendelssohn to Wagner: Memoirs of J. W. Davison, Forty Years Music Critic of the Times* (London, 1912), pp. 354–55.

Some Notes on an Anthem
by Mendelssohn

DAVID BRODBECK

[The research for this essay was made possible through generous grants from the National Endowment for the Humanities, the American Philosophical Society, and the Faculty of Arts and Sciences, University of Pittsburgh.]

In the early autumn of 1840, Felix Mendelssohn Bartholdy paid his sixth visit to England. Occasioned by the English première of the *Lobgesang* Symphony, this sojourn led to the creation of another, lesser-known work that was equally steeped in the English choral tradition. Just before returning to Leipzig, Mendelssohn accepted a commission from an eccentric musical and literary amateur named Charles Bayles Broadley, who requested of the composer a setting of one of his own metrical Psalm paraphrases, which he intended to publish in a lavish private edition. Serving as an intermediary between the two parties was Ignaz Moscheles, Broadley's composition teacher in London and one of Mendelssohn's dearest friends.[1]

Through Moscheles, Mendelssohn apparently was offered his choice of several texts; preserved in the composer's estate are Broadley's versions of Psalms 13, 100, and 126. The author described the first text as being "suitable for a Solo Anthem"; the other two, "for a Full or Choral Anthem."[2] In December Mendelssohn finally settled down to work, selecting the thirteenth Psalm ("Why, O Lord, delay forever") and setting this text, in Broadley's suggested manner, as an anthem for alto or mezzo soprano solo, chorus, and organ. A draft of the work—it took shape in three movements (Andante, Chorale, and Vivace finale)—was completed on 12 December, and two days later the composer produced a fair copy, which he dispatched to Moscheles on the twentieth of the month, together with a letter for

Broadley requesting permission to release a German edition on the date of the anthem's English appearance.[3] After asking his friend to explain to Broadley the customary practice concerning dual English and German editions, Mendelssohn turned briefly to artistic matters: "I do not know whether I have found the tone of the English anthem, but I have taken pains to do so and worked on the piece with more pleasure than I previously had imagined. Please give me your evaluation."[4]

Several weeks later, in a letter dated 9 February 1841, came Moscheles' belated response:

I have had to leave unanswered your letter of 20 December of last year, with the 13th Psalm, because I first wanted to hear about it from Mr. Broadley, who has been out of the city. On the day before yesterday he informed me of everything he wanted to say on the matter (and he expressed himself "broadly"). First I must convey to you my joy and special pleasure regarding your composition of the Psalm. It is noble, self-controlled, pure, and far from [showing] impractical embellishment and heterogeneous colors, that is, *sacred.* I must point out to you a favorite spot. The place in the alto solo "week [*sic*] and fainting" is truly poetic and later builds up splendidly in the choir. It affords me satisfaction that *you too* are pleased with the composition, since that proves to me that you are clear and at one with your intentions, and I hope you remain thus. My wife and I have performed the Psalm for my wise pupil B. and have moved him to rapture (over the composition, not the performance). [inserted later: Yesterday Miss Mason also rehearsed the solo part and finds it quite admirably suited to her voice.] He intends to have it performed on a suitable occasion in York Cathedral. I had settled with him to leave to you the arrangement of publishing it on 15 April of this year with English and German text; and he requests that on the title page stand [the words]: composed for C. Broadley Esqre by whom the english [*sic*] metrical Version of the Psalm is made.

His wish is to have, in addition, a prelude by you for the Psalm (approximately one page long) (which he wants to keep in his album), as well as some measures after the Chorale as a prelude to the last number, which he would like to have printed [originally: prefer not to have printed]. The comical manner in which he expresses himself to me in writing is so funny that I cannot keep it from you and enclose his letter. This document is one of the numerous of his peculiar half-deranged nature [see appendix 1]. As you can see, he envisions forming a trio of Psalms, by having me invite Spohr also to write one. Thinking about which role I am to play in this makes me anxious. I have finished a sketch of mine (the 93th). It consists of three numbers: a lengthy bass solo, with added four-part choir later appearing (D minor and D major), a chorus $\frac{6}{4}$ in B♭ major, and a figural chorale based on the tune of "Wachet auf ruft uns die Stimme."[5]

Moscheles' report gives evidence of a notable expansion in Broadley's ambitions. What had begun in the fall of 1840 as a commission of a single piece by Mendelssohn had grown by early 1841 into a planned collection involving works by three leading composers of the day.[6] Notwithstanding, Mendelssohn still intended to publish his work independently in Germany, and on 4 March he initiated discussion with N. Simrock, offering to send the anthem in "eine sehr gute Deutsche Übersetzung," and suggesting the title "Drei geistliche Lieder für eine Mezzo-Sopranstimme mit Chor und Begleitung der Orgel."[7] Simrock responded with an immediate interest,[8] whereupon Mendelssohn answered Moscheles' recent letter, again beginning with business matters and then taking up more substantive musical ones:

> And now to return to your two delightful letters. The first contained the enclosures from Broadley and instructions in reference to the German publication [see appendix 2]; they shall be punctually carried out. Please ask him to mention on the title-page of the English edition that Simrock of Bonn is the German publisher. May I beg you to communicate this to him without delay? Make my excuses to him (and yourself) for not having sent the short prelude. I would gladly do so; but really, with the best will in the world, I could not write a short prelude to suit that piece without altering the whole form and giving it a pretentious coloring, which it should not have. I would rather leave it to the organist to tumble his fingers about at random, making it long or short as he likes, and as rich or poor as he can afford.[9]

In preparing the score to be used in printing the German edition Mendelssohn simply worked over the autograph of 12 December, most notably by inserting the German text beneath the English words and placing above the original heading, "Anthem," the title "Geistliches Lied mit Chor." A wrapper, apparently added at this time, enlarged somewhat this inscription: "Geistliches Lied mit Chor und Orgelbegleitung componirt für Herrn C. Broadley in London," followed, in accordance with Broadley's stipulation, by the text: "This Music (except in Germany) is the Copyright of C. Broadley, Esq., the Author of the English words." When, on 31 March, Mendelssohn submitted the work to Simrock, he noted that the manuscript had been poorly copied ("schlecht abgeschrieben")—it had been his first draft, after all, not a fair copy—and thus requested proofs. Moreover, perhaps fearing that, despite his marking "non lento," the overly slow tempo that characterized German performances of chorales in the early nineteenth century might be followed in the second movement, he requested that this portion of the work be printed, not as it appeared in the manuscript, in *alla breve*, but in common time, with note values reduced by one-half. On the other hand, even though he had by now added to the score indications that the three movements were to be performed without pause between them, Mendelssohn was indifferent to the title of the composition, leaving to the publisher to decide between "Geistliches Lied mit Chor" (as the work was entitled in the manuscript) or "Drei geistliche Lieder mit Chor" (as the composer had otherwise described it).[10] Although Simrock worked quickly and already by 19 April was able to deliver a proof-copy of the musical text, his intention to produce an elaborate title page subsequently impeded progress; in August 1841 the work finally appeared, under the title *Drei geistliche Lieder für eine Altstimme mit Chor und Orgelbegleitung.*[11]

At the same time, Moscheles was attending to the details of the English edition, and in doing so found Broadley to be a fussy, meddlesome annoyance. As Mrs. Moscheles put it, "To him no paper is too fine, no engraver good enough, and so he constantly plagues my husband with this edition."[12] In spite of these distractions, Moscheles saw his work through, and on or near the appointed date of 15 April 1841 the anthem appeared in a handsome, large folio print, whose caption title on p. 2 presents a facsimile of Mendelssohn's handwriting taken from the autograph (see figures 1a and 1b).[13] The back wrapper of this edition bespeaks Broadley's ambitions and pretentiousness (figure 1c); not only are the other psalms in the projected series announced, but so too is a volume of Broadley's Psalm paraphrases (whose engravings, "as works of art, . . . have never been surpassed in any age or country"), as well as a collection of his own sacred music, all undertaken to be printed at his own expense. In the same month Spohr composed his setting of Broadley's version of Psalm 128, and shortly thereafter it too appeared in print.[14] By contrast, Moscheles evidently was slow to complete his psalm, which, de-

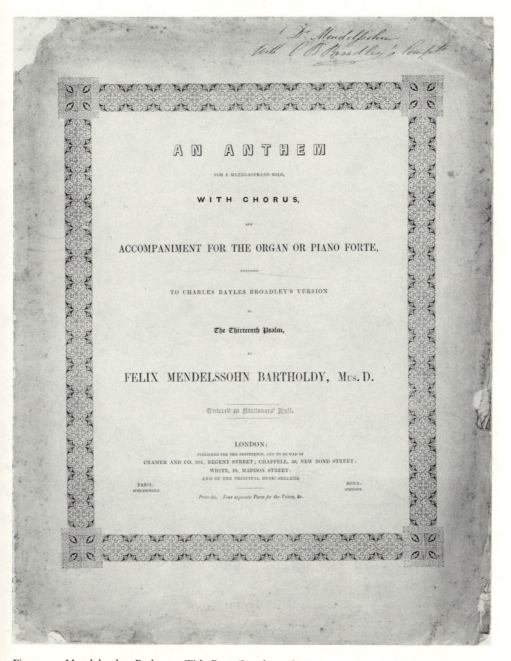

Figure 1a. Mendelssohn, Psalm 13, Title Page (London, 1841)

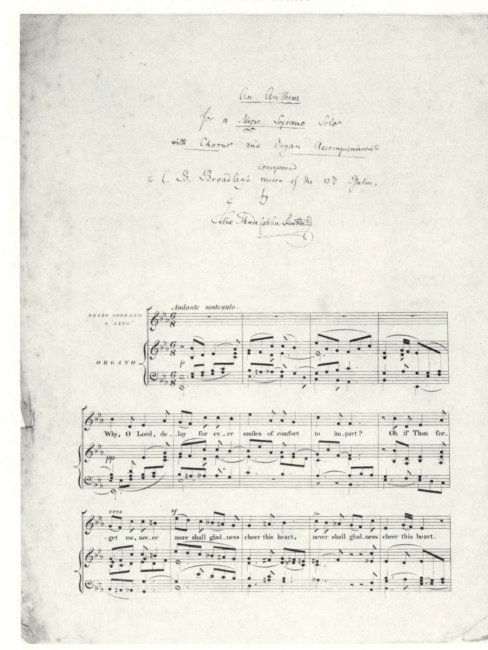

Figure 1b. Mendelssohn, Psalm 13, page 2

NOW READY,

FORMING THE FIRST OF A SERIES OF

𝕾𝖆𝖈𝖗𝖊𝖉 𝕸𝖚𝖘𝖎𝖈, 𝖈𝖍𝖎𝖊𝖋𝖑𝖞 𝕮𝖆𝖙𝖍𝖊𝖉𝖗𝖆𝖑,

Printed uniformly in size with the celebrated collections of DRS. BOYCE and ARNOLD, but with a fuller page,

AN ANTHEM,

COMPOSED BY FELIX MENDELSSOHN BARTHOLDY, MUS. D.,

A SECOND ANTHEM, COMPOSED BY I. MOSCHELES,

PIANIST TO H. R. H. THE PRINCE ALBERT,

AND

A THIRD ANTHEM, COMPOSED BY LOUIS SPOHR.

They are printed in Score, with Accompaniments for the Organ or Piano Forte, and separate Parts may be had for the Voices. The Words for the above three Anthems have been selected from a metrical Version of the PSALMS of DAVID, by CHARLES BAYLES BROADLEY, LL.B., of Trinity College, Cambridge. The three will be published *together*, in One Volume, and a few Copies may now be had separately.

Also, in the Press, and will be speedily published, in crown octavo, embellished with Line-Engravings on steel, after the Designs of T. STOTHARD, R.A., T. UWINS, R.A., CHARLES EASTLAKE, R.A., WILLIAM COLLINS, R.A., JOHN MARTIN, J. M. WRIGHT, HENRY CORBOULD, and other eminent Artists, by GOODALL, STOCKS, &c.,

SELECTIONS FROM THE PSALMS OF DAVID,

TRANSLATED INTO METRE,

BY CHARLES BAYLES BROADLEY, LL.B.,

OF TRINITY COLLEGE, CAMBRIDGE.

The price will be about half-a-guinea : Proofs, on medium or royal octavo, about double. Those who may be desirous of securing copies, with *early* impressions of the plates, are requested to send their names to the Proprietor, at D. T. White's, 28, Maddox Street, Hanover Square, London. It may be stated, without exaggeration, that, as works of art, the Embellishments have never been surpassed in any age or country. A few sets of choice Proofs, before the writing, may be had (apart from the letter-press) of Mr. D. T. White.

A VOLUME OF

CATHEDRAL AND OTHER SACRED MUSIC,

IN SCORE, WITH ACCOMPANIMENT FOR THE ORGAN OR PIANO FORTE, BY CHARLES BAYLES BROADLEY;

AND THE FOUNTAIN SONG,

From copper-plates, by BECKER, (with an Engraving on steel,) for a Mezzo-Soprano, or Alto Solo, with Piano Forte Accompaniment, the Music and Words by CHARLES BAYLES BROADLEY, are now engraved.

To be had at D. T. WHITE'S, 28, *Maddox Street, Hanover Square, London, and of the principal Music-sellers.*

E. CLAY, PRINTER, BREAD STREET HILL.

Figure 1c. Mendelssohn, Psalm 13, Back Wrapper

spite an announcement on the back wrapper of the Spohr edition, was not forthcoming until two years later.[15]

Meanwhile there arrived Broadley's request for orchestral versions of the composers' psalms, as a result of which, in late 1842, the anthem emerged once more in the correspondence between Moscheles and Mendelssohn. On 18 November, responding to Broadley's offer of ten guineas for the orchestration, Mendelssohn replied: "I will try to fit an orchestral dress on to the Broadley piece; and if I succeed, will send it to you without delay."[16] The composer quickly fashioned not only a new "dress," but also the beginning of a new, added fugal finale (the text of which he derived from the final verses of Broadley's original). Work on this addition was interrupted, however, by his mother's death on 12 December—ironically, the second anniversary of the completion of the anthem in its original guise—and not until 5 January 1843 did Mendelssohn complete the revised version.[17] The autograph was immediately given to a copyist, who prepared the score intended for Broadley.[18] Although Mendelssohn did not carefully proofread this source—a note in his hand to Moscheles added at the top of the score requests his friend's cooperation in checking for errors—he did make several corrections, added a number of articulation and dynamic markings, and, what is most significant, thickened the texture by means of instrumental doublings. On 16 January the score was forwarded to Moscheles, to whom Mendelssohn described the unexpected fugue as "the best piece of the whole . . . the gingerbread-nut they give into the bargain at the sweet-stuff shop."[19]

In a letter of 25 February Broadley thanked Mendelssohn for the manuscript and praised his work:

> I have received from Mr. Moscheles the Orchestral Parts to your Anthem composed to my version of the 13th Psalm, and feel much obliged by the additional Fugue, which I think exceedingly beautiful. The three first movements of the Anthem are frequently performed at the Chapel Royal, Windsor, by her Majesty's Command. Mr. Moscheles has been good enough to arrange the Fugue for the Organ. If it be not intruding too much on your kindness to request a few bars of Music with your signature on a small piece of paper (about the size of this note) to be inserted in a Lady's manuscript-Book of musical Autographs, you will further oblige, Sir, Your obedient Servant C B Broadley.[20]

In this letter Broadley evidently included a peculiar bilingual receipt for Mendelssohn to sign acknowledging payment "*received* für das *copyright* einer *additional fugue and for arranging the whole Anthem for orchestra.*"[21] Mendelssohn's response included a little three-part canon for Broadley's lady friend; the composer explained to Moscheles that, because the fugue had been offered as a gift, he could not sign the receipt as it was written, adding that none was really necessary. At the same time he informed Moscheles that Broadley could publish "die Fuge und das Ganze" according to his own preference, since he did not intend to publish the new version of the piece in Germany.[22] Indeed, within a few weeks' time Broadley had published the fugue in Moscheles' arrangement for organ accompaniment, and in later years he appears to have made some effort toward releasing the orchestration.[23] In the end, however, the instrumental setting transmitted in the Broadley manuscript—the only one that Mendelssohn prepared for publication—remained unpublished. The first edition of the orchestral version did not appear until 1852, five years after the composer's death. Published as *Hymne*, op. 96, this edition was based instead on the autograph, and it does not, accordingly, embody the significant changes that Mendelssohn had made in the final stages of revision.[24]

Mendelssohn's original three-movement form of 1840 is closely matched to the sequence of images contained in the five stanzas of Broadley's text (figure 2). The opening Andante provides a gentle terrain in which to explore the anxious questions that are posed in the first two quatrains; the earnest entreaties that follow are taken up in a sturdy, isometric Chorale; and a joyful Vivace, gradually building to an exuberant fugato, aptly expresses the final stanza's hymn of praise. In a manner that is reminiscent of the traditional English verse anthem, the solo voice and chorus engage in systematic alternations throughout, occurring at the level of two fused quatrains (in the chorale), the single strophe (in the beginnings of the first and last movements), and the half stanza (in the endings of the two outer movements).

If the patterns of solo-tutti alternation are quite straightforward, other aspects of the setting are handled with greater subtlety. The first movement, a rounded binary form in E♭ with a written-out repetition of the first part (A A′B A″), is a case in point. Following a simple, four-bar introduction in the organ, the main theme is given out twice, first by the soloist, whose setting of the opening stanza remains in the tonic (mm. 5–14), and then by the four-part chorus, in a varied repetition that tonicizes the dominant (mm. 15–24). At first this variation involves little more than the addition of certain chromatic de-

[NO. 1] ANDANTE SOSTENUTO
Why, O Lord, delay for ever
Smiles of comfort to impart?
Oh, if Thou forget me—never
More shall gladness cheer this heart.

Shall my soul still pine in sorrow?
Still shall foes their insults pour?
Weak and fainting—shall the morrow
Bring thine aid to me no more?

NO. 2 CHORALE, NON LENTO
On thy love my heart reposes
Hear me draw my falt'ring breath—
Raise me, lest mine eyelid closes—
Lest I sleep the sleep of death.

Lest my haughty foes prevailing
Proudly boast, "we laid him low."
Lest the scorner hear my wailing,
And he triumphed in my woe.

NO. 3 CON MOTO VIVACE
Lord! my heart's devotion raises
Off'rings to thy throne above:
Glad to sing thy hallow'd praises—
Aye rejoicing in thy love.

Figure 2.

NO. 1 ANDANTE
Lass, o Herr, mich Hülfe finden,
neig' dich gnädig meinem Flehn,
willst gedenken Du der Sünden
nimmermehr kann ich bestehn.

Soll mein Sorgen ewig dauern?
sollen Feinde spotten mein?
Schwach und hülflos, soll ich trauern,
und von dir vergessen sein?

NO. 2 CHORAL. NON LENTO
Deines Kind's Gebet erhöre,
Vater schau auf mich herab.
Meinen Augen Licht gewähre,
rette mich aus dunkelm Grab.

Sonst verlacht der Feind mich Armen,
triumphirt in stolzer Pracht,
sonst verfolgt er ohn' Erbarmen,
und verspottet deine Macht.

NO. 3 CON MOTO E VIVACE
Herr, wir trau'n auf deine Güte,
die uns rettet wunderbar,
singen dir mit frommem Liede,
danken freudig immerdar.

tails (e.g., the D♭ and A♭ in mm. 17–18); but at the point where the music begins to diverge from the tonic (mm. 19ff.), a significant new rising line is unfolded, one that not only adumbrates the head-motive of the following section (m. 25) but implies a contrapuntal texture that is realized only later (mm. 33ff.).[25]

Mendelssohn takes up Broadley's second stanza in the B section of the piece (mm. 24–47). Here the composer adopts a new, more urgent style. The psalmist's initial question ("Shall my soul still pine in sorrow?") is set using the rising stepwise motive presented in measure 19; by contrast, the second question ("Still shall foes their insults pour?") is etched angularly, with suitable leaps upward of a tritone on the word "foes" and downward of a diminished seventh on "insults." The two phrases are bound together by the throbbing but harmonically fluid accompaniment, which proceeds from a V^2/IV chord to a striking half cadence in the key of C minor (m. 28).

As Moscheles had noted, Mendelssohn's setting of the text begin-

ning "weak and fainting" (mm. 30–33), with its drooping melody, sequence of seventh chords, and Neapolitan cadence in the key of C
minor, is especially beautiful, as is the repetition of the entire stanza
in the chorus, which moves to a half cadence in G minor while building to a dramatic peak on the text "Still shall foes their insults pour?"
(mm. 40–41). Deftly handled, too, is the emergence of the reprise
(example 1). As the chorus subsides to a quiet full close in the new
key with the lament "shall the morrow bring thine aid to me no
more?" (mm. 42ff), the soloist enters softly on a sustained Bb (m. 47),
out of which the main theme slowly grows, supported now by a beautiful passing dominant seventh chord in second inversion that slides
back to the tonic for an abbreviated rehearsal of the opening material. The movement ends wistfully, with the thrice-stated text "nev-
ermore."

The modest second movement is in its way the most innovative of
the three: as Broadley observed to Moscheles, chorales were not a
regular feature of the English anthem.[26] The tune is Mendelssohn's
own, and the genre is one that he had long practiced.[27] Here the composer set Broadley's third and fourth stanzas to a simple thirty-two-
bar tune in Bb bearing the traditional phrase structure A A B C; as
before, the soloist presents the material first and then is echoed by
the chorus.

The melodic and formal simplicity of Mendelssohn's design only
throws into relief his subtle and expressive use of harmony. To wit,
no phrase is harmonized in precisely the same way twice. Consider
the first halves of the two A phrases (examples 2a and 2b). The one
offers a half cadence in the tonic (mm. 1–4); the other, in the submediant (mm. 9–12). Mendelssohn followed the same principle in
crafting the harmonization of the melody in the chorus. His handling
of the first half of the B phrase is typical (examples 3a and 3b). While,
as sung by the soloist, the tune had tonicized the dominant with a full
close (mm. 17–20), the chorus gives the music a new twist, as the melody comes to a dramatic pause by means of a Phrygian cadence in the
mediant (mm. 49–52).

The Vivace third movement recalls the opening Andante—not, to
be sure, in mood and tone, but in form and gesture. Again the structure may be described as A A'B A". As before, the soloist offers the
opening stanza in the tonic (mm. 1–10), to which the chorus answers
in a varied repetition that modulates to the dominant (mm. 11–26).
The ensuing B section (mm. 27–41), reserved for the soloist, not only
uses a rising stepwise figure that recalls the beginning of the comparable passage in the first movement, but modulates to the submediant, a key that had likewise figured prominently in the Andante. The

Example 1. Mendelssohn, "Why, O Lord, delay forever," First Movement, measures 42–49

a) measures 1–4

b) measures 9–12

Example 2. Mendelssohn, "Why, O Lord, delay forever," Second Movement

a) measures 17–20

b) measures 49–52

Example 3. Mendelssohn, "Why, O Lord, delay forever," Second Movement

a) measures 1–4

Let us sing his hal-low'd prais-es, aye re-joi-cing in his love——

b) measures 42–43

Lord! my heart's de-vo-tion rais-es

Example 4. Mendelssohn, "Why, O Lord, delay forever," Third Movement

A material returns in the chorus, which now develops the head-motive into a lively fugato (mm. 42–84), and the piece concludes with a clamorous coda (mm. 84–95), marked by prominent antiphonal effects between soloist and chorus.

In view of the composer's explanation that he "could not write a short prelude [to the first movement] without altering the whole form and giving it a pretentious coloring,"[28] his subsequent decision when scoring the piece for orchestra to append a full-blown concluding fugue to his original finale seems all the more puzzling. In truth, the added fugue, although effectively worked out, offends in both respects. It is, for one thing, thematically and formally redundant (example 4a). Not only does the third movement itself end with a joyful choral fugato on a similar subject (example 4b), but on its last pages it offers several emphatic signs of closure that scarcely need reiteration, especially coming at the end of a movement that might be described as a *perpetuum mobile*. At the same time, the fugue does seem to strike a pretentious tone, not least because of its text. Whereas in the last stanza of Broadley's original the psalmist extols God directly ("Lord! my heart's devotion raises off'rings to thy throne above: Glad to sing thy hallow'd praises—Aye rejoicing in thy love."), in Mendelssohn's textual derivative ("Let us sing his hallow'd praises—aye rejoicing in his love.") all humanity is exhorted to join in this doxology. The shifting to a more universal tone drew from Mendelssohn a loud musical response that borders at times on the bombastic.

In certain respects this "problematic" fugal finale calls to mind the composer's earlier (and widely popular) setting of Psalm 42 (op. 42). Conceived in 1837 in four parts, this great choral-orchestral work was subsequently enlarged by the addition of three central movements.

The similarity between psalm and anthem, however, concerns not only the expansion that both works underwent but the style and idea of their endings. Each concludes fugally, in a broad Handelian manner, with salient material that is taken from the immediately preceding section. More important, each offers—using the composer's own words—a hymn in praise of God: the doxology Mendelssohn fashioned for the orchestral setting of the anthem echoes the sentiment expressed in the words he had earlier tagged, in the manner of the *Gloria patri*, to the text of Psalm 42 ("Preis sei dem Herrn, dem Gott Israels, von nun an bis in Ewigkeit!"). Now the late Eric Werner, who was critical of op. 42 on account of its supposed "sentimentality" that effectively vitiated the strong, passionate images of the text, found little good to say about Mendelssohn's pseudo–*Gloria patri*.[29] Though this criticism seems overstated, the charge of sentimentality might more fairly be directed toward the composition at hand. For his part, Mendelssohn appears to have sensed a problem with his later addition—or at least a problem that might be evident to certain circles. If, when sending the piece for limited circulation in Victorian England, he could describe the fugue as "the best piece of the whole," his determination to withhold the orchestration from a wider distribution in Germany may well bespeak some misgivings about this new version. On the other hand, as we have seen, the composer clearly took pride and pleasure in his original work on the piece. And today, when measuring it against the repertory of anthems that followed, we cannot fail to recognize the hand of a master and have only to concur with Moscheles' judgment of the work as "noble, self-controlled, [and] pure."

APPENDIX 1

An unpublished letter from C. B. Broadley to Ignaz Moscheles
(Green Books, vol. 13, item 62)

Ibbotsons Hotel, Vere Street
8th Febr. 1841

Dear dear Sir,

I enclose a letter to Mr. Mendelssohn, and if you do not think it will be perfectly satisfactory, I beg you will suggest to me what I can say in addition thereto. If the title *Herr*, [*sic*] be not sufficiently complimentary, pray alter it, as I am ignorant of the etiquette in Germany in this matter. Unless you wish to suggest any thing to me, I shall not have occasion to trouble you for any answer by the Bearer. With reference to the Prelude, you were kind enough to say you would name to Mr. Mendelssohn, I beg to say that Organists in England generally indulge on those occasions in a style rather florid, at one time with an extra-low pedal bass at another time on the very top of the instrument either in thirds, or after the manner of some of the ad libitum passages in the Gems à la Paganini of yours; I think this has a very good effect for organ Prelude, especially on the *Swell*. If Mr. Mendelssohn will take the trouble to write me such a prelude, for my own private Album, without his publishing the same, or letting it be known, I shall be happy to pay him a proportionate *extra Fee*. I have written to Dr. Camidge for information as to whether the Cathedral tenor singers can sing from the Bass, and from the G treble cliff [*sic*]. Also whether he considers the introduction of the Chorale would be any impediment to the said anthems being used at the Church service in the English Cathedrals.

I enclose some observations for the Engraver and if you will have the goodness to press the same upon his notice, he will doubtless regard it more than any observations of mine.

Perhaps you will intimate to Mr. Mendelssohn for his prelude that English organs generally go from G to G 5 octaves: but that the York organ (with which I am acquainted) goes from C to C, six octaves (being half an octave higher, and half an octave lower than the G organ).

> I remain
> My dear Sir
> Very truly yours
> C B Broadley

We can leave the matter of the *Chorale* being introduced or not, into an anthem by Spohr to be arranged by us, after we hear from him that it will be agreeable to him to write an Anthem.

I trust you will be able to arrange with Spohr for a Prelude for my own private Album; without additional Fee.

APPENDIX 2

An unpublished letter from C. B. Broadley
to Mendelssohn
(Green Books, vol. 13, item 64)

London 8th Febr. 1841

Sir,

I beg to thank you very much for the successful manner in which you have treated my translation of the 13th Psalm: and I doubt not that all competent judges will consider your composition a *real treasure* to the Music of the Church, either for an Oratorio, or for the devotional service.

I have requested your friend Mr Moscheles to settle with you for the copyright for which I have paid him: and if you will have the following words printed with each copy of the Music, I consent to your publishing the same in Germany, or to your authorizing any Music-sellers or Publishers to publish the same in Germany, on and after Thursday the fifteenth (15th) day of April next, which I have fixed as my day of publication here.

Words to which the above refers:—

"This Music, except in Germany, is the Copyright of the Author of the English words."

> I have the honor to be,
> Sir,
> Your obedient Servant
> C B Broadley

NOTES

1. Moscheles described a typical lesson with Broadley in a humorous diary entry from 1841: "The colossus [*Riesengestalt*] was determined to create great works [*Riesenwerke*], and his head was always brimming with ideas. He brings to his lesson with me a newly baked Psalm, a motet, a song, and I correct [it] by taking an empty leaf, setting music to his text, which is often his own, and then asking: 'Is this what you meant to express?' Whereupon he always replies: 'Oh, yes, and just so.' " *Aus Moscheles' Leben, nach Briefen und Tagebüchern,* ed. [Charlotte Moscheles] (Leipzig, 1872–73), 2.82.

2. The texts are gathered as item 34 in vol. 27 of the so-called Green Books, in which Mendelssohn collected his correspondence. All twenty-seven volumes are preserved in Oxford, Bodleian Library, as part of the M. Deneke Mendelssohn Collection.

3. The draft, headed "Anthem" and "H. d. m." and dated "Leipzig d. 12ten Dec. 1840," is preserved in vol. 34, pp. 257–68, of the *Mendelssohn Nachlass* manuscripts (Kraków, Biblioteka Jagiellońska). The fair copy, which served as the *Stichvorlage* for the first edition, is preserved in London, British Library (Add. 31801); its wrapper contains the inscription: "An Anthem for a Mezzo Soprano Solo with Chorus and Organ Accompaniments composed for C. B. Broadley Esquire by Felix Mendelssohn Bartholdy. Leipzig 14 December 1840."

4. "Du erhältst mit diesem Briefe meinen Psalm für Broadley (so heißt er doch) und einen Brief an ihn. Ich bitte Dich, ihm beides zu übersenden, und mir seine Antwort auf die im Briefe enthaltene Frage, wegen der Publication in Deutschland, zukommen zu lassen. Wenn er mir nämlich den Tag des Erscheinens in England angeben kann, so würde ich's vielleicht auch mit deutschen Worten an demselben Tage hier herausgeben, schrieb ich ihm. . . .

Ich weiß nicht, ob ich den Ton der englischen Anthems getroffen habe, doch habe ich mir Mühe damit gegeben und mit mehr Vergnügen an dem Stück gearbeitet, als ich vorher gedacht hatte. Bitte, sag mir ja Dein Urtheil darüber" (*Briefe an Ignaz und Charlotte Moscheles* [Leipzig, 1888], pp. 204–5). The music and letters to Moscheles and Broadley were not sent directly to the intended recipients but were included in a package Mendelssohn forwarded to his London friend Karl Klingemann (*Felix Mendelssohn-Bartholdys Briefwechsel mit Legationsrat Karl Klingemann*, ed. Karl Klingemann [Jr.] [Essen, 1909], p. 254).

5. "Ich habe deinen Brief vom 20t Dec v. J. mit dem 13ten Psalm unbeantwortet laßen müßen weil ich von Mr. Broadley, der aus der Stadt war erst deswegen hören wollte. Vorgestern theilte er mir alles was er darüber zu sagen hatte (und er lässt sich *breit* Broad aus) mündlich mit. Zuerst muß ich Dir meine Freude und besonderes Wohlgefallen über Deine Composition des Psalms ausdrücken. Er ist edel gehalten, rein, u. fern von unnützer Ausschmückung und fremdartigen Farben, das heißt *geistlich*. Ein lieblings Stelle muß ich Dir herausheben. Die Stelle im Alt Solo "week [*sic*] and fainting" ist echt poetisch und steigert sich vortrefflich später im Chor. Es gewährt mir Satisfaction daß *Du auch* mit der Komposition zufrieden bist, denn das beweist mir daß Du mit Deinen Intentionen klar und einig bist, und ich hoffe Du bleibst es so. Meine Frau und ich haben meinem weisen Schüler B. den Psalm vorgetragen und wir versetzten ihn in Entzücken (über die Komposition, nicht durch den Vortrag). [inserted later: Auch Miss Mason probirt gestern den Solopart und findet ihn ganz vortrefflich ihrer Stimme angemessen.] Er gedenkt ihn in York Cathedral beÿ einer passenden Gelegenheit aufführen zu laßen. Ich hatte mit ihm verabredet daß er Dir die Disposition freÿ stellte ihn in Deutschland am 15t April d. J. mit englisch[em] und deutschem Text zu publiziren; und wünscht er daß auf dem Titel stehe: composed for C. Broadley Esqre by whom the english metrical Version of the Psalm is made.

"Sein Wünsch ist außer diesem ein Preludium von Dir (beÿläufig eine Seite lang) für diesen Psalm zu besitzen (das er in seinem Album bewahren will) auch einige Takte nach dem Choral als Vorspiel zu der letzten Nummer die er gern [originally: lieber nicht] drucken laßen möchte. Die drollige Weise in welcher er sich darüber an mich schriftlich ausdrückt, ist zu possirlich daß ich Dir sie nicht vorenthalten kann, u. lege seinen Brief beÿ. Dieses Document ist eines der zahlreichen seiner absonderlichen halfverrückten Natur. Wie Du siehst hat er im Sinne ein Kle[e]blatt von Psalmen zu bilden indem er Spohr durch mich auffordern ließ auch einen zu schreiben. Es wird mir Angst zu denken welche Stellung ich dabeÿ einnehmen soll. Ich habe meinen (dem 93ten) in der Skizze fertig. Es besteht aus dreÿ Nummern: ein großes Baß Solo mit später eintretendem 4 stimmigen Chor fugirt, [(] D moll u. D dur) ein Chor $\frac{6}{4}$ in B dur und einen figurierten Choral nach dem Text: 'Wachet auf ruft uns die Stimme.' " (Green Books, vol. 13, item 66).

Mendelssohn's decision to include a chorale-like movement seems to have raised some eyebrows yet proved influential. Although Broadley questioned the propriety of using such a piece in the anthem—the chorale was not a regular feature of English cathedral music—he apparently decided that Spohr might be asked to include one in his own setting (see appendix 1). And Moscheles, of course, made use of the well-known "Wachet auf."

6. In his diary Moscheles described the enterprise as "a completely novel piece of folly" ("eine ganz neue Marotte") (*Aus Moscheles' Leben*, 2.82). Moscheles' recollection appears incorrect in one respect: whereas he added that "Spohr, Mendelssohn, and I are each to write a Psalm with orchestra, for which he [Broadley] will pay £20 per piece," all three pieces were in fact originally written for organ accompaniment. Yet, as we shall see, each composer did eventually transcribe his piece for orchestra.

7. Letter of 4 March 1841, in Felix Mendelssohn Bartholdy, *Briefe an deutsche Verleger*, ed. Rudolf Elvers (Berlin, 1968), pp. 227–28. The origin of the German translation is not clear, although, as R. Larry Todd has argued in the case of the German version of the slightly later anthem *Hear my prayer* (whose original text is an English paraphrase by William Bartholomew of a part of Psalm 55), it may well stem from Mendelssohn himself. See the forward to Todd's critical edition of the orchestral version of *Hör mein Bitten* (Stuttgart, 1985), pp. v–vi.

8. Unpublished letter of 8 March 1841, in Green Books, vol. 13, item 116.

9. Letter of 14 March 1841, in *Letters of Felix Mendelssohn to Ignaz and Charlotte Moschles*, ed. Felix Moscheles (Boston, 1888), pp. 218–19.

10. *Briefe*, pp. 228–30.

11. The publication process can be followed in Simrock's letters of 19 April, 19 June, 28 June, and 9 August 1841 (Green Books, vol. 13, items 186, 261, 267, and vol. 14, item 32), and Mendelssohn's letters of 29 April, 4 June, and 12 July (*Briefe*, pp. 230, 233, and 234).

12. Quoting a letter of her own in *Aus Moscheles' Leben*, 2.82.

13. The accession date at the British Library was 8 May 1841.

14. Folker Göthel, *Thematisch-Bibliographisches Verzeichnis der Werke von Louis Spohr* (Tutzing, 1981), p. 210, correctly cites from Spohr's own handwritten *Werkverzeichnis* the date and place of composition—April 1841 in Kassel—but incorrectly lists the date of the Broadley edition as 1843. (The accession date at the British Library was 8 August 1841). In both Spohr's catalog and the Broadley print the psalm is designated op. 118; when, however, the piece appeared in a German edition, which *did* come out in 1843, it was given the revised designation op. 122.

15. Moscheles had doubted himself from the beginning. In the continuation of the letter to Mendelssohn of 9 February, cited in n. 5 above, he wrote: "Ach! hätte ich dabeÿ deinen Rath, deine Meinung! hätte ich ein gleiches Geschick mit F[erdinand] Hiller, der in Deiner Nähe arbeiten und sich von Dir winke holen durfte! Ich habe zwar das Bemüthseyn daß sich das Ding singen läßt, daß man es für kein Theaterstück halten wird—aber das ist nicht genug! Wenn Broadleÿ [*sic*] warten wollte mit der Publikation bis ich Dir ihn

zur Beurtheilung geschickt habe thue ich es gerne (voraussetzend daß Du nebst dem Freund auch die Stelle des Lehrers beÿ mir übersenden möchtest), aber das wird erst noch von ihm und Deiner freundlichen Erlaubnis abhängen." Mendelssohn responded: "I do wish I could hear your Psalm. You know how much I should enjoy it. But how could I venture to make suggestions, or even to *think* them, when I am so full of the beauties I find in your work, and so thankful, as we all have reason to be, for what you give us in so full a measure" (*Letters to Ignaz and Charlotte Moscheles*, p. 219). Mendelssohn evidently never went over the score, and Moscheles temporarily withdrew his work from the series. The piece seems to have been completed by 1842, when Moscheles played it for the composer Sigismund Neukomm (see *Recent Music and Musicians, as Described in the Diaries and Correspondence of Ignaz Moscheles*, ed. [Charlotte Moscheles], trans. A. D. Coleridge [New York, 1873], pp. 287–88), but it was not published until 1843, when it appeared in Broadley's series under the title *An anthem for a bass solo, with chorus and occasional solos for soprano, alto, tenor & bass, to which is added an accompaniment for the organ or pianoforte, composed to Charles Bayles Broadley's version of the 93d Psalm, by I. Moscheles, pianist to H. R. H. the Prince Albert. Op. 100*. (The accession date at the British Library was 3 June 1843.) The piece—the longest of the three psalms and not an unappealing work—has remained virtually unknown. It is not listed in either the *Thematisches Verzeichniss im Druck erschienenen Compositionen von Ignaz Moscheles* (1862; reprint ed., London, 1966) or the inventory of works appearing at the end of Mrs. Moscheles' biography of her husband (*Aus Moscheles' Leben*, translated as *Recent Music and Musicians*); the designation op. 100 was subsequently used for a four-hand piano ballad in E♭ minor.

16. *Letters to Ignaz and Charlotte Moscheles*, p. 234. Broadley's request was conveyed in an unpublished letter from Moscheles of 20 October 1842 (Green Books, vol. 16, item 79).

17. The autograph is preserved in vol. 38², pp. 1–31, of the *Mendelssohn Nachlass* manuscripts (Kraków, Biblioteka Jagiellońska). It is headed "Anthem" and "H. d. m."; at the end appears the inscription "Leipzig d. 5ten Januar 1843 für Herrn Broadley in London." Not surprisingly, the text of the first three movements, being based directly on the existing composition, is quite clean; the fugal finale, by contrast, shows much greater signs of compositional effort.

18. This *Abschrift*, with autograph corrections and additions, is preserved in London, British Library (Add. 31801), as are the psalms by Spohr, in an autograph dated September 1842 (Add. 31779), and Moscheles, in an undated autograph (Add. 31798). The orchestral versions of the pieces by Spohr and Moscheles remain unpublished; as we shall see, Mendelssohn's orchestration was published posthumously in a version based on the autograph in Kraków (see note 17).

19. *Letters to Ignaz and Charlotte Moscheles*, p. 236.

20. Unpublished letter in Green Books, vol. 17, item 101.

21. Quoted in Mendelssohn's letter to Moscheles of 15 April 1843 (*Briefe an Ignaz und Charlotte Moscheles*, p. 227).

22. Ibid.

23. The accession date at the British Library for Moscheles' arrangement of his friend's fugue was, like that of his own anthem, 3 June 1843. Appearing under the title *Fugue, being the fourth movement of an anthem for a mezzo-soprano solo, with chorus, and accompaniment for the organ or pianoforte, composed to Charles Bayles Broadley's version of the thirteenth Psalm, by Felix Mendelssohn Bartholdy*, this edition clearly was intended to be bound together with the print of the original, tripartite version of the piece, which, significantly, ran to thirteen pages. The later print has two paginations, one beginning "Mendelssohn's Anthem, p. 14"; the other, so as to account for both the empty verso of the last leaf in the 1841 edition and the title page of the new edition, simply "p. 16."

It is difficult to judge how far Broadley progressed in any plans to publish the orchestral version. It is clear, however, that he at least had parts copied and distributed. Bound together with the copyist's score is a note to a Mr. Goodwin dated 15 May 1848: "Please to send the Copy (Mendelssohn's Anthem) with the Music Paper, Covers, and written Instructions by Bearer— C B Broadley at Mr White's [a London publisher], 29 Gt. James Street Bedford Row." Moreover, on the verso of this leaf is a note, in an unidentified hand, indicating that a set of parts for an orchestral performance had been sent to a Miss Dolby (presumably the English contralto Helene Dolby [1821–1885]).

24. A similar situation holds for the Psalm *Richte mich Gott*, op. 78, no. 2, whose posthumous first edition of 1848 was based on the original version of the piece, dating from 1844, rather than on the rather different version that the composer himself had prepared in the following year for a planned (but aborted) publication of psalms, doxologies, and verses. For the first publication of Mendelssohn's revision of the psalm, see my new edition of the *Psalmen*, op. 78 (Stuttgart, forthcoming).

25. This anticipation of the B section is not limited to matters of theme and texture; the tonicizations of C minor (m. 11) and G minor (mm. 12 and 22) broach the keys used in the later section.

26. See the letter of 8 February 1841 quoted in appendix 1.

27. For an account of Mendelssohn's early study of the chorale, which included exercises in creating original tunes for texts of Gellert, see R. Larry Todd, *Mendelssohn's Musical Education: A Study and Edition of his Exercises in Composition* (Cambridge, 1983), pp. 27–39. In a number of later works the composer introduced original or altered chorale tunes; see the conclusion of the Prelude and Fugue in E minor, op. 35, no. 1 (1837), the Adagio of the Cello Sonata in D, op. 58 (1843), and the finale of the Piano Trio in C minor, op. 66 (1845).

28. Letter of 14 March 1841, cited in note 9.

29. "Not only do those 'optimistic' words of praise stand in contradiction to the problem-filled text, but the music belonging to them has an unpleasantly unctuous character which reminds us of bad preachers." Eric Werner, *Mendelssohn: A New Image of the Composer and His Age*, trans. Dika Newlin (London, 1963), pp. 346–47.

Mendelssohn and the Berlin Singakademie: The Composer at the Crossroads

WM. A. LITTLE

Carl Friedrich Zelter, Director of the Berlin Singakademie, died in Berlin on 15 May 1832. On the same day Mendelssohn, then in London, allegedly wrote to Charlotte Moscheles, telling her that he had just received news of Zelter's death and asked, "if you are quite alone at dinner and in the evening, I should much like to come to you."[1] Three days later, in reply to a letter from his father (written on 9 May), in which the latter had assured him that Zelter was recovering, Mendelssohn expressed his relief, but also prayed, "May God grant that by now Zelter may be safe and out of danger."[2] Thus begins, with characteristic incongruities, the murky saga of Mendelssohn's reluctant candidacy for the directorship of the Berlin Singakademie. If this tale were simply flawed by such relatively minor inconsistencies, they could be largely ignored or dealt with in footnotes. But it is not; Mendelssohn's relationship to the Singakademie at that time, and specifically as Zelter's possible successor, has been accorded such prominence by most of Mendelssohn's biographers, that it mandates a close and critical scrutiny of the entire affair.

In his *Mendelssohn: A New Image of the Composer and His Age*,[3] Eric Werner, discussing the effect on the composer caused by his allowing himself to become a candidate for Zelter's position, and the subsequent rejection of him by the Singakademie, writes, "He regretted the error; it induced the severest trauma of his life. The wound in Felix's soul never healed fully, and the unpleasant consequences for the family did not cease even after his death."[4] The evidence contained in Mendelssohn's correspondence, however, and in the memoirs of his friend Eduard Devrient and others, as well as in the papers of the Singakademie itself, suggest that the election results were considerably less permanently devastating to Mendelssohn than Werner would have us believe.[5] That is not to say that this incident in the composer's life was without its manifest frustrations, disappointments and bitterness; it was not, but to place them in perspective, it is important to understand something of the background that gave rise to them.

C. F. Christian Fasch (1736–1800) founded the Singakademie in Berlin in 1791 and directed its activities until his death, at which time his longtime assistant at the Akademie, Carl Friedrich Zelter, took over the directorship, a position he also held until his death in 1832.

From about the turn of the century the Mendelssohn family had maintained a strong and cordial relationship both with Fasch and Zelter, and they had participated actively in the ongoing functions and concerts of the Singakademie from about the time that Zelter became its director. In all there were nineteen members of the Mendelssohn family who were members at one time or another of the Singakademie in the first half of the century.[6] In the first decade of the century Sara Levy (Mendelssohn's great-aunt and a pupil of W. F. Bach) was sporadically harpsichord soloist for the Singakademie, primarily during the years 1806–1808.[7] Equally important, Abraham Mendelssohn (the composer's father) frequently brokered musical manuscripts for Zelter's personal collection and for the library of the Singakademie.[8] In 1811 he donated a number of important manuscripts, including manuscripts by J. S. Bach and C.P.E. Bach to the Singakademie.[9] Zelter's gratitude for these gifts was simply one part of the ligament that bound him and the Singakademie to the Mendelssohn family.

Felix Mendelssohn himself was the critical link. Together with his sister Fanny, they had joined the Singakademie on 1 October 1820.[10] Young Felix sang alto until 1824, when he moved into the tenor section.[11] His musical association with Zelter, however, went back to September 1819, when he had begun his studies in composition with Zelter. In 1820, Zelter also arranged for Mendelssohn to begin organ studies with August Wilhelm Bach, another of Zelter's pupils, a fellow member of the Singakademie and frequent accompanist at their rehearsals, and one of Berlin's most promising young organists.[12]

Zelter recognized early the extraordinary gifts of his young pupil, and he oversaw his progress and development with immense care. In 1821 he took his protégé to Weimar to introduce him to Goethe, and the friendship that developed between the seventy-two-year-old poet and the twelve-year-old prodigy lasted until Goethe's death.

During Mendelssohn's early years as a member of the Singakademie, he not only participated as a singer, but was also encouraged by Zelter to conduct, which he did with great eagerness and pleasure. Under Zelter's aegis the Singakademie became a forum where the young composer could conduct his own compositions. From 1821 (with a performance of his Psalm 19) onward, the Singakademie was the first and principal medium for most of Mendelssohn's major sacred choral works. Only a few weeks after the opening of the Singakademie in its new quarters in February 1827 Mendelssohn conducted a performance of his *Te Deum* (which was frequently performed there in later years). In 1828 he conducted his motet, *Tu es Petrus* (op. 111), and his cantata written for the Albrecht Dürer Festival. Early in 1829 he also conducted the Singakademie in a performance of his polychoral motet, *Hora est*.

By far the most important event in 1829 in the annals of the Singakademie was the first full-scale performance since Bach's death of the *St. Matthew Passion* on 11 March under the direction of Mendelssohn. Literally and metaphorically, that landmark performance signaled the beginning of the Bach revival that subsequently spread throughout the world and continues today. Historically, it represented the crowning achievement of Mendelssohn's youth, and it provided critical impetus for his future development, both as artist and composer.

Mendelssohn's involvement with the *St. Matthew Passion* antedates the performance by several years; his first encounter with it had occurred in the Singakademie, and in 1823 he had received a manuscript copy of it as a Christmas gift from his grandmother.[13] Over the next few years he studied it continually, though with little hope of ever hearing it performed. Beginning, however, in the winter of 1827, he gathered a small group of singers from the Singakademie, and they began serious rehearsal of the *Passion*. Even so, it was not until January 1829 that at the urging of his close friend, Eduard Devrient, they managed together to persuade Zelter to agree to a public performance of the work. Devrient was one of the leading tenor soloists in the Singakademie, and he was given the role of Christ.[14]

The performance itself was an unqualified success, and a second performance was scheduled ten days later, on 21 March, Bach's birthday. A third performance was set for the week of 12 April (Holy Week). Although it was intended that Mendelssohn should conduct all three, he could conduct only the first two, since his plans to leave for England on 10 April could not be changed, and consequently, Zelter conducted the third performance.

Mendelssohn's departure for England in April 1829 effectively marks closure to his active participation in the musical life of Berlin for slightly more than three years. With the exception of about four and a half months, between December 1829 and mid-May 1830, Mendelssohn did not again set foot in Berlin until 25 June 1832.

In that interval the Singakademie continued to grow and flourish under the direction of Zelter, with Carl Friedrich Rungenhagen as his able and well-liked deputy. Although now seventy-one years old, Zelter continued vigorously to rehearse and perform one major choral work after the other, and gave no indication that age had diminished his energies. With increasing frequency, however, death was thinning the ranks of his older friends, though it was not until one of his closest friends, Goethe, died on 22 March 1832, that the toll of years began to make itself visibly and tangibly felt. Zelter's friendship with Goethe went back to the late 1790s, and he was one of the very few surviving intimates of the great poet who had addressed him familiarly as *Du*. Despite this heavy loss, Zelter conducted the Singakademie's performance of Haydn's *Creation* on 31 March, then on 15 April the *St. Matthew Passion*, and on 20 April Graun's *Der Tod Jesu*. It was his last appearance as conductor; on 1 May he came to the rehearsal, but left almost immediately. As he noted in the Register of the Akademie, "Today, Tuesday, after the first number, the Director left."[15] The following day, after attending a concert in the Marienkirche and sitting for two hours on the stone steps to the chancel, he contracted a cold, then a fever, and he died on the morning of 15 May.[16] The funeral, attended by virtually all of Berlin's cultural and political leaders, took place on 18 May; Rungenhagen directed the Singakademie and Friedrich Schleiermacher[17] delivered the funeral oration. Also at the funeral the Berlin firm of Trautwein distributed to the mourners a memorial tribute to both Zelter and Goethe (see figure 1). Shortly afterward, on 7 June, the Singakademie held a memorial service at which several motets by Zelter were sung, followed by the Mozart *Requiem*, again under the direction of Rungenhagen. Mendelssohn was still in London.

Zelter's duties were now assumed by Rungenhagen, although the directors of the Singakademie initiated almost immediately the process of selecting a new director. Within a short time some thirteen applicants either announced their own candidacy or were proposed for the position.[18] Most names were soon eliminated from the list, as it became clear that the two serious candidates for the position were Rungenhagen and Mendelssohn. The constitution of the organization required, however, that three names be placed in nomination, and after both the Chevalier von Neukomm and C. G. Reißiger had declined, Eduard Grell allowed his name to be entered as the third candidate.

The search committee, composed of twenty members, was appointed by the board of directors and delegated the responsibility of submitting its proposals to the membership. Eduard Devrient was among those named to this committee, and he has provided a detailed, though obviously biased account of the Singakademie's selection of its new director. As Devrient acknowledges, "no one more ardently wished that the choice should fall upon Felix than I."[19]

As Mendelssohn's most outspoken advocate Deverient offered a proposal that Mendelssohn had already agreed to, and had possibly himself suggested. Essentially a compromise, it allowed for a joint directorship with Mendelssohn and Rungenhagen more or less as codirectors. A subcommittee of three, consisting of Schleiermacher, Köhler and Devrient, delegated with working out the details of this plan, formulated that "Rungenhagen was to be active and managing director in all matters concerning business and performances, and in the direction of musical affairs only was he to share with Mendelssohn, who was, however, to be chief authority in these."[20] This arrangement was clearly agreeable to Mendelssohn, and according to Devrient, it was also acceptable to Rungenhagen's supporters.[21] To Devrient's obvious astonishment, but hardly surprising otherwise, Rungenhagen himself refused, since he "considered that he had a right to the post on the conditions under which it was held by Zelter; and he was prepared to abide by an election by a majority of votes."[22]

After this general meeting in the first week of October 1832 Mendelssohn clearly saw the handwriting on the wall. Unfortunately, he was the only one who could read it. Devrient argued vigorously against Mendelssohn's intention to withdraw his name, as perhaps his family did also. In any case, Mendelssohn allowed himself only with great reluctance to remain in the contest. It was a serious tactical error, since it forced Mendelssohn into a competition he had been determined to avoid and for which he had no taste, and secondly, it pitted him openly against one of Berlin's most established and popular musical figures, and one with whom Mendelssohn had hitherto been on genuinely cordial terms.

At the time of this unhappy contest Carl Friedrich Rungenhagen was fifty-four years old. The son of an affluent Berlin merchant, Rungenhagen was forbidden by his father to follow a career in either music or painting, and under pressure he entered his father's firm. After his father's death in 1796, however, Rungenhagen became independently wealthy and free to do what he wished. From that point

Figure 1. *Das Gastmahl*. Memorial tribute to Goethe and Zelter, May 1832

Das Gastmahl.

1

Viele Gäste wünsch ich heut
Mir zu meinem Tische!
Speisen sind genug bereit,
Vögel, Wild und Fische!
Eingeladen sind sie ja,
Habens angenommen.
Hänschen geh und sieh dich um,
Sieh mir ob sie kommen.

2

Schöne Kinder hoff ich nun
Die von gar nichts wissen;
Nicht dass es was hübsches sei
Einen Freund zu küssen.
Eingeladen sind sie all

3

Frauen mag ich auch zu sehr
Die den Ehegatten
Wird er immer brummiger
Immer lieber hatten.
Eingeladen wurden

4

Junge Herrn berief ich auch
Nicht im mindsten eitel
Die sogar bescheiden sind und
Mit gefülltem Beutel.
Diese bat ich sonderlich

5

Männer lud ich mit Respect
Die auf ihre Frauen
Ganz allein, nichts neben aus
Auf die Schönste schauen
Sie erwiderten den Gruss

6

Dichter ist auch hier
Unsre Lust zu mehren,
Die weit lieber ein fremdes Lied
Als ihr eignes hören
Alle diese stimmten ein's

7

Doch ich sehe niemand gehn,
Sehe niemand rennen
Suppe gockt und redet ...
Braten will verbrennen.
Ach! wir habens fürcht ich, nur
Zu genau genommen.
Hänschen sag was mag das
Es wird niemand kommen.

8

Hänschen lauf und säume nicht
Ruf mir neue Gäste!
Jeder Leute wie er ist,
Das ist wohl das beste.—
Jeder ists in der Stadt bereits
Wohl ist's aufgenommen.
Hänschen macht die Thüren auf
Sieh nur wie sie kommen

6 B. 26 febr. 14.

Weimar d. 12 Octbr
1813.

Figure 1. cont.

onward he devoted himself primarily to his music. Despite early studies with Emil Fischer and Carl Benda, and later lessons under G. A. Schneider, Rungenhagen was predominantly self-taught. Although his creative gifts barely rose above mediocrity, he wrote prolifically and with some local success.

In addition to being socially well-connected, he possessed considerable charm and affability, both of which made him a welcome figure in Berlin's leading musical circles. He was highly regarded by Zelter (and apparently also by Carl Maria von Weber[23]), and after the première of his opera, *Die Fischer bei Colberg* (1814), Zelter invited him to become deputy director of the Singakademie.[24]

A member of the Singakademie since 1801, Rungenhagen had long been one of its strongest supporters. In 1825 he had been named *königlicher Musikdirektor*, and in 1828 on the occasion of Zelter's seventieth birthday, he had successfully solicited a cantata text from Goethe, which he set to music. Altogether, Rungenhagen— within his limitations—was a stable, competent and respected musician, who had proven himself over a period of more than thirty years.

To all but the most unperceptive observer the campaign for the directorship of the Singakademie was a reenactment of the classic contest between the tortoise and the hare, in which Mendelssohn was the very reluctant hare. Brilliant, mercurial and adroit, Mendelssohn was the romantic embodiment of "das Universal-Genie." As Liszt confided, with a certain degree of awe, to Marie d'Agoult some years later, "Mendelssohn sketches wonderfully, plays violin and viola, reads Homer fluently in Greek, and speaks four or five languages easily."[25] And Liszt had barely glimpsed beyond the threshold of Mendelssohn's immense warehouse of talents. They were, however, abundantly clear to those of his friends who supported his candidacy in 1832. Perhaps blindingly so, since they argued that with his gifts and charisma he would raise the reputation of the Singakademie to heights it had never dreamed of—forgetting for the moment that they were trying to hitch the Singakademie to a shooting star. Mendelssohn's position in this unequal and unwanted contest was at best ambiguous and at worst ambitious.

In a letter to his son in London (9 May 1832), in which he anticipated Zelter's death, Abraham Mendelssohn wrote, "there is no doubt that Zelter both wishes and requires to have you with him, because at all events it is quite impossible for him to carry on the Akademie, whence it is evident that if you do not undertake it, another must."[26] Shortly thereafter—and after Zelter had died—Fanny also wrote to her brother, urging him "to hasten his return, in order, if possible, to secure the position in the Academy."[27]

The position of Mendelssohn's family was clear: they were ambitious for him to become director of the Singakademie, and in this Devrient was their active ally. Mendelssohn, however, saw the situation somewhat differently: "the Director seems to me only an honorable post."[28] Unquestionably, he was aware of the honor that would accrue to him in that position; it would certainly be a matter of great personal pride to be invited to succeed his teacher and mentor, but it was not a position to which he viscerally aspired.

In three of the letters to his family, written in late May and early June, while he was still in London, Mendelssohn discusses in some detail his thoughts about the Singakademie and the possibility of his succeeding Zelter as director.[29] In the course of his remarks it becomes clear that three years earlier Professor Lichtenstein, one of the directors of the Singakademie (speaking for the Akademie?) had explicitly offered Mendelssohn the directorship (or so he believes), and now Mendelssohn expresses his willingness to accept it, if the board of directors again approaches him and reminds him of his earlier promise. Realistically speaking, of course, it is unthinkable that Lichtenstein could or would have offered Mendelssohn Zelter's post while Zelter was still the incumbent and Rungenhagen his deputy.

Since no records exist regarding this interchange, it seems reasonable to speculate, that probably around the time of Mendelssohn's performance of the *St. Matthew Passion* in the spring of 1829, Lichtenstein in a moment of exuberance or enthusiasm had suggested that Mendelssohn would be the ideal person to succeed Zelter, when the day came to fill that post.

Over the three intervening years the attitudes of father and son reversed themselves. Earlier Mendelssohn had favored accepting the proposal, while his father had argued that it was a sinecure for one's old age, but not the place for someone just beginning his career. Now, however, his father was almost importunate in urging him to secure the position, while Mendelssohn's attitude had become one of indifference, or at most velleity. He would accept the post if asked, but was adamant that he would under no circumstances apply for it.[30]

Mendelssohn did not hasten his return to Berlin, and when he did return, his thoughts about the Singakademie remained unchanged. Presumably, he was also now able to persuade his family of his reservations, since he could write Klingemann on 4 July that "my family, moreover, is quite in agreement with me, which pleases me."[31] Thus it devolved upon Devrient to prod Mendelssohn into allowing his name to be entered as a candidate, just as it did later when he was able to persuade him to remain a candidate, after the choice had been narrowed to him and Rungenhagen.[32]

From the beginning Mendelssohn had viewed the post as temporary at best, and he was determined that it should not interfere with his long-range professional plans. He also realized that the conditions he set for accepting the post would doubtless be unacceptable to the board of directors. Already on 4 August he stressed to Klingemann that "Rungenhagen will probably get—or rather keep—the post at the Akademie,"[33] but beyond that Mendelssohn vowed he would by no means accept "without stunning conditions: a fine salary, complete authority and leave to travel."[34]

Far from agonizing over the position at the Singakademie, Mendelssohn's entire correspondence during the latter half of 1832 eloquently affirms only his pained indifference and sporadic annoyance. Rather than tormenting him, as Eric Werner suggests,[35] the business with the Singakademie seldom seemed to amount to anything more than a rather persistent nuisance. Mendelssohn refers to it regularly in most of his correspondence with Klingemann, Moscheles, and even Charles Horsley, but always as a side issue, *always* buried in the middle of a paragraph, never at the beginning or end. At no point does he indicate that the matter is uppermost in his mind.

Undeniably, the latter half of 1832 was an unhappy and frustrating period in Mendelssohn's life, but only peripherally did it involve his concern about the Singakademie. During that summer and fall he longed still to be in England; he missed his friends there and the social bustle.[36] Subconsciously, he doubtless also missed being the musical epicenter of London—at a concert of the Philharmonic,

> I wished to go into the room to talk to some old friends; scarcely, however, had I gone down below, when one of the orchestra called out, "There is Mendelssohn!" on which they all began shouting and clapping their hands to such a degree that for a time I really did not know what to do; and when this was over, another called out "Welcome to him!" on which the uproar recommenced, and I was obliged to cross the room and clamber into the orchestra and return thanks.[37]

Nothing like that ever happened to him in Berlin.

From the joys, honors, and distractions of London, what had he returned to in Berlin? Eduard Rietz, one of his closest boyhood friends had died earlier that year, and now Zelter too was gone: "Yesterday I was at the Akademie for the first time, the hall without Old

Zelter and Rietz, I can't begin to tell you, . . . it was a sad impression."[38]

The cholera was abroad in Berlin, as his father had warned him, and not long after his return, another old friend, Friederike Robert fell victim to it. (And Bernhard Klein, though not a particularly close friend, died on 9 September.) Though herself spared this dread disease, Fanny was "almost continuously unwell"[39] the entire summer; his father had suffered colds and high fever, and Mendelssohn also felt physically unwell with stomach upsets and earaches.[40]

Beyond the very real and depressing matters of sickness and death, Mendelssohn returned to what was the coldest and wettest summer of his life, "the worst weather I have ever experienced, biting cold and pouring rain the whole day."[41] The leaves fell from the trees, fires had to be set, and flowers were killed by the frost.[42] The weather was dreadful and it clearly cast its pall on Mendelssohn's mood.

After more than two years away from home, Mendelssohn struggled, without much success, to readjust himself temporally and spatially to a situation that though familiar was no longer comfortable. "Time doesn't want to take on shape; I continue to hover between present and past, all memories of my trip are still so vivid in my mind; at every step here, in the streets or in the garden, old images spring up anew, and I cannot yet reconcile them. Internally, this makes me more uneasy and restless than I have ever been."[43] His efforts to move back into the musical life of the city produced only bland or negative reactions, whether at one of the concerts at Jagor's, or the Akademie der Künste or even at a Volksfest, where, "no happy face, no pretty girl, not even any happy children's faces were to be seen."[44] Given his depression and dreary state of mind, it is hardly surprising that his attempts to compose were sluggish and difficult. Nonetheless, he was hardly idle during these bleak months. The relatively routine "Morning and Evening Service" for Novello was completed; work continued on both the *Reformation* and the *Italian* Symphonies, as did his editing of Handel's *Solomon*. Moreover, during the early summer months he and his friend A. B. Marx renewed their friendship, and each agreed to write an oratorio text for the other. Mendelssohn was already formulating his thoughts for *St. Paul*, and Marx intended an oratorio on *Moses*. Although Marx never finished his *St. Paul's* text, Mendelssohn completed his text for *Moses* on 21 August 1832,[45] only to have Marx later reject it.

Also in mid-August plans began to take shape for a winter performance of Handel's *Solomon*, with Mendelssohn conducting the Singakademie, and he asked Klingemann for a new verse translation of the text. Although it arrived in time, the Singakademie had already rehearsed the German prose version and felt it was too late to change. "Mein ganzer Plan ist zu Wasser," Mendelssohn wrote to Klingemann,[46] and at the performance itself Rungenhagen conducted. (Even Rungenhagen recognized the weaknesses of the prose text, and Mendelssohn graciously lent him some of Klingemann's versions for the solos.[47])

Throughout the summer and early fall Mendelssohn wrote regularly to Moscheles, urging him to visit Berlin. To Mendelssohn's delight Moscheles agreed, and he and his wife spent nearly two weeks in Berlin (7–19 October), during which there were numerous parties, as well as a very successful recital at the Royal Opera House.[48] At least briefly, the dark clouds that had hung so low over Mendelssohn's head had dispelled.

As the election at the Singakademie now ominously approached, several small lights began to appear on Mendelssohn's horizon. Perhaps the most important of these came from W. Watts, Secretary of the Philharmonic Society in London, who invited Mendelssohn to compose and conduct "a symphony, an overture and a vocal work," for which he was to be paid one hundred guineas.[49] In addition to this piece of good news, Moscheles and his wife were expecting a child the following spring and asked Felix to stand as godfather.[50] Thus the prospect of escaping Berlin and returning to England the following spring suddenly crystallized, and Mendelssohn's depression dissipated proportionately.

At the time Watts's letter arrived from London Mendelssohn was already busy arranging a series of three benefit concerts that he planned to present in Berlin in November and December, with the proceeds going to the Funds for Widows of the Orchestra. (His original offer to give the proceeds to the Institute had been quite tactlessly declined.[51]) The three concerts that took place at the Singakademie—on 15 November, 1 December, 1832, and 20 January 1833 (rescheduled from 20 December)—included, among other works, the first performance of his revised *Reformation* Symphony (op. 107); the revised cantata, *Die erste Walpurgisnacht* (op. 60); the *Midsummer Night's Dream* Overture (op. 21); the *Meeresstille und glückliche Fahrt* Overture (op. 27); the *Hebrides* Overture (op. 26); the Piano Concerto in G minor (op. 25); the *Capriccio brilliant* in B minor (op. 22); Beethoven's G-major Piano Concerto and his Sonatas opp. 27 and 53; and Bach's Concerto in D minor.[52] It has been suggested that Mendelssohn had organized these concerts in order to advance his candidacy for the directorship of the Singakademie,[53] but that may not necessarily have been his primary goal. Certainly, it may have been a consciously perceived corollary to the series, but Mendelssohn was first and foremost a professional composer and musician, and it was only natural that he should compose and perform. He was also astute enough to realize that these concerts were hardly likely to sway the largely conservative membership of the Singakademie. Whatever the impetus for the series, their success was impressive. As the Berlin critic Ludwig Rellstab wrote, "These three musical evenings were more meaningful for the art than a whole year of the usual concerts."[54] In Leipzig the critic for the *AMZ* summed it up thus: "Through these most interesting concerts that he organized, Herr Mendelssohn has shown himself to be an extraordinary piano virtuoso of the highest calibre, an instrumental composer of genius and diligence, and a skillful orchestral conductor."[55] If any members of the Singakademie happened to read these reviews, they might well have asked themselves what more they could want.

The answer to that question soon became clear. After some three and a half months of speculation and rumination, the election of the new director took place on Tuesday evening, 22 January 1833, in the main hall of the Singakademie—more than eight and a half months after Zelter's death. One could hardly accuse the board of directors of having moved precipitately.

It was the first time in the history of the Singakademie that its director was elected by the membership at large, rather than by being appointed by the board of directors.[56] In January 1833 the total membership of the Singakademie numbered 520, of which 385 were "Thursday" or full members, and 135 were "Wednesday" or junior members.[57] Not all full members had voting rights, however, since all underage women, as well as all others who had not been full members for more than two years were ineligible to vote.[58] With these exclusions the ranks of eligible voters were quite drastically reduced. A total of 240 ballots were cast, and of those, 148 were cast for Rungenhagen, 88 for Mendelssohn, and 4 for Grell.[59] Thus Carl Friedrich Rungenhagen became Zelter's successor by a majority of 60 votes.

Of the election itself, only Devrient has left us a detailed description, and his must be read, keeping in mind his obvious and strong partisanship.[60] Since that moment represented the culmination of such lengthy and protracted negotiations, and because it was emotionally such a highly charged scene, Devrient's account warrants citation here:

An officer of rank . . . undertook the business of recording the names. So long as the majority was undecided the names were called quietly and properly, but no sooner had the majority of votes been declared for Rungenhagen, than the recorder began to emphasize his name with an offensive triumph, whilst that of Mendelssohn was mentioned in a desponding, and soon in a pitying tone, a proceeding which caused frequent laughter. I was indignant at this, not only on account of its indecent partisanship, but also because as an indecorum towards a considerable body of the members whose preference was registered in these votes. As none of the directors attempted to stem this scandalous conduct, I appealed to some acquaintances standing near me to protest against it. I was overruled, cautioned not to make a useless disturbance, and I was weak enough to follow their advice; to this day I repent that I did not raise a disturbance.[61]

The die had been unequivocally cast. Awkwardly, and obviously embarrassed by their stunning rejection of Mendelssohn, the Singakademie a week or so later tried to make amends by offering him the post of deputy director, but by then Mendelssohn had caught the whiff of freedom coming from England; he could not wait to be out of Berlin, and in a studiously polite letter of refusal he told them, "daß sie sich hängen lassen könnten."[62]

Now Mendelssohn's real bitterness began to calcify, and his anger that the Singakademie had elected Rungenhagen "mit Pauken und Trompeten" vented itself openly in his correspondence.[63] If nothing else, he was stung and humiliated to have been outgunned by a contender of such colorless and minimal talent. Altogether, it had been a startling though not surprising upset; however much Mendelssohn may have foreseen it, it came nevertheless as a numbing blow. But how to explain the lackluster tortoise overcoming the charismatic hare?

Eric Werner, by reading selectively and falling back on polemics, sees the entire episode in terms of a Judeo-Christian conflict, and more specifically as one more example of German-Judeo enmity.[64] Such a *reductio* falters, however, on both the facts and nuances of the case. Werner's comments are based solely on the remarks overheard by Devrient at a meeting "of the gentlemen members" of the Singakademie in August 1832: "I heard said near me, in an animated knot of talkers, that the Singakademie, from its almost exclusive devotion to sacred music, was a Christian institution, and on this account it was an unheard-of thing to try to thrust a Jewish lad upon them for their conductor."[65] The matter of Mendelssohn's ancestry as grounds for rejecting his candidacy is mentioned almost nowhere else, neither in Lichtenstein's nor in Blumner's histories of the Singakademie (though of course, in Schünemann's work, published in 1941, it is, as one might expect, very much a factor). Further, it is not mentioned as a concern in any of the correspondence or in any of the contemporary published accounts, though after Devrient's book was published it frequently recurs as a major theme.[66]

My point in exploring this question is not to reject Werner's assertion out of hand; Mendelssohn's race may indeed have played a role in the decision by the membership, but it was *not*, as Werner would have us believe, the central issue, if, in fact, there was a central issue. Far greater is the likelihood that his rejection by the Singakademie derived from a combination of issues involving a variety of problems.

In the first place, Mendelssohn's opponent for the directorship was already—and had been—firmly ensconced in his position as deputy director for seventeen years. During that time he had faithfully carried out his duties, and despite, or perhaps because of his bland ways,[67] had evidently made few enemies. Quite the contrary, he was generally well-liked and respected both in the Singakademie and the Liedertafel. He had devoted himself single-mindedly to the Singakademie and had demonstrated his affection for the society by composing numerous works for it. In short, he was *der treue Diener*, a known, a given; there were no hidden difficulties, and no potential for unpleasant surprises. Besides, after so many years' service, it would be blatant ingratitude not to appoint him to the post he had so long and patiently hoped for.

In virtually every way Mendelssohn represented Rungenhagen's diametric opposite. He was young, lightning-quick, and brilliant. In short, he was a genius. He had also, at twenty-three, established for himself an impressive and enviable reputation far beyond the confines of Berlin. Clearly, he would enhance the fame of the Singakademie, and they would have at their head a musician, composer and conductor of internationally recognized stature.

Like Rungenhagen, he was also a known or given, but not to the same extent or in the same way. From having grown up in the Singakademie and from having conducted it on numerous occasions, he was known to be a meticulous and demanding conductor, who knew what he wanted musically and how to achieve it. He was also known to be volatile in temperament; he did not suffer fools or contradiction gladly, and there were musicians—instrumentalists—in Berlin who refused to play under him. He had the potential in nearly equal measure for charm and intimidation. He was proud—and, some might also say, vain—but that, I think, was more appearance than substance.

What little is known of Mendelssohn's interaction with the Singakademie during the summer of 1832 does not suggest that he went out of his way to ingratiate himself with them. Quite the contrary, on his first visit to the Singakademie after returning from London, he made it clear to them that, "I will neither apply for the position nor campaign for it, which is what they wanted. If they wished to offer it to me, then I would accept it or not, . . ."[68] At the same meeting he also delivered some music that Charles Horsley had sent as a gift: "I stuffed it down their throat ("in den Rachen geworfen") and told them to send him a nice thank-you note."[69]

A not unimportant factor in this whole matter was Mendelssohn's family. Of immense wealth and influence, they, together with two or three other families to whom they were vaguely related, constituted for many years the nucleus and focal point of Berlin's cultural and intellectual life. Moreover, they were among the Singakademie's most important and generous patrons. Was it surprising that they promoted the scion of the family for the directorship? Was it surprising that in some measure they expected him to be elected? It was crucial to keep the family together, to keep Felix in Berlin, and the Singakademie post was not only fitting for him, but more important, it would achieve their primary goal.

For the members of the Singakademie who were eligible to vote, the choice was not easy, since not only did it involve two quite distinct personalities, but, equally important, it involved the direction they felt the Singakademie should take in the future. Certainly, they must also have asked themselves how serious Mendelssohn's commitment would be if he were elected. To all intents and purposes he had been away for three years before returning to Berlin the previous June. And one of the specific conditions he had stipulated was for ample travel time. It was clear he intended to spend considerable time away from Berlin and already he anticipated trips to England and Switzerland in 1833. (Rungenhagen, to my knowledge, made no stipulations.)

Then there was the inevitable question of age. Rungenhagen was a mature fifty-four, but could it legitimately be claimed that Mendelssohn was a callow twenty-three? Hardly. Mendelssohn's education had been the finest that could be had in Berlin; his homelife had stressed rigorous intellectual self-discipline, and he had the poise and bearing of someone far beyond his years. He had also traveled extensively and had already seen more of Europe and the British Isles than all but a small percentage of his compatriots. He was urbane, and his outlook, fashioned by wide experience, was broadly cosmopolitan.

Moreover, one's youthful age in Mendelssohn's day and before was not the obstacle it sometimes is today: at twenty-one William Crotch was appointed Professor of Music at Oxford, at twenty-two Longfellow was named Professor of Modern Languages at Bowdoin, and at twenty-three Schelling became Professor of Philosophy at Jena. Surely, at the same age Mendelssohn was capable of directing the Berlin Singakademie.

Devrient had argued his case on the merits of Mendelssohn's achievements, his youthful potential, his talent, and the enhancement of the society through Mendelssohn's leadership, to which the opposition parried that the Singakademie was a private institution, that its members came together because they liked to sing, not because they had a mission, and the public "were admitted on sufferance only . . . and were free to stay away"[70] if they did not like what was offered.

Ultimately, these were the arguments that carried the day for Rungenhagen. The Singakademie opted for the status quo; as Martin Blumner put it, "Respect for age [and] gratitude for loyal, well-intentioned work,"[71] were the decisive criteria. Devrient prophesied that the election of Rungenhagen "doomed the Singakademie to a long course of mediocrity,"[72] though that is not quite the impression conveyed by the membership figures, which grew steadily over the next decade, or by the list of major choral works performed during the same period.[73]

Devrient also reports that following the election the entire Mendelssohn family severed all ties with the Singakademie,[74] but that may be a slight exaggeration. Blumner seems unaware of such a move, and Mendelssohn's relationship with the society over the next ten years was always properly professional, though understandably cool. The Singakademie continued to perform his works regularly, and in 1838 gave the first Berlin performance of *St. Paul*. Early in 1842 Mendelssohn himself conducted *St. Paul* in the Singakademie, and on 15 March of that year he was named an honorary member of the association.[75] Although his father had died seven years earlier, this was an event the rest of the family lived to witness; unfortunately, their reactions have not been preserved. In 1854, when Mendelssohn's great-aunt, Sara Levy, died, she left her entire library to the Singakademie. Time had evidently healed some of the wounds.

Felix Mendelssohn's failure to win the post of director of the Berlin Singakademie can be seen, in the final analysis, as one of his great triumphs, since it liberated him from the need to commit himself to a specific institution and specific goals at a time when the freedom to grow and develop was critical to the full realization of his genius.

NOTES

1. Felix Moscheles, ed. *Letters of Felix Mendelssohn to Ignaz and Charlotte Moscheles* (London, 1888), p. 21.

2. Felix Mendelssohn Bartholdy, *Letters from Italy and Switzerland*, trans. Lady Wallace (Philadelphia, 1863), pp. 351–52. (MS: Bodleian Library, Oxford: M. Deneke M: d. 13, no. 19, fols. 115–16.) Hereafter cited as Mendelssohn-Letters.

3. Eric Werner, *Mendelssohn: A New Image of the Composer and His Age*, trans. D. Newlin (London, 1963). Hereafter cited as Werner (E.). A measure of the importance Werner attaches to this episode in Mendelssohn's life may be drawn from the chapter title, "Berlin Rejects; Europe Invites."

4. Ibid., p. 227. Werner further seems to suggest a conspiracy of silence in dealing with this matter, when he writes of "the almost universal, embarrassed silence of all Mendelssohn biographers, and, indeed, of most of the sources about this event" (p. 229). A perusal of Mendelssohn biographies from Lampadius (1848) onward reveals that this is not the case.

5. Werner also speaks of "the *traumatic* effects on Felix, which were catastrophic for him and of which he was at first unconscious" (p. 229).

6. Martin Blumner, *Geschichte der Sing-Akademie zu Berlin* (Berlin, 1891), p. 248. See also Prof. Hinrich Lichtenstein, *Zur Geschichte der Sing-Akademie in Berlin* (Berlin, 1843), p. 24, and *passim*.

7. Werner (E.), p. 9.

8. Georg Schünemann, *Die Singakademie zu Berlin: 1791–1941* (Regensburg, 1941), p. 67.

9. Ibid., p. 69.

10. Ibid., p. 53.

11. Ibid.

12. August Wilhelm Bach (1796–1869), organist of the Getraudenkirche in Berlin (1814–1816), then of the Marienkirche (1816ff.), organ instructor at the Institut für Kirchenmusik (1822ff.), and on Zelter's death, director, a post he held until his death. A figure of considerable stature and influence in Berlin in the first half of the nineteenth century; not a member of the Thuringian Bach family.

13. The MS is now in the Bodleian Library: MS M. Deneke M: c. 68. See also Schünemann, pp. 43–53.

14. Eduard Devrient, *My Recollections of Felix Mendelssohn-Bartholdy*, trans. N. MacFarren (London, 1869), p. 45. Devrient gives a full account of the genesis of this historic performance: pp. 45–63.

15. Schünemann, p. 63, with facsimile of Zelter's ledger entry (p. 60): "Heute Dienstag nach der ersten Nummer ging der Direktor ab."

16. Blumner, p. 84.

17. For Schleiermacher's relationship to the Singakademie, see W. Sattler, "Die Bedeutung der Singakademie zu Berlin für die liturgische Entwicklung Schleiermachers," in *Zeitschrift für Musikwissenschaft* 1/2 (Dec. 1918): 165–76.

18. The candidates were A. W. Bach (Berlin), H.A.B. Birnbach (Berlin), E. Grell (Berlin), B. Klein (Berlin), J. A. Lecerf (Berlin), C. Loewe (Stettin), F. Mendelssohn Bartholdy (Berlin), Fr. Musevius (Breslau), S. v. Neukomm, C. G. Reißiger (Dresden), C. F. Rungenhagen (Berlin), N. Schelble (Frankfurt am Main), and G. A. Schneider (Berlin).

19. Devrient, p. 147. Devrient provides a detailed account of the entire affair (pp. 145–56). Apparently reconstructed from diary entries (?) long after the fact, Devrient's very precise reminiscences are at times inaccurate as regards dates: a meeting "was called for Sunday, the 17th of August 1832, at 12 A.M." (p. 148); 17 August 1832 fell on Friday. A "meeting on Sunday 9 September" (p. 152) is likewise incorrect; 9 September 1832 fell on a Thursday. Whether his report contains more substantive errors is difficult to determine.

20. Ibid., p. 152.

21. Ibid.

22. Ibid., p. 153.

23. Schünemann, p. 75.

24. Ibid.

25. Marie d'Agoult, *Correspondence de Liszt et de la Comtesse d'Agoult*, ed. Daniel Ollivier (Paris, 1933), vol. 1, p. 414 (20 March 1840).

26. Mendelssohn-Letters, p. 352.

27. Ibid., p. 354.

28. Ibid., p. 355.

29. Ibid., pp. 351–359.

30. Ibid., p. 358. See also Karl Klingemann [Jr.], ed., *Felix Mendelssohn-Bartholdys Briefwechsel mit Legationsrat Karl Klingemann in London* (Essen, 1909), p. 95.

31. Klingemann, p. 95.

32. Devrient, p. 153.

33. Klingemann, p. 98.

34. Ibid.

35. Werner (E.), p. 228.

36. Karl Mendelssohn Bartholdy, ed., *Goethe and Mendelssohn*, trans. M. E. von Glehn (London, 1874). Letter to Charles Horsley, 4 August 1832 (pp. 96–98). See also Julius Schubring, *Briefwechsel zwischen Felix Mendelssohn Bartholdy und Julius Schubring* (Leipzig, 1892), p. 19 (25 August 1832).

37. Mendelssohn-Letters, p. 351.

38. Klingemann, p. 95 (4 July 1832).

39. Ibid., p. 96 (25 July 1832).

40. Ibid.

41. Ibid.

42. Moscheles, p. 24 (25 July 1832).

43. Klingemann, p. 96 (25 July 1832).

44. Ibid., p. 97 (4 August 1832).

45. Adolf Bernhard Marx, *Erinnerungen* (Berlin, 1865), vol. 1, p. 142.

46. Klingemann, p. 103 (5 December 1832).

47. Ibid.

48. *AMZ* 48 (1832), cols. 800–801.

49. George Hogarth, *The Philharmonic Society of London* (London, 1862), p. 59.

50. Moscheles, p. 48 (17 January 1833).

51. Klingemann, p. 102 (5 December 1832).

52. Ernst Wolff, *Felix Mendelssohn Bartholdy*. Berühmte Musiker (Berlin, 1906), p. 111. See also Susanna Großmann-Vendrey, *Felix Mendelssohn Bartholdy und die Musik der Vergangenheit* (Regensburg, 1969), pp. 51–52, who reprints the programs of the second and third concerts. Minor last-minute changes were made in the actual program.

53. Judith Silber, "Mendelssohn and His *Reformation Symphony*," in *JAMS* 40 (1987): 331–32.

54. Cited by Großmann-Vendrey, p. 52.

55. Ibid.

56. Schünemann, p. 73.

57. Blumner, p. 252.

58. Julius Eckhardt, *Ferdinand David und die Familie Mendelssohn Bartholdy* (Leipzig, 1888), p. 49 (letter from Mendelssohn's mother to David, 15 January 1833).

59. Schünemann, pp. 73–74.

60. Devrient, pp. 145–56. Devrient himself may have pressed his case too ardently with Mendelssohn, since the latter wrote to Klingemann on 26 December 1832 with undisguised annoyance, "Devrient has become a routine actor and a bad poet, and so much for that, . . . in short, he is a philistine." Klingemann, p. 105.

61. Devrient, pp. 154–55.

62. Klingemann, p. 110 (4 February 1833).

63. Ibid.

64. Eric Werner, *Mendelssohn: Leben und Werk in neuer Sicht.* (Zurich/Freiburg i.Br., 1980), pp. 256–57.

65. Devrient, p. 150.

66. So firm is Werner's conviction about this matter, that in reviewing Susanna Großmann-Vendrey's book (see n. 52), he chides her for "suppressing" it: "The ambigious at least, if not wholly hostile attitude of the Singakademie vis-à-vis Mendelssohn's candidacy, which had a very curious and unmistakable anti-Semitic background, is completely suppressed by the author. Why?" ("die mindestens zweideutige, wenn nicht gar feindselige Haltung der Singakademie gegenüber Mendelssohns Kandidatur, die sehr merkwürdige und unverkennbare antisemitische Hintergründe hatte, wird von der Verfasserin völlig unterdrückt. Warum?") Eric Werner, "Mendelssohniana," in *Felix Mendelssohn Bartholdy*, ed. Gerhard Schuhmacher (Darmstadt, 1982), p. 393.

67. "Bland" may not be quite accurate here. Mendelssohn's mother (though hardly impartial) recounts how Rungenhagen "bores the singers to

death with his phlegmatic manner and his wretched accompaniments." Eckhardt-David, p. 49 (15 January 1833).

68. Klingemann, p. 95 (4 July 1832).

69. Ibid., p. 96.

70. Devrient, pp. 149–50.

71. Blumner, p. 94.

72. Devrient, p. 155.

73. Blumner, pp. 252–53 and 213–22.

74. Devrient, pp. 155–56.

75. Bodleian Library, Oxford: MS M. Deneke M: a.1 (Roll), no. 6.

The Power of Class: Fanny Hensel

NANCY B. REICH

"Had Madame Hensel been a poor man's daughter, she must have become known to the world by the side of Madame Schumann and Madame Pleyel, as a female pianist of the very highest class. Like her brother, she had in her composition a touch of that southern vivacity which is so rare among the Germans. More feminine than his, her playing bore a strong family resemblance to her brother's in its fire, neatness, and solidity. Like himself, too, she was as generally accomplished as she was specially gifted."

HENRY F. CHORLEY[1]

The British music critic is speaking, of course, of Fanny Hensel *née* Mendelssohn Bartholdy,[2] the older sister of Felix Mendelssohn Bartholdy. The "accomplished" pianist gave only one public performance: a benefit concert in 1836; the "gifted" composer lived to see publication of only forty-two out of some four hundred works. Unlike her brother's music, hers was known only to a small circle and heard only at home musicales. When Fanny Hensel finally summoned up the courage to publish her work, defying the brother who disapproved of professional music making by a woman, sudden death cheated her of the satisfaction and triumph she surely would have had.

The constraints placed on Fanny Hensel were many: her gender, religion, family tradition, and prevailing intellectual beliefs all contributed to her position as a dilettante. Above all, as we learn from Chorley, the power of class was a potent force in keeping her work in the private realm.

The myths and legends about the Mendelssohns are gradually dispersing; access to heretofore unpublished letters have changed our perceptions of the family, and information about Fanny Hensel's creative output has led to examination and performance of her works. For over one hundred years, the major source of information about the Mendelssohns has been the family biography, written by Fanny Hensel's devoted son, Sebastian Hensel, and first published in 1879.[3] His book offers a portrait based on letters, diaries, and memories:

through Sebastian's eyes, we see the entire family, proudly beginning with the grand forebear, Moses Mendelssohn, the great German-Jewish philosopher. But it is precisely because Hensel gives what he refers to as a picture of a "good German bourgeois family"[4] that we must look further for the whole story. And that is what we are beginning to uncover.[5]

·

Fanny Caecilie Hensel, the eldest child of Abraham and Lea Mendelssohn and a granddaughter of Moses Mendelssohn, was given the same education as her brother Felix, three and one-half years younger. The two studied first with their mother and then were sent to Ludwig Berger for piano lessons and eventually to Carl Friedrich Zelter for theory and composition lessons. Zelter, a composer and conductor of the Singakademie, the Berlin choral society that Fanny and Felix joined in 1820, was the most influential Berlin musician of the time. The general education the Mendelssohn children received was thorough and intense: Fanny (1805–1847), Felix (1809–1847), Rebecka (1811–1858) and Paul (1812–1874), all had private tutoring from the finest scholars in Berlin. Besides music, they studied modern and classical languages, mathematics, history, geography, as well as drawing (in which Felix was particularly gifted) and dancing. The schedule—which also included physical exercise—drawn up for the young Mendelssohns left no idle time: beginning at five in the morning, every moment in the day was accounted for. In addition to the rigorous working schedule and the intellectual stimulation from distinguished friends, relatives, and guests, Fanny attended lectures on a wide variety of subjects given by Berlin's leading scholars.

The paths of the sister and brother diverged as they reached adolescence. All were musical—Fanny and Felix, exceptionally so—as Rebecka jokingly explained many years later: "My older siblings stole my artistic fame. In any other family, I would have been much praised as a musician and perhaps even have directed a small circle. But next to Felix and Fanny, I could not have succeeded in attaining any such recognition."[6]

Although it was clear to the family that Fanny had talents equal to those of her brother Felix, she was reminded by her father of the feminine duties and responsibilities that would not permit the professional activity open to Felix. When Abraham spoke of her future as a housewife, he envisioned, of course, a future as the mistress of a Berlin establishment befitting a member of the Berlin Jewish bourgeois aristocracy.[7] (The Mendelssohn children were converted to

Christianity in 1816 and their parents later, in 1822. Nevertheless, they were referred to as a Jewish family long after they left that faith.) After a lengthy engagement, Fanny married Wilhelm Hensel (1794–1861), a court painter and professor of art, and remained for most of her life a devoted and obedient daughter, wife, mother—and frustrated musician.

The prescribed role of the cultivated Berlin lady was familiar to Fanny Hensel. All her female relatives were educated and cultured women: grandmother, mother, aunts, and great-aunts on the maternal side were members of the very wealthy Itzig family who used their talents to establish salons, to build libraries, to support musicians, artists, and composers. It was expected that Fanny, a banker's daughter, would follow the tradition of her Itzig relatives.

The aunts on her father's side, Henriette Mendelssohn and Dorothea Veit Schlegel, daughters of Moses Mendelssohn, however, were not well-to-do. Both turned to intellectual pursuits and supported themselves by teaching and writing.[8]

Their father, Moses Mendelssohn, arrived in Berlin in 1743 and, as a Jew, barely gained entrance into that city. Recognized as one of the great thinkers of the Enlightenment, he carried on his intellectual labors only during the part of the day in which he was not engaged in his regular job, first as a bookkeeper in a textile factory, later as a partner in that enterprise. He was greatly concerned about the education of his children and took as much pride in the intellectual achievements of his oldest child, Dorothea, as in his sons. (Henrietta was only ten when he died.) But when Dorothea was eighteen, a husband was chosen for her without regard for her feelings or wishes.[9] Dorothea remained in a loveless marriage for sixteen years and ultimately divorced her husband to live with and later marry Friedrich Schlegel, the writer and critic. Yet, even before her marriage to her second husband, Dorothea worked as his copyist, editor, and writer, and, it seems, gladly took a subordinate position. In her journal is an entry: "[One goal for me] would be to be able to earn so much by writing that Friedrich need not write for money anymore."[10] To a mutual friend (Friedrich Schleiermacher) she wrote:

I feel myself so rich in many talents and gifts that it would be wrong of me and a sin if I permitted my lack of money to depress me too much. If only good fortune would favor me so that I could continue supporting my friend for several more years, then I would certainly be secure! . . . He too is working honestly and tirelessly, but how can one expect an artist to deliver a work of art each year just to be able to exist? He *cannot* create more. . . . To bring pressure on the artist to become a mere craftsman—I cannot do that. And it wouldn't succeed anyway. What I can do lies within these limits: to create peace for him and to earn bread humbly as a craftswoman until he is able to do so. And I am honestly determined to do just that.[11]

Her novel, *Florentin*, does not carry her name on the title page. Schlegel is listed as the "editor."

Henriette, a younger sister, never married. She founded a renowned boarding school for girls in Paris and then worked as the governess and companion to the daughter of the wealthy French general (later marshal) Sebastiani. After many years of teaching in Paris, she returned to Berlin in 1824, lived with the family of Lea and Abraham Mendelssohn, and died there.

Although Abraham and his family were fond, perhaps even proud, of the achievements of Dorothea and Henriette Mendelssohn, and offered them financial support when necessary, they were not Fanny's role models. The Itzig connection—her mother, grandmother, and great-aunts—served that function. Lea Mendelssohn *née* Salomon (1777–1842), was a granddaughter of Isaac Daniel Itzig (1723–1799) the court banker and probably the wealthiest man in Berlin. Powerful and privileged, his palace was opposite the king's own. He was a "protected Jew," and unique in that his children and grandchildren were permitted to inherit land and houses in the Prussian capital, a privilege that for other Jewish families extended only to one son, if at all. Itzig was the first of a small number of Jews to receive the rights of citizenship.[12] Of Itzig's eleven daughters (he also had five sons), we are particularly interested in four: Bella Salomon (1749–1824), the grandmother of Fanny, and three of her sisters: Sara Levy (1762–1854), Fanny von Arnstein (1758–1818), and Caecilie von Eskeles (1759–1818), the great-aunts after whom Fanny Caecilie Mendelssohn was named.

All the Itzig daughters were talented musicians and all appeared to be content with their roles as salonières, dilettantes, or patronesses. There is some controversy as to whether it was the grandmother, Bella Salomon, or the great-aunt, Sara Levy, who gave Felix Mendelssohn the handwritten score of the *St. Matthew Passion* in 1823, which led to the famous revival he conducted in 1829, but it could very well have been either, because all the sisters were well acquainted with the music of Johann Sebastian Bach at a time when little of it was published and still less performed publicly. Sara Levy, Fanny's great-aunt, studied with Wilhelm Friedemann Bach and was a friend and patron of Carl Phillip Emanuel Bach. Married to a banker chosen by her father, Madame Levy had amassed a large collection of Bach manuscripts donated to the Singakademie library. "Tante Levy" was not only an early member of the chorus but was reported to have performed as harpsichord soloist (unpaid, of course) with the Singakademie instrumental ensemble.

The Baronesses Fanny von Arnstein and Caecilie von Eskeles married Viennese court bankers and settled in that city. Fanny von Arnstein, a charming, witty woman over whom duels were fought, brought the intellectual tradition of the Berlin salon to the Habsburg capital. She was a pianist and befriended Beethoven and other Viennese composers. The musical soirées she gave during the Congress of Vienna were renowned, and benefit concerts she organized led to the founding of the Gesellschaft der Musikfreunde.[13] Her daughter, Henrietta Pereira-Arnstein (1780–1859), also a fine pianist, aided Haydn in his last years and continued the musical traditions of the Arnstein family.[14] Lea Mendelssohn particularly admired her aunt Fanny and there was close contact with the Viennese relatives who visited and corresponded regularly.

For most of her life, Fanny Hensel followed the pattern set by the Itzig women. She married, supervised a large home and the education of her one child, entertained family, friends and her husband's colleagues and students, maintained a large and lively correspondence with family members. Fanny did not travel widely, and, like many of the Mendelssohn family, had as her intimates her sister and other relatives, some converted Jews, others who remained Jewish. Almost all were musicians or music-lovers; many, with Fanny, participated in the choral activities of the Singakademie until 1833. When Felix was rejected for the post of conductor of the Singakademie, the family left that organization.[15] But the musical activity that engaged her energies and talents and that proved to be most rewarding, were the Mendelssohn family *Sonntagsmusik*—the Sunday musicales, held first in her parents' mansion on Leipzigerstrasse 3 and then later in the garden house on their property, where she lived with her husband and son. These private musicales became brilliant Berlin musical affairs attended by aristocracy and bourgeois music-lovers alike.[16]

Madame Hensel planned the programs, played, composed, and conducted both the choir made up of skilled amateurs and an orchestra of professional musicians hired from the Königstadt Theater. Her Sunday musicales introduced to Berlin audiences music of the Bach family and Gluck; her musicians performed scenes from Beethoven's opera, and sections of Handel oratorios; Fanny premièred many of her brother's works as well as her own. That she composed and conducted was perfectly acceptable so far as the family was concerned, since it was an amateur activity carried on in her own home and for which she was not paid. Publication of her works under her own name, however, was a different matter and one to which first her father and then her brother Felix strongly objected.

.

Moses Mendelssohn, the great Enlightenment philosopher, is often referred to as an emancipator. But the liberalism of the man who led the German Jews out of the ghetto and into German secular society did not extend to women. Like the *philosophes* and other Enlightenment thinkers whose influence was felt long after the French Revolution, Mendelssohn saw the roles of women primarily as those of mothers and wives. Bell and Offen point out that "after the French Revolution, discussions of female education took a distinctly conservative turn. . . . The secular political goals . . . were challenged by a resurgent moral conservatism that recast and reformulated female education in terms of traditional religious piety, chastity, and obedience."[17] This viewpoint coincided with the traditional Jewish position on women. For Moses, for his son Abraham, and for his grandson Felix, men for whom children and family life were of great importance, these sentiments made sense. They chose wives who fit a familiar pattern.

Abraham Mendelssohn had his children converted to Protestantism because, as he wrote to his daughter, "it is the creed of most civilized people, and contains nothing that can lead you away from what is good, and much that guides you to *love, obedience, tolerance and resignation* [my emphasis], even if it offered nothing but the example of its Founder, understood by so few and followed by still fewer."[18] Moreover, conversion to Christianity opened options to careers otherwise impossible for a Jew. As a son of Moses Mendelssohn, he had limited civil rights and career opportunities, but baptism made it possible for his grandsons to hold university posts, or for his son to take a position as a music director, for example, since all these posts were associated with state-supported institutions. These considerations extended only to the male members of the family, of course.

Why did Fanny Hensel remain a "dilettante" despite her skills? And why did her father and brother feel so strongly about public appearances and publication? Although there were a number of professional women pianists and composers active at this time (Clara

Schumann and Marie Pleyel, for example, cited by Chorley), they were not women from the bourgeois aristocratic class: they worked because of need. To the Mendelssohn men, a career as a musician placed a woman of Fanny's class in an untenable position: money would be exchanged, her name would be in print, and she would appear on stage. All the traditions of the family (Jewish, Christian, Enlightenment philosophy) united in prescribing "modesty" and "obedience" for females, qualities that could not be preserved while appearing in public and pursuing a career. In addition, it is difficult not to suspect that the social position of this Jewish-Christian family in Berlin also influenced their attitude.

Consequently, when six of Fanny's songs were published in early collections of Felix, they came out under his name—not to deceive the public or because he could not compose songs—but because her "modesty" would have been at stake.

Felix's objections to separate publication of his sister's works have been variously described as stemming from jealousy of his sister's talent; as "inherited" from his father; as a male chauvinist position intended to keep women in their place; as guilt at having succeeded in an arena in which she, equally gifted, was prevented from competing; and as a desire to protect his sister against the barbs of the critics. I believe there is some truth in all of these.

The musical kinship between sister and brother was very close; the two had studied together and the competition was a stimulus to each. Fanny reminded him of this in June 1837: "If you think back to the time when we were constantly together, when I immediately discovered every thought that went through your mind and knew your new things by heart even before they were notated, and if you remember that our relationship was a particularly rare one among siblings, in part because of our common musical pursuits."[19]

For many years, Fanny and Felix were musical confidantes: they discussed musical problems, criticized and trusted each other. At his request, she wrote detailed critiques of his works and took his place at Berlin rehearsals of *St. Paul* to assure a correct performance. He wrote comments on her work, and repeated to her praise of her playing and compositions from Kalkbrenner, Moscheles, and Goethe. Occasionally, he was caught between his prejudices and his musical judgments. While he was concerned about Fanny's "femininity" (to be "unfeminine," or "*unweiblich*," was anathema to the Mendelssohns), he could not help complimenting her on the fact that there was no trace of the feminine in her *Lobgesang*, a cantata composed in 1831.

The Mendelssohn men had a horror of *femmes savantes* like Rahel

Levin von Varnhagen and Bettina von Arnim, and Fanny shared their feeling. In a letter to the mother of Madame Bigot, their childhood piano teacher, Felix praises his sister's musicianship but takes pains to deny that she is an intellectual or "unfeminine":

> It makes me sad, that since her marriage she can no longer compose as diligently as earlier, for she has composed several things, especially German lieder, which belong to the very best which we possess of lieder; still it is good, on the other hand, that she finds much joy in her domestic concerns, for a woman who neglects them be it for oil colors, or for rhyme, or for double counterpoint always calls to mind instinctively, the Greek [language] from the *femmes savantes*, and I am afraid of that. This is, then, thank God, therefore not the case with my sister, and yet she has, as said, continued her piano playing still with much love and besides has made much progress in it recently.[20]

Although Felix could praise Fanny to others, he was not always so generous to her. One must suspect a certain amount of sibling rivalry when Felix, responding to her complaint that she had lost all inspiration after her child was born, wrote:

> You can hardly expect a man like me to wish you some musical ideas; it is just greediness for you to complain of a scarcity of them; . . . if you wanted to, you would already be composing with might and main and if you do not want to, why do you fret so dreadfully? If I had my child to nurse, then I would not want to write scores. . . . But seriously, the child is not even a half year old, and you already want to think of ideas other than Sebastian? (not Bach) Be happy that you have him, music fails to appear only when it has no place.[21]

Fanny Hensel was unable to ignore Felix's arguments and did not protest. Instead, she threw herself into the *Sonntagsmusik* with more energy than ever. The home musicales became her primary musical outlet.

The Music of Fanny Hensel

Only in the past two decades have we had the privilege of seeing and hearing a number of works by Fanny Hensel, recently described as "without doubt, the most significant woman composer of the nineteenth century."[22] Unlike her brother, Fanny was not given the opportunity to study string instruments (which would have facilitated her string and orchestral writing), to travel in order to hear new music and make contacts with foreign composers, to try out works for large audiences and make the necessary revisions after rehearsals, to hear painful criticism that would enable her to grow and develop as a composer. For most of her creative life, excepting her brother's comments, she heard only praise from the home musical circles around her—not necessarily a healthy situation.

The extent of her oeuvre has still to be determined, but it is known that she wrote keyboard music that includes sonatas, studies, contrapuntal works, and character pieces; works for organ; vocal music that encompasses solo songs, duets, trios, and choral works; works for chorus and orchestra, including an oratorio and several cantatas; an orchestral overture; and chamber music, including a piano quartet, a string quartet, a piano trio, and instrumental duos.[23] Although the bulk of her work remains in manuscript, there is no doubt that Fanny Hensel thought of herself as a composer. Except for an enormous need for her brother's approval, we find no traces of the self-derogation and lack of confidence about her creative efforts from which Clara Schumann, for example, suffered. The question remains: why did Fanny Hensel wait so long to accept publishing offers? She herself explains in a letter from July 1846 to her brother why she held her work back:

> I . . . have to tell you something. But since I know from the start you won't like it, it's a bit awkward to get underway. So laugh at me or not, as you wish: I'm afraid of my brothers at age 40 as I was of Father at age 14—or, more aptly expressed, desirous of pleasing you and everyone I've loved throughout my life. And when I now know in advance that it won't be the case, I thus feel *rather* uncomfortable. In a word, I'm beginning to publish. I have Herr Bock's sincere offer for my lieder and have finally turned a receptive ear to his favorable terms. . . . I hope I won't disgrace all of you through my publishing, as I'm no *femme libre*[24] . . . I trust *you* will in no way be bothered by it, since, as you can see, I've proceeded completely on my own in order to spare you any possible unpleasant moment, and I hope you won't think badly of me. If it succeeds—that is, if the pieces are well liked and I receive additional offers—I know it will be a great stimulus to me, something I've always needed in order to create.[25]

This revealing letter confirms what Fanny had often hinted at: that the very special bond with her brother had been a burden as well as a joy throughout her life, and that his approval was essential to her creativity.

Excerpts from Fanny's letters to her brother offer further support for this interpretation:

8 April 1835: "For I'm so unreasonably afraid of you anyway (and of no other person, except slightly of Father) that I actually never play particularly well in front of you, and I wouldn't even attempt to accompany in front of you, although I know I'm very good at it."[26]

12 January 1836: ". . . it's necessary for you to know everything in my life and approve of it. Therefore I'm also very sad, truly not out of vanity, that I haven't been able to be grateful to you in such a long time for liking my music. Did I really do it better in the old days, or were you merely easier to satisfy?"[27]

30 July 1836: "I don't know exactly what Goethe means by the demonic influence . . . but this much is clear: if it does exist, you exert it over me."[28]

22 November 1836: "I have to admit honestly that I'm rather neutral about it [publishing], and Hensel, on the one hand, is for it, and you, on the other hand, are against it. I would of course comply totally with the wishes of my husband in any other matter, yet on this issue alone it's crucial to have your consent, for without it I might not undertake anything of the kind."[29]

With this history, Fanny Hensel's decision to accept offers from publishers seems astonishing. The support of friends and her artist-husband, Wilhelm Hensel, certainly figured in her decision, but three other events in her life enabled her to overcome the "demonic influence" of her brother and the loyalty to family and class: her Italian trip of 1839–1840, her mother's death in December 1842, and her friendship with a young German musician and critic, Robert von Keudell.

Fanny Hensel's first Italian trip was an ecstatic experience that awakened her to a full realization of her musical powers. Her letters and diary give a detailed description of the sights and sounds and the liberating effect of the Mediterranean culture on her northern soul. Furthermore, she found herself, for the first time in her life, away from Berlin and its associations, from her mother, from her brother's influence, and—perhaps more importantly—freed from the heavy weight of prescriptive family conventions and expectations. She, her ten-year-old son Sebastian, and her husband Wilhelm Hensel spent much of their time with artists from the French Academy (the Prix de Rome winners) and three young Frenchmen—Charles Gounod and Georges Bousquet, composers, and Charles Dugasseau, a painter—all of whom evidently adored Madame Hensel. In his memoirs, Gounod described those glorious Roman days:

> Madame Hensel was a musician beyond comparison, a remarkable pianist, and a woman of superior mind; small and thin in person but with an energy that showed itself in her deep eyes and in her fiery glance. She was gifted with rare ability as a composer. . . . M. and Madame Hensel came to the Academy on Sunday evenings. She used to place herself at the piano with the good grace and simplicity of those who make music because they love it, and thanks to her fine talent and prodigious memory, I was brought to the knowledge of a mass of the chefs-d'oeuvres of German music of which I was completely ignorant at that time, among others, a number of pieces by Johann Sebastian Bach—sonatas, concertos, fugues, and preludes—and several Mendelssohn compositions which were, also, a revelation to me from an unknown world.[30]

Fanny had never been so much appreciated before, and her self-confidence as a musician blossomed. Her letters reveal a new and joyous woman.

The death of her mother, Lea Mendelssohn, broke another tie with the traditions of the wealthy cultivated Berlin salonières and the Itzig family. Although Lea had encouraged Fanny's composing and even urged Felix to give his approval, the change in the family constellation undoubtedly had an effect on the eldest daughter.

On her return to Berlin, she met Robert von Keudell, whose critical judgment and encouragement helped free her from her dependence on Felix. In her diary she wrote, "Keudell looks at everything new that I write with the greatest interest and points out to me if there is something to be corrected and in the main, he is correct. . . . He has always given me the very best counsel."[31]

In 1846, at the age of forty, Fanny Hensel chose, from the many hundreds of her works, a number of pieces for piano and songs. These were published by two Berlin publishers. Favorable reviews appeared in the leading music journals of Berlin and Leipzig. Heartened, Fanny continued to compose both for publication and for her Sunday musicales. During the summer of 1846, she wrote in her diary that she was always busy and felt gratified and successful. She added that perhaps never in her life—except for a short period during her first trip to Rome—had she felt so content and blessed.[32]

On the afternoon of Friday, 14 May 1847, Fanny Hensel was rehearsing her chorus for a Sunday performance of Felix's *Walpurgisnacht*, and suddenly felt ill. She quickly lost consciousness and died that evening.

Soon after her sudden and unexpected death, Felix (who died six months later) arranged to have a number of her compositions, including her Trio for piano, violin, and cello, published posthumously. Other works, however, remained in family hands until recently and were not published. Obituaries appearing in the Berlin newspapers lauded the musician:

> Fanny Hensel was an artist in the most exalted sense of the word; in her, the happiest gifts of nature always went hand in hand with the most careful cultivation of rare talents. Just as she shone as a gifted and accomplished pianist, so do the works only recently published under her own name testify to that heartfelt depth of feeling, which, precisely in this sphere, is fundamental to a lofty and noble creation.[33]

Her class was no longer a barrier.

NOTES

1. Henry F. Chorley, "Mendelssohn's Sister and Mother," in W. A. Lampadius, *Life of Felix Mendelssohn Bartholdy* (Boston, 1865), pp. 210–11.

2. The name Bartholdy was added to Mendelssohn when Abraham had his children converted to Christianity, but was not used consistently by the children. In this paper, the name will be given as Mendelssohn.

3. Sebastian Hensel, *Die Familie Mendelssohn 1729–1847: Nach Briefen und Tagebüchern*, 2d rev. ed. (Berlin, 1880). An English translation, *The Mendelssohn Family (1729–1847) From Letters and Journals*, trans. Carl Klingemann and an American collaborator, 2d rev. ed. (New York, 1881), followed almost immediately. References in this paper will be to the German edition (Berlin, 1880).

4. Hensel, vol. 1, p. v.

5. I refer here to recent sources such as letters, diaries, memoirs, and scholarly studies. For English readers, see, for example, the path-breaking dissertation by Victoria Ressmeyer Sirota, "The Life and Works of Fanny Mendelssohn Hensel" (D.M.A. dissertation, Boston University, 1981) and the work of Marcia J. Citron, "The Lieder of Fanny Mendelssohn Hensel," in *Musical Quarterly* 69 (1983): 570–93; her "Felix Mendelssohn's Influence on Fanny

Mendelssohn Hensel as a Professional Composer," in *Current Musicology* 37/ 38 (1984): 9–17; and her "The Letters of Fanny Hensel to Felix Mendelssohn in Oxford's Green Books," in *Mendelssohn and Schumann Essays*, ed. Jon Finson and R. Larry Todd (Durham, 1984), pp. 99–108. Especially valuable is her book, *The Letters of Fanny Hensel to Felix Mendelssohn*, collected, edited, and translated with introductory essays and notes by Marcia J. Citron (Stuyvesant, 1987), cited hereafter as Citron, *Letters*. Most useful, but unfortunately not translated into English, is the volume by the late historian Felix Gilbert (who was himself a Mendelssohn descendant), *Bankiers, Künstler und Gelehrte: Unveröffentlichte Briefe der Familie Mendelssohn aus dem 19. Jahrhundert* (Tübingen, 1975). Also in German, and particularly pertinent here, is *Fanny Mendelssohn: Italienisches Tagebuch*, ed. Eva Weissweiler, 2d ed. (Darmstadt, 1988).

6. Quoted from Johanna Kinkel's *Memoiren* in Konrad Feilchenfeldt, "Karl August Varnhagen von Ense: Sieben Briefe an Rebecka Dirichlet," in *Mendelssohn Studien* 3 (1979): 56–57.

7. This term, from William Weber, *Music and the Middle Class: The Social Structure of Concert Life in London, Paris and Vienna* (New York, 1975), p. 8, is a most appropriate classification for the family of Abraham and Lea Mendelssohn.

8. In their youth, Dorothea and Henriette were close friends of Henriette Herz and Rahel Levin, and much involved in the Berlin literary salons. For an insightful presentation of the Berlin salons, see Deborah Hertz, *Jewish High Society in Old Regime Berlin* (New Haven, 1988).

9. The great-grandson of Moses Mendelssohn, Sebastian Hensel, referred indignantly to this arrangement as an "oriental view of a woman as an object." Hensel, vol. 1, p. 44. It is interesting to note that "oriental" and "asiatic" were terms used by many, including Hensel and his great-aunt Dorothea Schlegel, as substitutions for "Jewish."

10. Quoted in *Florentin: A Novel*, trans., annotated, and introduced by Edwina Lawler and Ruth Richardson (Lewiston, 1988), p. xxviii.

11. Ibid., p. cxvi. My translation.

12. Gilbert, pp. xvii–xviii.

13. See Hilde Spiel, "Jewish Women in Austrian Culture," in *The Jews of Austria*, ed. Josef Fraenkel (London, 1967), pp. 97–102.

14. The musical salons of all three women are described by Johann Friedrich Reichardt in his *Vertraute Briefe geschrieben auf einer Reise nach Wien und den österreichischer Staaten zu Ende des Jahres 1808 und zu Anfang 1809*, 2 vols., ed. Gustav Gugitz (Munich, 1915), vol. 1, pp. 104–5.

15. See the discussion concerning the election, which, according to Werner, had anti-Semitic overtones, in Eric Werner, *Mendelssohn: A New Image of the Composer and His Age*, trans., Dika Newlin (New York, 1963), pp. 229–31.

16. In March 1844, Fanny wrote to her sister Rebecka that there were "twenty-two carriages in the court and Liszt and eight princesses in the room." Hensel, vol. 2, pp. 293–94.

17. *Women, The Family, and Freedom: The Debate in Documents.* 2 vols., ed. Susan Groag Bell and Karen M. Offen (Stanford, 1983), vol. 1, p. 83.

18. Hensel, vol. 1, p. 95.

19. Citron, *Letters*, p. 234.

20. Quoted from the letter of 1 June 1835 by Sirota, p. 85. It is interesting to note that "Tante Schlegel" was exempted from Felix's hostility toward women intellectuals. By the time Felix and Fanny knew her, Friedrich Schlegel had died and Dorothea was devoting herself to children and grandchildren. Moreover, Dorothea herself had always taken the Enlightenment position that her role was to nurture the creative (male) genius.

21. Quoted in Sirota, p. 59. I have modified the translation.

22. Franz Krautwurst, "Fanny Hensel," in *Die Musik in Geschichte und Gegenwart*, Supplement (1974), pp. 658–62.

23. For an extended discussion of her compositions, see Sirota, chapters 4, 5, and 6.

24. Here she refers to women like the *femmes savantes* who so distressed her brother.

25. Citron, *Letters*, p. 349.

26. Ibid., p. 182.

27. Ibid., p. 195.

28. Ibid., p. 209.

29. Ibid., p. 222.

30. Charles Gounod, *An Autobiography*, trans. Annette E. Crocker (Chicago, 1895), p. 125.

31. Hensel, vol. 2, p. 365.

32. Ibid., p. 375.

33. Reprinted from *Die Preussische Zeitung*, in *Signale für die musikalische Welt* (May 1847): 190–91.

Samplings

CLAUDIO SPIES

In memory of Professor Felix Gilbert

Pronouncements about the beauty of a piece of music may be informative as to the pronouncer's predilections, but are likely to yield little else of use—either to their utterer or to those thus addressed. No matter how emphatic such vociferations may sound, they are nonetheless bound to lack substance, unless whatever may be deemed beautiful is specifically defined, placed within a particular context, and gauged within the larger, overall, manifold dimensions of a composition. Each of us is apt to keep within easy recall a number of "places" in pieces of music that strike us as especially beautiful. Sooner or later, therefore, we may perceive an urge to delve into the reasons for which we find them so admirable, and to explore the various connections (to other portions or "places" in the particular piece) that we might thereby be encouraged to infer. Under such conditions, our notions as to beauty, or as to what we admire and love, are both clarified and enhanced, so that whatever may have been explained suffers no loss whatever in our perception, but instead gains greatly in those very qualities we are most drawn to. The result may indeed often be that one "place" yields offshoots, and that the singularly beautiful becomes multiply so.

In the experience of a lifetime, the music of Mendelssohn has always been especially rich in such delights, and I refer here also to much larger entities than merely those "places" whose details exert their constant yet ever-growing fascination. However, it is difficult to encompass a few remarks about the myriad felicities in Mendelssohn's music if not within a narrow frame of reference; I am consequently obliged to select a few "places"—chosen, perhaps, arbitrarily, but also because my joy in them could never decrease or grow stale—in his orchestral music.

It sometimes occurs in the orchestral works that a structurally significant return of musical material—a "theme" or a melody—will include the sudden appearance, seemingly out of nowhere (until a second thought/hearing/look shows us otherwise), of a countermelody of such compelling character, that it takes on, momentarily, a *primary* role, while leaving to the returning material itself the task of simply unrolling on its own. The countermelody that so sweepingly captures our attention is always placed in a cannily chosen register, and is given an instrumental assignment that insures both utmost clarity and a degree of orchestral surprise. Moreover, that surprising presence is apt to have more far-reaching consequences in the music's unfolding. An instance is found in the Intermezzo of the *Midsummer Night's Dream* music (op. 61, no. 5), measures 74–98 (example 1). The context, from the beginning of the Intermezzo, is of melodic material breathlessly tossed back and forth between two alternating instrumental groups, against a background of "sustaining" tremolando harmonic motion. The same alternating instrumental groups take part in a sequential passage ending in a dominant pedal that prepares for a return of the opening music. At this point, measure 74, the wonderfully contrasting countermelody appears, *sostenuto* but no less agitated, in cellos doubled by the first bassoon. Nowhere previous to measure 74 had the cellos been given any such melodic material, although—and here is where Mendelssohn's head works its magic—that bassoon had given a hint of the countermelody as early as in measure 10, and both bassoons had sustained alternating neighbor harmonies in measures 60–64. By the time the climactic high A is reached in measure 85, the first oboe adds an upper octave, and the marvelous chromatic descent that follows is twice assigned the widest registral span of any of the materials thus far presented—save for the octave doublings, predominantly in the first oboe and first bassoon(!) in measures 24–30. This kind of *instrumentally* supported continuity is made the more apparent by the gradual lengthening of those octave-doubled passages of countermelody fragments in oboe and bassoon: the first is stated in four measures (plus an upbeat), the next takes up six measures (again, plus the upbeat); then the full flowering of the countermelody (at m. 74) lasts eighteen measures, to which six more are added, following a two-measure interruption. Lastly, near the close, two hints of the fully stated countermelody occur in five-measure segments assigned to cellos, basses, and doubling bassoons (mm. 111–15 and 119–23). One further, telling detail must be mentioned: the second chromatic descent from the high A, in those aforementioned additional six measures (mm. 93–99), involves the (by this time) expected association of oboe and bassoon, doubled at the octave, but the cellos are now given an independent complementing line, so that what had provided the instrumental surprise in the appearance of the countermelody is now imbued with a subtler, more modest kind of surprise. It also, of course, bespeaks the composer's staunch allegiance to the notion that repetition should, whenever possible, be nonliteral!

Another sudden and unexpected melodic apparition occurs in measures 188–210 of the overture, op. 32 (*Zum Märchen von der schönen Melusine*, example 2), though here the surrounding circumstances and effects are altogether different from those governing the Intermezzo. The music is at this juncture developmental, with harmonic motion through the circle of fifths, but it also brings back the half-arpeggiating, upward tune in eighths with which the piece had opened. Prior to this, a secondary area with contrasting material in F minor and in A♭ had involved a larger orchestral ensemble at a predominantly higher dynamic. Into the sequential continuity that is redirected by the harmony (V of A) in measure 177 there intrudes, eleven measures later, a melody so ravishing as to threaten to obliterate the "main material" from our attention. The oboe, which had been silent for twenty-eight measures, is assigned this heart-wrencher with its own sequential patterning, its characteristic turns (mm. 191 and 195), and its duetting with the chromatically descending flute. Yet it also establishes a somewhat longer-range structural link to the subsequent return of the F-minor material (mm. 210ff.): after a one-and-a-half-measure interruption (during which the nonlegato, "nonbeginning" music breaks in), the oboe resumes the registrally highest position it had claimed with its previous melody. That, however, is now reduced to an embellished pedal on G, acting as a bridge across two-measure segments in which the overture's opening material and "nonbeginning" musics appear in alternation, with a gradual increase in dynamics, so that an arrival in F minor is heralded. Even so, the oboe's grace note B♭ (to A), elegantly hairpinned in both its occurrences, is bound to remind us of the previous ravishing tune, which, however, is never to return. Only much later, in measures 246–54, does the first clarinet play a tune whose transpositional kinship to the oboe's melody is made evident: the oboe's initial upward half step (D–E♭) is now the clarinet's C–D♭, and the grace note E♭ (to D♭) in measure 253 is plainly a dead ringer. If we now ponder the origin of that grace note, we can find it—if metrically displaced—in the first violins, measures 78 and 82, *where it is doubled by the first oboe*. Subsequent oboe doubling of this melodic segment (with the grace note) in the F-minor music under scrutiny, and even oboes *octave-doubling* (mm. 95–103), must be recognized as harbingers of oboe-things to come! (In this context, the turns in measures 191 and 195 are proof of Mendelssohn's inventive resourcefulness.) And if anyone should need to be reminded that good composers do not waste their materials any more than they shrug off connections among these, consider the chromatic descent in the flute (mm. 196–200): it brings to mind both a conspicuously chromatic rise in the F-minor bass (mm. 99–101) and in the violins' A♭-major tune that grows out of it (mm. 107ff.), so that it reflects the same chromatic pitch-class span (C to F) at its outset, and adds a second, smaller span (B♭ to D♭) a little later.

To anybody acquainted with the *Italian* Symphony, the long, sustaining high A in the oboe—all nine and a half measures of it, in the first movement—will be a familiar highlight, just as it will surely bring an irrepressible smile of pleasure to any musician's face. Yet it is not only by reason of its high-register pedal function, over an eventually descending bass, or its eloquently exclusive crescendo, that this lovely A is so memorable; it may have started as a *pp* doubling of a *p* pitch in the first violins, and it may have just "hung on" up there—but it ends up, once those very violins have rearticulated this pitch, *becoming a voice*: it descends stepwise in a diminuendo to a resolving F♯, and from there, a measure later, leads the upward motion, first to the clarinet's A, and then to the horns' C♯s, over the sequential bass that will soon convey the harmony to the crucial return of the symphony's opening melody. The sudden presence, here reduced to a single pitch (albeit the primordial pitch class), may possibly be seen as a subset of those unforeseen melodies discussed above. Still, the matter at hand, in measures 322–46 (example 3) is probably more subtle and, at the same time, more far-reaching in its various implications. Immediately preceding the entering oboe A is a thirteen-measure passage for strings alone: a prolongation of an important, *ff* C♯-major cadence involving the largest available registral span and including all parts except timpani (obviously) and trumpets (just as obviously, though by reason of their having alternated with the horns in two-measure segments, leaving the C♯ "tonic" ones to the horns, and lending *their* C♯s to the intervening "subdominant" measures). Once those thirteen measures for strings alone are past, *any* entrance by a single wind instrument would have been equally noteworthy, so that the oboe does not here require the insulation of a twenty-eight-measure silence, as in the *Melusine* Overture. But the choice of this oboe for that A is far from haphazard... First, however, the source for that important C♯-major cadence might be looked into—in keeping, naturally, with the position of that pitch class within the movement's tonic triad, and in light of the significance of E (major, as well as minor) at crucial points in the movement. A weak C#-minor way station first appears in measure 31, as part of a sequential passage leading to a restatement of the opening—though a varied version of it. Later on, a seven-measure sustained, quiet, stretch of C# minor I and V (mm. 159–66) can be heard as VI in reference to the subsequently strong cadence on E that brings on the first ending. In the fugato after the second ending, the strongly emphasized tutti (mm. 274–85) E minor leads to a tonicized F#-minor sequential "parallel" at measure 290, but the arrival there is preceded by a two-measure, octave-sustaining, *oboe* pedal of C#s. This curious "anticipation" provides the clue to the ambivalent "tonicization" of F#, for it soon appears that C# is the harmonic goal here, and that the apparently "dominant" C# yields to F# in its confirming ("subdominant," and, in mm. 302–3, *major* subdominant) role. One additional connecting feature in the ensuing music that has been examined in the foregoing is the chromatically rising bass line F#–A (mm. 332–36); A–C# (mm. 336–40); C#–E (mm. 344–46)—only cellos articulate the latter segment, following a four-measure interruption; only cellos *as part of a bass line*, yet now that is doubled, an octave higher, by both oboes! As for the high A that has given rise to this long paragraph, it, too, has its forerunners in the movement. First, that A is the highest, accented pitch in the oboe's quadruple response to the clarinets' and bassoons' thirds, in the first ending; and second, in the connective passage before the fugato begins in earnest, the first oboe articulates that A thrice (mm. 194–99), the last two times doubled by the second oboe at the lower octave, as both of them frame the clarinets.

Another passage for oboes, and yet a further sustained high A (though now doubled at the octave below) lies at the heart of one last "place" to be examined here: a little more than halfway through his *Hebrides* Overture, in measures 149–65 (example 4), Mendelssohn gives this octave A a unique function in making it the uninflected, *p*, pedallike foil for the whole remainder of the *pp*, *staccato e leggiero*, eventually and gradually swelling orchestral texture. This beacon octave is sounded through six measures and through six harmonic changes, but it does not *yet* become a voice, as it would have by moving down to G's over the resolving bass E. Instead, Mendelssohn postpones any linear deployment of those oboe octaves by a measure, and then proceeds upward diatonically in whole notes (now marked *cresc. sempre*, while the orchestral texture remains as before, when the A's were being sustained) over four measures, beginning on F#s, and then, joined for the next two and a quarter measures by unison-doubled flutes and clarinets, now in half notes, reaches its destination on a high E by means of chromatic motion. Why, then, that curious silence of the oboes in measure 158? The answer lies in a "second take," in that measure, on what is surely the most startling aspect of the music beginning three measures before the octave A's first enter here: the unprecedentedly non legato articulation, coupled with alternations in constant diminution, of the overture's main opening motive, now used for developmental purposes. Since nothing in the preceding 148 measures could have led anyone other than the composer to foresee so stupendous a change in texture, it stands to reason that measure 158 should be bereft of its sustaining oboes, by way of confirmation of this orchestral surprise. When they do reenter, the oboes no longer *merely* sustain or tie together; they are a vital participant in the polyphony, and it is their presence, furthermore, that allows for the gradual, subtle, and most elegantly wrought resumption of the composition's prevalently sustained articulation, through the ensuing fifteen measures, until the thoroughly altered return of the opening.

In this connection, by way of a brief aside, a good indication of Mendelssohn's intense self-criticism and scrupulous diligence is readily provided if one examines an early version of the overture from December 1830, now preserved in the Pierpont Morgan Library in New York.[1] There the oboes' octave A lasts only two and one-eighth measures (though the harmonic content "beneath" is the same throughout), leaving a much longer gap before the oboes return (i.e., four and seven-eighths measures); the ascent then proceeds in whole notes *entirely*, and includes an overlapping sequence; F♯–G–A♯–B–C♮–D♯–E. Moreover, the *octave* between the oboes' A's is anticipated by octave-doubled F–G♭–F in the oboes, over the two-measure descending scale in dotted rhythm in the strings, immediately before the passage under discussion!

The return at measure 180 soon yields a most telling link to that passage: when the harmony turns to III, four measures later there again is the octave A in the oboes, riding above everything else, and transferred to the violins after two measures. But it is this transfer that itself reinterprets a significant feature at the outset of the piece: the octave F♯s in the violins are succeeded by octave A's in the clarinets, two measures later, and, two after that, in turn, by octave C♯s in the oboes. Not only are *octaves* among instruments of the same kind thereby made to assume considerable structural suggestiveness, but so is the triad thus outlined, as well as the remarkably frequent appearance of such octaves, or those involving—if much less often—

instruments of differing timbre, in the first thirty-odd measures. What really clinches the argument that Mendelssohn has so brilliantly presented is the appearance, finally, of the tonic triad deployed in untransposed, tonal inversion, as F♯–D–B in octave-sounding mixtures of wind-instrument couples, *ff*, across a similar grouping of six measures toward the composition's conclusion, in measures 226–31. It literally "wraps up" the whole piece, this persistent octave-sound, yet it leaves until near the end the explanation, as it were, for the very beginning, as well as for that passage near the middle that has here been observed. And if a corollary were to be required, it is to be found at a glance in the final three measures: flute and clarinet start from a common F♯ and, by contrary motion, reach their respective goals of high B and low F♯, the clarinet's part spanning the F♯ octave that in the previous two measures had been placed at a higher octave's remove, so that the oboes' F♯ octave *continues* sounding the clarinet's higher span, while that instrument simultaneously extends it downward. The flute's high B, sustained beyond the duration of those two F♯ octaves, hovers at the end over an octave motion, up and back, in all the violins, *pizz.*, so that when the upper B occurs, all five octave locations of B's available to the overture's instrumentation are heard; then the violins' octave descent spells the ending.

In conclusion—but not, by now, in view of any further need to defend Mendelssohn's extraordinary compositional achievements from that ghastly, murderous twinning of ignorance and prejudice—I cite a recent classroom event. In a course on composers' arrangements, a student compared the two versions of Mendelssohn's String Symphony in D major of 1822. The degree to which, and the manner in which, the original conception for strings was reworked so as to become, impeccably, a fully *orchestral* composition gave evidence to everyone present not only of the breathtaking skill, ingenuity, adroitness and sense of appropriateness as heard and seen in the reregistered parts, in the reassigned instrumental lines (so that these might be perceived as never *possibly* to have been any different), or in the rethinking of phrase lengths, as well as in the actual recomposition of anything ranging from small details to entire sections of the work, but also proved that for this uniquely endowed thirteen-year-old those notions subsumed under the term "return" were, in the most unforced and utterly natural-sounding way, at the same time *bound* to include changes of various and varying kinds. In addition, his woodwind writing in this piece was shown frequently to instantiate stepwise linear linking across measures of rest. None of his tutors at the time could have taught Mendelssohn *those* things; he could have absorbed them only from intensively studying the music of Beethoven (then still alive!), Haydn, and Mozart. Can it then be astonishing that this superbly canny, acutely perceptive, and exceptionally intelligent musical prodigy developed into the certainly no *less* incredibly accomplished, painstaking, eloquent at the same time as elegant composer we "know"? . . .

NOTE

1. A facsimile is available in Felix Mendelssohn, *Die Hebriden*, ed. Hugo von Mendelssohn Bartholdy (Basel, 1947).

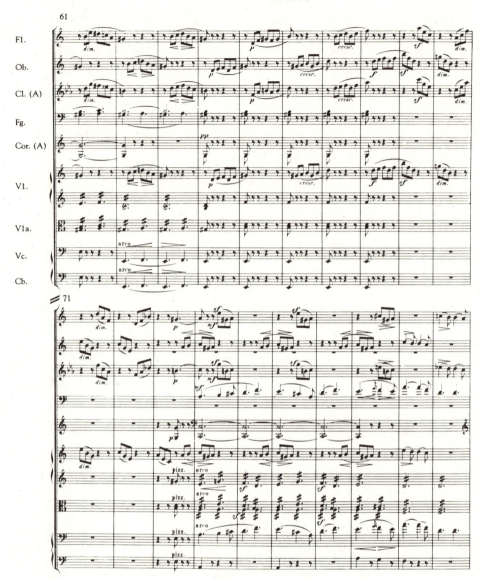

Example 1. Mendelssohn, Intermezzo from *Midsummer Night's Dream* music, Op. 61, no. 5, measures 74–98. Reproduced by arrangement with Broude Brothers Limited

81

Example 1, cont.

Example 2. Mendelssohn, Overture *Zum Märchen von der schönen Melusine*, Op. 32, measures 188–210

191

Example 2, cont.

Example 2, cont.

Example 2, cont.

204

Example 2, cont.

Example 3. Mendelssohn, *Italian* Symphony, First Movement, measures 322–46

Example 3, cont.

Example 4. Mendelssohn, *Hebrides* Overture, measures 149–65

Example 4, cont.

Example 4, cont.

Example 4, cont.

Elijah, Johann Sebastian Bach, and the New Covenant: On the Aria "Es ist genug" in Felix Mendelssohn-Bartholdy's Oratorio *Elijah*

MARTIN STAEHELIN

TRANSLATED BY SUSAN GILLESPIE

[This article was first published as "Elias, Johann Sebastian Bach und der Neue Bund. Zur Arie *Es ist genug* in Felix Mendelssohn Bartholdys Oratorium *Elias*," in *Beiträge zur Geschichte des Oratoriums seit Händel: Festschrift Günther Massenkeil zum 60. Geburtstag*, ed. Rainer Cadenbach and Helmut Loos (Bonn, 1986), pp. 283–96.][1]

The oratorio *Elijah* by Felix Mendelssohn-Bartholdy includes a section in the second part that attracts our interest primarily because in musical terms it follows unusually closely a work of Johann Sebastian Bach. I refer to the aria "Es ist genug," sung by Elijah, resigned and lonely, after his persecution and flight into the desert. It is evident that the musical model was the aria "Es ist vollbracht," from Bach's *St. John Passion*.

This relationship may long have been familiar to a few connoisseurs, but oddly enough, it has been largely overlooked in the published literature on Mendelssohn and *Elijah*;[2] and even when it has been mentioned in passing, the reference has generally been to the possibility of imitation, rather than to the fact.[3] The number and pronounced character of the correspondences that emerge from even the most superficial comparison between the two pieces are all the more remarkable. In considering the following comparison—which addresses only the most immediately obvious points of similarity—the reader is expressly advised to consult the scores of the two arias.⁴ Listening to the two arias will confirm the concordances beyond any shadow of a doubt.

Both pieces are tripartite in structure, with a measured part A followed by a spirited part B. The latter gradually rises in a crescendo of growing intensity. In each aria, the climax is reached in a high note of the vocal part, harmonically constructed upon a diminished-seventh chord. In Mendelssohn as in Bach, part B leads from the first motive — declaimed in an almost recitativelike manner — quite abruptly into a third part A', which corresponds in its similar musical material to the first part A in the manner of a reprise (but in each case more briefly than in A). Both works are orchestrated for strings alone; Mendelssohn calls for the addition of winds only in the middle part. Sections A and A' include a solo cello or viola da gamba. The beginnings of these instrumental introductions, and later the corresponding vocal parts, are identical in their structural pitches, although Bach varies them with passing tones. When, finally, we learn that Mendelssohn, in his drafts, considered the possibility of marking the two A sections in $\frac{3}{8}$ time, rather than the $\frac{3}{4}$ time he finally chose,⁵ the relationship to Bach's piece becomes even more apparent, since the latter is basically built on a musical movement in eighth notes.

It does not seem necessary to continue this recitation of stylistic features shared by the two pieces. For even if the romantic-classical work and the late baroque work differ in unmistakable ways—for example, in the way the voice is emphasized in solo parts; in the use of dialogue between voice and obbligato instrument; in the type of melodic phrasing; or in the general historical character of the two pieces—the correspondences enumerated in the preceding are so unmistakable that certainly they cannot be the result of chance. Rather, they demonstrate that Mendelssohn must definitely have modeled his aria along the lines of the preexistent Bach aria. If one recalls, for example, the astonishingly free manner in which the young Mendelssohn, in his String Quartet, op. 13, in A minor, came to terms with Beethoven's A-minor String Quartet, op. 132,⁶ then the result we have found might be surprising even in one of the composer's early works. But in a late piece like *Elijah*, the result is startling indeed and requires an explanation. The following is an attempt to provide one.

I

Mendelssohn's relationship to Bach's *St. John Passion* has always been overshadowed in the Mendelssohn literature by his incomparably more important relationship to Bach's *St. Matthew Passion*.[7] That Mendelssohn was also well aware of the *St. John Passion* is, however, not in doubt; as a member of the Berlin Singakademie from 1820 onward, and of Zelter's so-called *Freitagsmusiken*, he also knew it well from personal participation in rehearsals.[8]

This early acquaintance admittedly does not provide any clarification about the origins of the aria at hand. Our investigation of this question must begin at a much later date. According to the composer's correspondence with his friend, the preacher Julius Schubring,[9] who assisted in preparing the text not only of *St. Paul* but also of *Elijah* (the correspondence says nothing, it is true, about imitating Bach's model), the composition of the first version of the aria must have fallen in the period between December 1845 and May 1846.[10] The version that was finally printed differed from the first version in a number of details that are not germane to our investigation;[11] therefore, the following line of argument is confined to the original genesis of the work. The period mentioned in the preceding can be delimited even more precisely by reference to additional sources. First, we must note for the record that the text of the aria, which follows the words of the Bible in 1 Kings 19.4 and 19.10, was already present in an early variant in Schubring's draft of 17 November 1838[12]—if it was, indeed, not already extant in the early, lost libretto draft by Karl Klingemann.[13] Mendelssohn, however, cannot have done any musical work on the aria that early, for on 16 December 1845, when he took up the *Elijah* plan again after a hiatus of several years, he was still able to transmit for his friend's opinion and suggestions only "the text of Elijah, so far as I have it at present."[14] The remaining comments in this letter demonstrate how little of *Elijah*, even of its essential shape, stood firm at this point. For example "the second part, particularly its conclusion, is still very much in a state of uncertainty."[15] On 23 May 1846, Schubring learned that the composition of the first part of the oratorio had been completed, "and six or eight numbers from the second have already been set down on paper . . . What I . . . definitely have, is the scene in the desert (1 Kings 19.4–5)."[16] That is precisely the place where the aria in question is located.

A report from Eduard Devrient enables us to date the composition, in all probability, with even greater precision, specifically to January, perhaps early February 1846. Devrient had traveled to Leipzig in February for a brief stay to visit his friend Mendelssohn. Since the report also contains material pertinent to the question of the aria's relation to Bach, considerable sections are here quoted verbatim:

> In these two days that I spent with Felix, I was able to observe clearly the change that had occurred in his inner life. The bloom of fresh youthful cheer had been replaced by a certain annoyance, a weariness with life, that made everything appear different from before. . . . His direction of the concerts, everything that had to do with the business of organizing them, burdened him unbearably; he talked about leaving their direction entirely to Gade in the following winter. . . . As for himself, his habit of activity, which had become second nature, kept him continually composing. He called it "doing his duty." But I felt—quite apart from considerations of health—that he would do his duty better if he would write less and wait for the good hours of his imagination, which now seemed to come less frequently than before. I found, in recent times, that he was beginning to repeat himself in his compositions, involuntarily copying earlier masters, specifically Sebastian Bach, and employing a certain habitual manner in his writing. I said that to him, and he did not react sensitively, because he thought that I was entirely wrong and because he had a low opinion of those ideas that had to wait for a particular moment, or be contrived. When one felt in one's heart like writing music, he said, then whatever idea came involuntarily to mind was quite good enough, even if it wasn't striking or new, or even if it sounded like Sebastian Bach; that was just the way it would have to be.

> That didn't seem to me to accord with his strict criticism of his finished works and his tendency to revise them, and I ventured to say that he was confusing the drive to be active with the creative drive.

> I have not been able to change the opinion I formed at that time concerning most of his works from recent years. Even with *Elijah* the result is the same for me. If this work demonstrated beauties from its Master's best epoch, still, much of it seemed to be the product of effort. The exertion was noticeable to me, and I was sorry to miss the fresh stream of vivid impressions and feelings that characterize his *St. Paul*.[17]

Devrient's report, though this is not expressly stated, can only refer to the aria in question or at least have been inspired by it. In February 1846, Mendelssohn was working with the greatest intensity on *Elijah*, and he doubtless showed his friend whatever he already had in hand. Furthermore, Devrient refers to the aria in nearly the same connection in which he makes his remarks about Mendelssohn's imitation of Bach. No other piece with such a close relationship to a model by Bach is known either in *Elijah* or in anything else that Mendeissohn created during this period.

We may in all likelihood draw two conclusions from Devrient's report regarding the origin of the piece. First, a fairly precise dating of the composition of the aria can be established. Second, a reference to Mendelssohn's own opinion regarding his compositional mimicking of the Bach model can be identified. According to this reference, in Mendelssohn's view, the borrowing from the Bach model was an entirely involuntary event. This opinion corresponds more or less with a number of other, earlier remarks, in which Mendelssohn declared that such a thing occurred because during a particular composition he was in "a mood . . . like old Bach."[18] Such involuntary imitation was not something to be condemned, according to the composer, since not only forms were being copied, but a content as well, and a unique and honestly felt new content of the composer's own flowed into these forms.

From this viewpoint, an answer to the question before us would seem to lead us into the realm of intuitive creation, an area that is difficult to penetrate. If this explanation should prove to be on the right path, then one perhaps would want to consider whether an intuitive association with Bach might not have been brought about by the close verbal similarity of "Es ist genug" with "Es ist vollbracht." This is all the more likely, since the official 1829 hymnal of the Protestant congregation in Berlin, with which Mendelssohn was undoubtedly well acquainted, includes a church hymn in which each stanza begins with "Es ist vollbracht," immediately following a hymn with stanzas begining with "Es ist genug."[19] But when we attempt to imagine the musical procedure that would correspond to such an intuitive rationale, strong doubts immediately emerge. Above all, it must appear highly dubious that the composer Mendelssohn, who was an excellent connoisseur of Bach, would not have noticed such a close imitation of an existing model, or would have become conscious of it only after he completed the work. A work characterized by such a degree of imitation can only have been produced by him in clear awareness of this state of affairs. This recognition leads us, rather, into the realm of quite rational occurrences as a plausible explanation for this imitation. We must also look into the specific meaning that the Bach model may have given to Mendelssohn's aria.

II

The clarification of these questions must undoubtedly proceed from the texts. The wording of the aria shows Elijah in a state of complete resignation:

> It is enough; O Lord, now take away my life, for I am not better than my fathers! I desire to live no longer; now let me die, for my days are but vanity!

> I have been very jealous for the Lord God of Hosts! for the children of Israel have broken thy covenant, thrown down thine altars, and slain thy prophets—slain them with the sword: and I, even I, only am left; and they seek my life to take it away.

> It is enough; O Lord, now take away my life, for I am not better than my fathers!

> [Es ist genug! So nimm nun, Herr, meine Seele! Ich bin nicht besser denn meine Väter. Ich begehre nicht mehr zu leben, denn meine Tage sind vergeblich gewesen.

> Ich habe geeifert um den Herrn, den Gott Zebaoth, denn die Kinder Israels haben deinen Bund verlassen, und deine Altäre haben sie zerbrochen, und deine Propheten mit dem Schwert erwürgt. Und ich bin allein übrig geblieben: und sie stehn danach, dass sie mir mein Leben nehmen!

> Es ist genug! So nimm nun, Herr, meine Seele! Ich bin nicht besser denn meine Väter.]

This evident resignation contrasts with an entirely different mood in Bach:

> It is accomplished.
> O consolation of wounded souls!
> The night of grief
> Lets me count the final hour.

The hero of Judea is victorious through his might,
And concludes the battle.

It is accomplished.

[Es ist vollbracht.
O Trost für die gekränkten Seelen!
Die Trauernacht
lässt mich die letzte Stunde zählen.

Der Held aus Juda siegt mit Macht
und schliesst den Kampf.

Es ist vollbracht.]

That the two persons speaking in Mendelssohn and Bach are not necessarily comparable is not significant in the context that is being considered here. What is essential is only the content. Bach's text is not only filled with resignation of the same type that gripped Elijah, but in it the grief over the death of Jesus encompasses, with Christian consistency, the New Testament certitude of the victory over death. When Mendelssohn, through the use of musical means, refers so clearly to Bach's aria, he also clothes his work in a remarkable, suggestive way in the New Testament's message of salvation, and he does so even though the Old Testament Elijah, as the text of his aria illustrates, enjoys no prospect whatsoever of being saved.

A New Testament coloration or even interpretation of the figure of Elijah is not an isolated instance in the history of theology. If one excepts the "servant of the Lord," whose tasks and sufferings on behalf of mankind find expression in several of the later chapters of Isaiah, without a doubt Elijah is the figure in the Old Testament most closely allied with the Messiah. This is not only based on the fact that the life of Elijah contains elements that are comparable to the life of Jesus—his awakening of the dead, God's approach to him on the Mount of Transfiguration, his persecution, and above all his ascension to heaven—but it also follows from numerous nonbiographical references in the Bible, and even from various citations in the New Testament.[20] The postbiblical era also took special notice of these Elijah-Christ correspondences, and there is such a plethora of citations, particularly from early Christian and patristic art and culture,[21] that one must speak of an actual tradition—one that continues for an extended time, well into the literature of the eighteenth century.[22] Not so much because the composer Mendelssohn, on account of his own origins, might have been unfamiliar with such a Christian interpretation, but rather because the composer saw himself, in this connection, confronted with so many evidences of that tradition, are we compelled to ask whether or not we can identify the concrete source that inspired Mendelssohn.

Since the question at hand is now a theological one, we will look first to the theological literature; in particular, we must consider those works that originated in Mendelssohn's lifetime and geographical vicinity. For example, between 1829 and 1835 Professor Ernst Wilhelm Hengstenberg in Berlin presented an interpretation of the Old Testament from the vantage point of Christian salvation in his comprehensive *Christologie des Alten Testamentes*.[23] The supposition that Mendelssohn might have found his inspiration in this work must be set aside, however, since Hengstenberg's work is a thoroughly scholarly, specialized work and not at all easy for a lay person to read. Friedrich Schleiermacher, of whom one would naturally think next, also disqualifies himself, since he emphasizes the discontinuity of the Old and New Testaments, rather than their commonalities or points of unity.[24]

The rebuff to our investigation from these two theologians is probably a salutary hint that in order to resolve our pressing questions we should look less to the specialized theological literature and more to the world of devotional literature, particularly as it relates to sermons. In fact, there does exist a collection of Elijah sermons, apparently the only such work in the nineteenth century, which reached a total of seven editions between 1828 and 1903. Thus it must have been an unusually successful and widely known work. The volume in question is a collection of twenty-three sermons with the title *Elijah the Tishbite*, from the pen of the then-famous preacher Friedrich Wilhelm Krummacher (1796–1868).[25] Krummacher[26] was a son of the Reform pastor Adolf Wilhelm Krummacher, a representative of Rhenish-Westphalian late Pietism, and was active in his younger years in the Reform congregation in Frankfurt am Main. While there, he was probably introduced by a colleague to the family of Mendelssohn's later wife Cécile Jeanrenaud.[27] Later he went on by way of pastorates in Ruhrort, Barmen-Gemarke, and Elberfeld to become chaplain of the Church of the Trinity in Berlin in 1847, and, in 1856, even court chaplain in Potsdam. Goethe reviewed several of his texts and characterized them as "narcotic" on account of their tendency to pacify those listeners who were suffering the tribulations of life.[28] In any case, Krummacher must have been one of the most significant pulpit-orators of nineteenth-century German Protestantism, and he was accorded special mention in the collection of monographs on great preachers by August Nebe.[29]

In his tenth sermon, entitled *The Flight into the Desert*,[30] Krummacher chooses the words of 1 Kings 19.1–4 as the biblical text to be explicated. It concerns the persecution of Elijah by Queen Jezebel, his flight into the desert, and finally his desperate lament, as he sits under the juniper bush: "It is enough, now, O Lord; take away my life, for I am not better than my fathers." Krummacher, whose sermon follows closely the path taken by the biblical text, first paints Elijah's abandonment and desolation (in the third and final section) in the strongest hues and in great detail: "the dear servant of the Lord has enough of this vale of tears"; his soul is torn apart, "betrayed in its most beautiful expectations," and "now despairing of God and the world."[31] Not surprisingly, Krummacher also attempts to apply this situation to the churchgoing congregation: "'Lord, it is enough!' Alas, this little prayer is known to us as well. I know of many a workplace, many a chamber and bed of pain, whence almost ceaselessly, among many tears and fears, this sigh is resounding toward the heavens."[32] And from this starting point Pastor Krummacher easily enough offers solace to his congregation:

> But listen. As often as it will seem to you as if it were enough, as if the burden of life is no longer to be borne, do as Elijah did. Flee you, too, to the silence of solitude, and I will show you a juniper bush, and there you will cast yourself down. It is the cross. Yes, a juniper, covered with thorns and barbs that pierce the soul, girded about with points and nails that wound the heart and cause old nature [Eph. 4.22] pain and suffering. But this juniper also has a scent that refreshes the soul, and a perfume through which we become the Lord's sweet-smelling sacrifice. . . .
> In the presence of the cross you no longer think of complaining about the greatness of your sufferings. For here you see a suffering against which your own is as nothing; and a righteous man suffers it for the sake of you unrighteous man. In the presence of the cross you will quickly be forced to forget your distress, for the love of God in Jesus Christ for you poor sinner will soon draw all your thoughts and reflections away from everything else, and into it alone. Under the cross you are safe from the thought that what you experience in your unhappiness is something strange. . . . Under the cross you are preserved from impatience. . . . Under the cross your complaining will soon be absorbed in the peace of the Lord . . .

Peace and mercy stream	[Friede strömt und Gnade
Outward from the cross;	Von dem Kreuz herab;
Sorrow, woe, and harm	Jammer, Elend, Schade
Sink into the grave.	Sinkt in's ew'ge Grab.
Turn your tearful gaze	Blick mit nassen Augen,
Sinner! to the sky—	Sünder! in die Höh',—
Drink tranquility	Laß sie Ruhe saugen
From the Friend's distress.	Aus des Freundes Weh'.
Everything is done!	Alles ist vollendet!
Your battle is at an end,	Dein Kampf ist gekämpft,
Your suffering is over,	Deine Schmach gewendet,
Hell and world redeemed.	Höll' und Welt gedämpft.
Now you may receive,	Dir bleibt nur das Nehmen,
Take, as you believe!	Greif' denn gläubig zu!
Tremble not at ghosts!	Zittre nicht vor Schemen!
Be tranquil in the cross.[33]	Hab' im Kreuze Ruh'!]

We have intentionally quoted the concluding portion of Krummacher's sermon at great length. Only in this way does it become clear how much emphasis Krummacher places on the New Testament twist that is given to Elijah's Old Testament words. The suspicion that Mendelssohn read Krummacher's text and was inspired by it to model his *Elijah* aria after Bach's cannot be dismissed, if only because what is presented here is not—as in most cases—a New Testament interpretation of the entire Elijah figure, but rather, exactly as in Mendelssohn's case, one that focuses exclusively on a selected, single passage of Elijah's. This suspicion is strongly supported by the two choral stanzas that Krummacher appended to the end of his text and that may have reminded Mendelssohn of Bach's model.[34] Krummacher's "Everything is done!" resembles Bach's "It is accomplished!"; "Your battle is at an end," resembles Bach's "The hero of Judea is victorious through his might / And concludes the battle." In a more general sense Krummacher's "peace," deriving from the experience of Christ's death on the cross, and his "tranquil" feeling that lets everything ugly vanish correspond to Bach's similarly pacific "consolation of wounded souls."

Naturally it would be welcome if Krummacher's collection of sermons could be shown to have influenced the rest of Mendelssohn's *Elijah* setting in a way analogous to that suggested here for the aria under consideration. In that case, the isolated instance treated here could be confirmed with even greater certainty. Without presuming to predict the outcome of examining the remaining *Elijah* sections, however, one would have to assume that such a confirmation would be difficult to achieve. For Krummacher's sermon texts follow the Elijah story in orderly progression as it is told in 1 Kings 17–19 and 21.17–29, and 2 Kings 1–2.18, followed by the sections from 2 Chronicles 21.12–15 and Matthew 17.1–8; whereas Mendelssohn's text, especially in the second part, is interrupted by so many foreign elements—some of them from Isaiah—that in any event we cannot possibly draw conclusions from comparing the two program sequences. And since the musical considerations in *Elijah* will hardly elucidate a possible Krummacher influence any more clearly than has been done by the aria in question, it is unlikely that the music itself will offer more proofs of this sort. One is, therefore, all the more grateful for a circumstance that underlines the plausibility that Mendelssohn in fact did read Krummacher's texts. Namely, in the draft libretto he sent to Schubring on 16 December 1845, the composer had Elijah's helper Elisa, in 2 Kings 2.12—which was never actually set to music—call out erroneously during the ascension to heaven: "My father, my father, the chariot of Israel and its *fortress*!" (Mein Vater, mein Vater, Wagen Israels und seine *Burg*!) The correct text would indeed have been: "My father, my father, the chariot of Israel and the *horsemen* thereof!" (Mein Vater, mein Vater, Wagen Israels und seine *Reiter*!) Schubring immediately drew attention to the error,[35] but naturally he could not know that Mendelssohn's error must have derived from an excursus by Krummacher, who paraphrased Elijah's exclamation to say that Elijah was a veritable "*fortress* of wagons around the Zion of the true church" (eine Wagen*burg* um das Zion der wahren Kirche).[36] Thus this observation, too, strengthens the case for Mendelssohn's use of Krummacher's sermon collection.

And in case further proof of this use should seem necessary, it could be brought forth by the surprising announcement Krummacher himself made in his preface to the fourth edition of his *Elijah*. Here the author confesses the following: "It can only be a pleasant thought for me that, as has been revealed to me by a reliable source, these my lectures provided a part of the inspiration for the creation of the truly sacred and almost incomparable oratorio *Elijah* of Mendelssohn-Bartholdy."[37] We cannot know who it was that provided this information to Krummacher; perhaps it was Mendelssohn's widow, whose family had probably become close to Krummacher in his early years in Frankfurt.[38] The fact remains, however, that Mendelssohn consulted Krummacher's *Elijah* sermon texts during the composition of his *Elijah*.[39]

III

The proof of Mendelssohn's use of Krummacher's sermon collection is doubly instructive. First, it confirms Arno Forchert's portrayal, according to which Schubring was not so intimately involved in the creation of *Elijah* as was long believed.[40] To Schubring and Klingemann, whose role Forchert has correctly emphasized, we must now add Friedrich Wilhelm Krummacher, even though he was not associated with Mendelssohn in any personal, direct way. That the circle of influential individuals is not complete even then is suggested by a letter from Mendelssohn to his friend Eduard Bendemann of 8 November 1846, which has not been noticed before in this connection. In it, the composer expresses his thanks for Bendemann's written contributions to *Elijah*.[41]

Furthermore, the preceding may shed new light on the relationship between Old and New Testament, promise and fulfillment, Old and New Covenant, as Mendelssohn wished it to be understood in his *Elijah*. Forchert, again, criticized Schubring "on account of the dogmatic narrow-mindedness with which he unswervingly attempted to force a New Testament interpretation of the Elijah material on Mendelssohn, which the latter rejected."[42] That is likely a somewhat too radical verdict; for in the previously cited letter to Bendemann, Mendelssohn expressly conceded Elijah's "significance for the New Covenant, which after all must necessarily be included,"[43] although he gave it a much more restrained treatment in the actual oratorio than Schubring would have liked. For example, Mendelssohn felt unable to adopt Schubring's suggestions for visionary or real scenes with Christ, Moses, and Elijah—according to the transfiguration story in Matthew 17.3—or with Peter, John, and Jacob.[44] Probably, he did not want to anticipate his planned oratorio *Christus* (op. 97), which ultimately remained a fragment, and which was to bring together the Old and New Covenants in a manner that can no longer be clearly identified.[45] Thus, the composer contented himself with setting to music those prophetic texts from Isaiah and Matthew that form the basis of the last aria and the two last choruses of his oratorio (nos. 39, 41, and 42)[46]—texts, admittedly, whose essential function is to open a perspective onto the coming Messiah, and that neither portray nor emphasize the significance of Elijah, in particular, for the New Covenant, or the intimate relationship of Elijah and Christ. At best, this finds limited expression in the last, brief recitative (no. 40),[47] which refers back to Elijah, and which, based on its position between the previously named pieces, may perhaps be taken to portray the prophet as a kind of *precursor Christi*. Without any doubt, however, the Elijah-Christ pairing is emphasized in Elijah's "Es ist vollbracht" aria. By virtue of its particular setting, this work bears witness—admittedly only in a discreetly restrained manner and not with the posterlike outspokenness desired by Schubring—to the "significance for the New Covenant" that, in the composer's opinion, "after all must necessarily be included." By this token, the aria also demonstrates that it has a central place in Mendelssohn's *Elijah*.

NOTES

1. I would like to thank the following colleagues for their kind assistance: first Rudolf Smend (Göttingen), who gave me diverse and excellent advice in theological and Old Testament matters and who pointed me to and even lent me his own copy of the sermon collection by Krummacher in which the reference to its use by Mendelssohn could be found; Rudolf Elvers (Berlin), who offered helpful information concerning unpublished letters of Mendelssohn; and finally Ulrich Konrad (Göttingen), who in the course of several conversations made enlightening contributions to the subject discussed here.

2. So, for example, in the relevant contributions by Eduard Krüger (1847), Otto Jahn (1848), Frederick George Edwards (1896), Susanna Großmann-Vendrey (1969), Arno Forchert (1974), Eric Werner (1980), and Wulf Konold (1984).

3. See, for example, A. Kurzhals-Reuter, *Die Oratorien Felix Mendelssohn Bartholdys: Untersuchungen zur Quellenlage, Entstehung, Gestaltung und Überlieferung* (Tutzing, 1978), p. 191, note 18: "Stratton, *Mendelssohn*, London 1901, compares the theme [!] with that of the aria 'Es ist vollbracht' from the *St. John Passion* of Bach. It is possible that Mendelssohn was inspired by it"; Stratton's book was not available to me. Only H. C. Worbs, *Felix Mendelssohn Bartholdy in Selbstzeugnissen und Bilddokumenten* (Hamburg, 1974), p. 122, calls the aria "a solo for which the alto aria 'Es ist vollbracht' from Bach's 'Johannes-Passion' has obviously provided the model."

4. F. Mendelssohn-Bartholdy, *Elias*, Edition Eulenburg no. 989, pp. 186–92, no. 26; J. S. Bach, *Passion nach dem Evangelisten Johannes*, Edition Eulenburg no. 965, pp. 151–55, no. 58.

5. See the sketches in Berlin, Deutsche Staatsbibliothek, Music Department, mus. ms. autogr. Mendelssohn vol. 22, p. 69. The study by Donald Mintz, *The Sketches and Drafts of Three of Felix Mendelssohn's Major Works* (Ph.D. dissertation, Cornell University, 1960) was not available to me.

6. That is already evidenced by the fact that in op. 13 inspirations from other Beethoven works are taken up as well (for example, from op. 95 and op. 31 no. 2); on this process compare F. Krummacher, *Mendelssohn—der Komponist: Studien zur Kammermusik für Streicher* (Munich, 1978), esp. pp. 309–

18; more recently, also W. Konold, *Felix Mendelssohn Bartholdy und seine Zeit* (Laaber, 1984), pp. 111–38, and *Mendelssohn und der späte Beethoven*, Beethoven-Gesellschaft München (Mitteilungen), vol. 10 (1984).

7. See M. Geck, *Die Wiederentdeckung der Matthäuspassion im 19. Jahrhundert: Die zeitgenössischen Dokumente und ihre ideengeschichtliche Deutung* (Regensburg, 1967), esp. pp. 1–74.

8. See G. Schünemann, "Die Bachpflege der Berliner Singakademie," in *Bach-Jahrbuch* 25 (1928): 138–71, esp. 151–59.

9. *Briefwechsel zwischen Felix Mendelssohn Bartholdy und Julius Schubring, zugleich ein Beitrag zur Geschichte und Theorie des Oratoriums*, ed. J. Schubring (Leipzig, 1892).

10. See also notes 14 and 16.

11. See J. Bennett, " 'Elijah': A Comparison of the Original and Revised Scores," in *Musical Times* 23 (1882): 525–28, 588–91, 653–56; and ibid., 24 (1883): 6–10, 67–72, 123–25, 182–85, esp. 67–69.

12. *Felix Mendelssohn-Bartholdys Briefwechsel mit Legationsrat Karl Klingemann in London*, ed. K. Klingemann (Essen, 1909), esp. pp. 232f., and Schubring, pp. 125ff.

13. See Schubring, pp. 145f. It is very instructive to see that in the Berlin Sketchbook (see note 5) on p. 56 (top) a sketch still appears that contains the key words "Ich arbeite" [I labor] from the text, and thus shows that in the beginning Mendelssohn stayed even closer to this proposed text by Schubring, which included the quotation from Isaiah 49.4: "I have labored in vain, I have spent my strength for nought."

14. Schubring, p. 204.

15. Ibid., p. 206.

16. Ibid., pp. 219f.

17. E. Devrient, *Meine Erinnerungen an Felix Mendelssohn-Bartholdy* (Leipzig, 1869), pp. 263–66, esp. 264–66.

18. See F. Mendelssohn Bartholdy, *Reisebriefe aus den Jahren 1830 bis 1832* (Leipzig, 1864), p. 214 (to Eduard Devrient, 15 July 1831) and pp. 96f. (to Carl Friedrich Zelter, 18 December 1830).

19. See *Gesangbuch zum gottesdienstlichen Gebrauch für evangelische Gemeinen* (Berlin, 1829), pp. 416f., no. 730; and p. 417, no. 731.

20. See, for example, Malachi 3.23ff., Matthew 17.3ff., Matthew 27.47.

21. See the two-volume compendium *Elie le Prophète* (Paris, 1956), esp. vol. 1 (*Selon les écritures et les traditions chrétiennes*), and K. Wessel, "Elias," in *Reallexikon für Antike und Christentum* (Stuttgart, 1959), vol. 4, cols. 1141–71, with further bibliography.

22. See, for example, H. Werthemann, *Die Bedeutung der alttestamentlichen Historien in Johann Sebastian Bachs Kantaten* (Tübingen, 1960), pp. 156–65 (here also on the inclusion of the death of Lazarus). The text of the previously mentioned hymn "Es ist genug" (see above, note 19) shows, by the way, the manner in which Elijah's Old Testament resignation and the New Testament's consolation and absolution in Christ can interpenetrate each other.

The repeated stanza beginning "Es ist genug" [It is enough] points to Elijah, as, in the first stanza, does "so nimm Herr meinen Geist" [O Lord, take away my life], following 1 Kings 19.4, and probably also the concluding phrase "ich fahr ins Himmels Haus" [I am going to heaven's house], which evidently refers to Elijah's ascension to heaven in the fiery chariot (cf. H. Werthemann, ibid.). Christian elements in the hymn are, naturally, the mention of and argumentation using the cross and Jesus Christ. The hymn text, which goes back to Franz Joachim Burmeister, is quoted here according to the original version in Gottfried Vopelius, *Leipziger Gesang-Buch*, 3d edition (Leipzig, 1701), p. 491, Carl Gottlob Hofmann, ed., *Das priviligirte vollständige und vermehrte Leipziger Gesangbuch* (Leipzig, 1750). The Berlin edition of 1829 has been modernized at several points.

23. E. W. Hengstenberg, *Christologie des Alten Testamentes und Commentar über die Messianischen Weissagungen der Propheten* (Berlin 1829–1835).

24. See, for example, F. Schleiermacher, *Einleitung ins neue Testament* (Berlin, 1845) (*Sämtliche Werke* 1.8), pp. 25–28.

25. See F. W. Krummacher, *Elias der Thisbiter, nach seinem äussern und innern Leben dargestellt*, 1st edition (Elberfeld, 1828–1833), 3 vols.; 2d edition (Elberfeld, 1835–1839), 3 vols.; 3d edition (Elberfeld, 1846; hereafter collected into one volume and without subtitles); 4th edition (Elberfeld, 1851) [this edition cited in the following as Krummacher]. I was able to compare the first, second, third, and fourth editions and to establish the complete identity of the sermon texts.

26. On Krummacher's biography see R. Kögel, *Krummacher, Friedrich Wilhelm*, in *Realenzyklopädie für protestantische Theologie und Kirche* (Leipzig, 1902), vol. 11, pp. 152–53; and also F. W. Krummacher, *Eine Selbstbiographie* (Berlin, 1869). Also see note 29.

27. F. W. Krummacher (see note 26), p. 71.

28. J. W. von Goethe, *Rezension von: Blicke ins Reich der Gnade. Sammlung evangelischer Predigten von D. Krummacher, Pfarrer zu Gemarke* (Elberfeld, 1828), *Jubiläums-Ausgabe*, vol. 38 (Stuttgart, 1907), pp. 209–11, esp. p. 211.

29. A. Nebe, *Dr. F. W. Krummacher*, in *Zur Geschichte der Predigt: Charakterbilder der bedeutendsten Kanzelredner* (Wiesbaden, 1879), vol. 3, pp. 242–79.

30. Ibid., pp. 150–70.

31. Ibid., pp. 166 and 168.

32. Ibid., p. 168.

33. Ibid., pp. 169f.

34. Since little would be gained for our investigation, I have not attempted to identify the source of the two choral stanzas.

35. Schubring (see note 9), p. 213.

36. Krummacher (see note 25), p. 446.

37. Ibid., preface, p. 11.

38. See note 27. Unfortunately neither Friedrich Wilhelm Krummacher's *Selbstbiographie* (see note 26), nor Maria Krummacher, *Unsere Mutter* [Krum-

macher's wife Charlotte *née* Pilgeram] (Bielefeld, 1898) gives any helpful information on the subject.

39. It is also worth noting that Krummacher himself treated "Es ist vollbracht": *Fr. W. Krummacher, Es ist vollbracht! Charfreitags-Predigt* (Elberfeld, 1838); unfortunately this text was not available to me. Finally, it is not without its charm to learn several generations later of another Krummacher-Mendelssohn relationship: Friedhelm Krummacher, the great-great-grandson of the theologian, devoted a comprehensive and substantive book to Mendelssohn's chamber music for string quartet; see note 6.

40. A. Forchert, "Textanlage und Darstellungsprinzipien in Mendelssohns Elias," in *Das Problem Mendelssohn*, ed. C. Dahlhaus (Regensburg, 1974), pp. 61–77, esp. pp. 62–66.

41. F. Mendelssohn Bartholdy, *Briefe aus Leipziger Archiven*, ed. H.-J. Rothe and R. Szeskus (Leipzig, 1972), p. 43.

42. A. Forchert, p. 68.

43. F. Mendelssohn Bartholdy (see note 41), pp. 43f.

44. Schubring, pp. 213 and 216; see also the principles by which Schubring justified his advice, p. 222.

45. On this point, see A. Kurzhals-Reuter (see note 3), pp. 160–63 and 197–201.

46. Matthew 13.43; Isaiah 51.11, 41.25, 42.1, 11.2, 55.1, 55.3, and 58.8.

47. Malachi 3.23f.

The Incidental Politics to
Mendelssohn's *Antigone*

MICHAEL P. STEINBERG

For David Grene

"Of all the masterpieces of the classical and the modern world—and I know nearly all of them and you should and can—the *Antigone* seems to me to be the most magnificent and satisfying work of art of this kind." These confident words are Hegel's, spoken in the conclusion to the *Lectures on Aesthetics* (given between 1823 and 1829, published posthumously in 1835).[1] Hegel's judgment remained uncontested for a century. With reference to it, George Steiner began his 1984 book *Antigones* with the suggestion that from about 1790 (the year of Friedrich Schlegel's *History of Attic Tragedy*) to the turn of the twentieth century (when the Freudian referent of Oedipus claimed the spotlight), "it was widely held by European poets, philosophers, and scholars that Sophocles' *Antigone* was not only the finest of Greek tragedies, but a work of art nearer to perfection than any other produced by the human spirit."[2] The generation of the German idealists and romantics were perhaps the most ardent *Antigone* fans. Kant, Schelling, the Schlegel brothers, as well as Hegel, all revered the play. In 1787, while a student at Tübingen, the seventeen-year-old Hegel translated a portion of the play; he returned to it in the *Phenomenology of Mind* of 1807, the *Philosophy of Right* of 1821, and in the *Lectures on Aesthetics* of the 1820s. Friedrich Hölderlin, Hegel's intimate friend during their student days in Tübingen, ended his career in 1804 with a "translation" that has redefined the poetics of translation for modern criticism. August Boeckh and his pupil Johann Gustav Droysen—contributing founders not only of modern classical scholarship but of modern historiographical practice—came back to Sophocles' drama time and again throughout their long careers. Sovereign rulers who wanted to be intellectuals found their way to Sophocles too. The performance of Sophocles' *Antigone* that took place in the palace of Sanssouci on 28 October 1841, with incidental music by the newly appointed court composer Felix Mendelssohn, originated in the taste and wishes of Frederick William IV, who had ascended the Prussian throne in June 1840.

To speak, then, of "Mendelssohn's *Antigone*" is misleading both in a technical sense and in a way that addresses an issue crucial to German romantic creativity. The 1841 *Antigone* was a group effort involving the patronage of the king, the general mediation and the staging of his court "reader" (*Vorleser*) Ludwig Tieck, the translation of J. J. Donner, and the music of Mendelssohn. To be precise, therefore, is to refer with the rubric "Mendelssohn's *Antigone*" only to the orchestral introduction and choral settings he himself provided. But the more interesting point is that this kind of contribution is the rule rather than the exception for much artistic production of the period. The romantic cult of genius was developed precisely in the growing context of group efforts and institutional aesthetic and intellectual production and practice. Eighteenth-century patronage was expanding, during the first half of the nineteenth century, into networks of journals, artistic institutions (orchestral and choral societies, museums, etc.) and intellectual ones (primarily the modern university). The birth of the art industry is an important feature of modernity, and the fear of modernity's power did much to generate the projection of the cult of the romantic genius. Prometheus is the dream of Vulcan.

Inversely, however, the discussion of the work of the individual contributor—in our case, Mendelssohn—can be rendered more rather than less interesting by the presence of such a group dynamic. The group dynamic, together with the hidden voices of nonparticipants (Droysen, for example), informs themes and resonances that may not have clear lines of connection between an artist and his explicit artistic creation. Thus "Mendelssohn's *Antigone*" addresses questions fundamental to German romantic and liberal culture such as the cultural and political place of classical tradition, humanism, and scholarship, and—for Mendelssohn and Droysen—the cultural place of the Jews in both the classical and contemporary worlds—and in scholarly and cultural discourse about those worlds.

These issues involve the formal as well as the contextual aspects of Mendelssohn's contribution to the 1841 *Antigone*. It is and is not "incidental music"; it is and is not subservient to the Sophoclean tragedy.

It is a series of choruses for male voices that become the voice of the Sophoclean chorus. The onstage characters in drama are given their usual modern practice of "Worte ohne Lieder." The proximity of the music, but its simultaneous lack of control over the attendant drama, creates a kind of non-opera. Thus the question of the participatory quality of these musical settings in the actual tragic drama duplicates the fundamental question of the participatory versus commentary character of the Greek tragic chorus. The chorus remains outside the action. Mendelssohn's presence in the *Antigone* of Sophocles, Donner, and Tieck is that of a commentator through the voice of the chorus: an outsider in the court of Thebes as in the court of Prussia.

Frederick William's *Antigone* instantiates the conjunction in German history that Thomas Nipperdey has called "Bürgerwelt und starker Staat."[3] Significant in this dialectic of "bürgerlich" society— the adjective connotes bourgeois society but also the civil society that, for Hegel, mediates between the family and the state—and the state itself is the place of the assimilating, post-Enlightenment German Jewry. Its most renowned representative had been Moses Mendelssohn, the composer's grandfather. The father, Abraham, had chosen the path of full Protestant assimilation, including conversion and the change of the family name to Bartholdy. The relation of Felix to the question of German Jewry coincides with the increasing complications of the issue in his generation. He kept the name Mendelssohn against his father's explicit and stern wishes. The maturity that generated this decision is simultaneous with his devotion to Lutheran music. His relation, aesthetic, cultural, and religious, to Protestant music foreshadows Mahler's to Catholic culture and music two generations later. Subtlety can generate silence, and Felix Mendelssohn's relation to Judaism operated at a level of sensitivity approaching taboo. This was the practice of many in his intellectual circle, as will be discussed below.

The 1841 *Antigone* holds clues to this issue of assimilated enlightened Judaism and the uneasy Prussian state. Their infusion into Mendelssohn's presence in this realization of the play is intense and ambiguous, and speaks to the importance of classical drama as a nineteenth-century forum for the issues as it speaks to the importance of the issues themselves. The twentieth century has little inclination, knowledge, or patience for the hidden or silent presences of political issues within aesthetic forms. The conjunction of politics and drama fundamental to nineteenth-century cultural practice has been delegitimated as a trope by twentieth-century brutality. Even Wagner's gigantic Aeschylean cosmos offers illusions more than realities, to say nothing of Mendelssohn's spare Sophoclean one. There is no longer a place for an "incidental" aesthetics in its relation to real politics. For these reasons among others, this *Antigone*, along with other examples of its eclectic genre, has essentially disappeared.

I

First, a word on the political vagaries of the play's rich reception in romantic Germany. It is not hard to see why Sophocles' problematic of the confrontation of private, family religion and morality and the exigencies of modern state power struck a nerve among German intellectuals and theater publics in the nineteenth century, a period marked by the consolidation of state power and the perceived dissipation of traditional modes of community and culture. Germans were asking the same question posed in the tragedy: in the transition to modernity defined politically by the increasingly centralized state, where does one locate, and how does one preserve, legitimacy (the central political category) and authenticity (the central cultural category)?

In Sophocles, the modern state opposes the intransigence of traditional morality—and hence the definitions of legitimacy and authenticity—in the persons of Creon and Antigone. Creon is the restoring king who brings Thebes out of a threatened revolution, led by Polynices, brother of Antigone. To show that legitimacy rests with the state, he has forbidden burial ritual for the slain Polynices. Antigone resists and attempts to bury the corpse, in an insistence that legitimacy rests in a morality that is prior to and more constant than the life and the rights of the state. Creon remains confident in his attitude until the moment of the death of his son Haemon (a suicide for love of Antigone—*pace* Hegel, who said that the Greeks did not know of love in the romantic sense and that the suicide is not due to love).[4] The filial connection and its loss are ultimately more primal than the logic of the state. But Creon's grief does not solve the dramatic and political problem of the play. His grief may not necessarily prove the falseness of his prior position; it may indeed only call into question its intransigence and thus his ultimate incapacity to rule. In this way, the moral choice between Creon and Antigone occupied nineteenth-century readings of the tragedy.

For Hegel, the tragedy shows the way to synthesis and resolution of value conflicts (family versus city, moral law and tradition versus political necessity) beyond the abilities of the characters, and hence of the possibilities of the drama.⁵ For both Friedrich and August Wilhelm Schlegel, Antigone is the hero and Creon the villain; for Hegel the opposition is morally symmetrical and for that precise reason tragic. The harmonization of the ethical life of individual persons, families, and religions with the life and exigencies of the state is the process of history worked out throughout Hegel's work, with the references to *Antigone* a recurring presence. Hegel's reading cannot itself be read simply as an endorsement of Creon's position, just as his emerging philosophy of the state cannot be read simply as an endorsement of state (i.e., Prussian) power. But such a simplified reading was prevalent in the 1830s and 1840s, as it is still today. George Steiner therefore talks about the conservative, pro-Creon Hegel paradigm; such a paradigm belongs more accurately to the reception of Hegel than to his own position. This pro-Creon paradigm remained dominant, Steiner argues, until O. Ribbeck's *Sophokles und seine Tragödien* (1869) and Wilamowitz-Moellendorf on Antigone's martyrdom.⁶

The classicist August Boeckh (1785–1867), a colleague and a personal rival of Hegel's at the University of Berlin, worked as well within a state-oriented reading of the *Antigone*. Boeckh's essay "On the *Antigone* of Sophocles" dates from 1824 and was presented again in a Berlin seminar in 1828—a span simultaneous with Hegel's Berlin *Lectures on Aesthetics*.⁷ The crucial point Boeckh makes in this essay is that Creon's position is morally complicated and cannot be dismissed as that of the tyrant. Opposing the position of Schönborn, for whom Antigone was the clear heroine in a stand against tyranny, Boeckh argues that the line between legitimate state power and illegitimate tyranny is not clear. Antigone is not simply an innocent battling tyranny; she also undermines the state: "the action of this tragedy shatters the royal house and the state."⁸ He continues: "I do not have to restate that I have not ignored the tyrannical aspect of Creon; but who can ignore the fact that Sophocles represented him as a noble, solitary ruler in search of law and order?"⁹

The relative conservatism of Hegel and Boeckh's "Creonism" certainly inhabits the production of 1841, at least as far as Ludwig Tieck's participation is concerned. Steiner, for example, states that "there is, unquestionably, a Creon after Hegel. Already the celebrated Tieck-Mendelssohn staging of *Antigone* presents Creon as a noble, tragically constrained, defender of the law."¹⁰ But the scenario is complicated by the plurality of participants; not only Mendelssohn, but also Frederick William IV may be responsible for a larger degree of political ambiguity in the 1841 production than Steiner allows.

There is a strong and a weak interpretation of this ambiguity. The strong interpretation insists on an element of liberalism on the part of either Mendelssohn or the king, or both, which militates in favor of Antigone. The weak interpretation suggests that by 1840, the Hegelian promise of synthesis—the promise that the *Antigone* at least points the way to the resolution of morality and state power—has faded, and that the indecision, and hence the tragedy, of Sophocles' cosmos, must control the principles of its representation.

II

To pursue the question of the identity of "Mendelssohn's *Antigone*," we may, first, follow two chronologies—those of Mendelssohn and of his friend and teacher Johann Gustav Droysen (1808–1884). As to the question of the political identity, the reception of the work in the line of Hegel and Boeckh shows profound political ambivalence, and we are in a position to see how Mendelssohn adds new refractions to such ambivalence.

Felix's cultural and religious sensibilities can be understood according to (at least) three issues: his relationship to Judaism and to Jewish assimilation; his growing devotion to Protestant music; and the social taboo of the discussion of Jewish matters among the assimilated, largely converted Berlin intelligentsia. Abraham Mendelssohn's famous letter to his son of 8 July 1829 is a stern charge that his son adopt the name Bartholdy and drop the name Mendelssohn. Only thus could Felix reap the benefits of the Lutheran identity to which the family conversion entitled him. The letter bears quoting:

> My father felt that the name Moses ben Mendel Dessau would handicap him in gaining the needed access to those who had the better education at their disposal. Without any fear that his own father would take offense, my father assumed the name Mendelssohn. The change, though a small one, was decisive. As Mendelssohn, he became irrevocably detached from an entire class, the best of whom he raised to his own level. By that name he identified himself with a different group. Through the influence which, ever growing, persists to this day, that name Mendelssohn acquired a Messianic import and a significance which defies extinction. This, considering that you were reared a Christian, you can hardly understand. A Christian Mendelssohn is an impossibility. A Christian Mendelssohn the world would never recog-

nize. Nor should there be a Christian Mendelssohn; for my father himself did not want to be a Christian. "Mendelssohn" does and always will stand for a Judaism in transition, when Judaism, just because it is seeking to transmute itself spiritually, clings to its ancient form all the more stubbornly and tenaciously, by way of protest against the novel form that so arrogantly and tyrannically declared itself to be the one and only path to the good.[11]

This passage is a profound reflection of and on Jewish assimilation in Prussia in the first half of the nineteenth century. The historical logic is Hegelian: assimilation represents historical development and the maturation of spiritual life. Abraham did not see his conversion and name change as a rejection of his father's path, but precisely as a continuation of it. Moses had changed his name in accordance with the social changes of German Jewry; Abraham took the process one significant step further and expected his own son to respect this historical trajectory. Felix's rebellion must therefore be seen in terms of his general rejection of a Hegelian historical linearity—more on this will follow. Felix thus recomplicated the cultural identity in relation to which his father and grandfather had sought harmony and resolution.

With regard to this spirit of complication, Felix's determination to remain Mendelssohn must be understood in conjunction with the growing devotion to Protestant music—as a mark of his increasing insistence on a critical and self-forming cultural identity. The 1829 revival of the *St. Matthew Passion* is the strongest example. One might argue that Mendelssohn's relation to Protestantism and the integrity of its aesthetic representations foreshadows Mahler's attachment, two generations later (however more conflicted the latter's may be), to Catholicism and Catholic theatricality. Mahler roamed the contours of the German world, holding positions in Prague, Budapest, and Hamburg, and craved the return to the center, which meant the cultural, musical, and symbolic world of Vienna. His own conversion to Catholicism must therefore be understood as a dimension of a desire to participate in the majority culture of the Austrian Catholic baroque.[12] Similarly, Mendelssohn's itinerary had taken him from Hamburg, Düsseldorf, and Leipzig to the new cultural center of Berlin, and his Protestant devotion represented also a devotion to cultural traditions of northern Germany, with Bach as cultural as well as musical hero.

Nevertheless, the confidence and mastery Mendelssohn showed in 1829 were not free of Jewish self-consciousness, as noted in memoirs of Eduard Devrient. Devrient, an actor (Haemon in the 1841 *Antig-*

one) and close friend of Mendelssohn's, recalled Mendelssohn's remarks on the success of the *St. Matthew Passion*: "To think that a comedian and a Jew must revive the greatest Christian music for the world."[13] The fact that the performances took place in the Singakademie generated the recurring disapproval, in the nineteenth-century literature, of the alleged secularization of Bach.[14] Such uncertainties persisted. The Singakademie's rejection of Mendelssohn's candidacy for the directorship in January 1833 had clearly something to do with his Jewish origins.[15]

By 1833, one can suggest, the Jewish-Protestant symbiosis that Mendelssohn had internalized was in jeopardy on the outside as well. Another example of the inner symbiosis of Jewish memory and Protestant culture, but increasingly embattled from without, appears in Eric Werner's perceptive reading of the Jewish subtext in a January 1831 letter disparaging the frivolity of New Year's celebrations. The days around the turning of the year, wrote Mendelssohn, are *"real days* of atonement."* Werner attributes these thoughts to "his parental home, where the very serious attitude towards the New Year had simply been transposed from Jewish to Christian practice."[16] The same sensibility is revealed in the words to the concluding hymn of Goethe's *Erste Walpurgisnacht* (1831):

Und raubt man uns den alten Brauch,
Dein Licht, wer kann es rauben?

[And if we are robbed of our old customs,
Who can rob us of thy light?][17]

The Sophoclean theme of the robbing of custom must have been evident, perhaps even disturbing, to Mendelssohn. We can recall that for Hegel, the family as carrier of moral and religious values is illustrated in several relationships: brother and sister (Polynices and Antigone), and also father and son (Creon and Haemon). The latter relationship cannot survive the destruction of Antigone's family values. Where are we, then, on Hegel's historical path: the family and its values versus the state or integrated within it? I would suggest that Abraham Mendelssohn was in this sense the perfect Hegelian, and that he read the resolution of the Hegelian-Sophoclean dialectic of family and state in terms of the successful assimilation of the Berlin Jewish intelligentsia. By the time of Felix's maturity in the 1830s and 1840s, the synthesis had begun to show cracks. (It is worth remembering that Mendelssohn heard at least some of Hegel's lectures on aesthetics at the University of Berlin. According to a letter that Mendelssohn's teacher C. F. Zelter wrote to Goethe, Mendelssohn offered an accomplished imitation of Hegel's lecturing style.[18])

.

Felix Mendelssohn had, apparently, little sympathy for his patron Frederick William IV.[19] The king's political and cultural tastes remain underresearched and hard to fathom. The historian Heinrich von Treitschke called his entire reign, from 1840 to 1861, a "long chain of misunderstandings."[20] The association with Mendelssohn occurred during the "honeymoon" years of the reign. These early years were popularly successful, as the king's determination to be well liked led him to take the posture of the reformer. He thus reversed many of the repressive policies of 1819 and after. Censorship was "at least somewhat mitigated"; three of the liberal "Göttingen Seven" professors were called to Berlin. At bottom, however, Frederick William IV was a romantic conservative who believed in the divine right of kings and whose model of the Prussian state was grounded in an idea of a "Christian-German" moral community.[21] To that end he relied, in the 1840s, on the advice of Friedrich Julius Stahl, a converted Jew who worked out the model of the "evangelical state."[22] When, for example, David Friedrich Strauss wrote an essay called "Ein Romantiker auf dem Throne der Caesaren," the ostensible subject of Julian the Apostate was easily recognized as Frederick William IV. Nevertheless, the first years of his reign provided a certain honeymoon period for reinstated liberal intellectuals. The constitutional and parliamentary challenges culminating in the events of 1848 and after undid the king's liberalizing pretentions and persona.

How the king's taste brought him to Antigone is a difficult question but an interesting one. Apparently he found J. J. Donner's translation of the *Antigone* himself and gave it to Ludwig Tieck.[23] The elderly Tieck held the position of "Vorleser," or lecturer-reader, in the royal court. This was the king's first exposure to Greek tragedy, and the Berlin orientalist Christian Josias Freiherr von Bunsen reported him to be "delighted as with a new and brilliant discovery."[24] Tieck had argued to the king for a reading of the *Antigone* as a work presaging Christianity, an approach that irritated the historicist Boeckh. The spatial symbolism of Tieck's staging emphasized the orchestra while at the same time reflecting his view of the tragedy as pre-Christian. From the proscenium he built a double set of stairs leading down to the orchestra, which contained the instrumentalists and also the chorus and an altar.[25] Thus the stage action deferred to the levels of commentary emanating from the music and musical chorus; Greek drama deferred to the aesthetic forms of Lutheran church music. Tieck, who found "already the later Haydn too noisy, and Beethoven beyond the pale," did not like Mendelssohn's music.[26] Boeckh, on the other hand, defended the music as a legitimate evocation of the Attic poetic—metric—and cultural origins.[27]

One can reasonably assume that the king's personal wish to have *Antigone* staged in Sans-souci presupposed a given sympathy for the plight of Creon. How sensitive the king was to the text and what kind of political message he may have hoped it would give to the court audience are difficult questions to answer. The Mendelssohn-Tieck *Antigone* did originate with the king's own attraction to Sophocles' tragedy. What is the place of the person and moral intransigence of Antigone within the tastes and forms of a royal entertainment? Is the royal intention the tragedy of Creon, as Steiner suggests? Is it the Hegelian Antigone-Creon synthesis realized, a fitting aesthetic representation of a new liberal beginning? And how did Mendelssohn negotiate this hazy but high-staked symbolic context?

.

Where Mendelssohn's relationship with the classical world is at issue, his friendship with Johann Gustav Droysen is relevant, not only for his knowledge of classical literature but also for his sense of the contemporary political ramifications of classical allusion. The friendship dates from 1827, when Droysen, one year Mendelssohn's senior, replaced Karl Wilhelm Ludwig Heyse as the tutor for both Felix and Fanny Mendelssohn. They remained in regular contact until 1840, when Droysen was called from Berlin to a professorship in Kiel. Their closeness is revealed in their published correspondence, with the first extant letter from Mendelssohn to Droysen written in November 1829: a tourist report from London, with first names and the familiar address used throughout.[28]

Like Mendelssohn, Droysen had heard some of Hegel's Berlin lectures of the 1820s—in his case, the lectures on world history. These lectures contributed to the formation of Droysen's early conception of the history of fifth-century Athens as having "attained and set in motion a consciousness of freedom." "The conception of Athenian history as the manifestation of the idea of liberty," James McGlew has written, "is the basis of Droysen's interpretation of Athenian tragedy."[29] In 1832 Droysen published his two-volume study of Aeschylus (*Des Aischylos Werke*) and, in 1833, his life of Alexander the Great (*Geschichte Alexanders des Grossen*). The latter work displayed the first use of the term Hellenism in its now standard usage to mean the general culture of the period between Alexander and the rise of Christianity. The prior, traditional usage of the term had denoted the Greek dialect spoken by Jews in Egypt.[30] The work initiated a life-long interest in Hellenism, which yielded paradoxical results. On the one hand the idea of Macedonia as an ancient model for modern Prussia remained constant. On the other hand, the study of the Hellenistic period was never finished. Arnaldo Momigliano has suggested that this noncompletion had to do with Droysen's difficulty in engaging the question of the role of the Jews in the Hellenistic period. To be sure, the category of the Jews and its modern resonances complicates the linear sense of history grounded in liberal Hegelianism. But in the case of Droysen, as with Mendelssohn, there are personal and social criteria at work as well.

The first volume of the history of Hellenism (*Geschichte des Hellenismus*) appeared in 1836; the second in 1843. In the second volume's last chapter, Momigliano points out, "Judaism is mentioned for the first time as an important factor in the origins of Christianity. . . . [A]t least from 1838 onward Droysen became more interested in Judaism. He included books in the popular literature of which he intended to make a special study. He was not indifferent to the mounting research on Alexandrian Judaism, on the Essenes and on Paulism. He semed to be preparing himself for the next volume of the *History of Hellenism*. Yet nothing happened. . . . Once again we are faced with the question: why did he not pursue this obviously fruitful line?"[31] Momigliano's answer has to do with the "taboo . . . deeply ingrained" within the converted German-Jewish community of Berlin and their discussion of—and their silences about—Judaism.[32] Droysen's personal circle included many Jews and Jewish converts to Christianity. His first wife was Marie Mendheim, daughter of a bookseller, née Mendel. Other friends and associates, in addition to Mendelssohn, included E. Bendemann, Heine, Eduard Gans, the classicists G. Bernhardy and August Neander (né David Mendel).[33] Momigliano comments: "Droysen did some work on Jewish texts, but he never brought himself to face the whole problem of the relation between Judaism and Christianity. It was the problem which at a personal level had deeply concerned his best friends, his wife and his relatives—and it was going to affect his own children. He must have known that his friends were thinking about it in their silences. He remained silent, too. The *History of Hellenism* was never finished."[34] In March 1842, Droysen wrote to Mendelssohn of the success the oratorio *St. Paul* was enjoying in Kiel. (The audience was particularly enthusiastic, Droysen wrote, about the rendition of "Jerusalem" by

Amalie Niebuhr, "the daughter of the old Niebuhr.") Droysen heralded the return of "Protestant music" for the first time since Bach and Handel.[35] In view of Droysen's research on Paulism as an element of the Hellenistic transition from Judaism to Christianity, the silence on the work's Jewish references is significant.

•

On the occasion of Droysen's 1834 engagement to Marie Mendheim, Mendelssohn wrote a letter of congratulation that expresses nonetheless a sense of loss: "if we can no longer live in each other's company, let us not grow distant from one another."[36] Their next recorded correspondence occurs after a gap of almost three years. In December 1837 the two men corresponded about a possible Mendelssohn opera on the *Odyssey*. Droysen was interested in supplying the libretto, and entreated Mendelssohn not to plan an English opera: "Was haben wir schon alles in der Musik an das Ausland verloren!"—"Haven't we already lost enough music to foreigners?"[37]

Droysen first heard of the 1841 *Antigone* after the Potsdam première. In a letter to Mendelssohn of 1 November, he expressed astonishment that he had set the choruses to music, and great interest in hearing them. "You must have truly penetrated to the innermost core of this ancient splendor to be able to say just how they are musical. I cannot yet grasp it. . . . I have absolutely no idea how the ancient forms can adapt themselves to your sounds, something no musician has yet accomplished." The letter ends with the entreaty not to follow the inclinations of the Tieck circle and produce Euripides for the stage. It would be better, Droysen advises, "to bring to the boards the full preserved trilogy of Aeschylus; I think that this would provide the most powerful theatrical effect, and a great opportunity for music." A Wagnerian prophecy![38]

Mendelssohn answered (on 2 December) as follows:

> Should I tell you about the *Antigone*? Yes. If only you had been there! The thing was in fact a private amusement which I undertook, and which came out so well, that I have no desire to repeat it (you know my *esprit de contradiction* in such matters). There's no question of Euripides. . . . Deep in his soul even Tieck had no real interest in the thing [the *Antigone*], and then it was a question only of Count Redern and the actors! They all talk about it, because the King "wished" it, and for their part they wished only that I declare the music for such a thing an impossibility, as you do. But then one fine morning I read the wonderful three plays

and thought the devil on all this dumb talk and was beside myself
with the desire to see it before my eyes (for better or worse) and
I was most of all enchanted with the life that inhabits them still
today, and that the choruses are still today what we call musical
. . . and here the wonderful, natural, aboriginal verse made a
more overwhelming impression than I had ever dreamed possible. It gave me a boundless joy which I will never forget. The
more or less jolting words do not inspire concern; but the mood
and the verse rhythms are everywhere so truly musical, that one
need not think about the individual words but rather compose
only for those moods and rhythms—and the chorus is finished.
Even today one could hope for no richer a task than these multifaceted choral moods: victory and daybreak [i.e., Mendelssohn's chorus no. 1], peaceful reflection [no. 2], melancholia [no.
3], love [no. 4, first part], mourning [no. 4, second part], Bac-
chus's song [no. 6], and the earnest warning at the end [no. 7]—
what more could one want?[39]

A public forum for Droysen's reception of the *Antigone* came in a
newspaper essay following the public première of the work in the
Berlin Schauspielhaus on 13 April 1842.[40] The essay is a charged and
multifaceted polemic about the necessity of public culture and public
memory. Mendelssohn is embraced to those ends, but his name is
never mentioned.

Droysen's opening sentence exemplifies the cushioned political
barb, in this case directed against the king and court: "The *Antigone*
must not be a mere masterly and brilliant court festival, an artistic
pleasure for the small, select circle of the highly cultured. The work
is intended for the public theater, for the whole public." Attic tragedy
was a dimension of public culture, and its contemporary nineteenth-
century reprise is to serve the same ends. In this first of several in-
stances in this piece, Droysen's argument anticipates Nietzsche's.
Cleverly, Droysen flatters the members of Frederick William's circle
by referring to them not as the powerful or the privileged but as the
"Hochgebildete"—the highly educated and cultured. There may of
course be an element of personal resentment at work here—in regard
to Mendelssohn as well as the court—as Droysen only heard of the
Antigone project after the Sans-souci première. The Berlin performances, Droysen continues, became an event of great public interest:
"the city is full of talk about the piece." "The city" refers to Berlin,
but the category recalls Athens (or Thebes).

Antigone, Droysen continues, explodes "the renowned trivialities of the artistic taste" ["die bekannten Trivialitäten der Kunstkennerei"] of the Berlin public. He credits royal taste with the revival: "It was a royal idea to revive for our time the most splendid creation of Greek poetry." Here Droysen makes an impassioned argument for the place of interpretation as opposed to the illusory insistence on the literal representability of ancient forms. This argument for the place of interpretation is highly interesting as an early document in Droysen's developing ideas of historical methodology—the aspect of his work, culminating in the *Historik*, for which he is most remembered:

> Nicht die abgestorbenen Vergangenheiten sollen uns wiederkehren; aber was in ihnen Grosses und Unvergängliches, das soll mit dem frischesten und lebendigsten Geist der Gegenwart erfasst, von ihm durchdrungen zu neuer, unberechenbarer Wirkung in die Wirklichkeit geführt werden; kein Babel toter Trümmerstücke, sondern ein Pantheon der Vergangenheit sei unsere Gegenwart.

> [It is not the extinct ages of the past that are to be brought back to us; rather, it is for the freshest and liveliest minds of the present to grasp what is great and enduring in those ages and to lead them to unbroken effect in reality. Our own time should not be a Babel of dead lamentation plays, but a pantheon of the past.]

He then turns to the problem of music. The Greeks, he says, sang the choruses. Here he allows himself a Rankean moment: we simply do not know "wie sie gewesen"—what they were like. But Raphael had not seen Jesus or Mary with his own eyes, and no one reproached him for painting their likenesses. Of course what Droysen is sidestepping here is the epistemological problem of the relation of the limit of knowledge and representability—the issue over which Kantianism and Judaism meet. Just as Raphael saw the images of his subjects "mit der Augen des Geistes" (with his mind's eye; source: *Hamlet*), "just so did the composer read the drama of Sophocles, . . . and his hearing was itself a new and life-filled understanding." The result: "not ancient music, but the impression of ancient music." In addition, Droysen implies that the nineteenth-century audience possesses a musically constituted imagination, and that the use of music "warms" the audience to the tragedy. Music enables the modern spectator to enter into the "new, ideal world" of tragedy. Droysen is thus not making an argument for the adaptability or "modernization" of Sophocles. On the contrary, he is advocating the adaptation of the modern imagination to the world of Greek tragedy. The intention of tragedy,

Droysen argues finally, is not to overwhelm and abandon the spectator into "subjective discretion" but rather to "tear him out" of it into a state of self-forgetfulness. This position echoes the translation practice of Hölderlin's *Antigonä*, known to Droysen, which deliberately exoticized German idiom to a level of "otherness" appropriate to Greek tragedy.

This aspect of Droysen's discussion also allows us a point of entry into Mendelssohn's aesthetic, which Droysen does not discuss. Although circumstantial issues may indeed have determined the format of the incidental music to *Antigone*—principally the tastes and commission of the king, Mendelssohn clearly felt comfortable in the genre. It is the most modest category of the various choral categories that engaged Mendelssohn's attention: incidental choral music, oratorio (and sacred music), and opera. It restricts its reach on the dramatic material it engages: it comments and does not control.

III

The Greek tragic chorus that Mendelssohn set for his *Antigone* is, in Steiner's summary, "a device whereby the antique playwright can exactly calibrate and modulate the distances, the sight-lines, between spectator and scene. The chorus literally reaches back into the obscure instauration of ritual-dramatic performances. It also reaches forward, first into the section of the polis from which it is recruited, then into the audience as a whole, which is to say the body politic."[41] The term "stasimon" for choral song or interlude implies static commentary. But the thrust of Steiner's lines above shows that the chorus is a dynamic presence in the drama. Setting these parts of drama to music recognizes and emphasizes their dynamic quality. The chorus is also said to "sing" its verses and thus forms the locus of the unrecovered musical aspect of Attic tragedy. In his 1824 essay on the play, mentioned above, August Boeckh emphasized this musicality by focusing on the stasima and their musicality, for example the musical dactylic rhythm of the first stasimon (verses 579ff., in his reference). The rhythmic analogy to the lyric is indisputable, he said.[42]

Sophocles' drama contains an initial choral ode and five stasima. Using J. J. Donner's wordy 1839 translation, Mendelssohn sets these six choral passages and then concludes with an additional choral ode culled from the final dialogue between the chorus and Creon and the chorus's closing six lines. This final statement ends with a warning against the uttering of "big words" ("megaloi de logoi," line 1350) by great men. Donner's translation refers to "das vermessene Wort": literally, the overmeasured word, connoting both an arrogant utterance and a rhetorically overstated one. Whether Mendelssohn internalized this final warning is impossible to say, but I think it is clear that he incorporated the drama's final charge into his own attending compositional practice. His music is rhetorically understated. To an extent, this understatement may be a function both of the necessarily fragmentary structure of the choral settings and of the rhythmic predetermination of his music by the verse. But I want to speculate briefly here that Mendelssohn's modest rhetorical posture may have something to do with the moral and political thematic of the *Antigone* as he read it. First, there is the question of the piece as a court entertainment. The rhetorical ambivalence of Mendelssohn's choral writing reflects the ambiguity of the Greek chorus in relation to the dramatic action, but it also duplicates his own ambivalence to the court in general. Second, I want to ask whether the musical style and its inherent moral and political rhetoric might not be seen as a departure from, and an answer to, the entirely different rhetorical, moral, and political style of the *Lobgesang* Symphony (op. 52), completed a year earlier, in 1840.

Mendelssohn referred, as we have seen, to the first choral ode in terms of victory and daybreak. The words narrate the victory of the city of Thebes over the invading army; the point of view is antecedent to the whole Antigone problematic. The state is secure; the chorus proceeds in a secure C-major march. The ode has four parts: strophe 1, antistrophe 1, strophe 2, and antistrophe 2. (The second strophe is in C minor, the key of the orchestral introduction and its foreboding tone.) There are two referents to Mendelssohn's "daybreak," one in the words, the second in the music. The "sunrays over the seven-gated city" in Donner's first line provide the first. The second is the possible connotation of the ascending, arpeggiated figure that opens the chorus, reinforced by the harp arpeggiations in the two antistrophes.

The second chorus consists of Sophocles' first stasimon, uttered after the dramatic problematic has been revealed: the guard has informed Creon that Antigone has been caught throwing earth on her brother's corpse. The opening line is renowned; in Donner's version it reads "Vieles Gewaltige lebt, doch nichts / Ist gewaltiger als der Mensch" [Many powerful things live, but none more powerful than man]. (Modern English translations use "wondrous" rather than "powerful.") It concludes with a paean to civic loyalty and a denunciation of the opposite. We have the same major-minor relationship here, as the secure A-major chorus modulates to the minor at the shock of recognition when Antigone is brought in. So far the choral and musical rhetoric finds security, and advocates it, in the ballast of the (city-)state.

The third chorus ("melancholia") comments on the unyielding sorrow of the house of Oedipus, and ends with the signal to Creon that his son Haemon, soon to be robbed of his betrothed, enters. The fourth chorus is Mendelssohn's central one, and it is pivotal in his own rhetorical commentary on the drama. It is, first of all, broken into two parts, and so identified by his two descriptives "love" and "mourning" ("Totenklage"). When the tragedy is performed as Mendelssohn intended it to be, Antigone's lines about her own death are interspersed with the verses of the chorus.

The fifth chorus (fourth stasimon) comes after Antigone's final exit; it mourns her impending fate and prepares the scene, dramatically, for the sudden entrance of the blind prophet Tiresias. Mendelssohn emphasizes this anticipation and tension through an increasing tempo and use of chromaticism. Politically, the role of Tiresias is the pivot that justifies the reading of the play itself as favoring Antigone over Creon. Tiresias directly challenges the legitimacy of Creon's rule; he tells him that "all of the altars of the town are choked with the leavings of the dogs and birds" whose "feast was on that fated, fallen Polynices."[43] Creon is thus responsible for a literal, physical pollution of Thebes, but also for the pollution of religious values in favor of arbitrary political expediency: "you've confused the upper and lower worlds" (line 1068). Tiresias sways Creon, and also the voice of the chorus, which entreats him, successfully, to change course.

The sixth chorus (fifth stasimon) is a call to the god of the city to save it from the plague, and it comes just as Creon has taken the advice of the chorus to save Antigone and bury the corpse of Polynices. (The chorus advises, in a couplet not in the stasima and therefore not set by Mendelssohn: "The gods move very fast when they bring ruin on misguided men" [lines 1103–4].) Because the advice comes too late, the final chorus can only lament the successive suicides of Antigone, Haemon, and Euridice (Haemon's mother and Creon's wife). It also offers the warning about swollen words, as mentioned above. The understated C-minor conclusion—only five bars beyond the final choral statement—provides a clear counterpart to the fervent C-major opening of the first chorus, and thus reinforces the work's rhetorical modesty.

Mendelssohn was pleased with his *Antigone* music and remained closely identified with it during the final years of his life. An excerpt was played at his funeral in Leipzig's Paulinerkirche in 1847. What the piece—his music, its relation to the drama, and the drama itself—actually meant to him cannot be clearly understood. I would insist, however, that the resonances of this work are broad, even if they cannot be precisely determined. They start, but do not end, with the political ambivalences of Sophocles' text, its tradition of reception in romantic Germany, and its relationship to the court of Frederick William IV in the early years of his reign. The theme of eternal, religious law and custom versus the vagaries of the political and of the state recalls the Mendelssohn family saga of Jewish enlightenment (Moses), Protestant assimilation (Abraham) and subtly divided loyalty (Felix). We surely have the right to ask whether Felix's view of the character Antigone might have resonated with his own discomfort with the previous generation's modernizing, secularizing, state-oriented practice. This deep, personal involvement with the Antigone problematic informs the sensitivity of the musical settings, and it also sheds light on the clear difference in compositional style between this work and the *Lobgesang* of the previous year.

In a forthcoming essay, John Toews defines the political identity of the *Lobgesang* in a convincing argument that places Mendelssohn in a position entirely different from the one I am ascribing to him in the context of the *Antigone*. I want to conclude by addressing this reading of the *Lobgesang* and its refraction on the *Antigone* as a representation of the underside of Mendelssohn's relation to official Prussian culture. Thus the *Lobgesang*, in the spirit of the oratorio *St. Paul* (1836), reveals the public ethic of Christian reform, community, and adherence to the state; the *Antigone*, the private, moral, and public ambivalences in regard to these issues. Mendelssohn's public musical ethic, which led Alexander von Humboldt and Christian Bunsen to recommend to Frederick William IV that he be brought to Berlin, corresponded to Bunsen's view of music as, in Toews's formulation, "a significant component of religious reform by [its] recreating and revitalizing for public consumption the emotive core of traditional religious forms, both specifically liturgical and more broadly 'national' or communal."[44] This musical and moral-political ethic intensified, as Toews points out, after the sudden death of Abraham Mendelssohn in 1835. In a letter of December 1835 to Karl Klingemann, Mendelssohn wrote of the wish to "become like his father."[45] His determination to marry and to build a family thus spoke to his father's "longstanding wish"—again in Toews's formulation—"that he might emancipate himself from the subjective world of romantic fantasy and attain the solid ground of ethical responsibility." For his father, romantic, subjective solipsism was the partner of the cultural isolation of the Jew, as he had made clear in the famous letter of 1829.

The enormous public success of *St. Paul* and the successful relationship with the Leipzig Gewandhaus orchestra generated the aesthetic of the *Lobgesang*, which combines the Protestant ethic and the spirit of music with, in Toews's words, "a self-conscious attempt to remake or revise Beethoven's choral symphony in a manner which resolved its problematic relations between vocal and instrumental forms, and between immanent structures and transcendent yearnings."[46] There is certainly a convergence, in the years between 1836 and 1840, of a psychological internalization of Abraham's Protestant ethic and Felix's own aesthetic maturation as an independent musical presence, the latter bolstered by his success in Leipzig. One is led, therefore, to speculate whether the call to Berlin and to the court of the new king might have reactivated the rebellious individualism of the young Felix, and caused him to view the fatherly, Christian-German state of Frederick William IV with all the political, ethical, and psychological ambivalence evident in the *Antigone*—that of Sophocles and that of Mendelssohn.

NOTES

1. See *Hegel's Aesthetics: Lectures on Fine Art*, trans. T. M. Knox (Oxford, 1975), 2 vols., p. 1218.

2. George Steiner, *Antigones* (Oxford, 1984), p. 2.

3. Thomas Nipperdey, *Deutsche Geschichte 1800–1866: Bürgerwelt und starker Staat* (Munich, 1984). The terminology and tone of the phrase translate only with great difficulty. "Bürgerwelt" means "the world of the middle class" or the bourgeoisie, but with the positive connotation of citizenship and solidity. "Starker Staat" means, literally, "strong state."

4. See Hegel, *Aesthetics*, p. 564.

5. See the discussion in Martha C. Nussbaum, *The Fragility of Goodness: Luck and Ethics in Greek Tragedy and Philosophy* (Cambridge, 1986), p. 52.

6. Steiner, *Antigones*, p. 41.

7. August Boeckh, *Über die Antigone des Sophokles* (1824), 2d ed.: *Abhandlungen der historisch-philologischen Klasse der königlichen Akademie der Wissenschaften zu Berlin aus dem Jahre 1828* (1831), pp. 49–112.

8. Ibid., p. 77: ". . . die Handlung dieser Tragödie erschüttert Königshaus und Staat."

9. Ibid., p. 87: "Dass ich nun das Tyrannische in Kreon nicht verkannt habe, brauche ich nicht zu beweisen; aber dass ihn Sophokles als einen edlen,

Recht und Ordnung suchenden Alleinherrscher darstellte, wer kann das verkennen?"

10. Steiner, p. 182.

11. Eric Werner, *Mendelssohn: A New Image of the Composer and His Age* (Glencoe, 1963), p. 37.

12. See my discussion of this issue in its relation to Mahler and other thinkers in the chapter "The Catholic Culture of the Austrian Jews" in *The Meaning of the Salzburg Festival: Austria as Theater and Ideology, 1890–1938* (Ithaca, 1990), pp. 164–95.

13. Eduard Devrient, *Meine Erinnerungen an Felix Mendelssohn* (Berlin, n.d.), p. 56.

14. See Werner, p. 100.

15. Ibid., pp. 230–31. On the issue of the *Singakademie* election and Werner's account of it, see William A. Little's essay "Mendelssohn and the Berlin *Singakademie*: The Composer at the Crossroads," in this volume.

16. Werner, p. 171.

17. Ibid., p. 203.

18. Ibid., p. 79. Werner's summary of Hegel's ideas on the aesthetics of music and their possible influence on Mendelssohn's developing aesthetic is not convincing. Romantic platitudes about the emotionality of music form the principle of connection.

19. Werner cites an unpublished letter of 27 October 1840 (held, according to Werner, by the Library of Congress) in which Mendelssohn derides the king. Werner, pp. 82, 85.

20. Nipperdey, p. 397.

21. Ibid., pp. 396, 397.

22. See Walter Bussmann, *Zwischen Preussen und Deutschland: Friedrich Wilhelm IV, Eine Biographie* (Berlin 1990), pp. 159–90.

23. Roger Paulin, *Ludwig Tieck: A Literary Biography* (Oxford, 1985), p. 336.

24. Werner, p. 374.

25. Paulin, p. 336.

26. Ibid., 337.

27. Wulf Konold, *Felix Mendelssohn-Bartholdy und seine Zeit* (Regensburg, 1984), p. 215.

28. Rudolf Hübner, ed. *Johann Gustav Droysen, Briefwechsel*, 2 vols. (Osnabrück, 1929).

29. *Des Aischylos Werke* 1.163–64; James F. McGlew, "J. G. Droysen and the Aeschylean Hero," in *Classical Philology* 79/1 (January 1984): 4.

30. Arnaldo Momigliano, "J. G. Droysen between Greeks and Jews," in *Essays in Ancient and Modern Historiography* (Middletown, 1977), p. 310.

31. Ibid., p. 316.

32. Ibid., p. 318.

33. Ibid., p. 317.

34. Ibid., p. 318.

35. Hübner, 1.211.

36. Ibid., 1.71: "wenn wir auch wohl nicht wieder miteinander leben werden, so lass uns darum uns doch nicht von einander entfernen."

37. Ibid., 1.130.

38. Ibid., 1.200.

39. Ibid., 1.203.

40. The review is in the *Spenersche[n] Zeitung* of 25 April—*Kleinere Schriften zur alten Geschichte* 2 (1842): 146–52: "Die Aufführung der Antigone des Sophokles in Berlin."

41. Steiner, p. 166.

42. Boeckh, p. 69.

43. Lines 1016–18; trans. Elizabeth Wyckoff (Chicago, 1954).

44. John E. Toews, "Musical Historicism and the Transcendental Foundations of Community," forthcoming.

45. *Felix Mendelssohn Bartholdys Briefwechsel mit Legationsrat Karl Klingemann in London* (Essen, 1909), p. 195; quoted by Toews in "Musical Historicism."

46. Toews, "Musical Historicism."

The Unfinished Mendelssohn

R. LARRY TODD

When Robert Schumann lauded Mendelssohn in 1840 as the "Mozart of the nineteenth century,"[1] he acknowledged Mendelssohn as an enormously gifted musician who, having developed as a child prodigy, was blessed with a remarkable facility at composition. Five years before, Schumann had marveled at the arrival in Leipzig of "Meritis," as he dubbed Mendelssohn, to take up the leadership of the Gewandhaus Orchestra. Here was the composer of the Octet and the *Midsummer Night's Dream* Overture (completed in Mendelssohn's sixteenth and seventeenth years), firmly established at the forefront of European music, who in 1836 would release the oratorio *St. Paul*, for Schumann a decisive antidote to the philistinism then infecting the arts. After Mendelssohn's death in 1847 at the age of thirty-eight, Schumann prepared *Materialien* for a projected memoir of his friend, a sketchlike, aphoristic chronicle of their relationship. The tone of Schumann's jottings again suggests undiminished awe at Mendelssohn's versatility and fluency as a composer: "his life a consummate artwork," Schumann observed, and, with regard to the creative process, "his handwriting also an image of his harmonious inner self."[2]

The notion of Mendelssohn's harmonious inner self was reinforced in the years after his death by a wave of hero worship that found its most ardent expression in England. In Elizabeth Sheppard's fictional romance, *Charles Auchester* (1853), Mendelssohn was idealized as Seraphael, a composer who wrote "blissful modulations." And in Elise Polko's *Erinnerungen an Felix Mendelssohn Bartholdy: Ein Künstler- und Menschenleben*, which appeared in Germany in 1868 and in England in 1869, readers could find a freely embroidered biographical account presented, in the author's words, *con amore*.[3] But by 1875, Friedrich Niecks was taking up his pen to defend Mendelssohn against new, distinctly critical points of view, including Wagner's notorious anti-Semitic attack in "Judaism in Music."[4] Mendelssohn's compositional facility no longer inspired awe: "the serious beauty of

Mendelssohn's music has to most of us not the same charm as the rugged energy, the subtle thoughtfulness and morbid world-weariness of other composers. As the Romans of old took delight in the struggle and writhing agony of the gladiator, so we of the present day enjoy watching the beats and throes of the human heart as exhibited by our tone and word poets, the gladiators of modern times."⁵ Reviving Schumann's very phrase, Niecks referred to the "harmonious inner life of Mendelssohn, of which his works are the reflex." This harmony enabled the composer to gain in "perspicuity, roundness of form, and serenity of aspect," though it led him to lose, as if in compensation, in "depth, height, and intensity."

The view of Mendelssohn as a facile, perhaps superficial, genius has persevered despite occasional attempts at critical revaluation. The tenor of the age in which he lived—the *Restaurationszeit* in Germany and the early Victorian period in England—and the comfortable circumstances of his life surely contributed to the longevity of the view. But if we consider the primary documents of Mendelssohn's work as a composer, his manuscripts, we confront a fundamental contradiction. Despite the remarkably fluent orchestration of the *Midsummer Night's Dream* Overture, the seemingly effortless counterpoint in the fugal finale of the Octet, composition was not a matter of facility for Mendelssohn: his manuscripts typically teem with painstaking corrections, for to Mendelssohn the creative process was inextricably joined to revision. To return to Schumann's *Materialien*: "His painstaking corrections in the corrected proof—and the malicious comment of the engraver, 'this proceeds like a game of chess,' and his severe demeanor." What is more, Schumann found Mendelssohn's self criticism the "strongest, most scrupulous that ever appeared to me in an artist. He would change individual passages five or six times."⁶ The evidence of the manuscripts thus belies the notion of compositional facility.

Mendelssohn's habitual urge to revise was, in fact, an obsession. If we survey the compositional history of his major works, consistent signs of intense self-doubt, unrelenting scrutiny, and exacting revision emerge. Of the choral works, both oratorios, *St. Paul* and *Elijah*, underwent extensive reworkings. In the case of *Elijah*, revisions were incorporated even before its première in Birmingham, in August 1846, and before the London performances of the second version in April 1847;⁷ among the revisions was the addition of the masterful overture. Psalm 42, op. 42, was completed in July 1837 during Mendelssohn's honeymoon trip; a second, considerably expanded version followed in December 1837.⁸ The history of Psalm 95, op. 46, is somewhat more complex: completed in August 1838, it was performed in February 1839 and then revised in April 1839. Still not satisfied, Mendelssohn compared his inconstant progress on the psalm with Penelope's web and undertook yet another layer of revision in July 1841.[9] The cantata *Die erste Walpurgisnacht* was completed in February 1832; the revised version, which Berlioz heard in Leipzig, preoccupied Mendelssohn in 1842 and 1843.[10]

If we turn to the manuscripts of the instrumental works, a similar situation obtains. Mendelssohn typically spun his compositional web only to unravel it thread by thread. Thus, many of the *Lieder ohne Worte* were recorded in different versions;[11] and the so-called *Sonate écossaise*, evidently composed in 1828 *before* the Scottish sojourn of 1829, was reworked in 1833 and appeared in 1834 as the Fantasy, op. 28.[12] The six Preludes and Fugues, op. 35, present an especially intricate history. This work began as a series of unrelated, independent fugues composed between 1827 and 1836; in 1835 Mendelssohn conceived the idea of a group of etudes and fugues, and began to select, complete, and revise the fugues. In the final step the composition became a cyclical series of preludes and fugues; like the fugues, nearly all the preludes—most of which were composed in 1836—underwent multiple versions.[13]

Of the chamber works, the D-minor Piano Trio, op. 49, required two versions, which were accomplished in July and September 1839. The autograph of the Octet, op. 20, reveals several strategic excisions—for Mendelssohn, revision often entailed condensation—and, in the first movement, a critical rebarring from $\frac{2}{4}$ to common time.[14] The A-major String Quintet, op. 18, originally included a minuet and canonic trio in its autograph of March 1826; this was replaced in February 1832 by the deeply felt Intermezzo (*Nachruf*) composed in memory of Mendelssohn's friend and violin teacher, Eduard Rietz.[15] Perhaps most vexing of all is the String Quintet in Bb major of 1845, which appeared posthumously in 1850 as op. 87. Though in appearance the manuscript suggests a completed state, Friedhelm Krummacher has demonstrated how Mendelssohn encountered formidable difficulties with the formal design of the sonata-rondo finale, how he became dissatisfied with the contrasting material of the episode, and how he ultimately set aside or abandoned the work (as is not infrequently the case with the posthumous works, the published version does not reflect the *Fassung letzter Hand*).[16]

Nor did the orchestral works escape Mendelssohn's meticulous process of drafting followed by layer upon layer of redrafting. Of the symphonies, the first, op. 11, completed in 1824, was subjected to a curious experiment in 1829 when it was performed in London: Men-delssohn replaced the minuet—itself a recasting of a minuet from the C-minor Viola Sonata of 1824—by an arrangement of the scherzo from the Octet, and then restored the minuet when the symphony was published in 1834. The *Lobgesang* Symphony, op. 52, finished in June 1840, was subjected to revision in November 1840.[17] The *Scottish* Symphony, op. 56, the compositional history of which has still not been fully reconstructed, began as a sketch in Edinburgh in 1829;[18] not until 1842 was the symphony completed. The *Italian* Symphony, performed in England in May 1833, was revised extensively; new ev-idence suggests that the posthumously published version of the sym-phony, which appeared as op. 90 in 1851, does not represent Men-delssohn's final thoughts.[19] And the *Reformation* Symphony, op. 107, was of course withdrawn by the composer, who left instructions for it to be burned.[20]

Finally, the concert overtures, in which Mendelssohn made argu-ably his most significant contribution, were products of great travail. The account of Adolf Bernhard Marx rejecting an early draft of the *Midsummer Night's Dream* Overture and encouraging the composer to revise is borne out by the surviving manuscripts (though Mendels-sohn probably would have revised the draft without Marx's prompt-ing).[21] The lesser-known *Trumpet* Overture, op. 101, completed in March 1826, was recast in April 1833; similarly, *Meeresstille und glück-liche Fahrt*, finished and performed privately in Berlin in September 1828, was revised in March 1834. Most striking of all is the case of the *Fingal's Cave* Overture. Its opening theme was sketched in Scot-land in August 1829; the overture then underwent several incarna-tions before it appeared in print in 1835. Mendelssohn explored a range of different titles, including *Ouvertüre zur einsamen Insel, Die He-briden, The Isles of Fingal*, and finally *Fingalshöhle*. From this tangled chronology we may surmise that the composer faced a twofold di-lemma. First of all, Mendelssohn seems to have been concerned with capturing the proper tone for his overture, with achieving a quality free of artifice by removing vestiges of counterpoint in favor of the smell of sea gulls and train oil, as he put it.[22] Second, the series of titles suggests a concern with the programmatic content and meaning of the overture. Was it a seascape, a naturalistic tone painting, or was it meant to capture an Ossianic subject or character?[23] The very change in the titles betrays again that scrupulous self-criticism that Schumann observed.

During the 1840s, Mendelssohn discussed his views about compo-sition with J. C. Lobe, a Weimar musician and composer who served as editor of the Leipzig *Allgemeine musikalische Zeitung* from 1846 to 1848.[24] In 1855 Lobe published his "Gespräche mit Mendelssohn," set down in a style reminiscent of Eckermann's *Gespräche mit Goethe*.[25] According to Lobe's paraphrase, Mendelssohn observed that "in beginning a composition, one has a high idea of what will be created! Those ideas for which one proceeds to search take on much more lovely forms as shadowy presentiments than when they actually are put down on paper . . . If only those thoughts that correspond completely to one's requirements were accepted, then nothing or very little would ever be brought to fruition. Just for this reason I have occasionally begun works and left them unfinished."[26]

Mendelssohn's idealistic standards give only a partial explanation for why he abandoned so many compositions. After all, one is hard pressed to explain why the *Italian* Symphony did not measure up to the composer's expectations. Of course, other works, such as the oratorio *Christus* and the opera *Lorelei*, were left unfinished at the time of his death. But numerous rejected works, whether unpublished or unfinished, span Mendelssohn's entire career. They fall into two broad categories. First are those compositions that were completed on paper but that for a variety of reasons were withheld by Mendelssohn from publication. This group includes a large number of juvenilia (the thirteen string symphonies, for example), but also mature works such as the *Reformation* Symphony or *Trumpet* Overture, and the little-known concert aria *On Lena's Gloomy Heath* of 1846 or the Kyrie for five-part chorus and orchestra written for Luigi Cherubini in 1825. Presumably, had Mendelssohn lived long enough, a work such as the String Quintet, op. 87, would have been revised. But no doubt in some cases the decision not to publish was a deliberate one. According to Lobe, Mendelssohn admitted that he would occasionally force himself to finish a composition, even if it was not up to his expectations: "Though not an art work in the highest sense, it is still an exercise in forms and the representation of ideas. Here you have the reason why I have written so many compositions which have not and never should be printed." Evidently the Kyrie of 1825, a studious fugal exercise which included a learned application of mirror inversion, fell into this class.

In a second class are torsos of compositions, projects abandoned by Mendelssohn before he saw fit to complete them, regardless of whether they would have been realized ultimately as legitimate "artworks" or mere exercises. No full account of these fragments has yet been made, though they provide a wealth of information about the development of Mendelssohn's style, and shed light in several ways on other works as well. Thus, an unfinished draft for a piano con-

certo in E minor, on which Mendelssohn worked intermittently between 1842 and 1844, was abandoned in favor of the composer's
other E-minor concerto—that for violin, op. 64. Significantly, the two
concerti share certain formal features and thematic elements, so that
the first movement of the piano concerto can be heard as an adum-
bration of the opening movement of the violin concerto.[27] The subject of the following discussion, a little-known and undated draft for
the beginning of a piano sonata in G major, provides a stimulating
and intriguing example that allows us to consider in more detail the
meaning of the unfinished Mendelssohn.

．

The fragment, a ninety-seven measure draft for the exposition of the
first movement of a piano sonata, is preserved on a bifolio in the
M. Deneke Mendelssohn Collection at the Bodleian Library, Oxford
(b. 5, fols. 124–25; see figure 1). The handwriting is of the mature
Mendelssohn, though the manuscript offers no specific clues that
might lead to a definitive dating. On the first page appears the heading "Sonata," and, beneath it, the tempo designation "Allegro con fu-
oco." In the upper right-hand corner Mendelssohn has inscribed the
initials "L.e.g.G.," an abbreviation for "Lass es gelingen, Gott," one of
two invocations typically encountered in his first drafts. "L.e.g.G."
[Let it succeed, O Lord] tends to appear most often in the composer's
autographs from the 1820s, the student period; the other abbreviation, "H.D.m.," for "Hilf Du mir" [Help me, O Lord], tends to appear
in the manuscripts of the 1830s and 1840s. Still, these proclivities
alone are not sufficient to assign the fragment to, say, the early Berlin
or Leipzig periods. An early version of the *Hebrides* Overture (1830),
for example, bears the heading "L.e.g.G.," as does a draft of the lied
"Im Frühling" (1841);[28] so the appearance of the heading on the sonata fragment must be viewed as inconclusive evidence for the purposes of dating. The paper of the bifolio (sixteen staves, no water-
mark) is of a type commonly used by Mendelssohn during the
Leipzig period; but in the absence of an exhaustive study of Mendelssohn's paper types, the paper, too, yields no definitive clues that
might assist an attempt at dating.[29]
　To achieve a tentative dating we must turn to stylistic evidence
within the music; and it is this evidence, as we shall see, that may
ultimately explain why Mendelssohn abandoned the piano sonata.
Examples 1a and 1b give the main material for the first and second
thematic groups; example 2 offers a reduction of the tonal plan and
a summary of the sonata-form exposition of the fragment.
　The formal design of the fragment is clear enough: two thematic

Figure 1. Mendelssohn, Piano Sonata in G Major, Autograph (Oxford, Bodleian Library, M. Deneke Mendelssohn Collection b. 5, fol. 124r, mm. 1–21)

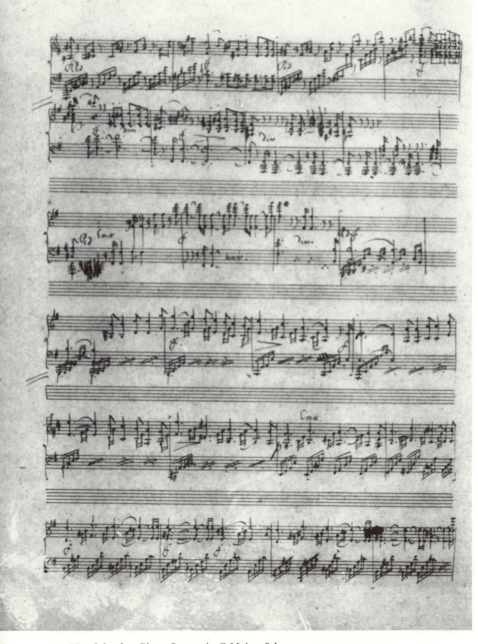

Figure 1, cont. Mendelssohn, Piano Sonata in G Major, fol. 124v, measures 22–45

125

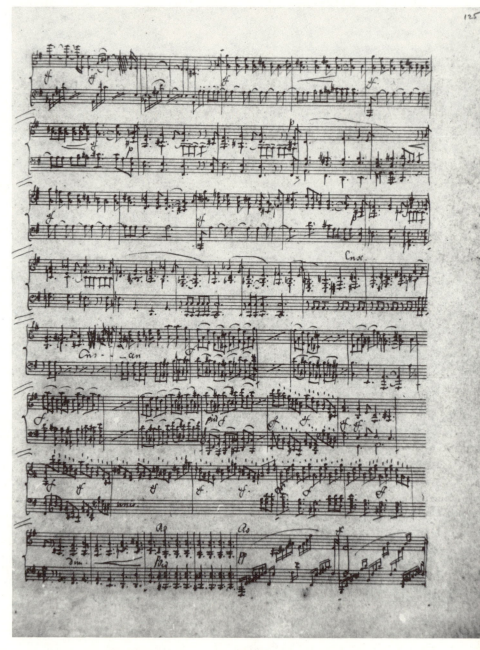

Figure 1, cont. Mendelssohn, Piano Sonata in G Major, fol. 125r, measures 46–89

Figure 1, cont. Mendelssohn, Piano Sonata in G Major, fol. 125v, measures 90–97

Example 1a. Mendelssohn, Piano Sonata in G Major, First Theme

Example 1a, cont.

Example 1b. Mendelssohn, Piano Sonata in G Major, Bridge and Second Theme

Example 1b, cont.

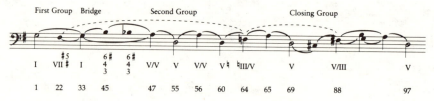

Example 2. Mendelssohn, Piano Sonata in G Major, Tonal Plan

groups in the tonic and dominant, G major and D major, linked by a modulating bridge and followed by a confirming closing section in the dominant. The first theme, rising in triadic fashion from the third scale degree (B–D–G), is accompanied by rolled arpeggiations in the bass register (G–B–D–G); we have here an example of a theme cut from the same cloth as its accompaniment.[30] Mendelssohn designs the theme as a balanced antecedent-consequent period. Questionlike, the first phrase moves from the tonic to ii $^6_5$; as if to answer, the following phrase tightens the ii $^6_5$ as a secondary dominant and then closes with a dominant seventh, returning us to the tonic. The theme and arpeggiated texture are extended for several measures, and the tonic is reaffirmed in measure 15. In the next measure, Mendelssohn introduces a contrasting texture: staccato, eighth-note chords now begin to interrupt the rolled, pedaled sonorities of the first theme. These chords then give way to a return of the opening material, transposed, however, to F♯ major, the leading-tone harmony (m. 22). Within a few measures, Mendelssohn establishes a pedal point on F♯; G-major chords appear above as the Neapolitan of F♯, or ♭II/VII (a subtle reversal of their primary role as the tonic); then, Mendelssohn reduces the texture to bare octaves on F♯.

The bridge commences by returning us momentarily to the opening theme in the tonic (m. 33). Through a series of chromatic inflections the secondary dominant, A major, is reached, in preparation for the second thematic group in the dominant. To attain V/V, Mendelssohn touches on a second-inversion E-major seventh chord (B–D–E–G♯). This is redefined, and emphasized by a sforzando, as a French augmented-sixth chord (spelled B♭–D–E–G♯).

The ensuing second theme (m. 48, see example lb) describes a descending stepwise line in trochaic rhythms above a syncopated pedal point on the secondary dominant A; a cadence on the dominant D major follows in measure 55. Mendelssohn then repeats the second theme, but in the minor mode. What is more, the expected parallel cadence in D minor is rejected in favor of a move to F major (mm. 60–64). In the local context, F major is the lowered mediant of the dominant D major. In the context of the whole fragment, however, it serves as a redefinition of F♯ major, the leading-tone harmony that figured prominently in the first group. In measure 65 the F-major passage gives way to a pedal-point passage on the secondary dominant, A major. The closing passage then commences in measure 69 by reasserting the dominant D major in a brilliant octave passage. In the final measures, Mendelssohn brings back the opening rolled texture of the movement, but now marked pianissimo, and once again in F♯ major. No longer the leading-tone harmony to G major, F♯ now serves as dominant of B minor (V/iii), and as mediant of the dominant (III/V). The reference to the opening theme and its sonorous texture brings us full circle; the fragment ends with a sforzando octave on the dominant D, with no clues as to the nature or course of the development.

Why did Mendelssohn abandon the piano sonata? Stylistic evidence suggests that the cause may have been his dissatisfaction with the opening theme. First of all, the $\frac{12}{8}$ meter, a meter not too frequently encountered in Mendelssohn,[31] proved a problematic choice. In the second and eighth measures (see figure 1) Mendelssohn misruled the barring by entering a line midway through the measure, as if to suggest his ambivalence about the $\frac{12}{8}$ versus a $\frac{6}{8}$ meter. In measure 2, the rebarring would have enabled the theme to begin with a strong downbeat. As the theme stands in $\frac{12}{8}$, it commences in the middle of the measure; and as a result, the consequent phrase is forced to enter on a downbeat (m. 5). Arguably a rebarring in $\frac{6}{8}$ would have resolved the inherent metrical ambiguity of the theme.

In 1843, Mendelssohn did publish a sonata whose first movement, marked *Allegro assai vivace*, is barred in $\frac{6}{8}$ time. More striking, the opening theme of this work—the Cello Sonata in D major, op. 58—bears significant similarities to the opening theme of the G-major piano sonata fragment. As examples 3a and 3b reveal, the cello sonata commences with a triadic theme that rises from the third scale degree, F♯; in the third and fourth measures, the triadic motion is completed by the arrival of the theme on the F♯ an octave above; this then moves by stepwise descent to an E, scale degree 2. In summary, underlying the robust cello theme is the simple melodic motion, $\hat{3}$–$\hat{2}$. Little analytical probing is required to demonstrate that a similar motion underlies the theme of the piano sonata. Scale degree $\hat{3}$, B, is established at the beginning, and the antecedent phrase closes on scale degree $\hat{2}$, A. Indeed, the initial outline of the theme, a triadic ascent from $\hat{3}$ followed by a stepwise descent (B–D–G–F♯–E–D–C–B), resembles closely the contours of the cello theme (F♯–A–D–C♯–B–A). Whereas the stepwise descent extends for an entire measure in the piano theme, that descent is considerably compressed in the cello theme (essentially one measure of $\frac{6}{8}$ time versus one measure of $\frac{12}{8}$ time).

In short, our comparison of the two themes argues for the cello theme as an improved reworking of the piano theme. Put another way, one would be hard pressed to imagine Mendelssohn beginning work on the piano sonata *after* the completion of the cello sonata; the

a) opening measures

b) reduction

Example 3. Mendelssohn, Cello Sonata in D Major, Op. 58

initial similarity between the two themes is simply too strong. If our interpretation is correct, then the cello sonata could serve as a *terminus ante quem* for the dating of the piano sonata fragment. In November 1842 Mendelssohn announced the composition of the cello sonata in a series of letters to Karl Klingemann, Ignaz Moscheles, and his mother Lea Mendelssohn Bartholdy;[32] the work was published by F. Kistner in July 1843.[33]

The first theme of the piano sonata fragment yields another comparison with a datable Mendelssohn work, and this second comparison may enable us to push back the *terminus ante quem* from 1842 or 1843 to 1841. The concluding, cadential phrase of the theme (mm. 13–15, see example 1) is strikingly similar to the concluding phrase of the second theme from the posthumous *Allegro brillant* for piano duet, op. 92 (mm. 92–95, example 4), a work that Mendelssohn dated on 23 March 1841.[34] Not only are the melodic contours especially close, but the two themes appear in G major and share similar harmonic accompaniments. (The common, slurred two-note figure in mm. 15 and 95, B–D, is one more link between the two passages.) Though we cannot know for certain, Mendelssohn probably borrowed the cadential phrase from the piano sonata for the *Allegro brillant*, a work that he at least finished and performed, even if he left it unpublished. Again, there would be little sense to Mendelssohn's beginning work on the sonata *after* the *Allegro brillant*—that is, borrowing the cadential phrase from op. 92—unless, of course, he intended to reject the *Allegro brillant* completely. If our assumption is correct, then the piano sonata fragment would predate March 1841.

The question of a *terminus post quem* for the fragment is less easily addressed. In this case, we must rely on stylistic evidence of a different kind, namely, on any unusual stylistic features that might suggest an external musical influence on Mendelssohn's creative mind. One passage in particular stands out in this regard: the close of the bridge leading to the second theme, in which Mendelssohn momentarily focuses on a French augmented-sixth chord (example 1b, mm. 43–47). The chord occurs twice as passing sonorities on weak beats (mm. 43, 45); then, in measures 46 and 47, the chord appears more emphatically on the downbeat. The particular stressing of the chord, and its paired presentation in measures 46 and 47, points compellingly to Schubert as a possible stylistic source for the passage. In Schubert's enriched harmonic vocabulary, augmented-sixth chords are featured prominently—and they often occur in his music in pairings.

According to conventional wisdom Mendelssohn was introduced to Schubert's music by Robert Schumann, who, upon visiting Ferdinand

Example 4. Mendelssohn, *Allegro brillant*, Op. 92, measures 88–95

Schubert in Vienna in 1839, discovered several unpublished works, among them the "Great" C-major Symphony (D. 944), which was sent to Leipzig and premièred by Mendelssohn at the Gewandhaus on March 21, 1839.[35] The year 1839 is thus rightfully viewed as a critical year for the posthumous reception of Schubert's music outside Austria. Without minimizing Schumann's role in disseminating Schubert's music, we should point out that Schubert's music was not completely unknown to Mendelssohn before Schumann's Viennese sojourn. As early as November 13, 1827, Mendelssohn accompanied the singer Carl Adam Bader in a performance of the *Erlkönig* in Berlin. But conservative Berlin tastes still inclined toward the simpler strophic settings of J. F. Reichardt and of Mendelssohn's teacher, Carl Friedrich Zelter. Despite the forceful performance, a reviewer submitted a report to the *Allgemeine musikalische Zeitung* that Schubert's *Erlkönig*, "although filled with modulations and bizarre turns, did not attain the level of Reichardt's or Zelter's settings."[36] Of course, it was Zelter who had recommended to Goethe in 1816 that he return unopened to Schubert a parcel of songs the composer had sent to him, a collection, devoted to Goethe's poetry, that included the *Erlkönig*.[37]

How much of Schubert's other music Mendelssohn knew before Schumann's trip to Vienna in 1839 is not clear; references to the composer in Mendelssohn's letters before 1839 do not appear in the standard sources.[38] But the arrival of the "Great" C-major Symphony early in 1839 no doubt turned Mendelssohn's attention to the cause of Schubert's music. What is more, as Peter Krause has recently emphasized, Mendelssohn himself was involved in the selection of the symphony for performance. We now know that, encouraged by Schumann, Ferdinand Schubert sent Mendelssohn on January 31, 1839 not only the "Great" C-major Symphony but also the "Little" C-major Symphony (D. 589); from these two, Mendelssohn selected D. 944.[39] Moreover, around this time, Mendelssohn received a copy of another Schubert work, the Piano Sonata in A minor, D. 784, about to be published by A. Diabelli with an honorary dedication to Mendelssohn as Schubert's op. 143.[40]

In the early months of 1839, then, Mendelssohn had the opportunity to study in detail at least three works of Schubert: D. 589, 784, and 944. And he could easily have known Robert Schumann's 1835 and 1838 reviews in the *Neue Zeitschrift für Musik* of Schubert's other piano music (including the sonatas D. 845, 850, 894, and 958–60).[41] Could Mendelssohn's knowledge of all these Schubert works have influenced the harmonic language and style of his G-major sonata fragment? Can we tentatively assign the early part of 1839 as a *terminus post quem* for the Oxford manuscript?

The most compelling evidence to support this thesis is that D. 589, 784, and 944 all contain passages with conspicuous presentations of reiterated augmented-sixth sonorities (see examples 5a, 5b, 5c, and 5d). In the first movement of D. 589, repetitions of a German sixth chord are employed to prepare the secondary dominant D major just before the entrance of the second theme; in the scherzo of the symphony, a similar progression occurs. In the finale of D. 784, pairings of Italian-sixth chords support a sequential passage. And, in one dramatic passage from the slow movement of D. 944, augmented-sixth

Example 5a. Schubert, Symphony in C Major, D. 589, First Movement

Example 5b. Schubert, Symphony in C Major, D. 589, Scherzo

chords in the winds are juxtaposed with bare octaves for the full orchestra.

Many additional examples of the paired augmented sixths could be adduced from Schubert's other works, though at least two in particular seem especially pertinent (example 6). The slow introduction to the overture of *Die Zauberharfe* (D. 644, formerly known as the *Rosamunde* Overture) concludes with a passage remarkably similar to the Mendelssohn: in an upper voice a pedal point is sustained in dotted rhythms against a bass line that oscillates between the dominant and the half step above. But even closer to Mendelssohn's passage is the

Example 5c. Schubert, Piano Sonata in A Minor, D. 784, Finale

Example 5d. Schubert, Symphony in C Major ("Great"), D. 944, Andante

conclusion of the development in the first movement of Schubert's Piano Sonata in G major, D. 894. Here the similarities are almost too striking to pass as coincidence. The two passages have the soprano pedal point, but now employ the exact same rhythmic values; the two have similar spacings of the augmented sonorites; and the two have the same essential bass, in this case, oscillating by descending step. Other comparisons suggest again that Mendelssohn may have known D. 894. Of course, the Schubert movement, like the Mendelssohn fragment, is in $\frac{12}{8}$ meter. Furthermore, Mendelssohn's turn to F♯ and his treatment of it as a pedal point may have been foreshadowed by

Example 6a. Schubert, Overture to *Die Zauberharfe*, D. 644

Example 6b. Schubert, Piano Sonata in G Major, D. 894, First Movement

Schubert's exquisite, extended pedal point on F♯ near the beginning of D. 894 (mm. 10–15).

We cannot determine the circumstances of when, and indeed if, Mendelssohn came to know D. 894. Be that as it may, the stylistic evidence suggests that Mendelssohn's assimilation of Schubert's style left its mark on the sonata fragment. And, because Mendelssohn's most concentrated period of studying Schubert's music occurred early in 1839, we may tentatively choose that year as a *terminus post quem* for the fragment, and provisionally suggest 1839–1841 as its date.

The influence of Schubert may explain one other feature of the Oxford fragment—namely, its expanded tonal compass. Of course, the middle ground motion from I to VII in the first thematic group, which we compared earlier to the opening of Schubert's D. 894, has some precedent in Beethoven, who used the device in such works as the first movements of the Piano Sonata, op. 31, no. 1 and the *Wald-stein* Sonata, op. 53 (though in each case the motion was from the tonic to the *lowered* leading tone, I–♭VII). But the treatment of the second thematic group, with its modal mixture of statements on the dominant major and minor, and its play on the mediant relationship between D major and F major (redefined in the closing group as D major and F♯ major) could be Schubertian in origin. A similar sort of expanded key relationships obtain in the second group of the first movement of D. 944.

The issue of Schubert's influence may help to explain why Mendelssohn had difficulty in completing the sonata movement. Indeed, the case of another instrumental composition Mendelssohn abandoned would seem to offer corroborating. evidence. In 1844 and 1845, the composer worked periodically on a symphony in C major, which, had he completed it, would have been his final symphony.[42] He drafted several pages in full score and left sketches for the exposition and opening of the development, and a few ideas for a slow movement, but then jettisoned the project. Here, as in the piano sonata movement, Mendelssohn approached and attempted to assimilate elements of Schubert's style; in this case, D. 944 looms large as a clear influence. A plausible argument is that Mendelssohn was not yet able to encompass into his style Schubert's "heavenly length," as Schumann had described it in his celebrated review of 1839.[43] And perhaps Mendelssohn was not yet prepared to come to terms with the implications of Schubert's expanded tonal practice (for example, in the first movement of D. 944 the modal substitutions of major and minor, and the play on raised and lowered mediant and submediant relationships as an extension of the traditional tonic-dominant axis).

But Mendelssohn was, after all, in good company. On 22 March 1845—just as he was laboring over his C-major Symphony—he acknowledged receipt of a special gift from Ferdinand Schubert, the sketches for Franz Schubert's unfinished Symphony in E major, D. 729:

Dear Herr Professor!

Yesterday I received from Dr. Härtel the sketches for your brother's symphony, of which you have made me a present. What joy you have given me through such a lovely, worthy gift, what hearty thanks I owe you for this remembrance of the deceased master, how I am honored that you would choose for me such a significant, even if unfinished, work from his estate—all of this you can of course say to yourself, though I am still obliged, if only with a few words, to express my gratitude for your gift! Believe me, I know how to value the full worth of this splendid present, that you could not have given it to anyone else to whom it would have brought a greater joy, who would be more sincerely thankful for it! It is as though I have gotten to know your brother more closely and reliably through the incompletion of the work, through its unfinished comments scattered here and there, than would have been the case through any of his finished compositions. For me it is as if I have seen him working in his study, and this joy I owe only to your unexpected generosity and friendship. Let me hope for an opportunity to meet you, whether in Vienna or these parts, and to make your acquaintance personally, and then to reiterate to you personally again all of my thanks.[44]

Mendelssohn's letter reads not only as an appreciation of Schubert's unfinished work but also as a testament to the faith he maintained in the ultimate mystery of the compositional process.

NOTES

1. In a review of the Piano Trio in D minor, op. 49. *Neue Zeitschrift für Musik* 13 (1840): 198.

2. Schumann's memoirs were first published in 1947 as *Erinnerungen an Felix Mendelssohn Bartholdy*, ed. G. Eismann (Zwickau). A revised, corrected transcription of the document has recently appeared in Robert Schumann, "Aufzeichnungen über Mendelssohn," in *Felix Mendelssohn Bartholdy*, ed H.-K. Metzger and R. Riehn (Munich, 1980). The passages cited here are from p. 106.

3. Elizabeth Sheppard, *Charles Auchester* (London, 1853); Elise Polko, *Erinnerungen an Felix Mendelssohn-Bartholdy: Ein Künstler- und Menschenleben* (Leipzig, 1868; London, 1869). Concerning *Charles Auchester* see E. D. Mackerness, "Music and Moral Purity in the Early Victorian Era," in *Canadian Music Journal* 4/2 (1960–61): 14–24.

4. [Richard Wagner], "Das Judenthum in der Musik," in *NZfM* 33 (1850): 101–7, 109–12.

5. Friedrich Niecks, "On Mendelssohn and Some of His Contemporary Critics," in *Monthly Musical Record* 5 (1875): 163. See also pp. 382–89.

6. Schumann, "Aufzeichnungen," pp. 102–3.

7. See A. Kurzals-Reuter, *Die Oratorien Felix Mendelssohn Bartholdys: Untersuchungen zur Quellenlage, Entstehung, Gestaltung und Überlieferung* (Tutzing, 1978), pp. 115–41.

8. See Douglass Seaton, "A Study of a Collection of Mendelssohn's Autograph Sketches and Other Autograph Material, Deutsche Staatsbibliothek Berlin 'Mus. Ms. Autogr. Mendelssohn 19'" (Ph.D. dissertation, Columbia University, 1977), pp. 136–79.

9. Letter of 14 July 1839 to F. Kistner, in *Felix Mendelssohn Bartholdy, Briefe an deutsche Verleger*, ed. R. Elvers (Berlin, 1968), p. 309. See also the "Vorwort" to my edition of Psalm 95, op. 46 (Stuttgart, Carus-Verlag, 1990).

10. See Douglass Seaton, "The Romantic Mendelssohn: the Composition of *Die erste Walpurgisnacht*," in *Musical Quarterly* 68 (1982): 398–410.

11. Alternate versions of op. 30, no. 4; op. 85, no. 6; and op. 102, no. 2 are included in Rudolf Elvers's edition of the *Lieder ohne Worte* (Munich, 1981). See also Christa Jost, *Mendelssohns Lieder ohne Worte* (Tutzing, 1988), and R. Larry Todd, "Piano Music Reformed: The Case of Felix Mendelssohn Bartholdy," in *Nineteenth-Century Piano Music*, ed. R. L. Todd (New York, 1990), pp. 196–98.

12. See "Piano Music Reformed," p. 200.

13. See my forthcoming "Mendelssohn as Contrapuntist: the Preludes and Fugues Op. 35 Reconsidered."

14. See the facsimile of the autograph now in the Library of Congress. *Octet for Strings, Op. 20*, ed. J. Newsom (Washington, D.C., 1976).

15. See R. L. Todd, "The Instrumental Music of Felix Mendelssohn-Bartholdy: Selected Studies Based on Primary Sources" (Ph.D. dissertation, Yale University, 1979), pp. 307–22.

16. See Friedhelm Krummacher, "Mendelssohn's Late Chamber Music: Some Autograph Sources Recovered," in *Mendelssohn and Schumann: Essays on Their Music and Its Context*, ed. J. W. Finson and R. L. Todd (Durham, 1984), pp. 76–80.

17. See Douglass Seaton, "Study," pp. 180–210, and the preface to his new edition of the *Lobgesang* (Stuttgart, 1990).

18. See D. Seaton, "A Draft for the Exposition of the First Movement of Mendelssohn's 'Scotch' Symphony," in *Journal of the American Musicological Society* 30 (1977): 129–35.

19. See the forthcoming study by J. Michael Cooper, "The Unfinished *Italian* Symphony Reconsidered."

20. On the history of this work, see Judith Silber Ballan, "Mendelssohn and the *Reformation* Symphony: A Critical and Historical Study" (Ph.D. dissertation, Yale University, 1987), pp. 205–18.

21. For Marx's account, see pp. 216–17. For a discussion of the rejected draft, see Todd, "Instrumental Music," pp. 417–27.

22. See my "Of Sea Gulls and Counterpoint: The Early Versions of Mendelssohn's *Hebrides* Overture," in *19th-Century Music* 2 (1979): 197ff.

23. See my "Mendelssohn's Ossianic Manner, with a New Source—*On Lena's Gloomy Heath*," in *Mendelssohn and Schumann*, pp. 137–49.

24. See pp. 187–205.

25. Johann Peter Eckermann, *Gespräche mit Goethe* (Wiesbaden, 1835).

26. Lobe, see p. 192.

27. See my "An Unfinished Piano Concerto by Mendelssohn," in *Musical Quarterly* 68 (1982): 80–101.

28. The autograph of *Die Hebriden* is in the Pierpont Morgan Library in

New York; a facsimile, edited by Hugo von Mendelssohn Bartholdy, one of the former owners, was published in Basel in 1947. The autograph of "Im Frühling," dated 20 April 1841, is in Band 35 of the *Mendelssohn Nachlass*, preserved in the Biblioteka Jagiellońska, Kraków.

29. Professor Douglass Seaton of Florida State University has begun an investigation of Mendelssohn's paper types.

30. Other examples of this type of derivation include the *Lied ohne Worte* in E major, op. 38, no. 3 and the Prelude in B minor, op. 104a, no. 2.

31. Some examples include the *Lieder ohne Worte*, op. 38, nos. 1 and 5, op. 53, no. 1, and op. 62, no. 2; the Prelude in B minor, op. 35, no. 3; the Organ Fugue in C minor, op. 37, no. 1; the Capriccio for String Quartet, op. 81, no. 3; and the finale of the String Quartet in D major, op. 44, no. 1.

32. 18 November 1842 to Ignaz Moscheles in *Letters of Felix Mendelssohn to Ignaz and Charlotte Moscheles*, trans. Felix Moscheles (Boston, 1888), p. 234; 23 November 1842 to Karl Klingemann in K. Klingemann, ed., *Felix Mendelssohn Bartholdys Briefwechsel mit Legationsrat Karl Klingemann in London* (Essen, 1909), p. 276; and 28 November 1842 to Lea Mendelssohn Bartholdy, New York Public Library.

33. In a letter of 17 June 1839 to Kistner, Mendelssohn referred to a new "Violinsonate," which Rudolf Elvers has assumed was the Cello Sonata, op. 58 (*Briefe*, pp. 308 and 309 n. 4). Conceivably, Mendelssohn could have meant the Violin Sonata in F major, drafted on 15 June 1838.

34. Paris, Bibliothèque Nationale, Conservatoire Ms. 208.

35. See O. E. Deutsch, "The Discovery of Schubert's Great C-major Symphony: A Story in Fifteen Letters," in *Musical Quarterly* 38 (1952): 528–32.

36. *Allegemeine musikalische Zeitung* 30 (1828): col. 42.

37. For details concerning the organization of Schubert's volume, see Walther Dürr, "Aus Schubert's ersten Publikationsplan: zwei Hefte mit Liedern von Goethe," in *Schubert-Studien*, ed. F. Grasberger and O. Wessely (Vienna, 1978), pp. 43–56.

38. And, what is more, Schubert evidently did not figure prominently in Mendelssohn's own library and does not appear in the list of *Musikalien* the composer prepared in 1844. See Peter Ward Jones, ed., *Catalogue of the Mendelssohn Papers in the Bodleian Library, Oxford, Vol. III* (Tutzing, 1989), pp. 285ff.

39. See Peter Krause, "Unbekannte Dokumente zur Uraufführung von Franz Schuberts großer C-Dur-Sinfonie durch Felix Mendelssohn Bartholdy," in *Beiträge zur Musikwissenschaft* 29 (1987): 240–50.

40. Diabelli's letter of dedication to Mendelssohn, dated 14 January 1839, is in the Green Books Collection at the Bodleian Library, Oxford (vol. 9, no. 22). The presentation copy of the sonata is in the Mendelssohn-Archiv, Staatsbibliothek Preussischer Kulturbesitz, Berlin. See *Catalogue of the Mendelssohn Papers in the Bodleian Library, Oxford, Vol. III*, p. 300.

41. See Leon Plantinga, *Schumann as Critic* (New Haven, 1967), pp. 219–24.

42. See my "An Unfinished Symphony by Mendelssohn," in *Music and Letters* 61 (1980): 293–309.

43. *NZfM* 12 (1840): 81–83.

44. "Briefe Felix Mendelssohn-Bartholdy's an Herrn Professor Ferdinand Schubert in Wien," in *Wiener allgemeine Musik-Zeitung* 8/4 (1848): 13–14.

PART

· II ·

MEMOIRS

Conversations with Felix Mendelssohn

JOHANN CHRISTIAN LOBE

TRANSLATED BY SUSAN GILLESPIE

Johann Christian Lobe (1797–1881) was born in Weimar, where he played in the court orchestra, composed operas, and befriended Goethe, at whose home he first met Mendelssohn, in November 1821. On that occasion Lobe participated in a performance of one of the young composer's piano quartets, presented in the company of Goethe and Carl Friedrich Zelter (see *Die Gartenlaube* 1 [1867]: 4–8). In 1842 Lobe arrived in Leipzig; from 1846 to 1848 he served as the editor of the *Allgemeine musikalische Zeitung*.

The conversations with Mendelssohn that Lobe recorded in his diary presumably occurred between 1842 and 1847—but in any event after 1838, the year in which Ferdinand Ries's *Biographische Notizen über Ludwig van Beethoven*, a work to which Lobe likely refers (see note 15), appeared. Lobe patterned his essay after Eckermann's celebrated *Gespräche mit Goethe*, as the quotations at the beginning suggest. [ed.]

[Source: *Fliegende Blätter für die Musik* 1, no. 5 (1855): 280–96.]

•

This collection of discussions and conversations with Goethe came about mostly as a result of my innate need to take possession of whatever experiences appear noteworthy to me by setting them down in written form.[1]

In both cases a reflection takes place, and it is extremely rare that in the process of passing through another individual nothing original is lost and nothing foreign is added.[2]

ECKERMANN, *Conversations with Goethe*

I have never had a particularly good memory. Whatever I found worth retaining of what I read, heard, or thought, I have had to write down as quickly as possible in my diary, and since I had a lot to write down, I had to do it in the fewest possible words. I regret this brevity especially since I pulled out the notes on my conversations with Mendelssohn, in order to share something of them. I can retrieve the main content, but not the particular expression. The deceased, however, not only thought very clearly, but also had the gift of expressing himself with precision, and he often knew how to hit the nail on the head with a quick tap. Therefore, the reader will hear Mendelssohn's thought not in his, but unfortunately only in my words. I do not know whether there is anyone who can boast of having had long conversations with Mendelssohn. So far as I knew him, they were not his cup of tea. Men of small knowledge and fine-sounding words tried in vain to draw him into conversation. He eluded them with a remark, or, if they attempted to hold him against his will, broke off curtly. Many an unsympathetic judgment about his works may have flowed from just such conversations rebuffed. People declared that he was proud and took their revenge in journalistic attacks.

I have always preferred to talk about our art with practicing musicians. Mere philosophers of art, even if they are the cleverest thinkers, can say nothing about many aspects of art, because they simply do not know them, or at least have not experienced them personally. No one doubts that Mendelssohn analyzed his art quite penetratingly from all sides. That was evident in every statement he made on the subject. But he usually tossed off the results of his analysis without deigning to give any particular reasoning. In Leipzig they wanted to give him responsibility, in addition to his direction of the Gewandhaus concerts, for lectures on music at the University. He turned them down. He said he was not confident that he had the necessary ability. That was not his real conviction. He knew very well that he was perfectly capable of doing this, too. But he lacked the inclination for it. He preferred composing to lecturing. At any rate, I flatter myself that I am among the people with whom he was not unwilling to engage in conversations about art. What I am about to communicate from these conversations is admittedly not strictly in the form they actually took. What appears here in unbroken succession I often had to glean, in fact, from widely separated moments of conversation.

On a walk our conversation once turned to the "school" and the disdain with which people were now (then) beginning to inveigh against it, as a drag on genius.

"This opinion," he exclaimed, "is an insult to both reason and experience! What concept do such people attach to the word 'school'? If someone has the greatest musical genius—can he compose without knowledge of chords and the rules governing their relationships?

Can he form a piece of music without having studied the laws of musical form? Can he orchestrate without knowing the instruments, without having had a hundredfold the experience of their inexhaustible combinations? And is all of this not schooling?"

"Perhaps," I interrupted, "what is meant by the limiting effect of schooling is not the technical things you mention, but rather the aesthetic blathering that brings the musician no practical advancement, but only confuses him with its contradictory demands and paralyzes his creative ability."

"No, no!" he continued. "This technical schooling *is* what they mean. I could list the names of people who later went looking for the thing they had just been despising, after they realized that they had only produced foolishness with their genius.

"And from an aesthetic point of view, too—can someone create something beautiful without consciousness of what is *done* in music? Why do I *change* a certain passage? Because it does not *please* me. Why does it not please me? Because it goes against some aesthetic rule or other that I have learned by studying the models. If I do not know this rule, then I do not recognize its absence and think the passage is good. Name me a single genuine, great master, not just in music, but in any other art, who did not undergo the most thorough schooling in technical and aesthetic matters. If we find weaknesses in an important artist, and there are such examples, what do we say? He is lacking *technique*, or he is lacking a firm artistic *insight*; in a word, he is lacking *schooling*. No painter, sculptor, or architect would ever think of looking at school as an obstacle, a drag on genius. Why does this absurd idea occur to so many musicians?"

"But you must admit," I objected, "that many artists who have their schooling completely under control do not create any significant works, while there are artists lacking schooling who accomplish important things."

"Well," he replied, "school cannot make talent; and if you do not have any, it will not help you. But that one can make anything sensible without schooling is something you will have to prove to me. I do not know of any examples. Someone can show talent without schooling, but so far as creating a genuine work of art, he should forget about it. Too bad, we say, that this artist has studied so little, or has so little true artistic insight. How much more important his works would have become *if he had learned more*. And such talents, who have never matured on account of their lack of study, have invented that sentence as consolation for their own inner accusations, and other lazybones have adopted it."

I

On another occasion I tried to obtain clarification on a point that was very important to me.

"I am told," I said, "that in your compositions you make many changes, often right up until the moment when you hand in the manuscript. Unfortunately, it is the same with me, and much worse; for I could not name a single one of my works in which I have not found deficiencies to complain about after it was printed, passages that now come to me more clearly, but that can no longer be banished."

Mendelssohn had two main ways of smiling. One was the incomparably lovely smile that played about his face when he had a satisfied, cheerful thought; the other contained a slight sarcastic admixture on occasions when he had something to criticize, without its seeming severe enough to make him feel bitter. The latter occurred very seldom with him in any case—or else, as a finely cultivated man of the world, he had learned to suppress it.

"The misfortune you complain about happens to me, too," he said. "In everything I have written down there is at least as much deleted as there is allowed to stand. We should take comfort from the greatest masters, who suffered no better fate. Ah, if it were only weak passages that the imagination, that wily dissembler, smuggled past an intoxicated judgment onto paper! She plays worse tricks than that on me! Sometimes she seduces me into writing an entire work that I later have to recognize is a piece of shoddy merchandise! Among twelve songs that I put together, I considered only six worthy of print, and threw out the other six.[3] My *St. Paul* originally had a third more numbers,[4] which never saw the light of day. What do you say to that?" he asked, smiling sarcastically.

"That in all probability you are too strict with your own works," I responded. "Many people would consider themselves fortunate if they had written and could publish what you throw away."

"Much obliged for your favorable opinion," he said with a laugh, "but not conceded. I can give you another good reason for the suppression of many of my compositions, which will make more sense to you. I am, namely, of the opinion *nulla dies sine linea.*[5] I never let a day pass without having done something. But what artist enjoys the muse's favor every day? Not I, but at any rate I can always produce *something*, and that is what I do *in order to stay in shape*. The same way a virtuoso loses skill and confidence if he leaves his instrument behind for any significant length of time, so do mental operations also lose their agility and freedom if certain exercises are often neglected. In order to stay on my toes, I always compose, but the spirit is not always willing. You should not think, by the way, as might appear by my comments, that I am satisfied with everything I have had printed. That is not the case. Quite a few things have slipped by that give me little pleasure and that I immediately realized are nothing special."

"Excepting such cases," I said, "why did you do it, since pecuniary considerations could not have been the cause? I have always thought the most lamentable fate for an artist was to have to create in order to earn his daily bread."

"There are other reasons for the artist who sees the world as it is," he remarked.

"I am curious to hear them," I said.

"The world *forgets very easily*," he remarked, "and the artist, once he has appeared in public, must try to forestall that forgetfulness through continuous publication of new works. He must not be absent from any fair catalog. In each one, his name must come before the eyes of the public, for it often takes a long time before the public responds to something. There are more and more composers. Disappear from the music catalogs for a few years, and you are lost, because forgotten."

"That may be true," I said, "and the public may not be entirely in the wrong. When someone allows a long pause to intervene before something else of his appears, then one assumes that his productive drive and creativity cannot be very strong and abundant."

"So it is," said Mendelssohn. "And since not every work the artist creates succeeds, and since he must always demonstrate that he is productive, he can and must let a weak performance get out from time to time along with the others, just to hold his place. If the thing is nothing special, he has nevertheless shown himself to be a vigorous worker, and so one hopes he will produce something better the next time. You can forgive someone you are interested in if he has a bad mood or is dry, but you will become indifferent to him if he comes too seldom, and finally you will not care about him at all, if he stays away entirely."

II

"How is it," he asked me once, "that you have fallen silent as a composer?[6] I have the impression that you have not published anything for several years now? That is a great mistake, as I have said to you previously. Your productivity can hardly have run out already?"

"The productivity perhaps not," I responded, "but the desire to produce. A single comment from a critical journal has frightened me off from composing, I believe forever, since unfortunately it seemed to me to be correct."

"Good gracious, what kind of a comment can that have been?" he asked with a smile.

" 'He has talent, *but he will not break any new ground.*' "

"Hmmm!" he said, "that frightened you off?"

"Indeed," I replied, "I found that everything I had done not only failed to surpass the best that was already in existence, but did not even come close to it. Now I really tried to improve. I resolved to be exceedingly original, from the first thought to the last, and to write more beautifully than could ever be expected. But my imagination did not bring forth what I desired. It did not show me a single thought that satisfied my demands, that would have made me appear as a traveler down a new path, so the pen finally dropped from my hand and I became resigned."

"Yes, yes," he said, "I know how that is. When you first start a composition you have a lofty idea of what you can and will create this time! The ideas for which you search always appear more beautiful in their vague presentiment than they are later on paper. I have experienced similar things, but I soon got a grip on myself. If we only wanted to accept the ideas that agreed *perfectly* with our desires, then we would accomplish nothing at all, or at most very little. For this reason I, too, have sometimes left works I had started unfinished and not completed them."

"That means nothing," I commented. "All artists have left torsos behind, as a result of the realization that they have blundered."

"That may be," he replied. "Such an unfinished work makes me extremely discomfited and hesitant to start another. I regret the time I have wasted on it. So I called a halt and swore that I would not stop working on any work I had begun, but would finish every one, no matter how it turns out. If it does not become a work of art in the highest sense, at least it is an exercise in forming and portraying ideas. Here you have the reason why I have made so many compositions that have not been published and never will be published."

"Well," I said, "as for compositions of your last type, I could produce a great many more of them; the ones that would appear to me as successful, as breaking new ground, would not be among them. And then, not everyone can work like you do, without asking whether or not the work will bring anything in. People like me, on whose pen, for the most part, the existence of their family depends, commit a sin when they make a mark without the hope of being paid for it. It is commendable to sacrifice oneself as an artist, but it is bad to make a family suffer for it."

"Granted, completely," Mendelssohn burst out, "*if* the renunciation of artistic destiny comes from a well-founded recognition of one's insufficient talent. But *your* reason for not wanting to write any more, because you do not hope to break any new ground, is—if you will pardon me—not reasonable. What does this phrase mean, actually? To clear a path that no one has walked before you? But first this new path would have to lead to much more beautiful, more charming territory. For just clearing a new path can be done by anyone who knows how to wield a shovel and move his legs. In every nobler sense, however, I deny forthwith that there are new paths to be cleared, for there are no more new artistic territories. All of them have long since been discovered. New ground! Vexatious demon for every artist who submits to it! Never, in fact, did an artist break new ground. In the best case he did things imperceptibly better than his immediate predecessors. Who should break the new ground? Surely no one but the most sublime geniuses? Well, did Beethoven open up new ground completely different from that of Mozart? Do Beethoven's symphonies proceed down completely new paths? No, I say. Between the first symphony of Beethoven and the last of Mozart I find no extraordinary [leap in] artistic value, and no more than ordinary effect. The one pleases me and the other pleases me. Today, if I hear Beethoven's Symphony in D major, I am happy, and tomorrow, if I hear the C-major of Mozart, with the final fugue,[7] I am happy too. I do not think about a new path in Beethoven's case, and there is nothing to remind me. What an opera *Fidelio* is! I do not say that every idea in it appeals to me completely, but I would like to know the name of the opera that could have a more profound effect, or offer more enchanting pleasures to the listener. Do you find in it a single number with which Beethoven broke new ground? I do not. I look at the score and listen to the performance, and everywhere I find Cherubini's dramatic musical style.[8] Beethoven was not imitating it, but he had it in mind as a favorite musical model."

"And Beethoven's last period?" I asked. "His last quartets, his Ninth Symphony? His mass? Here one cannot speak of a comparability with Mozart, or with any other artist before or after him."

"That may be, in a certain sense," he continued animatedly. "His forms are wider and broader, the style is more polyphonic, more artificial, the ideas for the most part darker, more melancholy, even when they want to be cheerful; the instrumentation is fuller, and *he went somewhat farther along the path he had already embarked on, but he did not clear a new one.* And let us be honest; where did he lead us? To regions that are really *more beautiful*? As *artists*, is the pleasure that we feel at the Ninth Symphony absolutely *greater* than what we feel at most of his other symphonies? As far as I am concerned, I will say quite openly: no! When I listen to it, I celebrate a joyous hour, but the C-minor symphony gives me occasion for a similar celebration, and what I experience with the former is perhaps not quite so unsullied, so pure, as with the latter."

III

On a subsequent occasion, I again brought the conversation around to the question of "new ground." The thought tormented me, and Mendelssohn's reasoning had not convinced or pacified me at all.

"Recently," I began, "I heard your overture to *A Midsummer Night's Dream*[9] for the first time. It seems to me to surpass all your earlier works in its originality, and I cannot compare it with any other piece; it has no sisters, no family resemblance. So one would probably be justified in saying that you have broken new ground with it?"

"Not at all," he retorted. "You have forgotten that what I understand by 'new ground' is creations that obey newly discovered and at the same time more sublime artistic laws. In my overture I have not given expression to a single new maxim. For example, you will find the very same maxims I followed in the great overture to Beethoven's *Fidelio*. My *ideas* are different, they are Mendelssohnian, not Beethovenian, but the *maxims* according to which I composed it are also Beethoven's maxims. It would be terrible indeed if, walking along the same path and creating according to the same principles, one could not come up with new ideas and images. What did Beethoven do in his overture? He painted the content of his piece in tone pictures. I tried to do the same thing. He did it in a broader overture form, and used more extended periods; so did I. But basically, the form of our periods follows the same laws under which the concept 'period' generally presents itself to human intelligence. And you can examine all the musical elements; nowhere will you find in my overture anything at all that Beethoven did not have and practice, unless"—he smiled roguishly—"you want to consider it as new ground that I used the ophicleide."[10]

"So you ascribe the originality of the invention to the particular subject matter you had in mind when you composed your overture?" I asked.

"Certainly," he replied.

"Then," I continued, "the world should be awash in original works, for there is no lack of titles that announce a substantive subject; but the music the titles refer to is often quite ordinary! According to your theory Herr A. and Herr B. and all the rest of the gentlemen right through to the end of the alphabet could have written your *Midsummer Night's Dream* Overture, if they had only set themselves the task of imitating the content of the play in tones."

"If they had attacked the problem with the same *seriousness*," he continued, "and immersed themselves in the play with the same zeal, they would all have brought forth *more sublime, more meaningful* works than would have been the case without this method.

"If someone has talent and still produces ordinary work, then it is always his own fault. The most ordinary cause of ordinariness is lack of self-criticism and desire to improve. If I had allowed everything to be printed *without changes*, there would be little originality to be found in it. If I am considered to have originality, I realize that I owe *most* of it to my strict self-criticism and my drive to change and better myself. I have turned and tested my ideas—how frequently I altered each one!—in order to transform their originally ordinary physiognomy into a more original, more meaningful and effective one. Just as it can happen that one or several notes, if their pitches or rhythms are treated differently, can give a particular idea an entirely different physiognomy and expression, so, in a larger context, a period that is inserted or omitted can make something ordinary and ineffective into something unusual and effective. My God, take a look at Beethoven's sketchbooks; just look at the sketch of 'Adelaide.'[11] Why did he make the change right at the beginning? Because the first variant was dull and ordinary, while the second is more lively, expressive and melodically pleasing. Give me an idea of the most ordinary kind, you may wager that I will turn it and twist it in shape and accompaniment and harmony and instrumentation long enough to make it into a decent piece. And as with a single idea, I believe I am capable, by means of changes and improvements, of turning an entire ordinary piece into an interesting one."

"I believe you," I said with complete conviction.

"And so?" he said, "What do you want? Roasted fowl do not fly into the mouth of even the most talented artist. It can happen occasionally, but seldom; as a rule, one must first catch and behead them, and then roast them!"

"And still you have set aside entire pieces because they were not particularly successful?" I asked.

"Yes," he replied, "Sometimes they come into the world so sickly that to turn them into healthy ones would require too much time, perhaps more than one would need to write a new one. Then it is preferable to make a new one."

"And is it not possible," I asked again, "that through excessive improvements, instead of making a work better, one can make it worse? Is not Goethe right when he says, 'You roasted your chestnuts too long in the fire; now they have all turned to charred embers'?"[12]

"That too," he said laughing. "Would Goethe have said something that did not have a basis in reality? But I prefer to roast a dish too long and have it turn to charcoal once in a while than to bring all my courses to the table raw."

IV

One day I succeeded in turning the conversation to that subject once again, and asking him whether a musician can do anything further with conscious intent that would strengthen his originality; whether he was aware of any specific mental procedures for this purpose.

"Besides sharp self-criticism while you are working, and careful alterations, I would not know what to add. But," he added after a short pause, smiling ironically at me and giving me a pat on the shoulder, "one thing that may help lead to originality is that one *composes more* and *worries less.* For, as with everything else in this world, there are secret agencies at work in the artist, and we can observe them in the phenomenon, but we earthlings will never worry the causes out of them. Through continued efforts one enables them to work themselves free; but by too much critical reflection one holds them back."

"That must be admitted," I said, "but, at the same time, one can make things too easy for oneself with this opinion. One might think that everything explainable about a certain phenomenon has been discovered at a point when that is actually not yet the case. By digging deeper, one would have discovered more."

"Have you tried that, and found more?" he asked pointedly.

I continued to think about this matter, but without coming up with very much. The following thought occurred to me:

"All our creativity, it seems to me, is made possible primarily by those things in the works of our predecessors that *attract*, and those that *repel* us, those that *please* us especially, or especially *displease* us. For if we wish to be quite clear in our minds about the impressions that musical works make on us, there are some that do not please us in the slightest; in fact, it is very rarely that we find one that satisfies us completely, in every respect. Here someone may feel the melodic portrayal of the idea is pleasing, but not the accompaniment, or the accompaniment is pleasing, but not the harmony, and so on. Someone else will be particularly attracted to the powerful ideas blared out by the brass section; a third person, with a finer constitution, will not like these but prefer the finer, softer colors, and so on. These attractions to and dislikes of artistic phenomena, with which we are born, are the essence of our original, individual predispositions. In their differing degrees and combinations, they resemble in a mental sense what external differences in form, gait, and features are physically. And in this regard all people, or certainly the greatest number, have individuality and the *predisposition* to originality."

"That's not bad," said Mendelssohn. "From that you deduce that the artist must allow his original predispositions free rein, and not change them around and modify them to go along with the authority of great artists or whatever opinions happen to be popular, and that in this way he can have a conscious effect on the development of his originality?"

"I do indeed think that," I continued. "As I said before, there are few people who do not originally possess individuality, but only a very few among them are such independent spirits that they develop themselves solely in accordance with their own nature. Most allow themselves to be snared by the influences of other people, by aesthetic arguments, criticisms of their works, masters who have a great following, and so on. They believe that they will proceed more surely by following the paths laid out by these others, than if they were to continue in the manner that was given to them; and as a result of the violence they impose upon themselves, they more or less become imitators."

"That is completely correct," Mendelssohn interrupted, "and I can claim this independence for myself, for I have been aware of it ever since my earliest youth. I cannot remember any occasion when I ever thought to myself, 'You want to write a trio like this one or that one by Beethoven, or by Mozart, or by any other master.' I wrote them according to my taste; in other words, whatever I imagined in general to be pleasing. For example, I do not like blaring brass instruments and have never emphasized them, although I often enough had occasion to notice the effect they have on many members of the audience. I love the finely woven voices, the polyphonic movement, and here my early studies in counterpoint with Zelter and my study of Bach may have had their principal impact;[13] purely homophonic methods of composition appeal to me less. And in this way, as I have tried to develop what satisfies me, what is part of my nature, whatever originality one will concede to me may have developed. Not bad, not bad," he added, his eyes sparkling with that incomparably engaging look he had whenever an idea caught his fancy. "Not bad," he repeated, after he had taken a few steps back and forth beside me, "if I keep these principles in mind, and *follow them consistently*, I can *lead myself* to the sphere of original creators."

"At the same time," I remarked, "this complete reliance upon oneself alone has its perils, if it is followed strictly—for example, in a case in which the individuality is set against the whole tendency of the period and of art. Then the artist remains lonely, he finds no public, he becomes a martyr to his originality."

"Better a martyr than an imitator," he said. "But where is the original and at the same naturally significant artistic nature that has not sooner or later been successful? *Everyone who is possessed of a really energetic originality finds his public. If only he perseveres.* But then there are many who fail because they do not continue what they have begun, because when they have observed for some time that they have not awakened any noticeable interest, they leave their own path and their nature behind and try to accommodate themselves to others who are looked upon as the heroes of the day. They become deserters, converts, and they turn back in exhaustion, perhaps close to the victory that they would have won if they had continued to fight on bravely. Do you think I am not aware that for a considerable time I found *no real interest*? True, there was no lack of apparent interest *when I was present*, but basically there was not much to it. I had to produce my own things; seldom did I find them already *there* when I arrived. And this experience was in truth not terribly encouraging. But I thought, 'What you have done you have done;[14] and now it will have to go forth and see how well it makes out in the world.' Eventually, even if it takes a long time, it will find the people who are sympathetic; after all, the world is so big and full of variety. And that is in fact how it happened. And it happened that way because I continued on my own path, without paying much heed to whether and when my works would find general acceptance."

"And would you really have held out if that acceptance had never come?" I asked. "Or were you not convinced, quite naturally, that your way really had value and *had to* prevail?"

"I do not want to make myself out to be stronger than I am," he said. "It is true that I never lost this conviction, or at least powerful hope. A single blow of the ax never fells a tree, I told myself, and if it is a strong one, sometimes several will not suffice. What every artist needs is *a single éclat*, one work that really makes an impact on the public. Then the matter is solved. Then he has captured attention, and from that point on the public is not only concerned with all the following works, it even inquires about the earlier ones that it has previously passed over without notice, and thus the whole thing begins to move. This, too, is what all music publishers count on. They continue for long periods to publish works by talented composers without expecting any return. They hope for the work, the éclat, that will make the earlier ones profitable too."

"And this éclat is what you demonstrated in the most fortunate way with your overture to *A Midsummer Night's Dream*," I said. "I remember very well what excitement this overture caused due to your surprising originality and honesty of expression, and how from that moment on you rose high in the opinions of musicians and lay people alike."

"I, too, believe that," he said, "and hence one must put a little trust in luck, too."

"Luck?" I asked. "I should think that such an overture is created not by luck, but by the artist's genius?"

"Talent," Mendelssohn said, modestly altering my expression, "is naturally part of it, but what I call luck here is the idea for the *subject* of this overture, which had the ability to provide me with musical ideas and forms that could appeal to the general public. What I was able to do as a composer, I was able to do before then. But I had never had a similar subject before my imagination. That was an inspiration, and a lucky one."

V

"In recent times one hears much about the influence that a composer's *Weltanschauung* is supposed to have on his works," I said to Mendelssohn. "I admit that I am unable to form a clear concept based on this sentence. You are a contemporary composer; what do you think of it?"

"Ah, there even I am unable to help you," he replied with a smile.

"I do not have the addiction, or, if you prefer, the spirit of making profound connections between heterogeneous things. Certainly many things that appear to be unrelated have an effect on one another and are mutually interdependent, but it is equally true that others have nothing to do with one another and have absolutely no interconnection."

"You are expressing the exact opposite of what is now maintained by many of our thinkers."

"I cannot help myself," he said with a shrug of his shoulders. "Besides, do you know a *composer* who expresses this opinion or agrees with it?"

I had to admit that I know none.

"There you have it!" he said. "And we too ought to be consulted about this statement!"

"But after all, the proof for this opinion has been constructed based on composers. Beethoven, for example . . ."

". . . wrote his opinion into the score?" he asked. "Right?"

"That is what they claim," I replied, "absolutely. *Weltanschauung* is supposed to mean nothing else but how somebody thinks about the phenomena in his life, what his opinion of them is, what views he holds. From these views a person's *mentality* is formed either in favor of or opposed to the things of this world. For the democrat, the current political system is invalid, he finds it inadequate measured against his idea of the state. He wishes it were arranged according to his idea, and the result is a *mentality*, hatred of anything and everything that is opposed to and opposes his idea. Let us assume that Beethoven had a political opinion of this kind and the mentality, the hatred, that goes with it; to what extent would this opinion and mentality have played a role in his *Pastoral* Symphony?"

"You are cleverly choosing a phenomenon of his that speaks *against* the statement. I would like to remind you, *in favor* of the statement, of his *Eroica*. We know that he wanted to glorify Napoleon as the hero of the revolution, as the republican, and that he tore up the title page when he heard that the consul had made himself emperor."[15]

"You are criticizing me for the very thing you allow yourself," he said. "My example *against*, your example *in favor*—if I am willing to admit that the music of the *Eroica* is democratic music, in other words, music in which one can hear the democratic *viewpoint* and *mentality* of Beethoven. But I would like to know whether you would hear such a thing if the title and the anecdote regarding it were not known? Beethoven wrote seven other symphonies in addition to this one, he wrote so and so many quartets, quintets, trios, sonatas, overtures, masses, an oratorio, an opera, and in them, so far as we know, he portrayed a great many subjects, materials, contents, which have nothing whatsoever to do with the democratic viewpoint and mentality. What about democracy in *Christ on the Mount of Olives*? In *Fidelio*? And in many other works of his?"

"But you will admit," I objected, "that no artist can escape his time, and that therefore his time has an influence on him?"

"Certainly, I admit that," he replied, "But that does not invalidate my opinion; it strengthens it. If one says that the artist is a child of his time, that means that he cannot escape from the view of art that is characteristic of his time. If someone composes a symphony in the current day and age, he will not have Pleyel, Dittersdorf, Wolf, and so on[16] on his mind, but Mozart and Beethoven. Beethoven wrote as he did because in his time Haydn's and Mozart's works were the shining examples, but he hardly drew his musical ideas from the political or religious spirit of his time. Can you tell from his Bb-major or F-major symphony, for example, that the revolution has broken out in France? All the political, religious standpoints of the time have not inspired him to use the clarinets, oboes, flutes, horns, and so on in a certain fashion, or to develop a theme in such and such a way; rather, he heard the use of these means in the works of his models, read them in their scores, abstracted his maxims from these sources, and continued to develop and then practice them after his own fashion."

"But now we see poets, for example, whom one can justifiably call political, since they treat the political interests of the times in their poems."

"Let the poets do it," he replied. "Such works are rhymed speeches; Poetry, the daughter of heaven, had no part in them. The composer, in particular, if he wishes to have an effect on all musical humanity, will have nothing at all to do with partisan ideas about politics or the state, but only with *feelings*, and purely human ones. The artist should be objective and universal. He must portray every kind of circumstance and the emotions that result from it equally faithfully and truly. Today he must be able to produce within himself a *revolt*, tomorrow an *idyll*, along with all the images and emotions that accompany them. If the secular viewpoints and opinions of his times were to tell him what to do, he would not be a free creator in art, but a bound servant.

"The artist, when he is creating, flees from ordinary life with its competing interests and enters the loftier, pure kingdom of art. What interconnection can exist for a political fanatic at the moment when he is to set his *love aria* to music? Is he permitted, in this moment of creation, to think of his democratic or aristocratic opinions, to awaken the hatred in his breast, and with this feeling to begin the musical description of the love of a tender maiden?"

"That would certainly turn into a strange piece of music," I remarked.

"The artist," continued Mendelssohn, "at the moment when he is creating, must *be* the thing he wants to describe, only that, and absolutely nothing else. His mentality may conform with a certain subject today; tomorrow it may differ from it. It is said that Goethe was an aristocrat. Even if we accept this as true—in *Götz von Berlichingen*, in *Egmont*[17]—nothing of this mentality is perceivable. There a heart seems to have burned for freedom. But then what mentality created *Iphigenie*? The *Elective Affinities*? *Tasso*?[18] Whatever political convictions and mentality he may have had, in his works it was not these that gave him his ideas, but the subject matter."

"I guess I agree with you," I said, "but then one must ask where an idea can come from, and find so many adherents, if there is basically nothing real in it?"

"It comes from a one-sided view of things. Because Auber wrote a *Muette de Portici*,[19] Beethoven an *Eroica* Symphony, Rossini a *Wilhelm Tell*, people have seen fit to extrapolate political music from them and to demonstrate that the composers must have *had* to write these pieces as a consequence of their political *Weltanschauung* and the times in which they lived. That Auber wrote a *Maurer und Schlosser*, a *Fra Diavolo*, Rossini an *Othello*, a *Tancredi*,[20] and so on; that Beethoven wrote a hundred works that have nothing to do with political *Weltanschauung*, is overlooked."

"If your reasoning is correct," I said, "then there is a further conclusion that can be drawn from it. Because the artist's work is made dependent upon his *Weltanschauung*, many people want to bring the development of art itself into a necessary relationship with political and religious life; political and religious ideas develop in such and such a way; *therefore* music had to develop in such and such a way. Handel *had* to write in a certain way in his time, because life was as it was; Gluck *had* to write the way he did; so did Haydn, Mozart, and so on, in conformity with the overall development of the general *Weltanschauung*."

"An opinion just as untenable," Mendelssohn said, "as the one about the works of the individual artist! After all, Beethoven's genius for music did not come into the world for the first time when he did. It is conceivable that it had existed several times previously, in earlier and very different times. But then it was confronted with other predecessors, other models, other artistic viewpoints. Our theorists generally accept Goethe's view that an artist who was born ten years earlier or later would have become a different artist, inasmuch as he would have encountered *other artistic views* that would have had a different effect on his training; but then they go right back to making the progress of art dependent on that of the world in general. The fact that Beethoven's genius took the shape it did is a consequence of the sequence in which it appeared. In Handel's time he would not have become our Beethoven. Haydn and Mozart would have been different people if they had come after Beethoven. And all this would most certainly have come about no matter how the world might have looked from a political or religious viewpoint. Whether we have this dogma or that political belief, war or peace, absolutism, constitutionalism, or a republic, it has *no effect whatsoever on the evolution of the art of music*. This evolution has only one cause—the fact that *the artist cannot develop and train himself otherwise than in keeping with the artistic moment in which he appears*. Imagine for a moment that today, for some reason, is the beginning of *a hundred-year hiatus in musical creation*, while the political, religious, philosophical world continues to march forward unchecked. Would the art of music, when it awoke from its long sleep, have moved forward along with the rest of the world; would the works of the next master be a hundred years ahead of the best works of our time? Not by a single step. In the best case, they would pick up where our best works left off, and continue the series that had been interrupted, no matter how far the world had progressed in every [other] area.

"In short, the development of the art of music has nothing in common with the development of science, of philosophy, of religion, of politics—it develops according to the natural laws of progression of the art in question, following the laws of creation, growth, and decay."

To my dismay Mendelssohn now caught sight of a friend, whom he greeted. "Adieu, Mr. Deep Thinker. Until the next time," he said, giving me his hand.

I had many objections to make to his last argument. Now I would have to wait for an opportune moment. For Mendelssohn was not always inclined to this kind of discussion, and when I noticed this I was careful not to bother him.

NOTES

1. Johann Peter Eckermann, *Gespräche mit Goethe* (Wiesbaden, 1835), "Vorrede." [ed.]

2. Ibid. [ed.]

3. During his lifetime Mendelssohn published four collections of six texted songs, opp. 19a (1833), 34 (1837), 47 (1840), and 57 (1843). [ed.]

4. For a discussion of the composition of *St. Paul*, see A. Kurzhals-Reuter, *Die Oratorien Felix Mendelssohn Bartholdys: Untersuchungen zur Quellenlage, Entstehung, Gestaltung und Überlieferung* (Tutzing, 1978), pp. 97–114, especially 113–14. [ed.]

5. Pliny the Elder, *Histories* 35.84: "No day without a line." [ed.]

6. Between 1819 and 1844 Lobe composed several operas, which were mounted in Weimar. [ed.]

7. Beethoven, Symphony no. 2 in D major, op. 36; Mozart, *Jupiter* Symphony in C major, K. 551. The *Jupiter* was a personal favorite of Mendelssohn; as a youth he composed a canon on the four-note motto theme from its finale and modeled the finale of his *Sinfonia* no. 8 on the *Jupiter* finale. See further R. Larry Todd, "Mozart according to Mendelssohn: a Contribution to *Rezeptionsgeschichte*," forthcoming in *Cambridge Studies in Performance Practice: Perspectives on Mozart Performance*, ed. R. L. Todd and Peter Williams (Cambridge, 1991), pp. 158–203. [ed.]

8. Cherubini's *Lodoïska* (1791), an example of the French rescue opera, served as one model for Beethoven's *Fidelio*; in addition, the libretto of Cherubini's *Les deux journées*, known in Germany as *Der Wasserträger* (1800), was written by Bouilly, the author of the French text on which *Fidelio* was based. Cherubini served as the director of the Conservatoire, where, in 1825, the young Mendelssohn met and presented him with a kyrie in D minor for five-part chorus and orchestra. [ed.]

9. Op. 21, composed in 1826. In 1843 Mendelssohn completed the incidental music, op. 61, for a production of the play in Berlin. [ed.]

10. The ophicleide is used in the overture to depict the boorish character Bottom. [ed.]

11. The song "Adelaide," op. 46. It is not clear to which sketches Mendelssohn had access. He was, however, a diligent collector of autographs, including Beethoven's. His dealings with the Viennese collector Fuchs are recorded on pp. 275–309. See also Rudolf Elvers, "Felix Mendelssohns Beethoven-Autographe," in *Bericht über den musikwissenschaftlichen Kongress Bonn 1970*, ed. C. Dahlhaus et al. (Kassel, 1970), pp. 380–82; and Douglas Johnson, Alan Tyson, and Robert Winter, *The Beethoven Sketchbooks* (Berkeley, 1985). [ed.]

12. Johann Wolfgang von Goethe, *Sämtliche Werke nach Epochen seines Schaffens*, ed. K. Richter et al. (Munich, 1987), vol. 9 (*Gedichte und Stammbucheintragungen: Sprichwörtlich*), p. 125. I am indebted to Prof. Wm. A. Little for this identification. [ed.]

13. Mendelssohn's work with Zelter, which began around 1819, included a thorough training in figured bass, invertible counterpoint, ornamented chorale, and canon and fugue. See R. Larry Todd, *Mendelssohn's Musical Education* (Cambridge, 1983). [ed.]

14. Verbatim expression of Mendelssohn. [Johann Christian Lobe]

15. The story describing Beethoven tearing the title page of the *Eroica* Symphony originated with Ferdinand Ries (1784–1838), the composer's secretary during the period of the symphony's creation. The anecdote appeared in the *Biographische Notizen über Ludwig von Beethoven*, prepared by Ries and F. G. Wegeler and published in Coblenz in 1838, and it is probably this work to which Lobe refers. For a critical revaluation of the anecdote and its significance, see Maynard Solomon, *Beethoven* (New York, 1977), pp. 132ff. [ed.]

16. Ignaz Pleyel (1757–1831), Carl Ditters von Dittersdorf (1739–1799), and E. W. Wolf (1735–1792). [ed.]

17. *Götz von Berlichingen* (1773); *Egmont* (1788). [ed.]

18. *Iphigenie* (1779, 1787); *Wahlverwandtschaften* (1809); *Torquato Tasso* (1790). [ed.]

19. D.-F.-E. Auber, *La muette de Portici*, grand opera premièred in Paris in 1828; its Brussels première in 1830 was reported to have sparked the Belgian revolution. [ed.]

20. Auber, *Le maçon* (1825) and *Fra Diavolo* (1830), examples of the *opéra comique*. Rossini, *Otello* (1816) and *Tancredi* (1813). [ed.]

From the Memoirs of
Adolf Bernhard Marx

TRANSLATED BY SUSAN GILLESPIE

Adolf Bernhard Marx (1795?–1866), noted German music theorist, studied in Berlin with Mendelssohn's composition teacher, Carl Friedrich Zelter. As editor of the *Berliner allgemeine musikalische Zeitung* (1824–1830), Marx contributed several articles about Beethoven, programmatic music, and aesthetics. In 1830, on Mendelssohn's recommendation, he was appointed professor of music at the University of Berlin. Marx's magnum opus is generally regarded to be the *Lehre von der musikalischen Komposition* (Leipzig, 1837–1847), which contains a widely influential discussion of ternary sonata form. In 1832 Mendelssohn prepared a libretto for Marx's oratorio *Mose*, but declined to perform the work when it was eventually finished in 1841. By 1839 the two friends were estranged, and Marx destroyed his correspondence with Mendelssohn. A highly partial account of their friendship was later published by Marx's wife, Therese: *Adolf Bernhard Marx' Verhältniss zu Felix Mendelssohn-Bartholdy* (Leipzig, 1869). (For Mendelssohn's view of Marx in 1834, see p. 235, note 43.) [ed.]

[Source: Adolf Bernhard Marx, *Erinnerungen aus meinem Leben* (Berlin, 1865), vol. 1, pp. 110–17, 131–44; and vol. 2, pp. 229–38.]

·

When I first saw him, Mendelssohn stood at the brink between boyhood and youth. Through his masterful performances and compositions, he had already made a name for himself that reverberated far beyond the city. I had occasionally glimpsed him in concerts and had taken pleasure in his fresh face, sometimes animated, sometimes dreamy; such a healthy bloom of youth, such warmth radiated from beneath the full head of long wavy hair! Several times one acquaintance or another had offered to introduce me to the household during the regular Sunday musical performances. I had always declined, partly because I did not enjoy visiting strange houses, partly because my position as editor made such an approach seem even more dubious. Finally it came about. Whether and by whom I was introduced, whether Felix or his father first approached me somewhere, I can no longer say. In any event, Felix visited me either immediately before or afterward; for I took the opportunity to play my 137th Psalm for him, which I had just completed and in which at the words "If I forget thee, O Jerusalem . . ." I had even been so bold as to attempt a fugue—a form concerning which I had achieved no greater clarity than that gleaned from Marpurg's[1] teachings and the enigmatic example of Bach's *Well-Tempered Clavier.*

Felix looked through the score, first with an astonished expression, then shaking his head; finally he could no longer contain himself: "That—that can't be! That isn't right! That [indicating the fugue] is no music at all!"

I was thrilled. I could not be hurt, for I was quite conscious that my burning desire and putative talent were lacking the third necessary element: artistic training. I was thrilled, because here I found openness! And that seemed to me the first requirement for every human relation.

Now there I was at one of those Sunday concerts, for which Felix had written a series of symphonies in three or four movements, the first movement a fugue, or fugato, the whole for stringed instruments alone; the piano, which Felix played in discreet accompaniment, and mostly or entirely as thoroughbass, took the place of the winds.[2]

Truly, I had no intention of making a clever reply; I was only being conscientiously serious when I answered Felix's question how I had liked the *sinfonia* by expressing my admiration for his skill in the movement, and then observed that there was nothing underneath it, that I had found no content to match the movement's proficiency.

So we faced each other, I knowing, he intuiting that the other might very well be right, both firmly convinced that every word was honestly meant. This was the cornerstone of our friendship, which was to mature quickly and solidly and take on a mutuality and strength that may be rare even between brothers. Who could have predicted (surely not I) that it would end, and without any external cause, in complete, deathly cold estrangement.

I soon made the acquaintance of a well-ordered and wisely led family, and learned what incalculable advantages attend one's birth into one, especially when old reputation (Moses Mendelssohn!), wealth, and extended connections are thrown in. I, poor soul, was the product of need and perplexity! Fate had set me down, a naive boy, innocent of all knowledge, at the crossroads of a hundred life paths, and had called out, "Go! Choose the one you like." Here I encountered someone whose every step was discussed and watched over by a father's judicious eye. From time to time, even relatively late, Felix would complain to me that his father had once again become doubtful about his profession, dissatisfied with the career of an artist, whose successes must always remain uncertain; that again and again he would suggest to him that he should become a merchant, or enter some other secure career. I would smile and pacify him by pointing out how wisely his father was acting when he encouraged him to examine himself again and again.

Later, I would tell my pupils, both in my writing and in person, that one should only become an artist if he cannot do otherwise. This conviction, to which I still very much adhere, may have its roots in those conversations with Felix. Another of his father's comments was to echo strangely in my thoughts, until I recognized the deep life experience out of which it grew. Somewhat later, after the father had become convinced of my loyal devotion to Felix, he once spoke his mind to me, saying that he did not believe his son possessed the highest talent (he meant genius) for music; but that his life might be all the happier as a result. Indeed, happiness in life and genius—how seldom they coexist in any lasting way! Was Schiller happy? Has it been forgotten that on his deathbed, his face averted, he pushed his favorite daughter away with his hand, his heart consumed with bitterness? Was Goethe, whom we call the fortunate one, really happy? He wanted to be the dramatist of his people—did he become that? And you, most noble one, who raised the performance-happy world of the instruments up into the realm of conscious spirit—Beethoven, last of our masters! Who can read your life without tears?

No, happiness in life and genius are rarely, if ever, united; they seem to avoid and flee from each other. In exchange, the chosen ones—many are called but few are chosen—experience the ecstasy of those moments in which the eye is emboldened to perceive undying visions that focus the burning passion of their entire whole spirit into a single moment—a burning entirely different from the heat of dedicated work, however praiseworthy and rewarding the latter may be.

No doubt he had seen and understood correctly, the discerning son of Moses Mendelssohn. And he was well qualified to speak on the subject of music; his entire life had prepared him for it. In his

younger years, he lived in Paris for a time and was exposed to continuous productions of Gluck's operas, which at the time still enjoyed
the high esteem of the French and were presented based on unbroken traditions handed down from Gluck's era. He also attended the
première of Cherubini's *Der Wasserträger*[3] and often talked about it
with pleasure. Until then, Cherubini had never had a resounding success. Now along came the *Wasserträger* with its suggestions of ideas of
the revolution. The response was an unprecedented, truly fearsome
one, the crowd inflamed to the point of madness. Mendelssohn went
backstage to see the composer even before the performance was over,
and found him stalking up and down in feverish excitement: "Ah! ç'a
frappé, ç'a frappé!" [That has struck home, that has struck home!]
he exclaimed over and over again, his voice hoarse. Auber,[4] his student, was not at all appreciated at that time, not even by his teacher.
Who would have guessed that the highly acclaimed master would
later (in his *Abencérages*[5]) become the emulator of his student!

Next to the father stood the highly intelligent, perhaps less-feeling
mother.[6] In her the traditions or resonances of Kirnberger[7] lived on;
she had made the acquaintance of Sebastian Bach's music and in her
home she perpetuated his tradition by continually playing the *Well-
Tempered Clavier*. It is odd that the father's great predilection for
Gluck had little impact on his family. Gluck was respected by all, but
not really beloved or kept constantly in mind. This honor was reserved for Mozart, Bach, and, to a much lesser extent, Handel. The
daughters and Paul,[8] the youngest son, with their similar convictions,
drew the family close together in a finely drawn circle. The oldest
daughter, Fanny,[9] was closest to Felix and took the liveliest interest in
his artistic studies. At the pianoforte, she lacked his skill and strength,
but not infrequently she was first in tenderness and sensitivity of interpretation, especially of Beethoven. Several of her songs, specifically the duet and some other songs from *Suleika*, found their way
into her brother's early published lieder under his name.[10] Other
works were published later, as is well known. The younger sister, Re-
bekka [*sic*], intellectually less remarkable than Fanny, was actually everyone's secret favorite—especially her brother's.[11] The impression
she made was like that of a half-veiled maiden; the less clearly she is
seen, the richer and tenderer one imagines her charms to be.

Paul was still very young, and held himself modestly aloof. When
Felix played, which was almost always without sheet music, the youth
with the passionate expression and short dark curls would occasionally steal up to his brother after it was over, tap him on the shoulder,

and say softly: "Felix! in the —th bar you played F; it should be F#. . . ."

Faced with this well-populated circle, one could observe how beneficial the rich society of the paternal home was for the future of the young composer. Here every song that had just ended, every masterfully performed new movement was attended by an expectant and well-disposed public; it was here that the performance of Bach's *Passion* was prepared;[12] here, finally, that the young artist made far-flung connections that were beneficial in the extreme. For the rich, respected house offered a hospitable, warm welcome to every musician of substance who visited Berlin and had the capability of supporting the visitor in anything he might undertake there.

Such was the nature of the soil from which Felix emerged; one should also take account of the influence of Louis Berger[13] as piano teacher, and also of Zelter, whose lessons had begun early enough to assure that the student did not neglect anything that the old school could not provide.

All that, taken together, was promising and fortunate enough. But every circumstance in which we humans find ourselves has its unavoidably necessary limitations and consequences. The guarantee of every educational means, combined with precocious success and influence, and then the circle of active and often gifted friends, the presence of a host of charming girls—all this had an effect on the youth, whose nature was already so fresh, like a continually refreshing, nerve-stimulating, and bracing bath. Quickness and cheerfulness became the keynotes of his character. This in itself was auspicious and at the same time augured future good fortune. It expressed itself in a peculiar musical trait of his. When he performed one of his compositions for the second or third time, one could observe that with each successive performance he speeded up the tempo—often significantly. Given his extraordinary skill one could not claim that he played slower the first times because of a lack of technique. Fanny was often in despair at this increase in the tempo, which was not always appropriate; but it was the expression of a growing excitement and impatience.

Much more dubious, if equally understandable, was the influence exercised by his pleasure-laden environment and the constant company of his sisters' young female friends. Felix, the clever Klingemann,[14] and I founded a garden newspaper in the expansive park surrounding the house. The capital for this undertaking consisted of a wooden table with a drawer, which stood day and night in one of the long shadowy arbors; whoever had something to contribute

would steal over to it. Drawings, tender poems, witty letters, everything imaginable found its way there, to the pleasure of all and sundry, to reveal its clandestine meaning to the lovely maiden who was
the object of special veneration. More than once I climbed with Felix—not without danger—onto the roof of an outbuilding, in order
to slip delicious peaches or swelling grapes onto the night table of a
young lady with a Polish name.

Was it surprising, was it otherwise possible than that the tender devotion awakened and simultaneously returned by so many should
have left that soft impress on the compositions one would later term
sweet, flirtatious, or tender, and that resulted in those "songs without
words" whose offshoots would reach from that period through the
whole life of the composer? At the time I took the greatest pleasure
in all this, as well I might. For it was only by dallying in this diminu-
tive and sweetly feminine sphere, by reverting to the easily understood motives of the barcarolle or of choralelike devotions, by seeing
how it was the weaker and lesser talents who were drawn to these
forms, which played with the intellect more than they embodied it,
that one could finally recognize the true significance of this tendency.

Another characteristic, also a necessary product of those happy circumstances, aroused an eerie feeling in my soul even before I understood its broader implications. It was expressed in a single word, but
words express—or betray—events occurring in the soul that are
meant to be revealed or sometimes hidden from others, even from
the speaker himself. "That gives me no pleasure!"[15] That was often
what I heard when the conversation turned to this or that in music,
painting, and so on; and in fact it resounded most often at those very
moments in which the most profound and solemn things, the greatest
powers of the spirit were being expressed. I remember hearing the
devastating expression applied to Dante, Michelangelo, even to Beethoven's compositions—and indeed his profoundest, namely, the
Ninth Symphony. And strange! As much as I admired and loved his
playing, his interpretation of Beethoven was seldom able to satisfy
me. We had words over it on several occasions, specifically over the
great B♭ major sonata.[16] But we got nowhere. I was not a strong
enough performer, and furthermore I had not achieved sufficiently
complete clarity on the matter for the discussion to bear fruit. . . .

Undisturbed by such considerations, our union grew so close and
fast that scarcely a day passed when we did not exchange visits and
notes. The content of the latter was unusual in that it consisted of
certain expressions and references that only we understood, musical
passages, and a crazy quilt of fantastic pictures; for Felix drew assid-

uously, especially landscapes, as I, too, practiced drawing human figures. We soon discovered that the truly social art is not music, but drawing. For the former imperiously puts an end to all conversation in its vicinity, whereas drawing has the effect of making it even livelier, especially when two dear friends are sitting close together, and if their subject matter should wane, a glance at the work of the other or a request for assistance always offers new material.

But even verbal exchanges between the two of us, whose lives had grown together so closely, could easily take on strange forms, particularly when they turned to subjects like instrumentation that do not permit an exact designation. I can still remember the astonishment in Droysen's[17] look, during a visit to my room, when he overheard me saying to Felix, "Here pure purple would have to be used; the horns were dampening the splendor of the trumpets"; and Felix replied, "No! No! That shouts too loud; I want violet."

And yet this relationship had to end.

Or, rather, the fundamental difference between our two characters, viewpoints, and artistic tendencies finally had to make itself more and more clearly felt and noticed by both of us, despite and in spite of all of the above. Had he fallen away from me? Or I from him? The latter would have been quite impossible to accomplish, even if I had had it in my nature to do so. For I had taken his side too often and too decisively, and expressed myself on the subject in my newspaper. As to the former—that is how I viewed the matter then, and the feeling that I had been deserted by him was bitter wormwood whose gall I was to taste for long years thereafter. Now, I think I see more clearly. The external separation was nothing but the necessary consequence of the inner division to which we had closed our eyes for so long.

Now they had to be opened.

I had finally acquired the necessary means and leisure to undertake the execution of my old pet project, *Moses*.[18] It was clear to me that *Moses* could not become a two-part opera, as I had once imagined in my early youth. Rather, it would have to have the outward form of an oratorio, and the Bible would have to provide the text. My close acquaintance with the Bible made me think that the creation of the libretto would not be difficult. I had often expressed myself to friends concerning my plan; now, when it had become serious—ah, it had always been serious for me, but my circumstances always intervened to hold me back—Felix was the first person in whom I confided. Only a few days later he came to me with the announcement that he also wanted to write an oratorio and draw his text from the Bible.

"That is a wonderful coincidence!" I replied. "I was afraid that the business of looking for the text would take away the freshness from composing; now we are both saved. You put my libretto together for me, and I will do yours for you, and we shall both have a fresh start with our work."

He happily agreed. Now I asked him about his subject matter. "I thought I would write about Paul."

I was taken aback. Paul, the teacher, the wise man—I might almost have said the Protestant, the rationalist. One must forgive my inaccurate expressions; I find no better ones to express my view of that noble, profound figure, if I were asked to imagine him as the subject of a musical treatment. The thinker, the painter, perhaps the poet can base their work on Paul; but the musician, whose creation belongs most immediately to the sphere of the inner life and emotions?

My awareness of the immediacy of artistic decisions was too strong for me to have dared to express my doubts at once. For such a decision is not at all (as outsiders often imagine) a matter of free choice. It grows out of a whole way of thinking, viewpoint, and mood, which attract an artist to this very subject and to no other; it expresses the necessary mutual relationship between the artist and his material, the magnetic attraction, as it were, that draws them together. For this reason, once the mind of the artist has got going in a certain direction, it can seldom be altered or improved; the groundwork must have been prepared by his entire cast of mind. Nonetheless, my firm conviction required that I make an attempt, at first in the form of a question, to bring at least some of my more superficial misgivings to his attention. Paul, I ventured, is a figure without a well-defined beginning or end. He is a teacher and a martyr, but not the first; Stephen precedes him as martyr. His end, according to legend, came by the sword in faraway Rome. But the high point of his life, for artistic representation, can only be the appearance of Christ. This is a task for painters and poets, but what should the musician do with the words "It is hard for thee to kick against the pricks" [Acts 9.5]? How should he demonstrate through them the sublimity of the holy one who speaks them—and the turmoil of him to whom they are addressed?

I advanced this and other arguments. I even suggested a second subject, Peter, the prince of the Apostles, of whom Christ said he was the rock on which he wanted to build his church—Peter, who before our very eyes betrays his wavering as a human being and then arises as a holy hero—Peter, finally, who in the eyes of the mother church continues to work through it, and the representatives of Christ; who gave to the church of Christ its first solid form. While we Protestants may not adhere to the Catholic doctrine of the presence of Christ through his representatives in the church (the artist, per se, is neither Protestant nor Catholic), the figure of the founder remains a most sublime one.

I am here publicly recording my view at that time, to which I still adhere, entirely without regard to the fact that *St. Paul* was composed, and that it was received with extraordinary acclaim. The work of art has such a manifold content, and success so many different sources, that the latter sheds no light on the former. This can only be achieved by thoroughgoing consideration of the work itself.

My protestations fell on deaf ears, and I wrote the libretto of *St. Paul* as well as I could.

Some time later Felix asked me whether I could not also work in some chorales. "What? Chorales in Paul's time? And in the events that make up his life?" I did not understand it and declined. The libretto, as it was later composed, was put together by Superintendant Schubring[19] in Dessau and the sympathetic theater director Eduard Devrient,[20] friends of the composer who were in Berlin at the time.

I had communicated the idea and the plan for *Moses* to Felix. Not long thereafter he brought me the libretto, entitled *Moses, an Oratorio, composed by A. B. Marx.* I have kept it as a memento; it bears the date 21 August 1832, at the end, along with the initials F.M.B.

I include here only the beginning and the conclusion, so as to give some basis for making a judgment:

MOSES

Part I

OVERTURE

And the Egyptians forced the children of Israel into servitude mercilessly, and made their life miserable with hard labor in the fields and with all sorts of drudgery, which they forced upon them mercilessly.

FIRST VOICE

O Lord, observe and see how miserable I have become.

CHORUS

Observe, all of you, and see whether there is any other pain like my pain. I am sore afraid!

A. B. Marx

A VOICE

Lord, hear my voice and my lament. Deliver my life from the cruel suffering.

CHORUS

Persecute them with fury, destroy them before heaven.

A VOICE

O, that help might befall Israel and God save his chosen people!

Conclusion

CHORUS

Hallelujah! Thank the Lord, for he is friendly. Then a thundering and lightning arose and a thick cloud upon the mountain, and a sound from a very loud trumpet, but the whole people was afraid, and the mountain Sinai smoked and quaked strongly, and the sound of the trumpet grew ever louder. Moses spoke and God answered him out loud: "I am the Lord thy God, who has led thee out of Egypt, out of the house of servitude. Thou shalt have no other God beside me. Thou shalt not make thyself any graven image. Thou shall not take the name of the Lord in vain. Be mindful of the Sabbath day, that thou hold it sacred. Thou shalt honor thy father and thy mother. Thou shalt not kill, thou shalt not commit adultery, thou shalt not steal, thou shalt not bear false witness. Thou shalt not covet women."

CHORUS

That is the love of God, that we should keep his Commandments.

. . . .

Mendelssohn had already had the desire before that, and actually all along, to move away from Berlin to somewhere else; Berlin was not to his taste, however many ties to family and friends might have bound him. After Zelter's death (1832), he was invited by the management of the Singakademie to apply for the vacant position of director. He did not wish to accept, however much that might have accorded with the wishes of his family. My exhortation, my emphasis on the many positive things he would be able to promote in this position, were finally decisive. He applied and was not chosen, in spite of the firm assurances he had been given that he would receive a large majority of the votes. Then he was hired as director, first in Düsseldorf, and then in Leipzig.

Mendelssohn had returned from his trips to England and Italy a different man from the one he had been during the time of our intimate friendship. When I made his acquaintance, he was deeply imbued with the power, profundity and truth of Sebastian Bach; repeatedly, with feeling, he had striven to demonstrate to me, for whom the pivotal works of the master had been unavailable up until then, the superiority of Bach over Handel. What I say here reflects his and perhaps also my thinking at that time; I have long since distanced myself sufficiently from such measuring of intellects against each other. At that time, too, Felix struggled for veracity and truthfulness in his own works. I can still see him [in 1826] entering my room with a heated expression, pacing up and down a few times, and saying: "I have a terrific idea! What do you think of it? I want to write an overture to *A Midsummer Night's Dream*." I expressed warm support for the idea. A few days later he, the happy, free one, was back again with the score, complete up to the second part.[21] The dance of the elves with its introductory chords was as one would later know it. Then—well, then there followed an overture, cheerful, pleasantly agitated, perfectly delightful, perfectly praiseworthy—only I could perceive no *Midsummer Night's Dream* in it. Sincerely feeling that it was my duty as a friend, I told him this in candor. He was taken aback, irritated, even hurt, and ran out without taking his leave. I let that pass and avoided his house for several days, for since my last visit, following that exchange, his mother and Fanny had also received me coldly, with something approaching hostility.

A few days later, the Mendelssohns' slim manservant appeared at my door and handed me an envelope with the words "A compliment from Mr. Felix." When I opened it great pieces of torn-up manuscript paper fell to the ground, along with a note from Felix reading: "You are always right! But now come and help." Perhaps the very understanding, thoughtful father had made the difference; or perhaps the hotheaded young man had come to himself.

I did not fail to respond; I hurried over and explained that, as I saw it, such a score, since it serves as a prologue, must give a true and complete reflection of the drama. He went to work with fire and absolute dedication. At least the wanderings of the young pairs of lovers could be salvaged from the first draft, in the first motive (E, D♯, D, C♯);[22] everything else was created anew. It was pointless to resist! "It's too full! too much!" he cried, when I wanted him to make room for the ruffians and even for Bottom's lovesick ass's braying. It was done; the overture became the one we now know. Mother and sister were reconciled when they saw the composer rushing around in high excitement and pleasure. But during the first performance at his house, the father declared in front of the numerous assembly that it was actually more my work than Felix's. This was naturally quite unjustified, whether it was merely to express his gratification at my behavior, or perhaps to give me satisfaction for the earlier defection of the womenfolk. The original idea and the execution belonged to Felix; the advice I had given was my duty and my only part in it.

Once, when we were taking our leave before his trip to England, Felix spoke to me with great emotion: "Listen. If anything should reach your ears over here that doesn't seem right to you, don't judge too hastily! I shall return." I did not understand his comment, but it gradually became clear to me.

In England he had performed his C-minor symphony,[23] but in place of the minuet he had inserted the scherzo from the Octet; it did not fit the character of the whole, but it seemed for him to be more attention-getting. How often he and I had earlier laughed and made fun of the bad habit the French had of mixing in foreign movements, for example of transplanting the scherzo of Beethoven's A-major symphony into that in D major!

When he returned from Italy he brought a new composition, the *Walpurgisnacht*;[24] at his request, Goethe himself had written a few verses for it. I found the composition charming, but I could not fail to notice the lack of verisimilitude on which this charm is based. It is true that the source of this problem has its origins in the poem itself, but there it goes unnoticed, while the more real art of music, which can only represent truth, not illusion, exposes every untruth to the light of day. As is well known, Goethe attributes to the original inhabitants, gathered on the mountaintop, a belief that is actually characteristic of Christendom—namely, the striving for eternal light, which they must then protect against the "stifling writings of the clerics." Therefore they disguise themselves as witches and goblins. Mendelssohn has clothed the narrative "Come with spikes and pitchforks, . . ." in pretty choruses of the witches; his orchestra, at the same time, rises in crescendo to the most boisterous clamor of actual witchery. And witchcraft is what is portrayed here; the fact that the whole affair is supposed to be an illusion is not expressed by the music, because music is incapable of doing so. The poet's imagination can indulge in lighthearted play; but for the musician it has to be in real earnest, even though the poem itself offers neither cause nor place for this. Hence the witchcraft never becomes real witchcraft, with its cruel power, but rather hovers between prank and reality. . . .

After he arrived in Berlin, Mendelssohn, at the suggestion of the king, composed the music to Sophocles' *Antigone*.[25] If this was to be done, there could hardly be a better place for it than here. Avoiding antiquarian detours, Mendelssohn without hesitation adopted Gluck's manner. It must be reiterated that there is nothing to criticize in the king's request; it was not his responsibility, but the musician's, to consider whether the task could be carried out in a way that would be in harmony with the nature of our modern music—and our stage and way of life—or whether it would demean them by inadequacy and untruth. Mendelssohn, however, had not been able to bring this up in the presence of the king.

However one may decide this question, neither this isolated activity, nor a number of compositions for the cathedral choir,[26] offered sufficient basis for a permanent position for Mendelssohn in Berlin. But they had called him there, and now the question arose what should become of him. Peculiar suggestions were made to him by various officials. He should perform church music. But where? For what purpose? He should arrange music festivals. He should found a conservatory. As he reported all this to me, I tried to win him over to the last suggestion, which was the only tenable one. But precisely this was the one he would not hear of. "There is Herr ——, and Herr ——, and ——; I can't go along with them, our paths are far apart, and I don't want to push them aside." In vain I attempted to prove that one could make use of each one in his post. In vain I drew his attention, half in jest, half seriously, to the fact that his point of view allowed only one way out—to wait for those three gentlemen to die; but by then they would either have groomed successors in their own image, or they would have already appointed them. All was in vain; Mendelssohn returned to Leipzig to his circle there.

NOTES

1. A reference to F. W. Marpurg, *Abhandlung von der Fuge* (Berlin, 1753), which contains a thorough discussion of canonic and fugal technique and a sympathetic treatment of J. S. Bach as a contrapuntist. [ed.]

2. Between 1821 and 1823 Mendelssohn composed thirteen string *sinfonie*, many of which are in a severe contrapuntal style reminiscent of Bach. [ed.]

3. Opera by Luigi Cherubini, known in France as *Les deux journées*, which was first performed in Paris in 1800. [ed.]

4. D.-F.-E. Auber (1782–1871), French opera composer. [ed.]

5. *Les Abencérages*, first performed in 1813. [ed.]

6. Lea Mendelssohn-Bartholdy (*née* Salomon, 1774–1842). [ed.]

7. J. P. Kirnberger (1721–1783), German theorist and pupil of J. S. Bach, author of *Die Kunst des reinen Satzes in der Musik* (Berlin, 1771–1779). [ed.]

8. Paul Mendelssohn-Bartholdy (1812–1874), who became a banker. [ed.]

9. Fanny Mendelssohn-Bartholdy (1805–1847); she married the Berlin court painter Wilhelm Hensel in 1829. [ed.]

10. A reference to the duet "Suleika und Hatem," which appeared as Felix Mendelssohn's op. 8, no. 12; see also p. 258, note 11. [ed.] Marx's "Duett und einige Gesänge von Suleika" is wrong. There is only one piece from *Suleika*— the duet, op. 8, no. 12. Fanny's other songs—op. 8, no. 2; op. 8, no. 3; op. 9, no. 7; op. 9, no. 10, and op. 9, no. 12—have texts by Robert, Grillparzer, Droysen, Heine, and Uhland, respectively. [trans.]

11. Rebecka Mendelssohn-Bartholdy (1811–1858); she married the mathematician Peter Lejeune Dirichlet. [ed.]

12. The preparations for Mendelssohn's revival of the *St. Matthew Passion* are recounted in Eduard Devrient, *Meine Erinnerungen an Felix Mendelssohn-Bartholdy and seine Briefe an mich* (Leipzig, 1869)—not, however, always a reliable source; see also Martin Geck, *Die Wiederentdeckung der Matthäuspassion im 19. Jahrhundert* (Regensburg, 1967). [ed.]

13. Ludwig Berger (1777–1839), pupil of Muzio Clementi. [ed.]

14. Karl Klingemann (1798–1862). [ed.]

15. Marx uses the French word *plaisir*, lending his observation a further note of frivolity. [trans.]

16. The *Hammerklavier* Sonata in B♭ major, op. 106. [ed.]

17. Johann Gustav Droysen (1808–1884), German historian, author of a multivolume history of the Prussian monarchy. [ed.]

18. The oratorio *Mose*, published as op. 10 in 1844. [ed.]

19. Julius Schubring (1806–1889), theologian in Dessau. [ed.]

20. Eduard Devrient (1801–1877), actor and singer. For accounts of Schubring's and Devrient's collaboration on *St. Paul*, see Devrient (note 12) and J. Schubring, *Briefwechsel zwischen Felix Mendelssohn Bartholdy und Julius Schubring* (Leipzig, 1892, rep. 1973). [ed.]

21. Mendelssohn announced his intention to compose the overture in a letter to his sister dated 6 July 1826, now preserved in the New York Public Library. An early, incomplete draft of the overture, presumably the one he showed Marx, survives in the M. Deneke Mendelssohn Collection, Bodleian Library, Oxford (cat. b. 5). It tends to bear out Marx's account, at least in part. The opening chords and "Elfentanz" appear in more or less their final form. But the bridge to the second theme, where the draft breaks off, differs markedly from the final version, as if to corroborate Marx's account. (See R. Larry Todd, "The Instrumental Music of Felix Mendelssohn-Bartholdy: Selected Studies Based on Primary Sources," Ph.D. dissertation, Yale University, 1979, pp. 419ff.) Mendelssohn completed the second, final version of the overture on 6 August 1826; that autograph is in the Biblioteca Jagielloń-ska, Kraków (*Mendelssohn Nachlass, Band* 32). [ed.]

22. See measures 458–60 of the overture; the chromatic descent is related

to the chromatic tetrachord E–D♯–C♮–B embedded in the four wind chords with which the overture commences. [ed.]

23. Symphony no. 1, op. 11, performed in London on 25 May 1829. [ed.]

24. The cantata *Die erste Walpurgisnacht*, op. 60. The first version was completed on 13 February 1832 and performed in Berlin on 10 January 1833. Mendelssohn revised the score in 1842 and 1843, and performed the second version in Leipzig on 2 February 1843, when it was heard by Hector Berlioz. [ed.]

25. Op. 55, performed in Potsdam on 28 October 1841. [ed.]

26. Including a setting of Psalm 98 for double chorus and orchestra, op. 91, performed on New Year's Day in 1844; a cappella settings of Psalms 2, 43, and 22, op. 78; the *Sechs Sprüche*, op. 79; and the incomplete *Deutsche Liturgie*. [ed.]

Reminiscences of
Felix Mendelssohn-Bartholdy

JULIUS SCHUBRING

Among the many friends with whom Mendelssohn maintained a regular correspondence was Julius Schubring (1806–1889), who arrived in 1825 in Berlin, where he became a pupil of Schleiermacher at the University. After returning to Dessau in 1830, he was appointed pastor of the Church of St. George; later he was awarded an honorary doctorate of theology from the University of Halle. In 1832 Mendelssohn turned to Schubring for assistance in preparing the libretto of his first oratorio, *St. Paul*, which was premièred in Düsseldorf in 1836. Schubring also collaborated on Mendelssohn's second oratorio, *Elijah*, first heard at the Birmingham Music Festival in 1846. In 1892 Schubring's son brought out much of the correspondence between the two in the *Briefwechsel zwischen Felix Mendelssohn Bartholdy und Julius Schubring*. [ed.]

[Source: "Reminiscences of Felix Mendelssohn-Bartholdy. On his 57th Birthday, February 3rd, 1866," in *Musical World* 31 (12 and 19 May 1866). Translated anonymously from the original German in *Daheim* 2 (1866): 373ff.]

∙

When, at Easter, 1825, I left the University of Leipsic to enter at that of Berlin, my respected professor, Wilhelm Müller (author of the *Griechenlieder*, etc.[1]) gave me a letter of introduction to the Mendelssohns, in whose house he had himself, a short time previously, spent some very pleasant weeks. Thanks to his recommendation, and still more to the extraordinarily hospitable spirit that reigned in the family, I was, during the whole period, five years of my stay in Berlin, received with a degree of kindness most gratifying and valuable to a man like myself, who would otherwise have led a somewhat lonely life and not have had many to advise him. The more I became cognisant how little I was calculated, by my habits and disposition, to contribute aught to so brilliant an intellectual circle, and that consequently I could not help receiving more than I gave, the more grateful must I feel for the kindly toleration with which I was treated.

The life at No. 3—now the "Herrenhaus"—in the Leipzigerstrasse was then indeed a brilliantly intellectual one. The family were as richly endowed with every kind of natural gifts as they were bountifully provided with earthly riches. The last were employed neither to maintain a vain system of ostentation nor of luxurious living, but, on the contrary, to promote every possible development of intellectual resources and keep up a truly refined tone. The parents and their four children—their happiness then unclouded by any untoward event—were harmoniously united to each other by unusual warmth of affection and congeniality of character, and produced a most pleasing impression upon every one who entered their house. Their existence was a domestic one, inasmuch as they felt little inclination to go out, being most partial, after the labours of the day, to spending the evening in familiar intercourse with one another. It was seldom, however, that they were found quite alone; they either had a number of young people who were on a friendly footing with them, or else their circle was filled up with another class of visitors. But it was seldom that there was what is called a regular party. Whoever felt so inclined went, and whoever took a pleasure in going was welcome. Science, Art, and Literature were equally represented. Humboldt[2] was a frequent visitor. Whenever he went, the rest of the persons present would gradually form a circle round him, for every other occupation or amusement soon yielded to his interesting conversation. He could go on, for hours together, without a pause, relating the most attractive facts from out the rich stores of his experience. Hegel[3] was another visitor, though he contributed little to the general entertainment, seeking rather, in a quiet game at whist, relaxation from his arduous intellectual labours. Except when he was there, I can hardly remember cards ever being played in the house. Celebrated and uncelebrated people, travellers of all kinds, and especially musicians, though not to the exclusion of other artists, found their efforts judiciously appreciated. The conversation was always animated and spirited.

The education of the children was carefully calculated to foster the rich stores implanted in them by the Creator. Felix was the general favourite, without, however, being, in the slightest degree, spoilt. If he ever gave his father[4] cause for dissatisfaction, he was spared neither the reproving look, nor the serious, but invariably calm, rebuke. We entertained the most unbounded reverence for the head of the family. When he glanced with his large, short-sighted eyes over his spectacles, he had the power, by a wonderful expression of his, of enforcing respect. The beautiful relations existing between the father and the son are very evident in the published correspondence. Willingly, however, would the father take part in the jokes of the young people, and derive pleasure from so doing. I still see his amazed appearance, when, on one occasion, at the conclusion of dinner, the youngest son intoned a four-part canon, written by Felix the same morning, and secretly handed round: "Gesegnete Mahlzeit, prost Mahlzeit, wohl bekomms!"[5] The boyish delight at surprising the father burst in with song, so suddenly upon the previous conversation, and the father gazed with such amaze at the little wag, that the first attempt was interrupted by a general fit of laughter. It was not till repeated that the movement could be properly executed.

That the boy Felix should not go to school, but be taught, partly with his sisters and partly alone, was quite in keeping with his peculiarly reserved and gentle nature, and advanced him the more quickly, because it enabled him to enter more deeply into the subject taught, and developed uninterruptedly his character.[6] On the other hand, however, I think I perceive in this fact the reason of his feeling easily offended and out of sorts, and of his never being altogether at home in general society. The softness of his disposition, never having been hardened, could not easily overcome disagreeable impressions. Perhaps this susceptibility might have been lessened had he, when young, gone through something of the rough training to be obtained among a number of schoolfellows.

He pursued his musical studies in company with his elder sister, Fanny, who was long his equal in composition and pianoforte-playing. There existed between the two a mutual appreciation and affectionate esteem, which were certainly unusual. They executed together scores so charmingly, that on one occasion when, after a lapse of many years they played him something—it was the ballet from *Die Hochzeit des Camacho*—their master, Berger,[7] who was not very liberal of his praise, sprang up from his seat, as though quite carried away, and exclaimed: "Why, my children, you play quite first-rate" ("Aber, Kinder, ihr spielt doch auch ganz famos!"). In the first book which he published of his *Lieder*, Felix included some of his sister's, though he joked her about the mode in which she had managed Grillparzer's ponderous text in op. 8, no. 3.[8] She, on the other hand, twitted him with the false octaves from *f* to *a* at the end of the first verse of *Lied* no. 5, and he defended himself by saying that the stringed instruments ought to close with the *f* in the soprano, and the wind instruments come in with the *a*.[9] The sisterly musical fidelity with which Fanny clung to her beloved brother all her life could not have had a more beautiful end than, during the rehearsal of his music, which she was conducting, and while she was in the midst of her delight that everything was going so smoothly, for her to be suddenly struck down in a fit, and give up her life without a pang.[10] With Rebecca, his youngest sister,[11] he read Greek, as far as Aeschylus, so that in this particular again the family was not wanting in common pursuits and good understanding. He was very fond of playing with the merry *Becky*, and used to pinch her cheeks when talking to her.

Felix was indeed a wonderfully gifted being. Leaving out of consideration Music, as the central point of his life, his natural gifts were exhibited in the most various ways, without any vain parade of them on his part. He was, for instance, a vigorous and skillful gymnast. The horizontal pole and the bars stood under the trees in the garden, and, shortly before the concerts which used to be given at home every fortnight, at twelve o'clock on Sunday morning, even when he had to play the piano, Felix thought nothing of having a half hour's good turn at gymnastics. On one occasion, he was summoned straight from the horizontal pole to the piano; but he had just run a small splinter into his finger, and the consequence was that he left marks of blood upon the keys during Beethoven's E-flat-major concerto,[12] and I carefully wiped them away while he was playing.—He was a very good swimmer. During all one hot summer, we used to bathe nearly every day at Pfuel's Baths, and I was annoyed because, when struggling against one another in the water, he always got the better of me, and sent me under, though I was the taller and stronger of the two. On account of the great distance of the baths, at the Silesian Gate, Mama provided a carriage, and the consequence was that I drove home with him nearly every evening that summer. After tea we regularly had music, which was best, perhaps, when we were alone. At that time, he never extemporised as he subsequently did. His own compositions he never played, as a rule, unless especially requested to do so. After tea was, in so far, an unfortunate time, because we generally went on till nine o'clock, and then the drummers of the guard passed under the windows beating the retreat from the Leipsic Gate to the offices of the Minister of War. It was by no means rare for this to come precisely in the *Adagio*, disturbing us, of course, in a very disagreeable manner. Even when the drummers were at a distance we could hear them gradually advancing, the nearer they approached the greater being the hubbub, until, when it reached its highest point, the window-panes rattled again. Any one who ever heard the melting tones of Mendelssohn's playing, and saw how his soul was absorbed by the magnificent creations of art—how he entered into them, and how his feeling for them was expressed on the gradually drooping lids of his beautiful eyes—will comprehend how such discordant sounds jarred upon our reverential feelings. When we got over the interruption, too, we knew we had to expect it on the march back. On one occasion, Mendelssohn jumped up in the midst of the movement, exclaiming angrily: "What stupid, monstrous, childishness!" It is true that we never thought of exercising ordinary precaution and going out of the way of the evil spirits.

Mendelssohn was, likewise, a good horseman. On the sole occasion I rode with him, we went to Pankow, walking thence to the Schönhauser Garden. It was about that time when he was busy with the overture to *A Midsummer Night's Dream*.[13] The weather was beautiful, and we were engaged in animated conversation, as we lay in the shade on the grass when, all of a sudden, he seized me firmly by the arm, and whispered: "Hush!" He afterwards informed me that a large fly had just then gone buzzing by, and he wanted to hear the sound it produced gradually die away. When the Overture was completed, he showed me the passage in the progression, where the violoncello modulates in the chord of the seventh of the descending scale from B minor to F sharp minor,[14] and said: "There, that's the fly that buzzed past us at Schönhauser!"[15] He was also an elegant dancer, a circumstance which, when he was a youth, procured him many friends. In consequence of this, his birthday was once celebrated, to please him, by a masquerade. Skating was the only thing at which he was not a good hand. On the one solitary occasion that I succeeded in prevailing on him to try it, he suffered so much from the cold, despite his large fur gloves, that he probably never repeated the experiment.

As in such pleasing exercises, so also in the sphere of the intellect, his natural gifts were variously exhibited. He played chess admirably, a game, by the way, of which his Father, also, was very fond. That he surprised his mother on her birthday with a translation which he had himself made of Terence's *Andria*, and which his tutor had sent to the printer's, is a fact with which I only became acquainted outside the house.[16] He never boasted of such things. Rösel[17] was his drawing-master; and, though I am not qualified to give an opinion of productions of this description, yet may I state that Mendelssohn possessed a feeling for the artistic conception of Nature as well as for

plastic art: he was capable of appreciating with intelligence and enthusiastic admiration the masterpieces of both ancient and modern
times. Anything connected with mathematics, however appeared to
be less in his way. In vain did I once attempt to make him understand
why the Polar Star, which happened just then to be shining beautifully clear and bright, was alone sufficient to guide us over the four
quarters of the globe. He could not master the line to be let fall, in
his mind, perpendicularly on the horizon, the extension of the line of
sight backwards through the eye, and its intersection at right angles
with the side-line.

How he composed, I enjoyed only one opportunity of witnessing.
I went one morning into his room, where I found him writing music.
I wanted to go away again directly so as not to disturb him. He asked
me to stop, however, remarking: "I am merely copying out." I remained in consequence, and we talked of all kinds of subjects, he continuing to write the whole time. But he was not copying, for there
was no paper but that on which he was writing. The work whereon
he was busy was the grand Overture in C major, that was performed
at that period but not published.[18] It was, too, a score for full band.
He began with the uppermost octave, slowly drew a bar-line, leaving
a pretty good amount of room, and then extended the bar-line right
to the bottom of the page. He next filled in the second, then the third
stave, etc., with pauses and partly with notes. On coming to the violins, it was evident why he had left so much space for the bar; there
was a figure requiring considerable room. The longer melody at this
passage was not in any way distinguished from the rest, but, like the
other parts, had its bar given in, and waited at the bar-line to be continued when the turn of its stave came round again. During all this,
there was no looking forwards or backwards, no comparing, no hum-
ming-over, or anything of the sort; the pen kept going steadily on,
slowly and carefully, it is true, but without pausing, and we never
ceased talking. The copying out, therefore, as he called it, meant that
the whole composition, to the last note, had been so thought over and
worked out in his mind, that he beheld it there as though it had been
actually lying before him. I subsequently saw other compositions
when half finished, at Friedrich Schneider's, for instance, but the bass
part was invariably written out, frequently figured, a musical figure,
too, being jotted down here and there in the various instruments, and
the remainder still unwritten. "I fill that up afterwards," observed
Schneider.[19] It is, however, a question whether the effect of this mode
of composing is not to produce too much filling-up, and cause a noisy
overloading of the work, while, in Mendelssohn's mode of proceed-

ing, every separate portion was definitely fixed, in connection with the onward flow of the whole, not merely with notes but with pauses as well?

Mendelssohn's character had a deep feeling of religion for its basis. That this wanted the specifically church colouring is a fact on which we disputed a great deal in our earlier years. As an unconditional Schleiermacherite,[20] I was then almost incapable of recognising Christianity in any other shape, and, consequently, wronged Felix. Wilmsen,[21] who had instructed and confirmed Mendelssohn, and his brothers and sisters, struck me as a man of no great capacity, and I let fall some hint or other to the effect that it would have been better had they gone to Schleiermacher. Felix was seriously angry, and gave me to understand he would not allow anyone to attack his spiritual adviser, for whom he entertained a feeling of affectionate reverence. It is true that he did not go very often to hear him perform Divine Service. When I recollect, however, with what a serious religious feeling he pursued his art, the exercise of it always being, as it were, a sacred duty; how the first page of everyone of his compositions bears impressed on it the initial letter of a prayer;[22] how he devoted the time, as he watched through the night by the bed of his dying friend, Hanstein, to marking in the first fugue, composed here, of the six he afterwards published—in E minor—the progress of the disease as it gradually destroyed the sufferer, until he made it culminate in the choral[e] of release in E major;[23] how the very best touches in his oratorios result from his delicate tact—for instance, the words for the air of Paul during the three days of his blindness, when he had just been converted before Damascus, for which Mendelssohn, dissatisfied with everything proposed to him, himself hit upon the 51st Psalm, that seems as though it had been written on purpose;[24] moreover, when I call to mind everything connected with my beloved friend, as regards his views and opinions on art and artists—whether he was standing at the conductor's desk, sitting at the piano, or taking the tenor-part in a quartet—religion and veneration were enthroned in his countenance; this was why his music possessed such a magic charm. On one occasion, he expressly said that sacred music, as such, did not stand higher in his estimation than any other, because every kind of music ought, in its peculiar way, to tend to the glory of God.

I once said to him, lamentingly, that I found it difficult to conceive Bach's music as aught but a dry arithmetical sum. To convince me that it was something more, he went and fetched the *Matthäus-Passion*, of which a copy had been given him, a short time previously, from Zelter's scores. We sang a good deal of it with his sisters, and when he perceived that the music deeply entranced me, albeit I was only an unprofessional, he took courage, and we arranged that the performance should be repeated with better resources. We soon enlisted the services of Edward Devrient and his wife,[25] who sang admirably; we soon, too, got together a small chorus of sixteen voices, and held weekly rehearsals. The delight of everyone, whether taking an active part in the matter, or only listening, encouraged and impelled him to get up the public performance of the following years, a performance which restored to the world this masterpiece which had long been consigned to oblivion.[26] If I am not mistaken, it was the first public performance he ever undertook, but it at once proved him a master in the art of conducting. His amiability could not fail to charm every one, and, despite the numerous faults committed at the rehearsals, owing to the great difficulties of the work, and the frequent repetitions necessary, on no single occasion did he lose his patience, or did we, who were the executants, ever feel tired of our task.

How thoroughly he had rendered himself master of this work was proved by his directing one of the later rehearsals at the piano, without any music before him, and by his remarking, at the conclusion of one movement: "In the twenty-third bar, the soprano has C and not C sharp." The *Passionsmusik* excited perfect enthusiasm in local musical circles. Mendelssohn told us, with hearty delight, a year subsequently, on his return from England, that Bader[27] had met him in the street, and hallooed out: "Oh! here you are again; when are we to sing the *Passion* a second time?" In addition to Devrient, who sang the part of our Saviour excellently, Stümer distinguished himself as the Evangelist.[28] But, however beautifully he rendered it, he did not at all care for the music. During the performance he had, in the pause between the parts, spoken to his wife, and expressed his amazement at observing traces of tears in her eyes. She replied that she had no reason to be ashamed, for all the gentlemen round her had cried. The circumstance produced its effect, and Stümer confessed to Mendelssohn that he then for the first time had a presentiment that there must be something in the music after all, and in the second part it did really affect him.

It was from this period that Mendelssohn, even at the little rehearsals at home, used the conductor's stick; he had hitherto modestly stated his opinion, from the piano or the desk of the tenor. He assumed a more independent bearing, too, as I remember was the case when, in Haydn's D-major symphony, he required the *tempi* to be taken at a slower rate than that to which we were accustomed. The orchestra kept continually hurrying on, but, with an iron will, and marking the time most forcibly with his stick, he held back, till even the faithful Edward Rietz,[29] the leader, began to grumble. For my own part, I must confess that quite a new light was then thrown upon the Symphony. I had always heard the last movement called the "Bear's Dance";[30] but, on the occasion in question, it was a most pleasing piece of composition. Good old father Haydn must not be hurried.

The amount of delicacy, and the nice and fine gradations Mendelssohn introduced into the orchestra are things so well known, that there is no necessity for me to say aught upon the subject. I think, that, on this particular, he learned a great deal from Weber. When the latter was in Berlin getting up his *Euryanthe*,[31] Mendelssohn frequently attended the rehearsals, and used to speak with astonishment of what the man did with a strange orchestra. It is true that he as little took as a model Weber's charming rudeness as his exaggerated wavering in the *tempo*. In this last particular, he rather preserved an equality, with tolerable strictness, and strove to attain effect more by clever gradation of light and shade than by changes of the time.

In the year 1830, I returned from Berlin to my native town, after fully enjoying the society of my beloved friend; during the period he was confined to his room by the measles.[32] In the ensuing spring he made the journey from which the now published *Reisebriefe*[33] date. He first paid me a visit at Dessau, accompanied by his father, who set out again the next day.[34] Mendelssohn attended a rehearsal, and, on being requested to do so, allowed them to try his *Meeresstille und glückliche Fahrt* Overture,[35] then not known here: afforded a small and select party, at Rust's, a rare treat by taking part in trios by Beethoven (D major), and Haydn (C major), besides extemporising on "Adelaide" and the commencement of the *Ninth Symphony*; and went to see the Duchess, from whom he received some commissions to execute in Rome. As a matter of course, we called at the house of Friedrich Schneider, the celebrated composer of the *Weltgericht*, but he was away, travelling. On driving into the country, on the third day, to visit my sister, whose acquaintance Mendelssohn was desirous of making, it so happened, that Schneider was in the place, residing close by at a friend's. We met in the village; I introduced the two; Schneider continued his walk, and, when he returned, some hours afterwards, we felt there was something wrong. Many years previously, Schneider had been once at the Mendelssohn's, and expressed his appreciation of the promising boy. But Bach's *Passion* had annoyed him. Enthusiasm had been excited about something which, though old, was unknown to Schneider; Marx had said, too, plainly, in the *Musikalische*

Zeitung: Any one who did not know the *Passion*, did not know Bach. Finally, the Duchess, after having been present at the performance, by which she was greatly moved, told Schneider she could not speak in terms of sufficient commendation of the impression it had produced, praising, moreover, the charming instrumentation, which was not so deafening as a great deal of other music. All this annoyed Schneider, so that he could never be induced to have a single movement of the *Passion* sung. Mendelssohn's name, too, was so intimately connected with the whole affair, that something of Schneider's dissatisfaction fell unconsciously on Mendelssohn. Schneider was then at the full height of his reputation, while Mendelssohn, then twenty-one, was just rising into notice. The consequence was that the former was rather haughty, and this did not please the latter. I must state that Schneider, to his credit, afterwards assumed a different tone towards Mendelssohn; when the corpse was conveyed through his place by rail, at midnight, Schneider greeted it on its way with a "Lament" which he composed on purpose.[36]

Subsequently to 1832, we frequently discussed the subject of oratorio texts. With regard to *St. Paul*, a considerable amount of preliminary labour had been got through before I knew anything about it: at Mendelssohn's request, I undertook a certain further amount of work of a subordinate kind, such as connecting and introducing certain suitable passages and songs. During this time, we were a great deal in communication with each other, sometimes orally and sometimes by letter.[37] He always proved himself a thoughtful artist, and strove to obtain a clear appreciation of each separate point, such, for instance, as the admissibility of the choral[e], of the narrative recitatives, etc. He rejected, also, much that was suggested, being so well acquainted with his Bible, that he obtained a great deal of valuable materials himself: for any assistance, he was, however, extremely grateful. That he would not accept my suggestions for the Paulinian doctrine of the justification by faith, but, at the appropriate place, substituted merely the general assertion: "Wir glauben all an einen Gott"[38] was something that did not satisfy my theological conscience, though, perhaps, any extension of the work in this direction would have made it too long. We arranged *Elijah* together from beginning to end, and he was pleased that I should, without any further introduction, have commenced the oratorio with the passage of Elijah, and marked the overture with no. 2, with the addition of "Muss drei Jahre dauern." Regarding the oratorio of *Christus*,[39] he never exchanged a word with me; on the other hand, we had often previously talked about St. Peter and John the Baptist. What I told him of the account given in the gospel of Nicodemus concerning the descent of Christ into Hell, interested him in an extraordinary degree, and, from what escaped him, I am inclined to believe he intended turning it, sometime or other, to musical account.

Some few circumstances concerning our relations with each other have been made known in the published *Letters*. Together with his musical doings, the loveable and fresh character of his youth is apparent to the world in the *Reisebriefe*, and his straightforward, manly earnestness in his later correspondence. I will, therefore, conclude my reminiscences by adding one little trait. When he played on the piano and sang to me, in Leipsic, as much of *St. Paul* as he had written, I thought that in the principal passage before Damascus, the voice of the Lord, which he had set for a soprano solo, was too thin. He said, in a tone of regret, that the matter struck him in the same light; that he had long endeavoured, though in vain, to hit upon something better; but that he could not at all reconcile himself to the notion of producing the effect of a very powerful bass voice. I suggested that he should set the phrase for four parts. After looking at me for a long time, he said: "Yes, and the worthy theologians would cut me up nicely for wishing to deny and supplant Him who arose from the dead." I replied that I would answer for the theologians, for they knew that the transfigured Lord of Heaven and Earth had a different voice from that of a mere mortal. Thereupon he altered the words into a four-part female chorus, and how overpowering was the effect![40] I was not, however, able quite to keep my promise with respect to the theologians. A sort of theologian, named Fink,[41] took offence, though, it is true, in the contrary sense to what was anticipated, in his musical paper, for he wanted the *vox humana* to be omitted entirely, and only indefinite sounds of the trombone heard. But that at the same time, he should take the opportunity of objecting to the words: "Ich bin Jesus von Nazareth, den Du verfolgst" ("I am Jesus of Nazareth, whom thou persecutest,") and of trying to prove that the Saviour, after his transfiguration and ascent to Heaven, was no longer He of Nazareth, but the Lord of Heaven, afforded us a most hearty laugh. The worthy Fink had undoubtedly been reading the *Acts of the Apostles*, Chap. 9, Verse 5, and found that the words "von Nazareth" ("of Nazareth") are not there; on this he based his criticism. He had, however, so far forgotten his theology as not to recollect how St. Paul himself, further in the *Acts of the Apostles*, twice gives an account of his conversion, and, in Chap. 22, Verse 8, expressly mentions the words to which objection is taken; so that the censure really fell upon the Apostle. Mendelssohn, who was well aware of the circumstance, laughed, but did not say much; friend Schleinitz,[42] however, in a playfully sarcastic manner, afterwards paid out master Fink very nicely.

Postscript.—I have just heard that an unfavorable opinion on a musician whose name is not printed—in a letter of the 8th of August, 1834, from Mendelssohn to myself—has been interpreted as referring to Schumann.[43] I can testify that this supposition is erroneous. Why there is no allusion to Schumann in the published correspondence is more than I know; one thing I know however, and that is, that Mendelssohn once spoke to me in terms of high appreciation of Schumann's musical significance, and that he was on a friendly footing with Schumann and his wife, not merely on account of the latter's pianoforte-playing; on another occasion, too, when I expressed my surprise at the F in the fifth bar of the fourth "Lied," Book Six of the *Lieder ohne Worte*,[44] he replied, also surprised, that he now knew what Schumann had meant the day before, by expressing from a distance an F with his fingers. He (Mendelssohn), he added, considered this F perfectly natural, but there must be something particular about it, as it had thus struck both Schumann and me. This little circumstance leads me to infer the existence of a kindly and friendly feeling between the two. A mere accident unfortunately prevented us from keeping the agreement we made at the time to meet at Rosenthal.

NOTES

1. Wilhelm Müller (1794–1827), also the poet of *Die schöne Müllerin* and *Winterreise*, set as song cycles by Franz Schubert. Müller was the father of the philologist F. Max Müller, whose memoirs of Mendelssohn are excerpted on pp. 252–58. [ed.]

2. Baron Alexander von Humboldt (1769–1859), scientist and explorer. Mendelssohn composed a festival cantata in his honor, which was performed in Berlin on 18 September 1828. [ed.]

3. G.W.F. Hegel (1770–1831). In 1827 Mendelssohn attended the philosopher's lectures at the University of Berlin. [ed.]

4. Abraham Mendelssohn-Bartholdy (1776–1835). [ed.]

5. It is the custom in Germany, after dinner, for the company at table to say to one another: "Gesegnete Mahlzeit" ("May Heaven bless the meal"), or words to that effect, amounting to a sort of secular grace, and it was this that Mendelssohn had set to music. [ed., *Musical World*]

6. In 1820 the eleven-year-old Mendelssohn set down this weekly regimen of tutored lessons: six hours of Latin (Caesar, Ovid, grammar, and exercises), mathematics (Euclid), history, arithmetic, geography, and German. Musical

activities included composition lessons with C. F. Zelter and the study of piano and violin. See R. Larry Todd, *Mendelssohn's Musical Education* (Cambridge, 1983), pp. 14–15. [ed.]

7. Ludwig Berger (1777–1839), the children's piano teacher during the early 1820s. Berger was a pupil of Muzio Clementi. [ed.]

8. See p. 219, note 10. [ed.]

9. "Pilgerspruch," op. 8, no. 5. Parallel ("false") octaves occur in the piano part of measure 14. [ed.]

10. Fanny died on 14 May 1847 while rehearsing her brother's cantata *Die erste Walpurgisnacht*. [ed.]

11. Rebecca Mendelssohn-Bartholdy (1811–1858). [ed.]

12. Piano Concerto no. 5 (*Emperor*). It is unknown when this work was performed at the Mendelssohn house. [ed.]

13. July and early August, 1826. Mendelssohn finished the overture on 6 August. [ed.]

14. Most likely measures 264ff. [ed.]

15. These words remind me of the significance people are so fond of attaching to modern music, and of their partiality for asserting that it conveys to them sharply defined ideas. Friedrich Schneider was exceedingly displeased at the system, and adduced the "freie deutsche Musik" ("Free German Music") as standing on higher ground than this Programme-Music, which he would acknowledge at most in Beethoven's *Pastoral Symphony*. Mendelssohn said that after Beethoven had taken such a step it was no longer possible to ignore it entirely. In the *Meeresstille und glückliche Fahrt* Overture, there is a most charming melody serving to reintroduce the first notes of the introduction; it begins on the third, then rises to the fifth, and ends upon the octave. I told Mendelssohn that it suggested to me the tones of love, which, thanks to the prosperous voyage, is entranced at approaching nearer and nearer the goal of its desires. He said that such was not his notion in composing it; he had thought of some good-natured old man sitting in the stern of the vessel and blowing vigorously in the sails, with puffed-out cheeks, so as to contribute his part to the prosperous voyage. [Julius Schubring] The passage referred to in the overture (op. 27) is probably measures 379ff., which mark the recapitulation. [ed.]

16. *Das Mädchen von Andros, eine Kömodie des Terentius in den Versmassen des Originals übersetzt* (Leipzig, 1826). Mendelssohn's tutor was Karl Wilhelm Ludwig Heyse (1797–1855), who contributed an introduction to the translation. The birthday of Mendelssohn's mother, Lea Mendelssohn-Bartholdy, fell on 15 March. [ed.]

17. Johann Gottlob Samuel Rösel (1768–1843). [ed.]

18. The so-called *Trumpet* Overture, posthumously published in 1867 as op. 101. Mendelssohn completed the first version on 4 March 1826 and performed the work in Berlin on 18 April 1828; a revision was completed on 10 April 1833, and a performance in London followed on 10 June 1833. [ed.]

19. Friedrich Schneider (1786–1853), oratorio composer, Kapellmeister of Anhalt-Dessau. See also note 15. [ed.]

20. F.E.D. Schleiermacher (1768–1834), German philosopher and professor of theology at the University of Berlin. [ed.]

21. F. P. Wilmsen (1770–1831). Mendelssohn's "Konfirmations-Bekenntnis," signed "Wilmsen. September 27, 1825," is reprinted in Karl Klingemann, ed. *Felix Mendelssohn-Bartholdys Briefwechsel mit Legationsrat Karl Klingemann in London* (Essen, 1909), pp. 358–62. [ed.]

22. Mendelssohn habitually used two invocations at the beginning of his manuscripts, "L.e.g.G." ("Lass es gelingen, Gott") and "H.D.m." ("Hilf Du mir"). [ed.]

23. The fugue in E minor, which later appeared as the first fugue in the collection of six preludes and fugues, op. 35 (1837). [ed.]

24. No. 17, the bass aria "Gott sei mir gnädig." [ed.]

25. Eduard Devrient (1801–1877) and Therese Devrient (1803–1882). [ed.]

26. The performance took place in Berlin on 11 March 1829. For a critical account see Martin Geck, *Die Wiederentdeckung der Matthäuspassion im 19. Jahrhundert* (Regensburg, 1967). [ed.]

27. Carl Adam Bader (1789–1870), tenor at the Berlin court opera and member of Zelter's Liedertafel. [ed.]

28. Heinrich Stümer (1789–1857), tenor at the Berlin court opera and member of Zelter's Liedertafel; as a youth he sang in Zelter's Singakademie. [ed.]

29. Eduard Rietz (1802–1832), Mendelssohn's violin teacher, and the dedicatee of the D-minor Violin Concerto (1822); the Violin Sonata, op. 4 (1823); and the Octet, op. 20 (1825). [ed.]

30. Unclear to which Haydn symphony Schubring refers; Symphony no. 82 in C major is known as the *L'ours*, on account of a supposedly ursine theme in its finale. [ed.]

31. Performed in Berlin on 23 December 1825. [ed.]

32. In March 1830. [ed.]

33. F. Mendelssohn, *Reisebriefe aus den Jahren 1830 bis 1832*, ed. P. Mendelssohn Bartholdy (Leipzig, 1861). [ed.]

34. In May 1830. [ed.]

35. Op. 27, finished in June 1828 and first performed in Berlin on 8 September 1828; the overture was revised in March 1834 and published in 1835 along with the *Midsummer Night's Dream* and *Hebrides* Overtures. [ed.]

36. The part-song for male choir, "Engelstimmen klangen," published in the *Musical Times and Singing Class Circular* 2 (1848): 134. [ed.]

37. Much of the correspondence later appeared in the *Briefwechsel zwischen Felix Mendelssohn Bartholdy und Julius Schubring*, ed. J. Schubring (Leipzig, 1892, rep. 1973). [ed.]

38. No. 35, in the chorus "Aber unser Gott im Himmel." [ed.]

39. Mendelssohn completed only a few numbers, which appeared posthumously in 1852 as op. 97. [ed.]

40. In no. 13, "Saul, was verfolgst du mich?" [ed.]

41. See Gottfried Wilhelm Fink, "Paulus," in *Allgemeine musikalische Zeitung* 39 (1837), cols. 497–506, 513–530, especially 515. Fink was the editor of the *AmZ*. [ed.]

42. Conrad Schleinitz (1802–1881), Leipzig lawyer. [ed.]

43. The letter appeared in the *Briefe aus den Jahren 1833 bis 1847*, ed. P. and C. Mendelssohn Bartholdy (Leipzig, 1863). We cite here a passage from the English translation that appeared in 1863, and then in numerous editions, *Letters of Felix Mendelssohn Bartholdy from 1833 to 1847* (London, 1878), p. 47: "I don't know what to say as to your opinion of X——. I think you are rather hard on him; and yet there is a good deal of truth in what you assert, too, and quite in accordance with what I find in his compositions. But my belief is, that you do him great injustice in pronouncing him to be a flatterer, as he never *intends* to flatter, but always fully believes in the truth and propriety of what he is saying; but when such an excitable temperament is not mitigated by some definite, energetic, and creative powers, or when it can bring forth nothing but a momentary assimilation to some foreign element, then it is indeed unfortunate; and I almost begin to fear that this is his case, for his compositions I exceedingly disapprove of." Mendelssohn was responding to Schubring's letter of 31 July 1834, in which we read: "The third, about whom you ask, is * [Adolph Bernhard Marx], and I want to say candidly how very much he has mispleased me during his recent, to be sure, only short stay. He behaved himself quite like a tasteless coxcomb . . . Recollect that I once said to you in Berlin that he seemed insincere to me and spoke as a flatterer, etc. Now that was the case here in the worst way. He fell in love with every young lady he encountered; with the greatest naivety—one might call it shamelessness—he threw into their faces, 'heavenly,' 'godly,' and so forth. One evening he was with us to hear a trio, along with three ladies, whom you also have seen, the * [die Müller], her sister and cousin. For example, to the sister (who made that lectern at which you marvelled) he said during the performance (Beethoven's Trio in D major): 'And you crown the performance.' 'How so?' 'By your listening.' This and other things in a seemingly underhand way, so that my wife later said to me, she would have departed, if such tastelessness was said to her face.—Then he said to * [die Müller], your piano is better than mine—(you know well her embattled casing), just to say something pleasant. To me again: With these trios (which were rather normal, partly without members of the audience, partly with my nearest acquaintance) I would fashion a center for good music in Dessau, in opposition to Schneider. To Schneider: He had not yet heard during his life symphonies played the same way as by him, etc., etc. In this way too he praised my sermon—of course in my presence; affected an enchantment with Dessau, etc. Now tell me in God's name, what does all this mean, and what should one say to it? We are not accustomed to this sort of thing here"

(*Briefwechsel zwischen Felix Mendelssohn Bartholdy und Julius Schubring*, pp. 72–73). Schubring's original letter survives in the Green Books Collection of the Bodleian Library, Oxford (vol. 3, no. 234), which reveals the object of these comments to be A. B. Marx. [ed.]

44. Op. 67, no. 4. [ed.]

Reminiscences of Mendelssohn by

His English Pupil

CHARLES EDWARD HORSLEY

The son of the English glee composer William Horsley (1774–1858), Charles Edward Horsley (1822–1876) first met Mendelssohn in 1832 in London. After a period of study in Kassel, Horsley moved to Leipzig in 1841; there he undertook composition lessons with Mendelssohn until 1843, when he returned to London. Horsley's reminiscences provide little-known glimpses of Mendelssohn as composer, pianist, organist, and conductor, and of concert life in Germany and England during the 1830s and 1840s. The panegyric tone of Horsley's prose is representative of the Mendelssohn worship that developed in England after the composer's death in 1847. [ed.]

[Source: *Dwight's Journal of Music* 32 (1872), 345ff., 353ff., 361ff.]

.

From this time [1832] Mendelssohn became the most intimate friend of my family. He used to come to us at all times when in London, and especially to breakfast, generally accompanied by his friends above named, Rosen[1] and Klingemann.[2] We had a small garden attached to my father's house, and it was Mendelssohn's great delight to spend hours in this, sketching the trees, &c., and talking not only about music, but about his travels in Italy, his intimacy with Goethe and Zelter,[3] and his future plans for his works. During these mornings we frequently heard the first germs of compositions that have now become immortal. The beautiful overtures to "Melusine" and "Isles of Fingal" were played at Kensington some years, I may say, before they were performed, and my sister possesses a copy of the first MS. totally different from those now published.[4] In like manner we heard scraps of "St. Paul," which was not produced until 1836, and many other works which then only existed in the great composer's head; and it was a matter of wonderment how so small a body could contain so many ideas, each belonging to a different composition, and yet all arranged in the most perfect and symmetrical order.

In 1832 the west end of London, especially that part commencing at Tyburn Gate and continuing down the Uxbridge or Oxford Road, wore a very different aspect from the present. . . . This part of London for many years after 1832 remained in a most desolate condition; but at the end of Albion St., Hyde Park, a church was built, which for a long time was the solitary oasis in this desert of suburban solitude. This church, dedicated to St. John, belonged to the Parish of Paddington, and contained a small but effective organ by Bishop. The revival and improved method of organ building in England had not then commenced, and this most desirable consummation was undoubtedly initiated by Mendelssohn. My friend Mr. George Maxwell, a pupil of Hummel, and a most talented pianist and organist, was appointed to this church, and it was at my father's house that he first met Mendelssohn. A conversation happening to turn on the then existing organs in London, Mendelssohn expressed a wish to try the instrument in St. John's.[5] Compared with the large organs of the present day, this was a very poor affair. It possessed but one full Manual, and a Swell down to Tenor C, and was what is technically termed a G organ; that is, the Pedals commenced on G, instead of the now indispensable compass of C; and there was only a 16 ft. open Diapason in the Pedal Organ. Such were the small means placed at Mendelssohn's disposal, but he made the most of them, and many happy afternoons were spent in hearing his interpretation of Bach's Fugues, his wonderful extemporizing, and the performance of his own Sonatas,[6] and other Organ pieces, then only existing in his memory. As the reports of these meetings became spread through the town, other and larger organs were placed at his disposal, and at St. Paul's Cathedral, Christ Church, Newgate St., St. Sepulchre's, and many other London churches he played on several occasions, giving the greatest delight to all who had the good fortune to hear him. I have heard most of the greatest organists of my time, both English, German and French, but in no respect have I ever known Mendelssohn excelled either in creative or executive ability, and it is hard to say which was the most extraordinary, his manipulation or his pedipulation,—for his feet were quite as active as his hands, and the independence of the former, being totally distinct from the latter, produced a result which at that time was quite unknown in England, and undoubtedly laid the foundation of a school of organ playing in

Great Britain which has placed English organists on the highest point attainable in their profession.

After the production of "St. Paul," at Düsseldorf in 1836, Mendelssohn came again to London and was everywhere received with the greatest enthusiasm. His oratorio was hailed with delight as opening a new phase of the art; his appearance at the Philharmonic[7] and other London concerts was the signal for crowded houses and enchanted audiences, and his presence at all social gatherings of his many private friends was the assurance of the certainty of most delightful evenings, where his geniality, his great kindness in displaying extraordinary gifts, both in music and general accomplishments, were the very life and soul of the entertainment. . . .

At the time I was in Leipzig [1841–1843], the fame of Mendelssohn was at its zenith. He was director of the celebrated Gewandhaus Concerts. He was in constant consultation with the King of Prussia concerning the progress of music in Berlin. Leipzig was the centre of music during his lifetime. No artist of any repute as a composer, a performer, or a singer visited Germany without paying homage to Mendelssohn. His orchestra, though not numerically great, was certainly by far the best in the North of Germany, and its performances of all the greatest works, especially Beethoven's Symphonies, were celebrated as the most complete that up to that time (1841) had been given. The Gewandhaus concerts took place every Thursday from Michaelmas to Easter. The management of these was entrusted nominally to a committee, but the direction was really in the hands of Mendelssohn, David (the orchestral leader),[8] and a most intimate friend of Mendelssohn, Schleinitz.[9] The concert programmes, according to notions prevalent now-a-days, were short. The first part, as a rule, contained an overture, a vocal piece, either solo or concerted, and a pianoforte or violin concerto, or a solo with orchestral accompaniment on some other instrument. The second part inevitably consisted of one Symphony. Thus the ear was not tired out by a selection of incongruous pieces, and the Symphony being placed at the last, the audience were not wearied by the length of the concert, and able to return home with a perfect sense of enjoyment of the feast of sound which had been so discriminately set before them. In addition to these full orchestral concerts there were two weekly rehearsals, and an evening devoted to Chamber Music, at which stringed Quartets, Trios, &c., formed the programme. These were also under Mendelssohn's direction, and he frequently played at them, but generally speaking young artists were allowed to appear, and both my friends Eckert[10] and Kufferath[11] had many opportunities for distinguishing themselves on the violin and piano. One great characteristic of Mendelssohn's disposition was his large-mindedness towards other musicians. Not only was his house and table open to all who knew him and brought letters to him, but his advice and in many cases his purse was at the disposal of all who required either; and had any artist written a work which pleased him, it was sure to find its way into the concert programmes without reference to the nation from which the composer sprang. Thus, Bennett[12] and Macfarren[13] as English writers, Miss Dolby[14] and Mme. Clara Novello[15] as English vocalists, Gade[16] from Denmark, and a whole host of German composers were encouraged to write and appear, with the certainty of having an admirable interpretation of their works and performances under Mendelssohn's direction; and I have always considered that it is to his generosity and open-heartedness to my countrymen, as well as to his frequent visits to England, that the foundation of that large re-action in favor of classical music, especially as regards the whole of Sebastian Bach's work, and the later compositions of Beethoven, which has taken place within the last forty years in the British Empire, may be traced. When those who had the right to call themselves pupils of Mendelssohn assert the fact, it must not be thought that he gave lessons in the ordinary acceptation of the word. In the first place I do not believe there is a single instance in which he received pecuniary recompense for his advice. Next, his instruction was not imparted in a formal manner. Speaking of myself as an example of the course he followed with others, I generally went to him three times a week. Previous to fixing an hour he would advise me to practice certain pieces, generally by Bach or Beethoven, and when I played them to him he would either criticize the performance, or more frequently play them to me. His favorite mode of giving advice was, however, by taking a walk during which he would invariably talk on musical subjects. One of his favorite haunts was a little Inn in a small forest near Leipzig, called the Rosenthal. I have frequently walked with him there, and during our wanderings he would invariably select for consideration a Symphony by Beethoven, an Opera of Mozart, or an Oratorio of Handel, or a Fugue of Bach. He would analyze these, point out the various beauties of their ideas, the ingenuity of their instrumentation, or the subtleness of their counterpoint in a most masterly manner. At the rehearsals of the Gewandhaus, to which all his pupils were free, he would always provide us with the scores of the larger works, and we had generally afterward to undergo a pretty keen examination as to the construction and peculiarities of each. . . .

I do not remember a single instance in which his compositions failed to meet with great and lasting success. I do not however think that full justice has yet been done to his marvellous powers as an executive musician. As an Organ and Pianoforte player he has never been excelled. His playing on the Organ has been already mentioned, but his management of the Piano was if possible still more marvellous. His mastery over the instrument was little short of miraculous. His powers of execution were quite as great as those of Rubinstein[17] and Liszt; his delicacy of touch and tone was not exceeded by Thalberg[18] or Chopin; and when to all these qualities are added the wonderful scope of his own mind in grasping the Pianoforte music of all schools, I do not in the least exaggerate when I assert that, of all pianoforte players of and since his time, Mendelssohn stands by far on the apex of greatness. During my stay in Leipzig various great pianists arrived on visits, and it was refreshing to observe the great attention paid them by Mendelssohn, the great deference and admiration showed to them by him, and the eagerness with which he sought to make himself acquainted with their peculiarities of style and method. One day I received a note from him asking me to come to dinner, as Thalberg had arrived the previous evening, and would be his guest. We were a trio, and after dinner Mendelssohn asked Thalberg if he had written anything new, whereupon Thalberg sat down to the piano and played his Fantasia from the "Sonnambula," then very recently composed, and in MS.[19] This composition is one of the most individual and effective of all Thalberg's works. At the close there are several runs of Chromatic Octaves, which at that time had not previously been heard, and of which peculiar passages Thalberg was undoubtedly the inventor. Mendelssohn was much struck with the novel effect produced, and greatly admired its ingenuity. When we separated for the evening he told me to be with him the next afternoon at 2 o'clock. When I arrived at his study door I heard him playing to himself, and practising continually this passage which had so struck him the previous day. I waited for at least half an hour listening in wonderment to the facility with which he applied his own thoughts to the cleverness of Thalberg's mechanism, and then went into the room. He laughed and said: "Listen to this, is it not almost like Thalberg?"—and he proceeded to play all sorts of passages founded on these double scales. He never introduced the effect, however, in his writings; but the last "Lied ohne Worte" in Book 4,[20] which he dedicated to my sister, Sophy Horsley (1st Edition published in London and Leipzig), contains an accompaniment somewhat founded on this idea, which was written about the time I am describing. Mendelssohn's life in Leipzig was that of a true artist. He was an early riser, and generally in his library by nine o'clock. He had a very large correspondence, both professional and private, and was most regular in answering all letters addressed to him. In accordance with German early hours the concert rehearsals were always in the forenoon, and his usual time for his own pursuits was after the early family dinner at 1 o'clock. His evenings, when not publicly engaged, were always spent with his wife and children.

Mendelssohn's home was truly happy. Mme. Mendelssohn was a charming lady, very beautiful in person and very accomplished in mind. She was devoted to him; of a calm, unexcitable temperament; and as he was of a precisely opposite disposition, the extremes in this case met to mutual advantage. His children were admirably brought up, and have now all become most excellent members of society, though strange to say, none have in the least inherited a taste for music. Perhaps this is well, as neither of his boys could have been placed in the position of Mozart's surviving son,[21] who, though a really sound and learned musician (this on Hauptmann's[22] authority, who knew him in Milan) constantly complained of want of success in his profession, alleging as the reason, that the superlative greatness of his father caused every one to imagine it impossible that any scrap of the Mozartean mantle could have fallen on the shoulders of his son. . . .

This very happy time of my life could not last forever, so it was decided I should return to London and enter on the sea of troubles and vicissitudes connected with the active duties of professional life in England. The last week of my stay was devoted by Mendelssohn to all sorts of musical and social hospitalities. He arranged for a special private party at the Gewandhaus, where he gave us (my sister had arrived on a visit) a performance of the "Hymn of Praise" which we heard for the first time; and as an afterpiece Beethoven's Ninth Symphony with chorus. Every evening in the week was devoted to some species of music, and the last night before we left we had a musical party, at which Mendelssohn played Beethoven's Trio in C minor, and Mme. Schumann Mendelssohn's Trio in D minor. His sister, Mme. Hensel, was present, and played magnificently on this occasion. She had much of her brother's fire and style, and was a most talented and intellectual person.[23]

After this, I returned to London, but frequently corresponded with Mendelssohn and passed many happy hours with him both in England and Berlin. Many memorable evenings were passed on these occasions; for, from 1843 to 1847, "The Walpurgisnacht," "Athalie," "Œdipus," the music to the "Midsummer Night's Dream," the Trio in

C minor,[24] many Quartets, and numerous smaller works, were produced in London, at the Philharmonic Society, at Exeter Hall, and in various private houses, especially at that of Moscheles, in Chester Place, Regent's Park, at my father's house, and at Mr. Alsager's,[25] a most distinguished amateur, whose lamentable suicide greatly shocked his numerous friends. I was a member of the "Society of British Musicians," and on one occasion we invited Mendelssohn to be present at a performance of some of our own works. He came and listened most attentively, and, after our own share of the programme was concluded, he sat down to the piano and improvised in a most extraordinary manner, introducing many themes he had recollected from the music (all in manuscript) which he had heard.

In 1844 Mendelssohn sent to England Joseph Joachim, then a lad of 12 years old. The playing of this boy was astonishing, and it is well known to all that his extraordinary gifts have matured to an extent which now places him at the head of all violinists in the world.[26] Great as Mendelssohn's pianoforte triumphs were, there was one occasion in which he excelled them all. A concert had been arranged at the Hanover Square Rooms, at which Thalberg, Moscheles, and Mendelssohn were announced to play Sebastian Bach's Triple Concerto for three pianofortes, in D minor.[27] As it was known to none better than himself, that Thalberg was not accustomed to extemporizing, it was agreed that no cadences should be made. The piece proceeded in a most satisfactory manner until the orchestra made a pause and, much to the surprise of those who knew the compromise, Moscheles commenced a cadence, and in his usual felicitous, musician-like and admirable manner, delighted the audience. Then came Thalberg, who, though completely taken by surprise, acquitted himself excellently well, albeit his style hardly assimilated with the ideas of the great Leipzig Cantor. During these two performances I watched Mendelssohn's countenance. At first when Moscheles began, he looked much annoyed, but he gradually accepted the situation, and bided his time. When Thalberg had finished, Mendelssohn waited for the long and deserved pause to subside. He then shrugged his shoulders and commenced. I wish I had the pen of a Dickens, or a Scott (had either of them had any knowledge of music) to describe in fitting terms this performance. It began very quietly, and the themes of the Concerto, most scientifically varied, gradually crept up in their new garments. A crescendo then began, the themes ever newly presented, rose higher and higher, and at last a storm, nay a perfect hurricane of octaves, which must have lasted for five minutes, brought to a conclusion an exhibition of mechanical skill, and the most perfect inspiration, which neither before nor since that memorable Thursday afternoon has ever been approached. The effect on the audience was electrical. At first perfect silence reigned, but as the cadence continued, symptoms of excitement were shown; when the rush of octaves commenced those present rose almost to a man, and with difficulty restrained bursts of applause; but when the end came rounds of cheers were given for the great artist, which sounded like salons of artillery. I walked with Mendelssohn in Hyde Park after this triumph, and on congratulating him he replied: "I thought the people would like some octaves, so I played them."

Very many pages might be filled with descriptions of occurrences similar to the above, but one must be sufficient, as both time and space are closing in. The last season Mendelssohn spent in England before the production of "Elijah" was perhaps the most brilliant of all. He was everywhere received with the utmost enthusiasm. The Queen and Prince Albert paid him the most marked attentions, and every one from the highest to the lowest vied in showing honor to the great genius and thoroughly excellent man. But all this adulation, however justly deserved, had little or no effect upon his simple and modest character. His motto seems throughout life to have been "Excelsior" and, one art triumph reached, completed, another and a still higher flight of genius was immediately contemplated. Although the first families in England eagerly sought his society, and although he not unfrequently paid them visits, yet his heart was always with his own relatives and his old friends. On one occasion, when staying with Madame Mendelssohn's aunt at Denmark Hill near London,[28] an excursion to Windsor was planned; he pleaded a slight indisposition and did not join the party. It would seem that he employed the day after his own way, for when his friends returned he delighted them in the evening by playing the result of his labors, the charming "Lied ohne Worte," in A major, No. 6 of the 5th Book, in the first London Edition,—one of the freshest, most pleasing, and universally popular of the whole collection.[29] . . .

"Elijah" has passed into a realm far beyond the reach of criticism. In popularity it vies with the "Messiah" and "Creation." As a masterpiece of genius and musical craft, in its faultless construction, its wonderful delineation of the character of the great Prophet and his contemporaries, in the gorgeousness of its instrumental clothing, in its various touching episodes, and in its masterly contrapuntal treatment, although there is not a set Fugue in it for the delectation of ultra Handelians, the production of "Elijah" is the great event of Oratorio writing since "Israel in Egypt." There is only one work which can be named in comparison to it, viz., "St. Paul." While the latter in many ways may be and is considered the superior work by reason of its undoubtedly greater contrapuntal learning, yet I cannot wonder at "Elijah" being the greatest favorite; and this arises, if I may say so, from a very obvious cause. In "St. Paul," Mendelssohn had to give to his music a stern, uncompromising early Christian coloring; excepting in the raving of the indignant Jews, against the taunts of Stephen and the outpourings of Paul, there was no opportunity for any great dramatic treatment. The reverse is the case in *Elijah*. Were it to English habits seemly, the whole oratorio without any material alteration might be placed on the stage with the greatest propriety, with scenery, costume and dramatic action. There is not a scene in the work which is not capable of the highest stage effect, and I fancy that, had Mendelssohn lived, something approaching to a dramatic performance would have been attempted; an undertaking similar to those described by him in his letters from Düsseldorf, where "Israel in Egypt" was performed with scenery and action.[30] Such an exhibition of sacred subjects is however quite contrary to English feeling, and an attempt at introducing it would inevitably be forbidden by the law, but the real dramatic tendency of "Elijah" will always remain the chief secret of its great popularity.

I have said that "Elijah" was the culminating triumph of Mendelssohn's genius. He received the universal homage of multitudes with the calmness and absence of vanity which was the chief characteristic of his mind. I saw him at the house of his old friend Mr. Moore[31] an hour after the first performance at Birmingham.[32] All he replied to my hearty congratulations was: "I know you like some of 'Elijah,' tell me what you do not like," and no sooner had he returned to his beloved Leipzig for the Gewandhaus Concerts of 1846, than he set to work to make sundry alterations and improvements; the greatest of which was, perhaps, the substitution of the unaccompanied trio for Soprani: "Lift thine eyes" for an accompanied Duet to the same words [no. 28]. During this autumn and winter his letters show that not only was he employed in preparing "Elijah" for the press, but he was sketching out various plans for future works, amongst others the "Christus,"[33] thereby showing his wish to add another to the numerous works on the same subject, which more than any other has engaged the minds of all great composers.

The London season of 1847 now drew near, and it was known that its principal honors would be given to Mendelssohn and the "Elijah." Many performances were held in the provinces and in Dublin, at most of which he presided; and at Exeter Hall his new Oratorio, and his appearance was the signal for crowded audiences and enthusiastic receptions. During this time in London he was excessively occupied with all sorts of public and private engagements,—but he never forgot his old friends. He lived chiefly at the house of his friend, Charles Klingemann, in Hobart Place, Eaton Square, and many were the delightful evenings spent in that agreeable circle. His last appearance in London was at a Philharmonic concert in July [*recte* April], at the Hanover Square Rooms. Few present on that occasion will forget the evening. Both the Queen and the Prince Consort were present. Mendelssohn played Beethoven's Concerto in G, and directed his own Midsummer Night's Dream music. Two days after this he left England for the last time.[34] It has been asserted by an author writing on "Music and Mortals," that "Elijah" destroyed Mendelssohn. This is not the fact. It is true that at the close of the London season he was excessively tired by the constant ovations offered him; but there is no reason to suppose that, if he could have had the quiet and repose in Switzerland he had planned for himself and his family, he would not have recovered his usual health. All was prepared for a happy holiday in the Bernese Oberland, which he always declared was the most beautiful country he knew; the sketch books and color boxes were packed, the last proofs of "Elijah" had been corrected and sent to the press; plans were formed for the continuation of "Christus" and many other works lying unfinished in his portfolio; everything pointed to a happy period of some weeks of perfect quiet with his wife and children when an event occurred which laid the foundation of his fatal illness. Mendelssohn had been most fondly attached to all the members of his family, but especially to his sister Fanny Hensel. This lady, as I have already stated, was gifted with the highest musical attainments; she was an admirable pianist and an excellent composer, and she has left many works which show she possessed much of her brother's genius. Nothing can show the love which the brother and sister entertained for each other better than Mendelssohn's own letters.

It was either on the day fixed for Mendelssohn's leaving Frankfort-on-the-Main, or close upon it, that Mme. Hensel died suddenly in Berlin.[35] The painful news was communicated to Mendelssohn in a very abrupt manner, and the effect was such as to completely stun him, and to cause a slight attack of the malady which afterwards in so short a time proved fatal. However he was still urged by his friends and physicians to carry out his plans for change of scene and repose, and he did so. His letters during this closing period of his life are very sad. In one to his friend [Edward] Buxton, of the firm of Ewer

& Co., the London publishers of his works, he speaks in a gloomy manner of returning to Leipzig "to set his house in order," and it is evident that the great grief caused by his sister's decease had the effect upon his mind and body which subsequently caused his death. In the fall of the year, he returned with his family to Leipzig, and commenced preparations for the musical season, and especially for a grand performance of "Elijah" at Vienna, which he was especially engaged to conduct. Soon after he arrived in Leipzig,[36] it became necessary for him to go to Berlin, in order to arrange his late sister's musical MSS. and other papers which had been left in his charge. This was the last drop which caused the cup to overflow. His early life in Berlin, his never ceasing affection for his mother, who died in 1844 [*recte* 1842], and for his sister so recently taken from him, was all brought back to him. On his return to Leipzig he became frequently subject to fits of unconsciousness, and on the very day that he was to have conducted a Gewandhaus concert, and a week before the time fixed for his journey to Vienna, he fell into a stupor from which he never recovered, and died calmly and painlessly on the 4th of November, 1847.

The cause of his death was ascertained by a *post mortem* examination to be an affection of the brain. The year following his death I was in Leipzig, and I saw the physician who attended him. He told me that had it been possible to save his life his reason would probably have been so affected, that melancholy madness would have been the result. It is needless to add that death was a preferable alternative to such a life of misery for such a mind.

News in 1847 did not travel so fast as now, but such an occurrence was not long in reaching London, the scene of Mendelssohn's many triumphs and successes. The unexpected event, and the necessary confusion and excitement in Leipzig rendered it impossible for private letters to be written. The first intelligence therefore came through the public prints, and I became acquainted with the fact by reading the *Times* newspaper of the 7th of November, 1847. It was aptly said by Mr. Chorley in the *Athenaeum*,[37] that since the death of Scott no event had made such an impression as the death of Mendelssohn. Scott, however, died at a mature age, and after such a wonderful exercise of his powers as might well try the mind of any man over sixty years of age. Mendelssohn died in the thirty-seventh [*recte* thirty-eighth] year of his age. A few months previously he had quitted London in the full possession of all his faculties. He had left under many promises to return; plans were made for the production of new works; new triumphs were in store for him; and England, next to Germany the home of his choice, was already girding herself up for the dispensing of further honors and proofs of love. No wonder then that the 4th of November was a black letter day in the history of music in Great Britain. . . .

"*Si monumentum requiris, circumspice.*"[38] This most pertinent but perhaps too oft quoted phrase from the inscription to Sir Christopher Wren, in the Cathedral Church of St. Paul, London, most fittingly applies to Mendelssohn. His works are his monument, and most truly will they follow him. These I leave to the admiration of all who would learn what is good and great in music. If he had not the learning of Bach, the massiveness of Handel, the versatility of Mozart, the grandeur of Beethoven, was not his style, his very mannerism, a happy combination, in addition to his own exhaustless invention, of all the great men, his compeers who preceded him? Where shall we find better and more satisfactory evidences of learning than in "St. Paul," "Elijah," the many Psalms and the Church music written for the Cathedral in Berlin? Where shall we find in modern composition greater massiveness than in the Chorus: "Arise, shine," in *St. Paul*, or in "Thanks be to God" or "Be not afraid" in *Elijah*? Where can greater versatility be discovered than in the writings of a man whose mind could range from the composition of the "Antigone" and "Œdipus" choruses, the Italian and Scotch Symphonies, down to the wonderfully serio-comic funeral march of "Pyramus and Thisbe" in the "Midsummer Night's Dream?" And in grandeur or fancy can many better specimens of both be found than in the Druid's choruses in the "Walpurgisnacht" or in the pseudo Witches' chorus in the same work? The fact is, that the more Mendelssohn's works are studied the more they will be believed in, and far from waning, I feel certain that long after many stars have set that now are shining, Mendelssohn's fame, as a planet fixed in the admiration of true believers in all that is sterling and great in art, will remain in its proper hemisphere, to be the wonder and instructor of all ages.

Of my dear friend's character as a man it is difficult to speak but in terms that might almost savor of exaggeration. In all relations of life, as a son, a husband and a father, he was humanly speaking perfect. I never met with a man who came up more to the standard of a Christian, a scholar and a gentleman. In his art opinions he was essentially catholic, and sought for good in all schools. His great models were Bach and Beethoven, but he was at all times willing to admit talent wherever he found it. Thus he rescued Schubert from the undeserved neglect, if not total ignorance, into which his works had fallen.[39] He was the fast friend of Robert Schumann, who during his life time was living in Leipzig, and greatly indebted to Mendelssohn for artistic advice and friendly counsel. The "Music of the Future" had, at Mendelssohn's death, not permeated musical society to the extent that it has since obtained; but I have heard him speak of Wagner's early works with great respect and hopes for the future, and although I cannot for a moment believe that he, as so consummate an artist, would have been pleased with all he heard from the disciples of the "Musik der Zukunft," yet I feel sure that he would have done justice to the splendid orchestration, and the great strivings and yearnings of the school to strike out new paths of art, and would have gladly recognized the immense talents required to do this, as worthy of all praise.

Thus, I have endeavored to record my imperfect tribute of love and admiration to the memory of a man who was certainly the greatest musician of his time. As I said at the outset of my remarks, I trust the interest of the subject will be the excuse for all the faults with which I have executed my task. In America, Mendelssohn has long been the object of the greatest homage. This, the country destined to the greatest future yet attained by any nation of the earth, does well to cherish the memory of the great men of Europe; and amongst them all, whether as an artist, or as a man, few will be found worthier of admiration than Felix Mendelssohn Bartholdy.

New York City, Oct., 1872

NOTES

1. Friedrich Rosen (1805–1837), Professor of Oriental languages in London. [ed.]

2. Karl Klingemann (1798–1862), member of the Hanover legation in London. Mendelssohn composed lieder to several texts by Klingemann, who also provided the libretto for the Singspiel *Heimkehr aus der Fremde*, op. 89, inspired by Klingemann's and Mendelssohn's walking tour of Scotland in 1829. [ed.]

3. Both Goethe and Zelter died in 1832. Carl Friedrich Zelter, the musical confidant of Goethe, had introduced young Mendelssohn as his *Meisterschüler* to the poet in 1821. [ed.]

4. Overture to *Die schöne Melusine*, op. 32, performed in London on 7 April 1834; *Isles of Fingal*, a version of the celebrated *Fingal's Cave* (*Hebrides*) Overture, performed in London on 14 May 1832. A manuscript, entitled "Overture to the Isles of Fingal. Arranged as a duet for two performers on the pianoforte. FMB," was inscribed by Mendelssohn on 19 June 1832 to Marie

and Sophie Horsley, and it is perhaps this manuscript to which Charles Edward Horsley refers. See *Catalogue of the Mendelssohn Papers in the Bodleian Library, Oxford*, ed. Peter Ward Jones (Tutzing, 1989), vol. 3, p. 208. [ed.]

5. At least one performance on the organ took place on 27 June 1833. See *Mendelssohn and His Friends in Kensington, Letters from Fanny and Sophy Horsley, Written 1833–36*, ed. R. B. Gotch (London, 1934), p. 28. [ed.]

6. Mendelssohn's six Sonatas for Organ, op. 65, composed chiefly in 1844 and 1845, appeared in 1845; for some of his material Mendelssohn drew on earlier organ works from the 1830s. His other major work for organ, the three Preludes and Fugues, op. 37, appeared in 1837. [ed.]

7. Mendelssohn directed a performance of *St. Paul* at the Birmingham Music Festival on 20 September 1837; a London performance took place at Exeter Hall on 12 September. See the *London Times*, 13 September 1837, p. 3; and 22 September 1837, p. 3. He appeared with the Philharmonic as conductor or pianist in 1829, 1833, 1844, and 1847. Full details are in M. B. Foster, *History of the Philharmonic Society of London 1813–1912* (London, 1912), pp. 92ff. [ed.]

8. Ferdinand David (1810–1873), violinist. [ed.]

9. Heinrich Conrad Schleinitz (1802–1881), Leipzig attorney. [ed.]

10. Carl Eckert (1820–1879), violinist and pianist. [ed.]

11. Johann Hermann Kufferath (1797–1864), violinist. [ed.]

12. William Sterndale Bennett (1816–1875), English composer and pianist. On Bennett's relationship with Mendelssohn, see J. R. Sterndale Bennett, *The Life of William Sterndale Bennett* (Cambridge, 1907). [ed.]

13. George Macfarren (1813–1887), English composer; his overture *Chevy Chace* was performed by Mendelssohn in Leipzig in 1843. [ed.]

14. Helene Dolby (1821–1885), English contralto engaged by Mendelssohn for the 1845–1846 winter concert season of the Gewandhaus orchestra. [ed.]

15. Clara Novello (1818–1908), English soprano, daughter of the music publisher Vincent Novello. [ed.]

16. Niels Gade (1817–1890), Danish composer; he served as Mendelssohn's assistant conductor in Leipzig. [ed.]

17. Anton Rubinstein (1829–1894), Russian pianist and composer. [ed.]

18. Sigismond Thalberg (1812–1871), German pianist and composer, recognized for developing the so-called three-hand technique, in which a melodic line is placed in the middle register of the piano, with figuration above and below. [ed.]

19. Thalberg performed his Caprice on Themes from Bellini's *Sonnambula* in Leipzig on 8 February 1841. See the *Allgemeine musikalische Zeitung* 43 (1841), col. 137. [ed.]

20. The *Lied ohne Worte* in A major, op. 53, no. 6, composed on 1 May 1841. [ed.]

21. Franz Xavier Wolfgang Mozart (1791–1844). [ed.]

22. Moritz Hauptmann (1792–1868), theorist and composer. [ed.]

23. Mendelssohn was visited in Leipzig by his two sisters Fanny Hensel and

Rebecka Dirichlet in February and March 1843, and it may be this visit to which Horsley refers. [ed.]

24. *Die erste Walpurgisnacht*, op. 60, a cantata, composed in 1832, revised 1842–1843; incidental music to Racine's *Athalie*, op. 74 (1845); incidental music to Sophocles' *Oedipus at Colonos*, op. 93 (1845); incidental music to *A Midsummer Night's Dream*, op. 61 (1843); Piano Trio no. 2 in C minor, op. 66 (1845). [ed.]

25. Thomas Massa Alsager (1779–1846), English journalist. See David B. Levy, "Thomas Massa Alsager, Esq.: A Beethoven Advocate in London," in *19th-Century Music* 9 (1985): 119–27. [ed.]

26. Joseph Joachim (1831–1907), violinist. His English debut occurred in March 1844. [ed.]

27. The concert took place on 1 June 1844 and was reviewed in the *AmZ* 46 (1844): cols. 454–56. [ed.]

28. In June 1842, at the home of Henriette Benecke (1807–1893) and Friedrich Wilhelm Benecke (1802–1865), the aunt and uncle of Mendelssohn's wife, Cécile (*née* Jeanrenaud). [ed.]

29. The famous *Frühlingslied* in A major, op. 62, no. 6, composed on 1 June 1842. [ed.]

30. Performed at a fête in honor of the Crown Prince of Prussia (the future Frederick William IV). See Mendelssohn's letter of 26 October 1833 to his sister Rebecka in Felix Mendelssohn, *Letters*, ed. G. Selden-Goth (New York, 1972), pp. 217–19. [ed.]

31. Joseph Moore (1766–1851), manager of the Birmingham Music Festival. [ed.]

32. On 26 August 1846. [ed.]

33. Mendelssohn completed only a few numbers for *Christus*, which were published posthumously in 1852 as op. 97. [ed.]

34. The concert took place on 26 April 1847. On two other counts Horsley is in error. On 5 May 1847 Mendelssohn gave an organ concert at the Hanover Square Rooms, probably his last English appearance. He left London on 8 May. [ed.]

35. Fanny Hensel died on 14 May 1847. [ed.]

36. On 17 September 1847. [ed.]

37. Henry Fothergill Chorley (1808–1872), critic and journalist. [ed.]

38. "If you require a monument, look around." [ed.]

39. A reference to Mendelssohn's première of Schubert's "Great" Symphony in C major, D. 944, performed in Leipzig on 21 March 1839. A copy of the symphony was sent to Mendelssohn by Robert Schumann, who discovered the autograph in Vienna. [ed.]

From the Memoirs of

F. Max Müller

The son of Wilhelm Müller, the poet of Schubert's *Schöne Müllerin* and *Winterreise*, Max Müller (1823–1900) studied Sanskrit and comparative philology at the Universities of Leipzig and Berlin. With the backing of the Baron von Bunsen, he prepared an edition of the *Rig Veda*, which was published by Oxford University Press in 1846.

As a youth Müller studied music with a pupil of Friedrich Schneider in Dessau; when he arrived in Leipzig, Mendelssohn advised him to "keep to Greek and Latin." In later years, Müller's musical tastes remained conservative, as he himself admitted: "I have passed through a long school. I began with Haydn, Mozart, and Beethoven, lived on with Mendelssohn, rose to Schumann, and reached even Brahms; but I could never get beyond, I could never learn to enjoy Wagner except now and then in one of his lucid intervals. No doubt this is my fault and my loss, but surely the *vulgus profanum* also has its rights and may protest against being tired instead of being refreshed and invigorated by music." [ed.]

[Source: F. Max Müller, *Auld Lang Syne* (New York, 1898), pp. 1–33.]

·

How many memories crowd in upon me! I heard Liszt when I was still at school at Leipzig. It was his first entry into Germany, and he came like a triumphator. He was young, theatrical, and terribly attractive, as ladies, young and old, used to say. His style of playing was then something quite new—now every player lets off the same fireworks. The musical critics who then ruled supreme at Leipzig were somewhat coy and reserved, and I remember taking a criticism to the editor of the *Leipziger Tageblatt* which the writer did not wish to sign with his own name. Mendelssohn only, with his well-tempered heart, received him with open arms. He gave a *matinée musicale* at his house,[1] all the best-known musicians of the place being present. I remember, though vaguely, David,[2] Kalliwoda,[3] Hiller;[4] I doubt whether Schumann and Clara Wieck were present. Well, Liszt appeared in his Hungarian costume, wild and magnificent. He told Mendelssohn that he had written something special for him. He sat down, and swaying right and left on his music-stool, played first a Hungarian melody, and then three or four variations, one more incredible than the other.

We stood amazed, and after everybody had paid his compliments to the hero of the day, some of Mendelssohn's friends gathered round him, and said: "Ah, Felix, now we can pack up (jetzt können wir einpacken). No one can do that; it is over with us!" Mendelssohn smiled; and when Liszt came up to him asking him to play something in turn, he laughed and said that he never played now; and this, to a certain extent, was true. He did not give much time to practising then, but worked chiefly at composing and directing his concerts. However, Liszt would take no refusal, and so at last little Mendelssohn, with his own charming playfulness, said: "Well, I'll play, but you must promise me not to be angry." And what did he play? He sat down and played first all of Liszt's Hungarian Melody, and then one variation after another, so that no one but Liszt himself could have told the difference. We all trembled lest Liszt should be offended, for Mendelssohn could not keep himself from slightly imitating Liszt's movements and raptures. However, Mendelssohn managed never to offend man, woman, or child. Liszt laughed and applauded, and admitted that no one, not he himself, could have performed such a *bravura.* . . .

And Mendelssohn also, whom I had known as a young man, said good-bye to me for the last time in London. It was after the first performance of his "Elijah" in 1847.[5] He too said he would come again next year, and then came the news of his sudden death. I saw him last at Bunsen's[6] house, where he played at a *matinée musicale* always ready to please and oblige his friends, always amiable and charming, even under great provocation. Only once I remember seeing him almost beside himself with anger, and well he might be. He possessed a most valuable album, with letters, poems, pictures, compositions of the most illustrious men of the age, such as Goethe and others.[7] The binding had somewhat suffered, so it was sent to be mended, and I was present when it came back. It was at his sister's house, Fanny Hensel's, at Berlin. Mendelssohn opened the album, jumped up and screamed. The binder had cut off the blue skies and tree-tops of all the Italian sketches, and the signatures of most of the poems and letters. This was too much for *Felix*, he was for once *infelix*. Still, happy and serene as his life certainly was, for he had everything a man of his talents could desire, there were bitter drops in it of which the world knew little, and need not know anything now. There are things we know, important things which the world would be glad to know. But we bury them; they are to be as if they had never been, like letters that are reduced to ashes and can never be produced again by friends or enemies.

He was devoted to his sister Fanny, who was married to Hensel[8] the painter, an intimate friend of my father. When I was a student at Berlin, I was much in their house in the *Leipziger Strasse*, and heard many a private concert given in the large room looking out on the garden. Mendelssohn played almost every instrument in the orchestra, and had generally to play the instrument which he was supposed to play worst. When he played the pianoforte, he was handicapped by being made to play with his arms crossed. All the celebrities of Berlin (and Berlin was then rich in celebrities) were present at those musical gatherings, and Mendelssohn was the life of the whole. He was never quiet for a moment, moving from chair to chair and conversing with everybody.

Boeckh,[9] the great Greek scholar, lived in the same house, and Mendelssohn had received so good a classical education that he could hold his own when discussing with the old master the choruses of the Antigone. Mendelssohn was, in fact, a man *teres et rotundus*.[10] He was at home in classical literature, he spoke French and English, he was an exquisite draughtsman, and had seen the greatest works of the greatest painters, ancient and modern. His father, a rich banker in Berlin, had done all he could for the education of his children. He was the son of Mendelssohn the philosopher, and when his son Felix had become known to fame, he used to say with his slightly Jewish accent: "When I was young I was called the son of the great Mendelssohn; now that I am old I am called the father of the great Mendelssohn; then, what am I?" Well, he found the wherewithal that enabled his son, and his other children too, to become what they were, all worthy of their great grandfather, all worthy of the name of Mendelssohn.

Felix was attached to both his sisters, Fanny and Rebekah (Dirichlet), but he was more particularly devoted to Fanny (Hensel). They had been educated together. She knew Greek and Latin like her brother, she played perfectly, and composed so well that her brother published several of her compositions under his own name.[11] They were one spirit and one soul, and at that time ladies still shrank from publicity. Everybody knew which songs were hers (I remember, for instance, "Schöner und schöner schmückt sich die Flur"),[12] and it was

Figure 1. Fanny Hensel, "Die glückliche Fischerin," Autograph

only later in life that she began to publish under her own name. I give the beginning of a song which she wrote for my mother.[13] The words are my father's, the little vignette was drawn by her husband, who was an eminent artist at Berlin.

The struggles which many, if not most men of genius, more particularly musicians, have had to pass through were unknown to Felix Mendelssohn Bartholdy. Some people go so far as to say that they miss the traces of those struggles in his character and in his music. And yet those who knew him best know that his soul, too, knew its own bitterness. His happiest years were no doubt spent at Leipzig, where I saw much of him while I was at school and at the University. He was loved and admired by everybody; he was undisputed master in the realm of music. He was at first unmarried, and many were the rumours as to who should be his bride. News had reached his friends that his heart had been won by a young lady at Frankfurt; but nobody, not even his most intimate friends, knew for certain. However, one evening he had just returned from Frankfurt, and had to conduct one of the Gewandhaus Concerts. The last piece was Beethoven's Ninth Symphony.[14] I had sung in the chorus, and found myself on the orchestra when the concert was over, the room nearly empty, except his personal friends, who surrounded him and teased him about his approaching engagement. His beaming face betrayed him, but he would say nothing to anybody, till at last he sat down and extemporised on the pianoforte. And what was the theme of his fantasy? It was the passage of the chorus, "Wer ein holdes Weib errungen, mische seinen Jubel ein."[15] That was his confession to his friends, and then we all knew. And she was indeed "ein holdes Weib" when she arrived at Leipzig. One thing only she lacked—she could not express all she felt. She was soon called the "Goddess of Silence" by the side of her devoted husband, who never could be silent, but was always bubbling over like champagne in a small glass. They were a devoted couple, not a whisper was ever heard about either of them, though Mendelssohn had many friends, the greatest of all being his sister Fanny. With her he could speak and exchange whatever was uppermost or deepest in his heart. I have heard them extemporise together on the pianoforte, one holding with his little finger the finger of the other. Her death was the heaviest loss he ever suffered in life. He was so unaccustomed to suffering and distress that he could never recover from this unexpected blow. Nor did he survive her long. She died on the 14th of May, 1847; he followed her on the 4th of November of the same year.

During most of the time when Mendelssohn celebrated his triumphs as director of Gewandhaus Concerts, young Robert Schumann was at Leipzig, but he was little seen. Mendelssohn, so bright and happy himself, wished to see the whole world around him bright and happy, and was kind to everybody. The idea of jealousy was impossible at that time in Mendelssohn's heart. Neither could Schumann, as a young and rising musician, have thought himself to be in any sense an equal or rival of Mendelssohn. But there were natures which like to be left alone, or with very few intimate friends only, and which shrink from the too demonstrative happiness of others. It is not envy, it is often modesty; but in any case it is not pleasant. Schumann was conscious of his own strength, but he was still struggling for recognition, and he was also struggling against that adversity of fortitude which seems to decree poverty to be the lot of genius. . . .

It was in the last year of his life that Mendelssohn paid his last visit to England to conduct his last oratorio, the "Elijah." It had to be performed at Exeter Hall, then the best place for sacred music. Most of the musicians, however, were not professionals, and they had only bound themselves to attend a certain number of rehearsals. Excellent as they were in such oratorios as the "Messiah," which they knew by heart, a new oratorio, such as the "Elijah," was too much for them; and I well remember Mendelssohn, in the afternoon before the performance, declaring he would not conduct.

"Oh, these tailors and shoemakers," he said, "they cannot do it, and they will not practise! I shall not go." However, a message arrived that the Queen and Prince Albert were to be present, so nothing remained but to go. I was present, the place was crowded.[16] Mendelssohn conducted, and now and then made a face, but no one else detected what was wrong. It was a great success and a great triumph for Mendelssohn. If he could have heard it performed as it was performed at Exeter Hall in later years, when his tailors and shoemakers knew it by heart, he would not have made a face.

It was at Bunsen's house, at a *matinée musicale*, that I saw him last. He took the liveliest interest in my work, the edition of the Rig Veda, the Sacred Hymns of the Brâhmans. A great friend of his, Friedrich Rosen,[17] had begun the same work, but had died before the first volume was finished. He was a brother of the wife of Mendelssohn's great friend, Klingemann, then Hanoverian Chargé d'Affaires in London, a poet many of whose poems were set to music by Mendelssohn. So Mendelssohn knew all about the Sacred Hymns of the Brâhmans, and talked very intelligently about the Veda. He was, however, subjected to a very severe trial of patience soon after. The room was crowded with what is called the best society of London, and Mendelssohn being asked to play, never refused. He played several things, and at last Beethoven's so-called "Moonlight Sonata." All was silence and delight; no one moved, no one breathed aloud. Suddenly in the middle of the Adagio, a stately dowager sitting in the front row was so carried away by the rhythm, rather than by anything else, of Beethoven's music, that she began to play with her fan, and accompanied the music by letting it open and shut with each bar. Everybody stared at her, but it took time before she perceived her atrocity, and at last allowed her fan to collapse. Mendelssohn in the meantime kept perfectly quiet, and played on; but, when he could stand it no longer, he simply repeated the last bar in arpeggios again and again, following the movements of her fan; and when at last the fan stopped, he went on playing as if nothing had happened. I dare say that when the old dowager thanked him for the great treat he had given her, he bowed without moving a muscle of his inspired face. How different from another player who, when disturbed by some noise in the audience, got up in a rage and declared that either she or the talker must leave the room.

NOTES

1. In March 1840. [ed.]

2. Ferdinand David (1810–1873), violinist and concertmaster of the Gewandhaus orchestra. [ed.]

3. Johann Wenzel Kalliwoda (1801–1866), Bohemian composer. [ed.]

4. Ferdinand Hiller (1811–1885), German composer; on Mendelssohn's friendship with Hiller, see F. Hiller, *Felix Mendelssohn Bartholdy: Briefe und Erinnerungen* (Cologne, 1874, rep. 1972). [ed.]

5. On 16 April 1847. [ed.]

6. Christian Josias Freiherr von Bunsen (1791–1860), Prussian emissary and scholar, transferred to the London Embassy in 1842. [ed.]

7. Several albums belonging to Mendelssohn and his wife are preserved in the Bodleian Library, Oxford. See *Catalogue of the Mendelssohn Papers in the Bodleian Library, Oxford*, ed. M. Crum (Tutzing, 1983), vol. 2, pp. 73ff. [ed.]

8. Wilhelm Hensel (1794–1861). [ed.]

9. Philipp August Boeckh (1785–1867). [ed.]

10. Horace, *Satirae* 2.7.86: "polished and well rounded." [ed.]

11. Including *Das Heimweh*, op. 8, no. 2; *Italien*, op. 8, no. 3; *Suelika und Hatem*, op. 8, no. 12; *Sehnsucht*, op. 9, no. 7; *Verlust*, op. 9, no. 10; and *Die Nonne*, op. 9, no. 12. [ed.]

12. *Italien*, op. 8, no. 3, on a text by F. Grillparzer. [ed.]

13. "Die glückliche Fischerin." [ed.]

14. Performed in Leipzig on 13 March 1837. See A. Dörffel, *Geschichte der Gewandhausconcerte zu Leizpig von 25. November 1781 bis 25. November 1881* (Leipzig, 1884, rep. 1972), p. 89. [ed.]

15. "Who has won a noble wife may join in the rejoicing," measures 273–76 of the finale to Beethoven's Ninth Symphony. [ed.]

16. 23 April 1847. [ed.]

17. Friedrich Rosen (1805–1837), professor of oriental languages in London. [ed.]

From the Memoirs of Ernst Rudorff

TRANSLATED AND ANNOTATED

BY NANCY B. REICH

The memoirs of Ernst Rudorff (1840–1916), entitled *Aus den Tagen der Romantik: Ein Bildnis einer deutschen Familie*, were edited by his daughter and published in Leipzig in 1938, but the pages on the Mendelssohn family were omitted from the published book. They remained in typescript and appear here for the first time.[1] *Aus den Tagen der Romantik* was based on reminiscences, published letters, family records, and the diaries of Ernst Rudorff's father, Adolph Rudorff (1803–1873), a professor of jurisprudence at the Berlin University; his mother, Friederike Dorothea Elisabeth Rudorff *née* Pistor (1808–1887), known as Betty; and his own *Tagebücher*.

Ernst Rudorff, a composer, conductor, and editor, was head of the piano department of the Königliche Hochschule für Musik in Berlin from 1869 to 1910. In the 1880s, he became interested in the relationship of modern life and nature, an issue that led to the founding of the *Heimat- und Naturschutzbewegung*, organized to protect historical landmarks and preserve the natural environment. He is perhaps best known today for his contributions to environmental protection.

The following excerpt, a translation of the omitted pages of the 1938 book, is based on the diaries of Betty Pistor, an unusually musical girl who was invited by Carl Zelter to join the Singakademie when she was only fourteen. Here Rudorff writes about his mother and her relationship to the Mendelssohn family.

From *Aus den Tagen der Romantik*

Betty Pistor first became acquainted with Felix Mendelssohn at the Friday rehearsals, held for a small group of carefully chosen members of the Singakademie.[2] At first, he was still a boy who sang beside his sister Fanny in the alto section, but very soon thereafter he was seated permanently at the piano and accompanied the group with amazing skill. Betty and Felix were both at the turning point between childhood and youth when they saw each other for the first time. Felix still wore the boyhood clothing—so often described—the deeply cut-out jacket wide open at the neck.[3] Betty, one year older than he, was delighted to learn that her birthday, 14 January, was the same as Felix's name day. Some time later, Mendelssohn's younger sister, Rebecka, also appeared regularly at Zelter's on Fridays.

Since 1825, the Mendelssohn family had lived in the large, grand house with a splendid garden behind it, at no. 3 Leipzigerstrasse. The way home for the three Mendelssohn children led from Zelter's home almost past the Pistor's house [34 Mauerstrasse], and it soon became a regular thing to walk back together with Betty. As a result, a particularly friendly relationship developed between Betty and Rebecka. They visited back and forth and engaged in all sorts of things together. They also worked with each other at their Italian studies. Manzoni's novel, *I promessi sposi*, had recently appeared and made a great stir.[4] Both girls set about reading it in the original language.

The friendly relations among all the young people became ever more lively and the Mendelssohns invited Betty to all sorts of social events—musicales, charades, balls. Eduard Rietz, the distinguished violinist, who was Felix Mendelssohn's beloved childhood friend[5] was utterly indispensable in all these activities and was also a welcome and frequent guest in the Pistors' house.

Betty's diary entries in the years 1826–1827 record almost daily her sisterly relationship with Felix and Rebecka. When Betty made her first long journey in August 1827 with her mother to Wernigerode, where her cousin Sophie Reichardt, married to the pastor Ernst Radecke, lived, Felix promised that he would visit his friend there and he kept his word.[6] He wandered through southern and western Germany for a few more weeks, and Betty was invited to the Mendelssohns' on the first evening of his return home in the middle of October. A few days later Felix appeared at the Pistors' in the morning, and in the afternoon they were together again in the Singakademie. And so for a few months the routine continued in the old way. Betty's diary recorded many pleasant hours spent together—an evening at the Pistors', for example, when Felix and Rietz played the Kreutzer Sonata from memory—an event that aroused the greatest enthusiasm.

A special circumstance gave Felix a motive for coming alone in the mornings to the Pistors' even more frequently than he otherwise would have. I cannot state with certainty the exact time at which a large portion of the musical estate of Friedemann Bach was put up for public auction in Berlin after it had been in the hands of a second party a few years earlier.[7] The collection included full scores of thirteen of the church cantatas of Johann Sebastian Bach in his own hand, as well as an autograph fragment of one other. Furthermore, there were many instrumental and vocal parts of cantatas written out [from the scores] by a copyist but bearing traces of Bach's perusal in the markings pertaining to performance. Indeed, here and there, there was a page or several lines in Bach's own hand. Finally, there was a large number of valuable copies of Bach's work of every kind written by Johann Ringk, Friedemann Bach, and various other contemporary copyists. In addition to these manuscripts, several copies of the original prints of the so-called *Clavierübung* were included in the collection.[8]

Zelter and my grandfather Pistor were both present at the auction. They bid against each other with stubborn persistence until at last Zelter was reduced to silence and Pistor received the nod. Delighted, he returned home with his treasures, enough to fill a good-sized chest. The next morning Zelter sent a message saying that he had decided to meet Pistor's price, and offered to buy the autographs from Pistor. My grandfather thanked him very kindly for the good intentions, but replied that he preferred to keep the things for himself. And so the matter stood.[9]

Mendelssohn naturally learned of the precious acquisition very soon and expressed the greatest desire to examine the things thoroughly himself. At the same time, he offered to sort out all the materials, which were still in complete disarray. Pistor not only accepted the offer with thanks but also presented him with the score of one of the autograph cantatas as recompense for his efforts.[10] (I still have the bundles with wrappers of thick blue paper on which the pieces found by Mendelssohn were listed by him.)[11]

On a morning in January 1828, Felix showed up again at the Pistors' door intending to work on the Bach autographs. Betty's friend Marie Schinkel and her cousin Mine Stelzer were visiting, and the girls were engaged in cheerful conversation. Now and then a joke called forth loud laughter. At Mendelssohn's ring, the door was opened and laughter could be heard coming from the sitting room. With the words "Oh, I can hear you have visitors; I won't disturb you," he left the entrance hall quickly. When, a few days later, he saw Betty again, he treated her so coolly that she returned home perplexed and quite concerned. On her birthday, 14 January, a day on which Felix had always come to bring her his personal greetings, Rebecka came but he did not show up. Betty speculated about everything that could have offended him, and could only conclude that at his last visit he must have imagined that the girls' laughter was aimed at him and his relationship to her. Naturally it was impossible to come to an understanding or bring up this particular point, and so the matter remained unexplained.

The two saw each other again in the Mendelssohn house only after several weeks had gone by. It must have become clear to the sensitive young man that he could not hold Betty responsible in any way for what had happened, and so he visibly took pains to show her his undiminished cordiality. Nonetheless, his usual visits to Mauerstrasse were awaited in vain. Evidently, he did not want anything more to do with what went on at the Pistors', and that conformed completely to the growing extreme vulnerability that was characteristic of him.[12]

Soon after all this came Felix's birthday on 3 February, which was to be celebrated with a dance. At Zelter's, two days before the event, the Mendelssohn siblings invited Betty to take part in the festivities and pressed her to come. This time, however, Father Pistor refused to give permission, because he found it unsuitable for a young girl to be invited to share in the birthday celebration of a young man, and Betty had to decline. The next day Rebecka came to her friend in great agitation, and implored her not to fail to come, particularly this time. Her family, she said, had known very well—and for some time—the real basis for her absence. With these words she played on the anti-Semitism of some branches of the Reichardt and Alberti families,[13] who looked askance at Betty because of her relationship with the Mendelssohn family and mockingly called her "the music- and Jew-loving cousin."

In contrast to these relatives, the Pistor parents were totally free of any anti-Semitic impulses. Their rejection of Rahel Varnhagen had nothing to do with such feelings. Insofar as she was concerned, they had the same attitude as Felix himself to whom that type of clever female was just as objectionable.[14]

Both girls wept bitter tears when Pistor adamantly refused to alter his view of the birthday party. At the same time, he decided to visit Frau Mendelssohn and to make clear to her why his daughter had to comply with his wishes and reject the invitation. This explanation was of little or no use. Mendelssohn's parents did not believe the sincerity of Pistor's reasoning; they assumed it was just a pretext with which to cover the true reason, and Felix was again so deeply hurt that when he met Betty shortly afterward, he did not say a word to her. The next Friday, Betty met Rebecka at Zelter's and learned of the elder Mendelssohn's state of mind. This made her so unhappy that she was barely able to keep her composure and sang only with great difficulty. She resolved to go herself to Mendelssohn's mother the next morning, and the impression of her guiltlessness in all that had recently taken place was so strong that the reconciliation with the family was complete.

As before, she returned as a heartily welcomed guest in the Mendelssohn house. As before, Rebecka appeared at the Pistors' home, and Felix behaved toward Betty just as he had in the past. But he never entered the house in the Mauerstrasse again.

The *St. Matthew Passion*

During the first weeks of 1829, Bach's *St. Matthew Passion* was studied regularly on Fridays at Zelter's. Soon, however, Felix organized weekly rehearsals of the work with a selected chorus that met in his parents' home. Out of these rehearsals grew a desire to make this completely forgotten, greatest, and most Protestant of all church music known to the world through a public performance. How he was encouraged to do so by Eduard Devrient and was constantly urged on by him; how the two friends succeeded in breaking down Zelter's opposition; and how, finally, the affair was brought to a most magnificent and victorious conclusion—all this is described in such clear detail by Devrient in his memoirs about Felix Mendelssohn that it would be superfluous to embark upon a discussion of the particulars here.[15]

From beginning to end, Betty took the liveliest and most active interest in the events, did not miss a single rehearsal, and found the excitement of participating in the rebirth of one of the most sublime masterpieces of all time reverberating in the very core of her soul.

Mendelssohn sat at the piano, and his magnificent and eloquent interpretation of the orchestral accompaniment created the indescribable impression that each individual instrument was speaking in the most expressive terms. From rehearsal to rehearsal, the music seemed to become greater, more powerful, and more gripping to the participants—and the first public performance of the *St. Matthew Passion* on 11 March 1829, under Mendelssohn's direction in the Singakademie, may well be called a historic artistic event of the first and foremost significance. No person there—musician or listener—had ever experienced a purer, more profound, or more sacred artistic inspiration.

A repeat performance had to be given on 21 March, Bach's birthday. On 10 April Felix left for England, visited Scotland with Klingemann,[16] and did not return to Berlin until the early part of December because of an accident that kept him in bed and delayed his homecoming.[17] In the meantime, Fanny had married the artist Wilhelm Hensel in October.[18] The young couple lived in the Mendelssohns' garden house at no. 3 Leipzigerstrasse. In her diary entry of 17 October 1829, Betty described an evening that she had spent at the Mendelssohns' during which Hensel was reworking a sketch he had previously made of her. Later, this drawing was presented to the Pistor family but received a very negative response because it bore little resemblance to Betty. Though Betty did not share her family's reaction, she returned the picture to Rebecka and so it remained with the Mendelssohn family. In any case, it may not have been Hensel's intention to give the sketch away, and the return left no hard feelings on either side. They remained on the most cordial terms, and on 28 November Betty was invited to the Hensels' for dinner and felt very much at ease there. In the evening they all went over to the older Mendelssohns', and Betty's diary entry adds, "Beckchen [Rebecka] was most delightful . . . Felix is returning next week; they are beside themselves with joy."

As is well known, Hensel made portraits of almost everybody in the circle of friends and acquaintances, and so collected in his sketchbook [Album] an extensive series of splendid portraits of the most diverse personalities of Berlin society. Because in later years he worked little, the malicious Berlin wits called him the "Albummler."[19]

On 26 December 1829, the Mendelssohn parents celebrated their silver wedding anniversary. For the festivities, which began on the eve of Christmas day, Felix had composed the *Liederspiel, Die Heimkehr aus der Fremde.*[20] We can assume that Betty was among the 120 guests who assembled that evening at the Mendelssohns' home. Unfortunately, the diary leaves us in the dark here. (There were many omissions just at this time.) Nevertheless, it does seem strange that there is not even a brief mention of her participation in such an event . . . But it is certain that she was present at a later repetition of the delightful work in the Mendelssohn home. In her old age, not only did she still speak with excitement about the impression the *Liederspiel* had made on her in her youth, but a written testimonial to Betty and the event still exists. This will become clear very shortly.

On 4 January 1830 Betty wrote the following entry in her diary:

"In the afternoon I went with Rebecka and Felix to the Akademie; we were *very* merry along the way." On 15 January, the day after her [twenty-second] birthday, she met Felix at Zelter's and he gave her a manuscript copy of the huntsman's song from the *Liederspiel*. He had written it out for her on fine blue music paper in his own particularly beautiful hand. The first page was adorned by Hensel with a charming vignette portraying the hunter with his rifle.[21] (See figures 1 and 2.)

During the next few weeks, there were several other pleasant meetings at Zelter's and in the Mendelssohns' home until Felix, who was preparing for the long journey that would take him to Italy via Weimar, Munich, Vienna, and so on, caught the measles from Rebecka and had to postpone his trip until 7 May. . . .

Some time before all these events—it must have been in the beginning of the year 1829—Felix told Betty with a smile, "I am composing a quartet for you." However, the possibility of anyone's dedicating a composition to her—particularly a large work like a quartet—seemed so remote to her that she interpreted the remark as merely teasing and just answered with a laugh. But, as a matter of fact, Mendelssohn was indeed composing his lovely String Quartet in E♭ major, op. 12— the one with the charming Canzonetta in G minor—with her in mind and placed the initials of her name, "To B. P." as a silent dedication to her at the head of the score.

He took the sketch along with him when he went to England in April and completed the piece in London. Klingemann, who was with Felix daily, wrote to Fanny in Berlin on 7 July 1829: "I am really delighted with what I know of the symphony [perhaps the *Reformation*, op. 107] and am looking forward to what is still to come. He is in the middle of the Adagio of a new quartet, to B. P., in E♭ major; he has just worked out something new that makes me very happy and he was pleased that I understood it." And again on 29 August, Felix wrote to Klingemann from an English country estate about a bouquet of carnations "which is lying near me on the score of the quartet for B. P." In a letter to Fanny from London on 10 September, he wrote, "I am in the middle of the last movement of my quartet and I think it will be finished any day now." He planned to send it to his family as soon as it was completed. The last page of the handwritten score ["to B. P."] is inscribed: "Felix Mendelssohn Bartholdy. London, 14 September 1829."

Mendelssohn gave the score of the quartet to the violinist

Figure 1. Mendelssohn, "Wenn die Abendglocken läuten," Autograph (page 1)

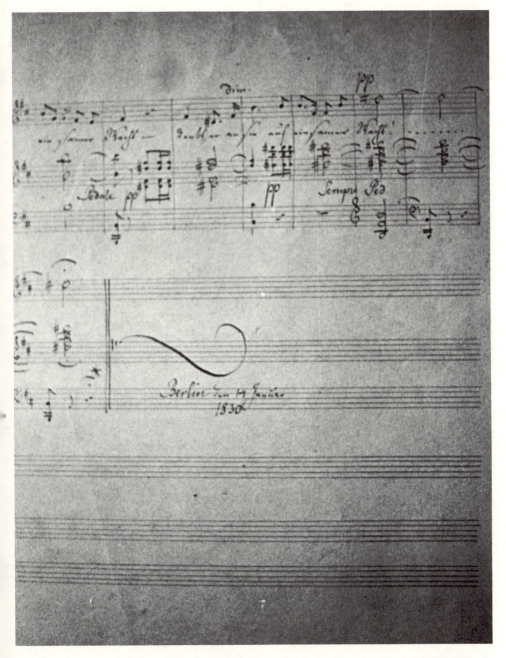

Figure 2. Mendelssohn, "Wenn die Abendglocken läuten," Autograph (page 6, containing date of Betty Pistor's birthday)

Kudelsky[22] at the end of January 1830. He took it with him to Dorpat where he was to deliver it to David, who, Mendelssohn assumed, would have the best opportunity to play it.[23] David had been engaged by the Baron Liehard[24] [*sic*] to play first violin in a string quartet established by this wealthy and cultured music-lover on his estate near Dorpat. Kudelsky was to play second violin or viola.

From his darkened room [while recovering from the measles] Mendelssohn dictated a letter on 14 April 1830 to his friend Ferdinand David in Dorpat in which there appears the following passage:

> Do you want to know the latest news from Berlin? Not until I first learn it myself since I know as little about what is going on as I would if I were in Dorpat. But still I do know *one* thing which would distress you if you didn't have new consolations and would upset me if I hadn't already given up courting and girls and resolved to be an old bachelor. Hear now and take alarm: Betty Pistor is engaged. Totally engaged. She is the legal property of Dr. and Professor of Jurisprudence Rudorff. I authorize you to transform the B. P. on the score of my quartet in E♭ to a B. R. as soon as you get confirmation of their marriage from the Berlin newspapers. It will take just a skillful little stroke of the pen—it will be quite easy.[25]

Once more, one and a half years later, the quartet to B. P. appeared in Mendelssohn's letters. On 20 December 1831, he wrote to Rebecka from Paris: "It gave me the greatest pleasure to hear [Baillot] play my quartet. He played it with spirit and fire." Then it vanished from the correspondence—that is, from the published correspondence.[26]

Soon after his return, he became, as is well known, the director of music in Düsseldorf and, later, conductor of the Gewandhaus Concerts in Leipzig. He did not come to Berlin for any kind of lengthy stay until the beginning of the 1840s, when Friedrich Wilhelm IV, soon after his accession to the throne, attempted to interest him in coming to Berlin. At that time, Marie Lichtenstein, my mother's most intimate friend, had many opportunities to meet with him.[27] She was sitting next to him at a large evening gathering and the two began to talk of Betty Pistor, now Betty Rudorff. "Yes," said Mendelssohn warmly, "*that* was a musical soul. . . ."

·

Thirty years passed without my mother's having had the least idea of all that had gone before with the quartet. How she finally learned that Mendelssohn had indeed written the beautiful string quartet for her—actually his most beautiful—will be told in the proper place. At this point, however, it may be said that Betty's feelings for Felix Mendelssohn were never mixed with any elements of passion. And this seems natural because of the age difference between them. She was the elder of the two, and it is known that in early youth, a girl is uninterested in *younger* men. She certainly admired the wonderful musical talent and exceedingly engaging personality of the youth, who was as noble and loveable as he was gifted. She was favored with his affection and continually received fresh tokens of his attachment, which were reciprocated with the most cordial and sincere friendship. She had no thought beyond that. As long as she lived, the memory of the dear friend of her youth, of all the wonderful ways in which he enriched her existence and inner life, remained an incomparably dear and sacred possession.

NOTES

1. With the kind permission of the Rudorff-Archiv, Lauenstein. I am grateful to the Rudorff-Archiv for many courtesies. See my article, "The Rudorff Collection," in *Notes of the Music Library Association* 31 (December 1974): 247–61.

2. Fanny and Felix Mendelssohn evidently attended the Friday rehearsals at Zelter's even before they officially entered the Singakademie in October 1820. A letter of 1 May 1819, from Lea Mendelssohn to her cousin Henriette Pereira-Arnstein in Vienna, confirms the fact that Fanny and Felix took part in the Friday musicales "where instrumental works of Handel, Bach, and, in short, the more serious things were performed." See Susanna Grossmann-Vendrey, *Felix Mendelssohn Bartholdy und die Musik der Vergangenheit* (Regensburg, 1969), p. 15.

3. Rudorff is referring to the famous description by Eduard Devrient in *Meine Erinnerungen an Felix Mendelssohn Bartholdy und seine Briefe an mich* (Leipzig, 1869), p. 10. It is available in English as *My Recollections of Felix Mendelssohn Bartholdy and His Letters to Me*, trans. Natalia MacFarren (London, 1869), p. 2. References to Devrient in this excerpt will be to the English translation.

4. Alessandro Manzoni (1785–1873) wrote his best-known novel, *I promessi sposi*, in 1825–1826. It had an immediate and lasting popular success.

5. Eduard Rietz (1802–1832), sometimes spelled Ritz, was also Felix's violin teacher.

6. An unpublished letter from Felix to his parents, dated 30 August 1827 (New York Public Library, Mendelssohn *Briefe*, no. 38), describes the visit. Written during a hiking trip he made in the company of several friends, the

letter attests to the high spirits of the young men as they traveled through Thuringia. The letter reads, in part: "The following day Ritz [Rietz] and I dined with Pastor Radicase [*sic*] where I also met up with the goal of my journey (*teste matre cum Caecilia*); I mean, naturally, the Pistors. We broke up at one o'clock and went on to Ilsenburg am Ilsenthal joking and laughing all the way."

7. Wilhelm Friedemann Bach (1710–1784), the eldest son of Johann Sebastian Bach; he died in Berlin.

8. The Pistor collection, along with many other rare items collected by later members of the family, was sold by Ernst Rudorff to the music library of the publisher C. F. Peters in 1916. At the present time remnants of the Pistor-Rudorff collection are in the Musikbibliothek der Stadt Leipzig and are described in *Handschriften der Werke Johann Sebastian Bachs in der Musikbibliothek der Stadt Leipzig* (Leipzig, 1964), pp. 43–53.

9. Zelter evidently forgave Betty her father's victory. Included in the Leipzig collection today is the J. S. Bach Concerto, BWV 1058 (in the hand of a copyist), which was a gift from Zelter to Betty Pistor and inscribed to his "dear devoted Betty, 10 March 1832." See *Handschriften der Werke Johann Sebastian Bachs*, p. 52.

10. The cantata, *Ich freue mich in dir*, BWV 133.

11. The 1964 inventory in *Handschriften der Werke Bachs* of the Leipzig music library notes that Mendelssohn's handwritten lists on the blue paper are still in the library.

12. In his *Mendelssohn: A New Image of the Composer and His Age* (New York, 1963), p. 40, Eric Werner discusses Mendelssohn's "sensitivity," describing it as "defensive" and attributing it to "a number of rather disappointing experiences during his youth and early manhood."

13. Betty Pistor's mother, Charlotte Pistor *née* Hensler, was the daughter of Johanna Hensler Reichardt *née* Alberti (1755–1827), and thus the stepdaughter of Johann Friedrich Reichardt (1752–1814), the German composer and writer.

14. Rahel von Ense Varnhagen, *née* Levin (1771–1833), had a leading literary and artistic salon in Berlin. She, like the Mendelssohn family, was born Jewish but converted to Christianity. According to Devrient, Felix "could not bear celebrated women" like Rahel Varnhagen and Bettina von Arnim. Devrient, p. 37.

15. See also the excerpt in Hans T. David and Arthur Mendel, *The Bach Reader*, rev. ed. (New York, 1966), pp. 376–86.

16. Karl Klingemann (1798–1862), an intimate family friend, was secretary to the Hanoverian delegation in London from 1827 onward. In the summer of 1829, he and Felix journeyed to Scotland and it was during this trip that the *Fingal's Cave* Overture, op. 26, and the *Scottish* Symphony, op. 56, were conceived.

17. Mendelssohn injured his leg in a coach accident in London.

18. Wilhelm Hensel (1794–1861), court painter, was married to Fanny Mendelssohn on 3 October 1829.

19. A play on the words *Album* and *Bummler* (loafer). Actually, Hensel was a productive artist and was continually busy with commissions and teaching until Fanny's death. He never recovered from this blow and ceased painting at that time.

20. *Die Heimkehr aus der Fremde*, a comic opera for which Klingemann wrote the libretto, was composed during Mendelssohn's stay in England. At the performance of 26 December, family members and close friends, Devrient among them, made up the cast. According to Devrient (pp. 92–93), *Die Heimkehr* was so intimately related to Felix's feelings about his family that he declined to have it published or performed publicly during his lifetime. It was not published until 1851 (as op. 89).

21. Rudorff was mistaken; it was the song of the watchman, not of a hunter: "Wenn die Abendglocken läuten."

22. Karl Matthias Kudelsky (1805–1877), German violinist.

23. Ferdinand David (1810–1873), German violinist and a boyhood friend of Mendelssohn. Later, he was Mendelssohn's concertmaster in the Leipzig Gewandhaus orchestra, and teacher in the Leipzig Conservatory.

24. Carl von Liphart (1778–1853). David married his daughter Sophie.

25. The original letter, still in the possession of the Rudorff estate, differs somewhat from the published versions, which are based on a copy in Leipzig. See "The Rudorff Collection," p. 253.

26. Although Rudorff had obviously read all the published Mendelssohn letters, there were many letters to which he did not have access. In the collection of Mendelssohn letters in the New York Public Library, there are several letters from the years 1829–1832, in which Betty Pistor and the quartet are mentioned.

27. Marie Lichtenstein (1817–1890), was Rudorff's first piano teacher. She was the daughter of Heinrich Lichtenstein (1780–1857), professor at the Berlin University, zoologist, and a leading member of many Berlin musical institutions.

PART

· III ·

LETTERS

Letters from Felix Mendelssohn-Bartholdy

to Aloys Fuchs

EDUARD HANSLICK

TRANSLATED BY SUSAN GILLESPIE

The celebrated critic Eduard Hanslick (1825–1904) played a crucial role in Viennese musical life of the second half of the nineteenth century. Today he is chiefly remembered as the author of a treatise on musical aesthetics, *Vom Musikalisch-Schönen* (*On the Beautiful in Music*), which appeared in 1854 and ran to many editions; and as the arch supporter of Brahms and the persistent detractor of Wagner, Liszt, and the movement known as *Zukunftsmusik* (Music of the Future), for which role Hanslick was parodied in Wagner's *Die Meistersinger* as Beckmesser. Hanslick's treatise propounded a view of music as an absolute, ultimately self-sufficient art; for Hanslick the beautiful in music lay not in its expressiveness, or its uncertain ability to carry a programmatic meaning, but in its independent relations of form and structure. Hanslick found in the music of Brahms, and, before him, of Mozart, Beethoven, Schumann, and Mendelssohn, a familiar and especially rich tradition of instrumental music with which to support his views.

Hanslick's introductory essay to Mendelssohn's correspondence with Aloys Fuchs is illustrative of the critic's witty and eloquent prose style. These little-known letters reveal a facet of Mendelssohn still relatively unexplored today: his frenetic activities as a collector of musical autographs and his unwavering efforts to resuscitate interest in music of earlier historical periods. [ed.]

[Source: "Briefe von Felix Mendelssohn-Bartholdy an Aloys Fuchs, mit Einleitung von Eduard Hanslick," in *Deutsche Rundschau* 57 (1888): 65–85.]

I have before me twenty letters by Felix Mendelssohn, in the familiar, fine, graceful hand that has so much similarity to that of his antipode Richard Wagner. The letters span a period of fourteen years (July 1831 to December 1845) and are addressed to Aloys Fuchs in Vienna. Who is Aloys Fuchs, our readers will ask. His name, once much cited in serious, more selective musical circles, is now as good as forgotten; it requires an explanation. Fuchs is not one of the great, famous figures of music; he was neither a composer nor a virtuoso—he was a collector. A collector of autographs and portraits of famous musicians. He collected with a passion, not for mere amusement, still less out of speculation. Thoroughly educated in musical matters and a competent singer in the church choir, he pursued his quest for autographs out of scholarly interest and in the spirit of scholarship. Since all his thoughts and endeavors were directed toward this single end, he soon succeeded in making his collection grow from modest beginnings to full bloom, and in earning the great respect of music historians. Seldom did a musician or music historian of any significance leave Vienna without having paid a visit to Fuchs's autograph collection and, when appropriate, solicited his advice. The visitor would find the modest-mannered owner, always eager to please, ready to display and explain his well-ordered treasure at any time. Through his collecting, Fuchs gradually evolved into a competent music historian, and every piece of information he offered about the genuineness of a signature, about the life and work of a musician, whether famous or half-forgotten, was considered reliable.

Aloys Fuchs was a bureaucrat. Naturally, one will say. In Austria before the period of the 1848 Revolution everyone was a bureaucrat who was devoured by the love for artistic creation, and would not have had anything to devour himself were it not for the comfortable government job he occupied on the side. Our poets and writers: Collin, Grillparzer, Friedrich Halm, Mosenthal, J. N. Vogl, Tschabuschnigg, and so on, were bureaucrats.[1] Our music writers: Kiesewetter, von Mosel, Anton Schmid (the biographer of Gluck), Ambros—bureaucrats.[2] True, our Aloys Fuchs did not rise as high as Kiesewetter and Mosel, to the position of privy councilor; he occupied an insignificant post in the Royal Council of War. His bureaucratic service from 9:00 until 2:00 provided him with his livelihood; the afternoon and evening, and the early morning too, belonged to music—and the autographs.

Fuchs was born in 1799 in Raase, Austrian Silesia, the son of a schoolteacher, from whom he inherited his musical talent and love of order. Nothing else. At seventeen he came to Vienna, where as a student he lived a rather wretched existence. Once safely moored in the haven of officialdom, he pursued his musical studies avidly and set himself the goal of assembling "a universal collection of autograph scores of the classical composers of all periods and countries." Conscientiousness, talent, and luck as a collector brought him unexpectedly quick successes. His hobby first took hold in 1820, and by 1834 he already possessed something approaching seven hundred musical autographs and five hundred portraits. The majority of the manuscripts were whole, valuable pieces, complete scores; only a few composers were represented by fragmentary sketches. Later he saw the collection increase by twice that amount. His modest means allowed neither expensive purchases nor costly trips; most of what he had was acquired cheaply, either through trade or through gifts and exchange of services. His honest sobriety, his modesty and unboasting, engaging personality explain why numerous friends were glad to exert themselves on his behalf; even a Felix Mendelssohn, whether at home or traveling, was always mindful of increasing Fuchs's autograph collection. In his modest apartment in the suburban Leimgrube (no. 184, fourth floor), he had systematically arranged his exemplarily cataloged collection. According to his plan, the collection was to retain a truly art-historical value in the future, to provide insight in questionable cases into the genuineness of orthography, and so on. Unfortunately, it shared the fate of so many valuable collections: it did not remain together. Fuchs himself was forced by frequent severe illnesses to sell off his treasures piece by piece. Holberg purchased the majority of the autographs;[3] Grasnick in Berlin the portrait collection; the monastery in Gottweih the library; the bookseller Butsch[4] in Augsburg the remainder of the papers and biographical articles. Aloys Fuchs died at the age of fifty-four on 21 March 1853 in Vienna, and left behind a widow and four sons.

Fuchs counted Mendelssohn's friendship among the greatest honors and treasures of his life. Mendelssohn, who had made his acquaintance during his sojourn in Vienna in August, 1830,[5] inspected Fuchs's collection with great interest at that time, and volunteered to help with it to the best of his ability. The enriching of this collection through manuscripts or portraits is the main theme of the correspondence we have before us; but, as we shall see, it is not the only one. Mendelssohn's first letter (from Milan, in July 1831) documents his inexhaustible amiability. He sends Fuchs original scores by Durante and Paisiello, along with autographs of Rossini, Bellini, Mercadante,[6] and Staffa.[7] He also suggests that Fuchs write directly (mentioning Mendelssohn's name) to Cottrau, who, as the leading music publisher in Naples, could easily obtain all desired autographs of Italian composers. Guillaume Cottrau, whom Mendelssohn praises as "a very friendly and punctual man," played a significant role in the world of Italian music. Born in Paris in 1797, he lived in Naples continuously from the time he was three, where he founded a flourishing publishing firm and became popular as the composer of many Neapolitan canzonettes and romances. He died in 1847 in Naples. His son Jules Cottrau recently published his father's letters under the title *Lettres d'un Mélomane* (Naples, 1885); in them Mendelssohn's Neapolitan sojourn of April 1831 is mentioned. While there, Mendelssohn made frequent visits to the soprano Fodor,[8] with G. Cottrau and Donizetti. In Rome, Mendelssohn had worked very conscientiously; in Naples he was more inclined to follow his fancy. "Il fut pris par la fainéantise et délaissa un peu la musique." ["He was taken by idleness and somewhat abandoned music."] Cottrau reports that Mendelssohn valued Donizetti's talent very highly and later "had almost all the pieces from *Lucia* and *La Favorite* at his fingertips."[9] Chancellor Kiesewetter, to whom Mendelssohn addresses the manuscripts that are meant for Fuchs, is the famous music historian Georg Raphael von Kiesewetter (b. 1773 in Hölleschau in Moravia; d. 1850 in Baden near Vienna), whose private performances of old music were highly regarded in Vienna. "Our Hauser," whose welfare Mendelssohn inquires after so solicitously, is the eminent singer Franz Hauser (b. 1784 near Prague), who, after originally gracing the opera in Dresden, Kassel, and Vienna, later (in 1838) settled in Vienna as a voice teacher, and finally (from 1846 to 1864) developed an influential role as director of the Munich Conservatory. Among his students were Henriette Sontag, Frau Vogel, Staudigl, Joseph Hauser, and v. Milde in Weimar, among others.[10] After Hauser retired, he became a pensioner in Freiburg im Breisgau, where he died in 1870. Mendelssohn thought a great deal of Hauser and in almost every one of these letters he asks to be remembered to him with heartfelt greetings.

The two following letters (nos. 2 and 3) are concerned chiefly with Fuchs's collection. Mendelssohn asks Fuchs for an accurate list of all those musicians of whom he does not yet possess a clear autograph. Mendelssohn hopes to be able to acquire some things from Despréaux.[11] For the moment he is sending manuscripts of Rossini, Auber, Hiller, Liszt, Herz, Adam, Carulli, Karr, and Tolbècque.[12]

Fuchs thus received much, and many valuable items, from Mendelssohn. Eventually, however, it is Mendelssohn's turn (in letter no. 4) to appear "as a supplicant with my hands out." Mendelssohn asks Fuchs to choose a new piano for him from the firm Graf, and to send it to Berlin.[13] The instrument—one of the finest—is not to cost more than 300 gulden! One can see what a revolution in prices has taken place since 1832; today in Vienna a grand piano from Ehrbar or Bösendorfer costs at least three times that much. The following letters (nos. 5, 6, 7, and 8) deal with the purchase of the piano. Mendelssohn thanks his friend for procuring it so quickly and especially, also, for his friendly letter. He wants to "think up and go to great lengths to invent all kinds of requests for Fuchs in the future," in order to receive another such letter from him. Mendelssohn wants the exterior of the piano to be as plain as possible, but the bass notes must reach low C and the soprano F. Nowadays every self-respecting piano has four more keys in the high register (F♯, G, G♯, A) and three more in the low (B, B♭, A). On 15 November 1832, Mendelssohn played the Graf piano in a concert in Berlin, and proclaimed it excellent.[14] Once more, from Düsseldorf, he addresses the same request to Fuchs. He would like—as soon as possible—to possess a piano on the Rhine, one that is as outstanding as the Graf piano that had remained in his father's house in Berlin. In case Graf does not have an exquisitely fine instrument on hand, then he asks for a Streicher. For this instrument, "which must be very, very beautiful," and of mahogany, he can, however, not spend more than 300 florins, approximately 400 gulden including transportation. When he discovers that the piano costs 450 florins in Vienna, without transportation, he writes back and forth twice more, finally deciding to pay the price. Mendelssohn again finds the new instrument from Graf excellent; he writes that on the day before Christmas he "had a delightful time with it and romped and rumbled all over it." And yet a third piano must be procured by the faithful Fuchs! It is destined for Mendelssohn's brother in Berlin, who is getting married and wants to give the piano to his bride as a wedding present. This piano, too, is selected as well as may be and earns the most complete satisfaction from the Mendelssohn family.

During this eagerly pursued piece of piano business the subject of autographs does not vanish completely. From Berlin, Mendelssohn sends Fuchs manuscripts of Righini[15] and inquires whether he would be interested in those of Neukomm[16] and Marx.[17] "I would like to send you something again!" Fuchs, for his part, sends a treatise on Gluck's manuscripts (letter no. 6), which is of the "greatest interest" to Mendelssohn. This "treatise"—if one may apply the title to a series of bibliographic and antiquarian notes—exists as a lithograph in the archive of the Gesellschaft der österreichischen Musikfreunde [Society of Austrian Friends of Music] and bears the title "Bemerkung über die in meiner Autographensammlung befindlichen Original-

handschriften des Chr. v. Gluck und über die verschiedenen Anga-
ben seines Geburtsjahres, begleitet von einer möglichst vollständigen
Aufzählung seiner Oper" ["Remarks on the Original Manuscripts of
Chr. v. Gluck in My Possession and on the Various Claims about the
Year of His Birth, with His Operas Listed as Completely as Possi-
ble."][18]

Fuchs reports in his essay that in his search for a manuscript by
Gluck he looked everywhere until chance finally brought him together with a fellow who had often associated with Gluck during the
last years of the composer's life. This man (according to Schmid's information it was an old musician by the name of Piering) owned five
music notebooks that were written entirely by Gluck himself: sketches
and complete pieces from *Alceste*, *Iphigenie in Tauris*, *Telemacco*, and
Aristeo (two Italian operas from Gluck's first period).[19] Fuchs purchased these extremely valuable sketches, which he refers to as the
"crown jewels" of his collection. Musical works in Gluck's own hand
are known to be among the greatest rarities, not only because in earlier times they were treated extremely carelessly and heedlessly, but
also because Gluck had the habit of destroying his own sketches as
soon as the copyist, working under his direction, had completed a
clean copy. It is striking that Fuchs called Gluck's scanty and incoher-
ent notes "the first authentic thing" he had seen concerning Gluck's
life. It is true that the first complete Gluck biography (by Anton
Schmid in Vienna) did not appear until 1854.[20] Still more remarkable, almost disconcerting for us is Mendelssohn's remark that he
"considers [Gluck] to be the greatest musician."

There follow more packages of autographs from Mendelssohn to
Fuchs: compositions by Attwood, Moscheles, Clementi, Righini, and
Riem.[21] In a postscript, Mendelssohn announces that he has received
an old letter and a very polite new letter from Mechetti,[22] who "wants
to make a quick engraving of the symphony," adding: "It is *your* work,
isn't it?" Mechetti must nonetheless have made inquiries about printing one of Mendelssohn's symphonies; not one of the master's symphonies ever appeared with Mechetti, however.[23]

Mendelssohn makes efforts to enrich Fuchs's portrait collection, as
well, but with less success. "Here they scarcely know what Mozart
looked like," he writes from Düsseldorf. Mendelssohn himself had
not yet had his portrait engraved, and he commented that if he had
his way, it would not happen. "I would prefer to get it down in the
form of notes before it appears in facial expressions." Not until 1837
is he able to send his friend his own portrait (letter no. 17), indeed

both one published by Breitkopf and another by Simrock. A third that is to be published in Cologne "will follow very soon."

In letter no. 10, Mendelssohn acknowledges with thanks the receipt of a brochure by Herr Fischhof concerning Fuchs's collection. This is a description of the autograph collection that originally appeared in the January issue of *Mittheilungen aus Wien* [*Notes from Vienna*], a long-defunct little monthly put out by Franz Pietznigg. Josef Fischhof (b. 1804 in Moravia; d. 1857 in Vienna) was a professor of piano at the conservatory and one of the best known and loved musical personalities of pre-1848 Vienna. He was one of those practical musicians—at that time still a rarity—who possess a general education, knowledge of foreign languages, and social graces. Fischhof, who made an elegant and self-assured impression in the salon, knew how to address the questions of his art in a graceful manner, touching on them rather than exhausting them. His manner toward foreign artists was one of gracious amiability, and he maintained wide and estimable relations with the musical notables of other countries. In December 1847, Robert and Clara Schumann stayed with Fischhof. The latter invited all the musical and literary lights of Vienna (among them the poet Joseph von Eichendorff[24]) to an intimate morning concert at which Schumann's glorious Variations for Two Pianos were performed for the first time by Clara and Rubinstein, playing from manuscript.[25] One of the most enraptured listeners was Aloys Fuchs, whom I saw on that occasion for the first time—the very picture of the good-natured petty official, shy in manner, dressed with threadbare meticulousness. Fischhof felt very flattered when Richard Wagner visited him in the summer of 1848, and equally hurt when his guest spoke to him of political and social reforms but not at all about music. It eventually emerged, as I can authentically attest, that Wagner had thought the professor of piano to be the same person as Dr. Adolf Fischhof,[26] who had played a prominent role in Vienna in the revolutionary movement of March 1848, and was well known as one of the most gifted leaders of the Democratic party. Fischhof dedicated himself with admirable zeal to making Mendelssohn known and appreciated and Vienna, at a time when the composer of *St. Paul* was still quite unknown to our musical circles.

Not all autograph collectors were so gracious and broadminded as Aloys Fuchs. Pölchau, in Berlin,[27] flatly refused to allow Mendelssohn access to Mozart's arrangement of Handel's *Acis und Galatea*, which Mendelssohn wished to perform (letter no. 11). Pölchau did not even want to permit Mendelssohn to copy down the wind parts that Mozart had added. Then Mendelssohn, in his extremity, turned to

Fuchs, and the latter immediately procured for him a copy of the Handel-Mozart cantata taken from an original score in Vienna.[28]

Of great interest is Mendelssohn's lively eagerness to find out "how much truth or untruth there is in the new Beethoven pieces that everyone is talking about so much" (letters nos. 11, 12, 18). He has heard about a posthumous tenth symphony, then about a third overture to *Leonore* or *Fidelio*.[29] He asks Fuchs to procure him a copy if at all possible, regardless of the price. Mendelssohn asks, further, when the long-announced Haslinger publication of a cantata and the new overture by Beethoven will appear? It sounds strange enough to us that in the year 1835 people still believed in a posthumous tenth symphony of Beethoven. The rumor persisted for some time until people became convinced that Beethoven had written no tenth symphony, although he had had ideas for one. The new cantata that Mendelssohn mentioned is the *Glorreicher Augenblick* [*Glorious Moment*], composed in the year 1814, published by Haslinger in the year 1836. So far as the overture to *Leonore* (*Fidelio*) is concerned, Mendelssohn is only familiar with two of them: the one in C major, with the trumpet solo (now known as no. 3); and the fourth, in E major.[30]

Haslinger, of whom Mendelssohn writes that he knows him as "imprecise and not very detailed" in his answers to written questions, is the well-known Viennese music publisher Tobias Haslinger.[31]

Mendelssohn's respect for the classic artists always goes hand in hand with the most lively interest in new creations. He wishes (letter 13) to receive from Fuchs the orchestra parts to Lachner's *Preissymphonie* before the end of the Leipzig concert season, in order to perform the work as soon as possible.[32] A great stir was created in those days when the (not at all spiritual) management of the Viennese "Spirituelconcerte" offered a prize of 50 ducats for the best new symphony. The prize committee had very respectable prospects: Weigl, Gyrowetz, Eybler, Gansbacher, Umlauf, Seyfried and Conradin Kreutzer,[33] the last being the sole romantic blemish on this "white ermine of the old school." The prize was won, as is well known, by Franz Lachner (currently retired general music director in Munich) for his *Sinfonia appassionata* in C minor, which was given a most festive première on 19 February 1836, in Vienna. Thereupon it had the good fortune to be conducted by Mendelssohn at a Leipzig Gewandhaus concert, and the bad luck to be criticized mercilessly by Robert Schumann.[34]

With the fifteenth letter, the correspondence takes quite an unexpected turn. Mendelssohn, who until now has tirelessly supplied Herr Fuchs with autographs, now asks for some for himself! He has just become engaged to Cécile Jeanrenaud, about whom he writes from Leipzig on 18 November 1836: "My fiancée is so good and beautiful and lovable that I would fall in love with her all over again every day, if I had not already done so on the very first day." As a Christmas present he wants to give her a pretty musical album, for which he already has quite a bit of material in hand. "But right up front, as an introduction," he would like to have Mozart and Beethoven, and he entreats the faithful Aloys Fuchs to get hold of a handwritten piece by these two masters—"The request is a big one!" The latter is free to expend "as much money and as many good words as you wish; that is, actually money only up to about 12 florins, but good words *ad libitum*." Fuchs, however, expends neither the one nor the other, but takes from his own collection three musical autographs of Haydn, Mozart, and Beethoven and sends them to the joyfully surprised Mendelssohn, for his beloved bride.[35] Mendelssohn feels "what a great sacrifice it has been for Fuchs to part with these priceless things," and in truth we do not believe that he would have made the sacrifice for anyone but Mendelssohn. The latter cannot express his thanks often enough, along with his wish to demonstrate his grati-tude. He attempts to do this by sending autographs of L. Berger,[36] Löwe,[37] and Lobe.[38]

Lamentations by Mozart, about which Fuchs has asked Mendels-sohn, are not known to him, and he thinks that the matter is a mere misunderstanding (letter no. 16). Correctly so; in Köchel's catalog there is no lamentation by Mozart. Probably what was meant was a still-unknown *Litanei*, which Mendelssohn's later letter (letter no. 18) seems to corroborate. Mendelssohn made his friend a nice present with the as-yet-unpublished great *Psalm* (in twelve to fifteen numbers) by Handel (*Dixit Dominus*), of which a single copy now exists in the Royal Library in London. Mendelssohn himself made his copy dur-ing a long sickness in London "to while away the time."[39] The condi-tion imposed upon him—namely, that he not allow anyone else to make a copy of the *Psalm*—he had to pass along to Fuchs. Mendels-sohn also takes advantage of J. B. Streicher's[40] presence in Berlin to send portraits of Curschmann,[41] Bennett,[42] and others to Fuchs (let-ter no. 19). The last letter (no. 20) is from Leipzig, dated 11 Decem-ber 1845. In it, Mendelssohn thanks Fuchs for the "singable and beautiful verses of J. N. Vogl,"[43] which Fuchs had sent him with the request that he set them to music. But Mendelssohn is "so unbeliev-ably pressured by work—business—interruptions of every sort," that many days pass in which only with difficulty can he claim a half hour for himself and collect himself. "But arrange things in such a way," he says with true Mendelssohnian sensitivity, "that he at least does not doubt my good will." How many hundreds of poems may have been sent to the much-harried master "to be set to music"!

In his numerous letters to Moscheles, F. David, Hiller, and others, Mendelssohn often accuses himself of being a neglectful, lazy letter-writer who does not deserve the forbearance of his friends, and so on. Mendelssohn did himself a great injustice by saying this. We are, on the contrary, amazed at the great number of detailed letters from him, rich in content, that have already been printed. As incomprehensible as the wealth of musical compositions that Mendelssohn created in a life of such brief duration is the extensiveness of his correspondence, which accompanied his strenuous activity as composer, conductor, virtuoso, and organizer. And in all the numerous letters from him to the most diverse individuals, in the most varied circumstances of life—always the same indestructible amiability, the same golden naturalness and grace, the same seriousness softened by the most thriving humor! We have found these qualities in rich profusion in the letters presented here, which offer us the image of this glorious human being so truly and in such fresh vivid colors.

·

Milan, 19 July 1831[44]

Dear Herr Fuchs!

You will receive in the enclosure a little packet of manuscripts that I have uncovered for you; unfortunately the greater part, which consists of a batch of manuscripts (music) by newer composers that I found in Naples and that the owner promised to forward to me, has not yet arrived, and since I can no longer postpone my trip you will have to be so good as to forgive the slimness of this package. It includes a magnificat by Durante and a piece by Paisiello; I found these two in Naples, and one of the best local *dilettanti* has given me assurances that they are genuine, since I know less than nothing about it and have no opinion on the subject. I am also sending the signatures of Rossini and Mercadante and notes by Bellini and Staffa; at the same time I hope soon to receive music by all of the above, and by Pacini,[45] Donizetti, and others on your list; or rather I shall write and ask that they be sent to you directly. Perhaps you would be so good as to write a few lines yourself to Naples about this, since it seemed to me that the owner would be flattered if you would ask him directly for these manuscripts, which, by the way, he was very willing to part with. In this case I would ask you to write your letter in French to Herr Cottrau, addressed to "Musikhandlung von Girard, Strada Toledo," and simply to mention me and the oral commitments he made to me. This would seem to be the best course from another point of view, as well, for from this man you can obtain with ease *all* the manuscripts your heart desires by Italian composers, since he is in contact with all of them and, as the leading music publisher of Naples, is himself in possession of much music by them. He promised me that he would be delighted to send you whatever manuscripts you might wish to have, and although he has not kept his promise to send them on to me, I know him otherwise to be a very friendly and punctual man, and so I do not doubt that he will carry out your requests at once. I am addressing this to Chancellor Kiesewetter, since I do not know your address and do not want it to be lost. May I ask you to send me a few lines in response, and especially to let me know how our Hauser is doing, whether he is still in Vienna and in good health, and so on. I have already sent him two letters without receiving an answer and am quite concerned about him. My address until the end of August is still Lucerne in Switzerland, *poste restante*, and from there to Munich to Baron von Kerstorf.[46] Forgive these hurried lines, but I am about to set off by coach and I am writing this surrounded by the great commotion of departure. Be well and healthy and be assured that I shall always recall your friendship and goodness with gratitude.

Always, your
Felix Mendelssohn Bartholdy

.

Dear Herr Fuchs![47]

In great haste and in the complete confusion of a Parisian morning, when one's head is simply buzzing with visits and music and politics and people, I write a few lines to you to request some assignments relating to your music collection. In your last letter, you sent me a list of musicians whose autographs you wished to have, and I began to ask some people for them; but then I learned that several of the people I consulted had already sent something to you, and others had already given your manuscripts to Herr Despréaux for you. I am only too eager to procure some things for your collection, since I am in touch with most of the musicians here, and since I would like to show my gratitude for all your friendship; therefore I would like to ask you now for an exact list of all those musicians whom you do not possess, either through Despréaux or anyone else, and I promise to send you the manuscripts if it is at all within my power to do so. Forgive the hurried lines, but I am entirely too pre-occupied and rushed. Your Beethoven sketchbook[48] is attracting attention among musicians here. Farewell; if you see Mme. Hauser, greet her warmly from

> Your most devoted
> Felix Mendelssohn Bartholdy

Paris, 23 January 1832
Address: [c/o] Mr. Auguste Leo, rue Louis le Grand, no. 11
P.S. Have you already got Rossini? He is available.

·

n.d.[49] (from Paris, 1832)

Dear Herr Fuchs!

Just back on my feet after an illness and on the point of departure, I write to send you a few words in haste. I was just about to begin searching for [some things for] your collection, and could have sent you more if my sickness had not prevented me; so you must bear with me; all my plans have been upset, including this one. But today I am handing a packet of manuscripts over to Herr Filliard to forward it to you or to Artaria. It contains a canon by Rossini with the words "pour Mr. Fuchs par J. Rossini," and also by him a sketch for a Stabat mater that he has just composed.[50] It is fairly interesting, and even without his signature you will easily recognize his handwriting. I had something of Auber's for you, but I remember your manuscript from the *muette de Portici*,[51] and it is undoubtedly genuine; he writes just as small and graceful a hand as on that sheet. Then there are also manuscripts by Hiller, Liszt, Herz, Adam, Carulli, Karr, and Tol-bècque, all with the signatures. I would have liked to send more and better, but as I said it was not possible.

Now my thoughts are already in London, where your letters will reach me at the address: Mess. [*sic*] Doxat et Co. If you want anything by London composers, write soon to let me know. A thousand greetings for Hauser.

> Your
> Felix Mendelssohn Bartholdy

·

Dear Herr Fuchs!

Today I approach you as a supplicant with my hands out. You will already have learned from Hauser that it was not possible for me to get hold of a manuscript of Handel's for you, not even through trade for the Beethoven; the principal collection of his things belongs to the king and it is impossible to pry loose even a single sheet. Those private individuals who have anything have paid so dearly for it that they would not give it up for any price. Although I have thus had little success, I am coming to you as a supplicant and asking you for a great favor. I know your great kindness and therefore I do not hesitate to make demands on you. Namely, I wish to have a piano from Graf sent to me here, and although I know Graf personally and believe he would send me a good instrument, still I would prefer to have someone look at and approve it beforehand—someone in whom I can place complete confidence, since, as you can easily imagine, I depend a great deal on having a flawless instrument. Would you therefore perhaps be so good as to do this for me and in the process to hand the enclosed letter to Graf, ask him to show you what kind of instruments he has, and, if there are two equally good ones, select the one that pleases you more? It matters a great deal to me that I have one of his best instruments, and in my letter to him I ask him myself for one. Only the importance this matter holds for me excuses the fact that I am bothering you with it. Could you then perhaps be so friendly as to send me a few lines of confirmation—whether, when, and what quality of instrument I may expect here?

I have been meaning to ask you for a long time whether you possess a manuscript by Righini? I have a requiem that he is reported to have written for the Singakademie, in his handwriting, and would be delighted, in case you don't yet have anything of his, to have it sent to you at the first opportunity. What is the address of your forwarding agent here?

Excuse me again and let me have the pleasure of a speedy reply.

Your devoted
Felix Mendelssohn Bartholdy

Berlin, 20 July 1832
P.S. I would like to ask you to send me the price that Graf quotes at once, and in case it is not more than 300 florins and you find a perfect instrument, to claim it and have it sent here right away.

.

Berlin, 21 August 1832

Dear Herr Fuchs!

My most sincere thanks for the great goodness and favor you have done me once again, and also for the friendly letter you wrote me. In the future I shall think up and go to great lengths to invent all kinds of requests, just so I may receive another letter like the last one, which can't help but console a person for many unpleasantnesses in the world, and restore one's trust. Thank you again most warmly. I am delighted that Graf will send me an especially good instrument, for that is very important to me; now my only request is to have it sent to me as soon as possible, not, that is, to be in a hurry when it comes to perfecting every detail, but to lose no time, since we need it here. I ask him to send the instrument, as soon as it is ready, to my father: Councilor A. Mendelssohn Bartholdy, and to collect the money for it from Messrs. Arnstein and Eskeles,[52] who will be informed of the necessary particulars from here. I believe I have already specified that I would like the exterior to be as plain as possible, and without many features; however it is necessary that in the lower register it should go to low C and in the high register to F; these are both indispensable to me. I hope now I will hear soon that it is finished and has been sent off, and I already look forward to it and thank you for it. Neukomm was just here. He will stay for a few weeks and perform his oratorio *The Ten Commandments*. Do you already have something from his hand? If not, I could easily get you something decent, since he is very forthcoming and friendly. And do write to me, in addition, whether there is another Berlin manuscript that you might be interested in? Do you already have Marx? I am very eager to have your treatise on Gluck's manuscripts. Please send it to me as soon as it is finished; you know how much it interests me. In some of the papers it is said that Hauser is sitting in prison on account of the bankruptcy of the English theater director. There is not a true word in any of this; last week he arrived happily in Hamburg together with Moscheles and Neukomm, and by now he is probably already back in Leipzig, calm and cheerful. I write this to you so that you will not be shocked by this stupid rumor too. Farewell.

Your
Felix Mendelssohn Bartholdy

•

Dear Herr Fuchs!

As a great sinner I appear before you, for the instrument and your kind package arrived safely and I have still not sent you a reply. But my great excuse is written in the newspaper, where it says that yesterday I gave my first concert here, and that I must give two more in the next few weeks, all for charitable purposes. How much running, worrying, ordering, and chasing around this entails you could scarcely believe; I didn't have time for myself, much less for a letter. Then, what's more, I thought it would be nice to have introduced the Graf piano in public in order to be able to write to you in detail about its success. Yesterday that happened and so today I hasten to bring you news; above all, though, I must ask you to forgive me my sins of omission in correspondence and not to be angry with me on that account; I thought about it every day, and every day the mail went out without my having been able to write. For that reason I had to fear you might lose patience with me, and so I want to tell you today, although I am pressed, with many thank-you visits and the like, in a great rush, how very indebted I am for your great kindness and friendship. The instrument you selected for me is quite outstanding and created the greatest possible pleasure in the whole house. It was exceptionally clear and distinct and songful yesterday and came across splendidly against the orchestra, to the approbation of all. Please thank Graf very warmly on my behalf and tell him how gladly I perform on his instruments; you yourself are most warmly thanked for your friendly response to my request and for the beautiful instrument that you procured for me. I wish with all my heart that an occasion may arise when I might be in a position to return the favor, and I hope that then you will give me precedence before your other correspondents here and will let me have the pleasure of helping you out in any way possible.

For the notes on Gluck I must thank you quite particularly; they are of the greatest interest to me, because they are the first authentic thing I have read concerning his life, and because I consider him to be the greatest musician. Concerning a few passages I must reserve the right to ask you at another time because I do not have the brochure here, but have lent it to some friends, who are also very much interested in it.* Thank you very warmly and please be so good as to tell me in your reply whether I may keep this copy or whether I should send it back to you when I have an opportunity? With the first traveler I run into you shall also receive several weak autographs; your interesting catalog puts me in a position to promote your cause properly, and only my running around for the concert has been able to prevent me heretofore.

Now just one more *pater peccavi*; that is, I am very lazy but you are very friendly and will not be angry with me. And so farewell

Your most devoted and respectful
Felix Mendelssohn Bartholdy

(Berlin) 16 November 1832
* They do not steal and are discreet people, or I would not have entrusted them with anything.

•

Düsseldorf, 6 September 1833

Dear Herr Fuchs!

Please above all forgive my long silence; it was not intentional, but really enforced, because during the entire time that has passed I had unusually much to do. To top it all, my father fell ill in London;[53] I was there solely to care for him, and although he is now quite recovered, I must accompany him back to Berlin to make sure that he arrives safe and sound. Then I must return here, where I shall spend the whole winter and the following year, and with all this traveling to and fro and the various worries, I have found time for neither note nor letter writing. Nevertheless I have a manuscript by Moscheles, one by Clementi, the one by Righini, and one of my own lying here waiting for you, and I ask you to let me know, when it is convenient, how I should send them to you, or whether I should wait for a private opportunity.

Undoubtedly you can already tell that once again I have a request to make of you. I am almost ashamed to come out with it, and if I did not know your friendliness I wouldn't do it. But I know you, and I am doing it. Would you have the kindness, again, to select a piano for me? I would like to have one on the Rhine, and because the Graf piano turned out so excellently, I cannot deny myself the opportunity to turn to you once more. In case Graf doesn't have an exquisitely good piano on hand, and Streicher does, a Streicher would be perfectly agreeable to me, since I would like to have the instrument by the end of October at the latest; but it must be very, very beautiful. But to whom am I saying that? You know it better. I cannot afford to spend more than about 300 florins (ca. 400 gulden) for it, *including transportation*, but I would like, on the other hand, to have a mahogany case, but without any bronze fittings. Would that be possible, do you think?

Please write to me by return post, just a line to let me know whether you wish to do me the favor at all, and if so, whether it will be Graf or Streicher, how much it is to cost, when it can arrive here, and so on. Then I will immediately give you the address to which I wish you to have the instrument sent here, and see to all the other details. On my return from Berlin I will pass through Frankfurt am Main[54] and I beg you to send your reply to Frankfurt *poste restante*, since I shall be spending several days there. All subsequent letters (from the first of October on) I ask you to send to my name in Düsseldorf.

I expect to see Hauser on my way through Leipzig, and will write you about him from Frankfurt. I shall await your answer as to the manuscripts in Frankfurt, as well, but if I find a good opportunity in Berlin I shall already send them from there. And now excuse me again, write me a line in reply, and remain a friend to

Your devoted
Felix Mendelssohn Bartholdy

•

Düsseldorf, 18 October 1833

Dear Herr Fuchs!

I have just returned from a business trip on which I visited several libraries on the Rhine to find your latest letter of the seventh and hardly know how I can ask your pardon and excuse myself sufficiently for writing back so tardily. And yet I can't help it. Your first letter took a long time to reach me (it was two weeks ago), because I was away then, too. You write that the instrument would cost 450 florins *there*; actually I had counted on that much including *all* transportation costs and as a result I had to write back and forth two more times before I could say with certainty that I would take it at that price. And when I had barely reached this decision, suddenly so many things to write descended upon me in my new surroundings, and this trip, that I say *amice peccavi*, or *pater*, or whatever you want, and must only ask you not to be angry.

As for the instrument, at the prices you wrote to me earlier, I now ask you to have it packed and sent off as soon as possible, for I wish very much that it should arrive early this winter. Please excuse me to Graf for my tardiness and give him my thanks for being so willing to entrust it to me; I hope it is not too late and he has not yet given it away.

The address to which I would like you to have it sent is: Herr Mendelssohn in Bonn.[55] Then it is certain to arrive; the money will be paid by Messrs. Arnstein and Eckeles. Please accept my thanks, Herr Fuchs, for all your care, and excuse the hasty letter. Soon more and better, for if I have not had a chance before the end of next week I shall send your manuscripts by coach, as you wish, and write at the same time. Farewell.

Always your
Felix Mendelssohn Bartholdy

My address is now permanently Düsseldorf.

In the last few days I received a very old letter from Mechetti and a polite new one. Now they want to print the symphony right away. This is not your work by any chance?

·

Dear Herr Fuchs,

I no longer ask your pardon for my long silence, for I am such a stubborn sinner that no one will believe me any more. But I am living at the moment so happily at work, so deeply immersed *in musicalibus*, that I only get around to writing a letter after the holidays, or the like, as now. What is more, I have just returned from Bonn, where your fine Graf had just arrived, like me, on the day before Christmas; so then I had a delightful time with it and romped and rumbled all over it. Thank you for your friendly care in selecting it. The instrument is really very beautiful. If I might be permitted, from this great distance, to make a small observation to Graf, it would be that in several of his new instruments, in which I am most interested, and in this one in Bonn, too, the middle pitches approximately within this octave [the octave f¹ – f² was notated here] are not as strong as the others in duration or volume of sound. Above and below them, they are perfectly beautiful again, but in this range, for example, the F [f¹], if it is played strongly, is so much weaker than the tones beneath it, that it sounds toneless or at any rate not pleasant. I consider it my duty to say this, precisely because otherwise the instruments are so good. Thank you again for all your trouble and kindness. Hauser wrote to me about four weeks ago; he is well and happy, amiable, as ever, and is furiously collecting Bach.[56] I haven't answered him either, though every day I intend to. I received both of your catalogs too, but there is little hope of any portraits here; here they scarcely know what Mozart looked like, and so one can hardly expect novelties. My own portrait has not been engraved yet, as far as I know, and it won't either, if I have my way. I would prefer to get it down in the form of notes, before it appears in facial expressions.

Today I am delivering to the mail coach, wrapped in waxed canvas and marked A. F., the following manuscripts for the collection: 1) a canon by Clementi, written for Moscheles; 2) an étude by Moscheles from the second volume[57] of the engraved edition, with preface, fingering, and so on; 3) a requiem by Righini on the death of Queen Louise;[58] 4) a canon by Attword [Attwood], an outstanding student of Mozart's, who is now organist and music director at St. Paul's in London; 5) a quartet of mine, in a green binding.[59]

Some business is arriving and I must close. When I have something again I shall send it at once. Live happily and have a Happy New Year.

Your

Felix Mendelssohn Bartholdy

Düsseldorf, 4 January 1834

P.S. The money was sent immediately from Berlin to Arnstein and Eskeles (from Mendelssohn and Co.). I hope everything is in order. If the musical things arrive in good shape, I hope to receive a few words as a receipt.

Dear Herr Fuchs!

Thank you very much for the interesting package, for which I am indebted to your kindness. I received it here just a short while ago and have read Herr Fischhof's brochure on your collection with great pleasure. It is nice that it is now becoming quite well known and the public is made aware that such a curiosity exists; for your fervent, long-lasting, and unceasing efforts certainly deserve every recognition. Unfortunately, I cannot send you anything from here that would be of any significance. There are no significant musicians on the Rhine, and hence no manuscripts of theirs. But in July I am thinking of taking another trip of several months' duration,[60] and if any significant manuscript crosses my path I will snap it up and off it will go to Vienna. My portrait at the Congress of Great Men in Berlin is shameful in the extreme; I did not even sit for it; but the only other one that exists, an English one,[61] is even more repulsive. If a decent one ever comes out I shall send it to you at once, since you would like to have one.

Today I have another request. Namely, whether you would be so good as to choose a piano for me from Graf? It is for my brother, who is getting married and would like to give his wife a Graf instrument as a wedding present, and since the first one you chose for me turned out to be so very excellent he asked me to request the same favor for him, which I do herewith. I would therefore like to ask you very kindly to select from Graf a good instrument, free of imperfections, that *completely satisfies* you. If he doesn't have one ready, I would prefer that you wait until one can be found. But if there is one that you can term excellent, then I ask you to choose it, the sooner the better, and have it packed up and sent off, since it should be in Berlin by the end of May, if possible, and since my brother is looking forward to it. I wish this instrument to be as simple as possible on the exterior; I am concerned only with the excellence of its tone and touch. So if there is a walnut case on hand, that would be all right with me; if not, then simple mahogany, no bronze. It must have six and a half octaves; if Graf can be persuaded to let me have it for the same price as the previous two, I would be pleased. I ask you to speak with him about this, and to close the deal as *you* find best; since I have already bought several pianos from him I hope he will not set the price too high. My brother has opened a credit with Arnstein and Eskeles for the cost of a piano, and I ask you, after you have come to an agreement with Graf, to tell him that he can collect the amount (which you will specify) from Arnstein and Eskeles, against his signed receipt. You see that I am putting the whole business in your hands; forgive the liberty I am taking and the trouble I am causing you; but I am convinced that this is the best way, and that the instrument, selected and tested by you, will give the greatest joy to my brother and to all of us.

Please address the instrument to Mendelssohn and Co. in Berlin. Once more I beg of you to take this matter up without delay, so that the instrument can be bought and packed up at once if one of the finished ones is to your taste—only if that is not the case would I ask you to wait. But if you forsee that it could take longer than mid-May, then I would request that you inform me immediately.

You have already rendered so many favors and friendly services for me that I could almost be called presumptuous; but for that very reason I am not, and will only be more and more in your debt for all your friendship.

Now farewell, be happy, dear Herr Fuchs, and think with friendship of

Your devoted
Felix Mendelssohn Bartholdy

Düsseldorf, 10 April 1831 [*recte* 1835]

.

Dear Herr Fuchs!

A thousand thanks for your punctual response, once again, to my last request; I arrived here a few days ago (and only for a few days) and immediately tried out the Graf instrument that you selected for my brother. To my great pleasure I found it extraordinarily excellent. I take pleasure in playing it every time I am at my brother's, and it gives him and his wife the greatest joy; they join me, therefore, in expressing many, many thanks to you for your great favor and for the care with which you have selected such a beautiful instrument for us.

Today once more I have a number of questions and requests for you, but this time they go more toward the subject in which you have taken such an active and successful interest. Herr Pölchau, whom you have probably also met, has in his collection Handel's drama *Acis und Galatea* with a supplemental arrangement by Mozart (like those for *Messiah* and *Alexanders Feast*).[62] He has the Mozart manuscript, which Mozart wrote in little notes on a copy of the original score by Handel, and he showed me this interesting piece a few years ago. Since I had intended to perform it, some time ago, I made Herr Pölchau aware of my wish to receive a copy of the Mozart wind instruments. I promised to make the copy myself if necessary and never to give it out of my hands except during rehearsals, and in this way to be accountable for any possible dissemination of the manuscript, other than by performance, since I anticipated that Herr Pölchau himself would wish to keep any future publication for himself. However, he flatly refused to allow me access to the work at all. I now wish to know whether there is another copy of this arrangement (which, if I am not mistaken, was commissioned by Baron van Swieten[63]), in Vienna or elsewhere, and whether a copy can be obtained? You are without a doubt among all possible people the one who is in the best position to give me information on this, and since, if you haven't already heard of it, it would surely be very interesting for you to track down a work by Mozart, I ask you very sincerely whether you would inquire about this from the principal sources and please let me know the result. I would be very much in your debt.

Further, I would very much like to know how much truth or untruth there is in the new Beethoven pieces that everyone is talking about so much. There is talk of a tenth symphony that has been found (and that, if I am not mistaken, is said to be in Haslinger's possession); of several unpublished piano sonatas; and finally of a third overture to *Leonore* or *Fidelio*, also in Haslinger's possession. Is there any truth in all this? And if there is, is it possible to receive these things in copy form, at whatever price, or are they being published, and when? Further, when will the Beethoven cantata, which Haslinger has long since announced, and his new overture appear? On all these points I fervently hope for a prompt reply. A conversation with Haslinger would surely elicit complete answers to all my questions; I would write to him directly, but I know him too little, and I also know that his answers to such questions are imprecise and not very detailed. So you can do me a great favor by shedding light on all these points; and if you were thinking of being annoyed about the trouble that I am once again causing you, then do not forget that you must ascribe all that to your own oft-repeated obligingness. Be well and happy and please pass on greetings to your wife sometime from one who doesn't know her but remains

Your respectfully devoted
Felix Mendelssohn Bartholdy

Berlin, 9 August 1835
P.S. Please send your answer to Breitkopf and Härtel in Leipzig. And please! Write to me soon!

.

Dear Herr Fuchs!

I received your friendly letter of 17 August here today. It waited for several days in Leipzig, where I was expected, and finally it was sent on to me, and although I am leaving here tomorrow for Leipzig, where I shall remain through the winter, I make haste to answer from here.

Above all you have my sincere thanks for your great favor, which pleases me immensely. You may believe me when I say that your kindness is of the greatest value, and that I am very sincerely grateful for it. If only I could manage to prove this to you soon by my deeds! Thus I was very gratified to receive along with your letter the list of autographs that you would like to receive from Leipzig, and hope with certainty that it will be possible for me to send some of them quite soon indeed.

I ask you to have a copy of the Mozart-Handel cantata *Acis und Galatea* prepared as quickly as possible by your copyist, and to send it to me in Leipzig by coach. For this I will be very indebted to you. The cost, if it runs to as much as 12 francs CM or more, will be remitted at once, and with sincere thanks.

If it were possible for you to send me at the same time a copy of the third Beethoven overture to *Fidelio*, which is completely unknown to me up to now (I know the two in E-major and

my joy would be great. If that is not possible, then please enclose the piano reduction of this third overture, which you mentioned has appeared from Haslinger.[64] However I would naturally *much, much* prefer to have the score. With all these things I merely ask you to tell me the price right away, so that I need not remain in your debt for too long. And please let me hear soon in detail from you, and send me the score, which I am looking forward all too eagerly to possessing, really, really soon. How happy I am that I turned to you, whose kindness has not allowed a single request to remain unanswered. My address remains with Messrs. Breitkopf and Härtel; forgive my hasty lines, and farewell. With warm greetings to your wife from your unknown (to her) and

most devoted
Felix Mendelssohn Bartholdy

Berlin, 28 August 1835

·

Dear Herr Fuchs!

It is quite unfair of me that I have not written to you for so long, and have not expressed my thanks for kindly sending *Acis und Galatea*, with which you have given me the greatest pleasure. But I would so much have liked to send you one of the manuscripts that you wrote to me about, and I thought I would certainly be able to procure one of them from Messrs. Breitkopf and Härtel. These gentlemen kept me waiting from one day to the next, promised to look around, to find something, and so on and on; in short, a few days ago they had the impoliteness all at once to turn me down flat, and the day before yesterday to announce an auction of old manuscripts, at which, as I hear, many autographs are to be found. This is really going too far, and I hold it against the gentlemen; but I shall go to the auction (which is in several weeks) anyway and try to get something. But I ask you to write me at once how high I should go in the price in your name, in case there should be something significant by Bach or one of the composers you mentioned to me. An autograph of Attwood's, whom you once wished to have, is lying here for you; but because I do not know whether you have found another one in the meanwhile, I want to ask you first whether it is worth the postage. It is a pretty, canonic church piece for four voices. Your interesting package of *Acis* material has already given me very great and frequent pleasure. Have you received the cost of the copying, which I instructed Arnstein and Eskeles to pay out at once, in good order?

I also thank you very much for the piano reduction of Beethoven's third overture to *Leonore*, but when will the orchestral parts finally be available? And in this connection, another question occurs to me: could I get the parts to Lachner's new symphony, which captured the prize in your city [Vienna], before the end of the concert season here (the last one is scheduled for 20 March) for a performance? Since a prompt performance here would surely be quite good for the dissemination of the work, perhaps Haslinger could be persuaded to send a copy, and at the same time do me a great favor. May I ask you to inquire about this, and if Haslinger is willing, to send me the parts very soon—or if not, then to send me an answer to that effect in your next letter. I remain, with best regards for Frau Fuchs,

Your devoted
Felix Mendelssohn Bartholdy

Leipzig, 8 February 1836

·

Dear Herr Fuchs!

I just received your letter of the twenty-third, and hasten to reply that unfortunately it will be impossible for me to carry out your instructions, since I am leaving Leipzig next Sunday and will not return until September. When I last wrote to you, I believed that the auction would take place in March or April, but since it will be in the summer, I will not be able to be present, as I have a number of travel plans[65] that I intend to work out more fully on the Rhine (for which I am now departing). I shall pass the two lists you sent me along to Herr Kistner, the music dealer, and if later on you give this commission to someone else, he can pick them up there and you will be spared the trouble of writing them down twice.

I am also giving Herr Kistner, to be sent for you to Haslinger's music shop, two songs in Riem's handwriting and the aforesaid canon by Attwood. It is admittedly not much, but only a rogue gives more than he has! Forgive these hasty lines, but I am already packing my things again; and farewell.

Your devoted
Felix Mendelssohn Bartholdy

·

Most honored friend,[66]

After a long silence I turn to you once again with a great request, which can be fulfilled by no one so easily as by you, and which I would therefore not make of anyone else, even if I did not already have so many examples to prove your obligingness and friendship. But the request is a big one. Namely, I wish to have a page of manuscript by Mozart and one by Beethoven, if possible with both of their signatures. It need only be something very brief, but of unquestion-

· 298 ·

able authenticity. If it should be possible for you to procure this for me, you would do me the greatest favor, and I beg of you to expend as much money and as many good words as you wish—that is, money actually only up to about 12 gulden—but good words *ad libitum*. I imagine that this cannot be too hard for you. Now listen to the reason *why* I want these pages—

Like you, most honored friend, I also intend to enter into the state of matrimony, and have gotten engaged, and my dear fiancée is so good and beautiful and lovable that I would fall in love with her all over again every day if I had not already done so on the very first day. But unfortunately she is not here, but in Frankfurt, and I cannot visit there until nearly Christmas. Then I would like to give her a pretty musical album, for which I already have various pieces. But right up front, as an introduction, I would like to have the names of Mozart and Beethoven, and that is why I am making this request of you. You will also see from this what great value I place on its fulfillment, and can also deduce from it what kind of manuscript I most wish to have, namely above all some song or other, if such a thing is to be found, or if not that, then a trifle for the piano; if not that, then something else, whatever that may be. If you can do this service for me, I ask you to send the things here by coach, and you will have my heartfelt thanks. But there is quite some urgency about it, since I am planning to leave for Frankfurt on the fifteenth of December. In any case I ask you to send me right away a few lines in reply, and not to be angry with me that I am once more taking advantage of your kindness and amiability. But you know that out of love for one's bride one would happily leap into the fire, much less—. Farewell, and do not forget

Your devoted
Felix Mendelssohn Bartholdy

Leipzig, 18 November 1836

.

Most honored friend.

How splendidly you have surprised me with your package, which I just received. I must write to you immediately to thank you, because it is entirely too marvelous. And how appropriate precisely these things are. I knew very well to whom I was turning with my request, and that it would be carried out better than if I had done it myself. And now you have even added in Haydn. Truly, you are too good, and I thank you most warmly for the great joy you have given me. But tell me, how can I show my appreciation?

I know what a great sacrifice it was for you to part with these price-less things, therefore I am only too eager to do some small service for your manuscript collection, but I am hardly in a very good position to do so. Then it occurred to me that I do possess something novel—the question is only whether you will regard it as such. Namely I had occasion to make a copy in London of a great psalm by Handel (in twelve to fifteen numbers), from which there is only a single copy in the king's library, and which has never been published. I copied it at that time under the condition that I would not pass it on to anyone else, and would send you my copy only with the same restriction—for I am convinced that you would keep the promise not to pass it on further, the question being only whether it is interesting for your col-lection, since it is, after all, not Handel's autograph.

Send me your answer soon, and tell me how I should begin to prove how much in your debt I am for your kindness, and how grate-ful I am to you. For the business with the lamentation is unfortu-nately only a misunderstanding. I am aware of no lamentation by Mozart, no unknown composition by him, and cannot even imagine what could have been the cause of this misunderstanding, since so far as I know I never spoke with Hauptmann[67] about anything like that. The collection of André[68] in Offenbach, where the originals of the *Magic Flute*, *Don Juan*, and several unfinished Mozart operas, and so on, are to be found, is undoubtedly known to you.

Just now I am accidentally in a position to send you manuscripts by Berger, Löwe, and Lobe; at least I will go to the greatest possible lengths to see that they don't slip out of our grasp this time. The letters from B. and Lobe are set aside for you, but I would prefer to include them in the larger package, since unfortunately I cannot send anything by post to Vienna. Wouldn't you like to give me the name of a book dealer through whom I could have it sent to you? Then I would also include three different editions of my portrait, which all suddenly came out at the same time, as I know that you collect such things, too. Now enough for today; again many thanks for your ex-cellent present which has given me so much joy; farewell and do not forget

Your
Felix Mendelssohn Bartholdy

Leipzig, 2 December 1836[69]

·

Dear Herr Fuchs,

Today I am sending the package for you to Hermann and Lang-bein and hope you will receive it in good order. Included in it are: 1)

my copy of Handel's *Dixit dominus*, which has some value for me due to the fact that I made it during a long illness in London, to while away the time, and was only able to take the original home under special dispensation—for which reason, so far as I know, no other copy of it yet exists, and for which reason I must also once more attach the condition that no one but you should receive the copy. Not until today did I receive the copy that I am keeping back from the copyist, and that is why I was not able to send the package off earlier; it is a longer piece than I had thought, because I write so small; 2) a copy of my portrait by Breitkopf and Härtel; 3) another one published by Simrock. A third one that has appeared in Cologne will follow shortly, for unfortunately I cannot send the Berger manuscript that I have for you yet today, but you will receive it in two weeks at the latest. It is an eight-part male chorus in several movements, which, however, has yet to be published, and must be copied here first (it is supposed to be published) before I can send it to you. In the meantime, I enclose a letter of Berger's; I expect to get Löwe and Taubert, too, by that time.

For today farewell and excuse the hasty lines. Give my best regards to your wife and do not forget

Your devoted
Felix Mendelssohn Bartholdy

Leipzig, 31 January 1837

The concerto of S. Bach I will send at the earliest; it is nothing but misery with the copyists here; they need more time for copying than I do for composing.

•

Leipzig, 13 April 1838[70]

Dear Herr Fuchs,

Many thanks for your most recent, friendly letter, which I should long since have answered. Multiple business matters prevented me from doing so, and then it disturbs me that I can only give you such scanty information. Of Handel's works I know only what is to be found in the Arnold[71] edition, nothing more (except for the *Dixit dom.* that I have sent you), and all of the operas you name are quite unknown to me. Further, I am not quite certain which Mozart aria you mean; I have unfortunately misplaced your letter and do not remember it exactly; of the litany only a couple of pieces in a piano reduction are available here, and I had their owner (Attorney Schleinitz[72]) bring them by today, but there is no aria among them. The score is said to be in Munich, in the library, from where Councilor Rochlitz[73] once borrowed it and had the above-mentioned piano reduction made. I enclose a letter from Bennett to me; unfortunately I have no musical manuscript from his hand, but he is coming here again in September, as he informs me, and then he should send you something proper. If you would like me to write him about the Handel operas and make inquiries, then please send a few lines to me in Berlin (Leipzigerstrasse no. 3), where I am traveling in the next few days, and tell me what you mean by "indication of the themes" of the operas—the themes of the overture, or of all the individual numbers? One more thing, you can surely tell me whether another copy of the Beethoven overture to *Leonore* exists somewhere, which (as it seems) is the first longer and more serious version of the great one in C major (by Breitkopf and Härtel), with the same theme, the same conclusion, the trumpet call in the middle, and so on. From Herr Schindler[74] in Aachen, Breitkopf and Härtel here have acquired a copy of this overture, with notes in Beethoven's handwriting—but at the end two to four lines are missing, and Herr Schindler claims they are nowhere to be found, since this copy is the only one that exists of the overture. Is that true? Or do you know ways and means to replace the missing piece from some other copy, or perhaps even from the manuscript? It is the last two or three hundred measures (after the beginning of the last Presto) that are in question. You don't mind sending a line or two in answer to me in Berlin?

And now farewell. When I shall come to Vienna, only the gods know; I wish it would be soon, but I fear that it is not. My best greetings to you, your wife, and the little foxes,[75] from me, my wife, and my little son (who is now ten weeks old). See, now I too have dignity and know how to behave accordingly. Again farewell.

Your devoted
Felix Mendelssohn Bartholdy

·

Dear Herr Fuchs,

Since Herr Streicher is passing through here today and is returning to Vienna, I could not miss this chance to restore myself to your good graces, and I know that the best way to do that is by means of autographs or portraits. Today I have the latter to send you, and not of the best quality, either, but I hope that it will suffice for that restoration, and then its purpose will have been accomplished. Hence you receive Curschmann, in a lithograph that has just come out here; Bennett, published in Leipzig; the heads of Liszt, Thalberg, Henselt, Chopin, and my own on a single page, published by Schubert and Neimeyer in Hamburg, and my portrait printed separately from that page and most repulsive. If you think I look different, at least you will think of me once more, and that is, as I said, all I wish to accomplish.

Streicher's impending departure does not leave me time for more, other than a thousand greetings to you and all the friends there.

Always your devoted
Felix Mendelssohn Bartholdy

Berlin, 14 October 1841

.

Leipzig, 11 December 1845[76]

Most honored Sir,

It gave me great joy to see your dear handwriting, well-known from earlier times, after so long, and I am very grateful to you and Herr Vogel [*sic*][77] for that and for the confidence that you kindly place in me.

If only I could express this gratitude in deeds and send the singable and beautiful verses of Herr v. Vogl back to you with a melody attached! But it is quite impossible for me; I am so unbelievably pressured by work—business—interruptions of every sort, that many days pass in which it is only with difficulty that I can claim a half hour for myself and collect myself in it! So for now I cannot take on anything new, no matter how much I would like to, or even if it would require so little time as in this case.

I ask you to transmit my apologies to Herr Vogel, but to arrange things in such a way that he at least does not doubt my good will; if my time were only a little more my own now, if I were not burdened in so many ways by other demands, I assure you my music, as well as I can make it, would not be wanting.

Keep me in your good, unchanged remembrance, as I am always and remain

Your truly devoted
Felix Mendelssohn Bartholdy

NOTES

1. Heinrich Joseph Collin (1772–1811), poet; Franz Grillparzer (1791–1872), dramatist, poet, author of Beethoven's funeral oration and Schubert's epitaph; Friedrich Halm, pseudonym for E.F.J. von Munch-Bellinghausen (1806–1871), poet, playwright; S. H. von Mosenthal (1821–1877), play-

wright, librettist; J. N. Vogl, see note 43; Adolf Ritter von Tschabuschnigg (1809–1877), statesman, poet. [ed.]

2. Raphael Georg Kiesewetter (1773–1850), musicologist, author of a history of music (1834), who organized a series of historical concerts, held at his home, devoted to music of the sixteenth through the eighteenth centuries; I. E. von Mosel (1772–1844), composer and writer on music; Anton Schmid (1787–1857), musicologist, author of studies of Petrucci and Haydn, and of *Christoph Willibald Ritter von Gluck: dessen Leben und tonkünstlerisches Wirken* (Leipzig, 1854); and August Wilhelm Ambros (1816–1876), musicologist and critic, nephew of Kiesewetter, and author of a four-volume history of music issued between 1862 and 1878. [ed.]

3. For a more accurate assessment of the disposition of Fuchs's library, see Richard Schaal, *Quellen und Forschungen zur Wiener Musiksammlung von Aloys Fuchs* (Vienna, 1966), pp. 78ff. The greater part of the collection was acquired by the Deutsche Staatsbibliothek in Berlin. [ed.]

4. Friedrich August Grasnick (1798–1877), autograph collector in Berlin; Fidelis Butsch (1805–1879), book dealer in Augsburg. [ed.]

5. Mendelssohn arrived in Vienna in mid-August. On 16 September, Fuchs presented him with a Beethoven sketchbook containing sketches for the *Missa solemnis* (the Wittgenstein sketchbook). For a facsimile of Fuchs's dedicatory note, see *Letters of Felix Mendelssohn to Ignaz and Charlotte Moscheles*, trans. Felix Moscheles (Boston, 1888), p. 49. [ed.]

6. Francesco Durante (1684–1755), Italian composer of sacred music; Giovanni Paisiello (1740–1816), Italian opera composer; Saverio Mercadante (1795–1870), Italian opera composer. [ed.]

7. Baron Joseph Staffa, born in 1807, Neapolitan nobleman, dedicated himself as an amateur to composition and wrote operas. The poor success of his last works, especially the opera *Alceste* (1851), caused him to abandon composition. He died in Naples in 1877. [Eduard Hanslick]

8. Mendelssohn arrived in Naples in mid-April. Fodor was the French soprano Josephine Fodor-Mainvielle (1789–1870). [ed.]

9. Donizetti, *Lucia di Lammermoor* (1835), and *La Favorite* (1840). [ed.]

10. Henriette Sontag (1806–1854), German soprano; Therese Thoma Vogl (1845–1921), soprano, wife of the tenor Heinrich Vogl (1845–1900); Joseph Staudigl (1807–1861), Austrian bass, who first sang the part of Elijah in Mendelssohn's oratorio at its première in Birmingham in 1846; Feodor von Milde (1821–1899), Austrian baritone. Hanslick discussed the correspondence between Mendelssohn and Franz Hauser in "Briefe von F. Mendelssohn," *Aus neuer und neuester Zeit* (Berlin, 1900, reprint 1971), pp. 281–94. [ed.]

11. Despréaux (Guillaume Ross), born in Clermont in 1803, was a pupil of Berton and Felix at the Paris Conservatory and mounted two small works in the *Opéra comique* without success (*Le souper du mari* and *Le dame d'honneur*). [Eduard Hanslick]

12. Henri Herz (1803–1888), German virtuoso pianist and composer; Adolphe Adam (1803–1856), French opera composer [ed.]; Ferdinand Ca-

rulli, guitarist and composer, born in 1770 in Naples, died in 1841 in Paris. Henri Karr (father of the writer Alphonse Karr), born in Deux-Ponts in 1784, died in Paris in 1842, remained in vogue for a while as a composer of light piano music; he wrote so much and so carelessly that he offered his manuscripts to publishers for a few francs. Jean-Baptiste-Joseph Tolbèque, born in Belgium in 1797, died in Paris in 1869, was the most popular composer of dance music before Musard, and ball-orchestral director in Paris. [Eduard Hanslick]

13. Conrad Graf, in his time the most celebrated piano manufacturer in Vienna, was born in 1782 in Riedlingen (Württemberg). He established himself in Vienna in 1804, where he died in 1851 as the royal piano manufacturer. [Eduard Hanslick]

14. At a benefit concert held at the Singakademie for the widows of members of the orchestra. Presented during the concert was the first performance of Mendelssohn's *Reformation* Symphony, op. 107, and performances of the *Midsummer Night's Dream* Overture and the Piano Concerto no. 1 in G minor, op. 25. See the *Allgemeine musikalische Zeitung* 35 (1833): col. 22. [ed.]

15. Vincenz Righini, born 1756 in Bologna, Kapellmeister of the Italian Opera in Vienna, then in Berlin in 1793, composer of the once highly esteemed opera *Tigranes*, died 1812 in Bologna. [Eduard Hanslick]

16. Sigmund Ritter von Neukomm, born 1778 in Salzburg, pupil of Michael Haydn, then of Joseph Haydn; he lived primarily in Paris as a friend and associate of Talleyrand. In 1832 he came to Berlin, where he performed his oratorio *Das Gesetz des alten Bundes*. He wrote over one thousand compositions and died in Paris in 1858. [Eduard Hanslick]

17. Adolf Bernhard Marx, famous writer on music and composer of the oratorio *Moses*, born 1799 in Halle, died 1866 in Berlin. [Eduard Hanslick]

18. Fuchs later published a "complete" thematic catalog of Gluck's music in the *Neue Berliner Musikzeitung* 5 (1851): 207ff. [ed.]

19. *Alceste* (Vienna, 1769), *Iphigenie in Tauris* (German version, 1781), and *Telemacco* (Vienna, 1765). *Aristeo* is the second act of *Le feste d'Apollo* (1769). [ed.]

20. See note 2. [ed.]

21. Thomas Attwood, born 1767, died 1838 at his manor in Chelsea, studied in Italy, then with Mozart in Vienna, returned to England in 1787, wrote operas and church music. He had dealings with Mozart and Felix Mendelssohn! [Eduard Hanslick] Mendelssohn met Attwood in 1829 during his first English sojourn and later dedicated the Three Preludes and Fugues for Organ, op. 37, to him. [ed.] Friedrich Wilhelm Riem, organist and composer, born 1779 in Kolleda (Thuringen), died 1857 in Bremen, as director of the Singakademie there; he wrote organ compositions and chamber pieces. [Eduard Hanslick]

22. Pietro Mechetti (1777–1850), born in Lucca, came to Vienna in 1798 and was one of the most distinguished music dealers and publishers here. After his death his firm was dissolved during the 1840s. [Eduard Hanslick]

23. Mendelssohn indeed originally intended to publish the Symphony no. 1 in C minor, op. 11, with Mechetti. See Felix Mendelssohn-Bartholdy, *Briefe an deutsche Verleger*, ed. Rudolf Elvers (Berlin, 1968), pp. 291–93. Nevertheless, the work appeared in 1834 from the Berlin firm of A. M. Schlesinger. [ed.]

24. Joseph von Eichendorff (1788–1857). [ed.]

25. Perhaps the Andante and Variations in B♭ major, op. 46. Rubinstein was the Russian pianist and composer Anton Rubinstein (1829–1894). [ed.]

26. Adolf Fischhof (1816–1893), Austrian political activist. After the dissolution of the Reichstag in 1849 he was arrested and imprisoned for several months. In 1867 he received a full amnesty. Along with Josef Unger, Fischhof is credited with suggesting a dual monarchy as a solution to the political crisis (*Zur Lösung der ungarischen Frage*, 1861). This solution was realized in 1867 with the foundation of the Austro-Hungarian Empire. [ed.]

27. Georg Pölchau, born 1773 in Lievland, moved to Hamburg where he laid the foundation of his great music collection through the purchase of the musical *Nachlass* of Philipp Emanuel Bach. In 1813 he settled in Berlin, where he died in 1836. His remarkable collection was purchased by the Royal Library in London and the Berlin Singakademie. [Eduard Hanslick]

28. Mozart's arrangement (K. 566), completed in 1788, called for additional woodwinds. Unknown to Hanslick was the fact that Mendelssohn himself had prepared an arrangement of *Acis and Galatea* which he finished on 3 January 1829. For a brief description of the manuscript, preserved in the M. Deneke Mendelssohn Collection at Oxford, see *Catalogue of the Mendelssohn Papers in the Bodleian Library, Oxford*, ed. Margaret Crum (Tutzing, 1983), vol. 2, pp. 41–42. [ed.]

29. Concerning the sketches for Beethoven's Tenth Symphony, see Barry Cooper, "Newly Identified Sketches for Beethoven's Tenth Symphony," in *Music and Letters* 66 (1985): 9–18. [ed.]

30. The Overture in C major now known as no. 1 appeared in 1832 [*recte* 1838] from Haslinger as op. 138. At the time this was to be published, only two *Leonore* overtures were known in Vienna: the one classified as no. 3, from the year 1806; and the fourth, in E major, from the year 1814. Nothing precise was as yet known about the actual first overture [no. 2], from the year 1805; for this became known only as a result of performances in the Leipzig Gewandhaus in 1840 and was published in the year 1842 as the second. (Nottebohm, *Beethoveniana*, p. 73) [Eduard Hanslick] The chronology of the various overtures to Beethoven's *Fidelio* is especially complex. In the nineteenth century, Gustav Nottebohm was the first to propose that "no. 1," op. 138, in fact dated from a projected 1807 performance of the opera in Prague, and thus, in postdating "no. 2" (1805) and "no. 3" (1806), was actually the third. Other Beethoven scholars rejected this redating on stylistic grounds, arguing that op. 138 was less developed in form and style than the other overtures and therefore must have preceded them. More recently, Alan Tyson has supported Nottebohm's argument, and suggested a dating

of fall 1806–1807 for op. 138. See "The Problem of Beethoven's 'First' *Leonore* Overture," in *Journal of the American Musicological Society* 28 (1975): 292–334. [ed.]

31. Tobias Haslinger arrived in Vienna in 1810 and was a book dealer, then an associate of the Steiner music firm, and finally an independent publisher. After his death (1842) his son, Carl Haslinger, also known as a composer, took over the business. He died in 1868. [Eduard Hanslick]

32. Franz Paul Lachner (1803–1890), *Preissinfonie* in C minor, op. 52. [ed.]

33. Joseph Weigl (1766–1846), composer; Adalbert Gyrowetz (1763–1850), composer; J. L. Eybler (1765–1846), composer; Johann Gansbacher (1778–1844), composer; Michael Umlauf (1781–1842), composer and conductor of the 1814 performances of Beethoven's *Fidelio*; Ignaz Seyfried (1776–1841), composer; Conradin Kreutzer (1780–1849), composer. [ed.]

34. Performed by Mendelssohn on 27 October 1836. The symphony evidently did not impress. See *AmZ* 38 (1836): col. 746. [ed.] Schumann's *Gesammelte Schriften*, part 3, p. 199. [Eduard Hanslick]

35. The album was presented to Cécile Jeanrenaud on 24 December 1836, and survives in the M. Deneke Mendelssohn Collection at Oxford (c. 21). The three autographs are Haydn's Presto for a Musical Clock, Hob. XIX:31; Mozart's Allegro in G minor, K. 312; and Beethoven's Ecossaise and Trio in D, WoO 22. See *Catalogue of the Mendelssohn Papers in the Bodleian Library, Oxford*, vol. 2, pp. 78–79. [ed.]

36. Ludwig Berger, born 1777 in Berlin, died there in 1839, was Mendelssohn's piano teacher, as well as Henselt's and Taubert's [Adolf Henselt (1814–1889), pianist and composer; Wilhelm Taubert (1811–1891), composer, pianist, and conductor]. Of his compositions many songs, male choruses, and piano works are esteemed. [Eduard Hanslick]

37. Carl Löwe, the celebrated ballad composer, born 1796 in Lobejun, died 1869 in Kiel. [Eduard Hanslick]

38. Johann Christian Lobe, theorist and composer, born 1797 in Weimar, died 1881 in Leipzig. [Eduard Hanslick] See also pp. 187–205. [ed.]

39. A copy prepared from Mendelssohn's copy survives in the M. Deneke Collection at Oxford (c. 75) with the heading "Dixit Dominus von Handel copirt in London den 6ten Nov. 1829." See *Catalogue of the Mendelssohn Papers in the Bodleian Library, Oxford*, vol. 2, p. 42. [ed.]

40. Johann Baptiste Streicher, celebrated piano manufacturer in Vienna, born 1794, died 1871, son of Andreas Streicher, the devoted young friend of Schiller, who was helpful to the poet when he fled the Karlsschule and later, as the spouse of Nanette Stein from Augsburg, founded the Viennese piano firm. [Eduard Hanslick]

41. Karl Friedrich Curschmann, song composer, born 1805 in Berlin, died 1841 in Danzig. [Eduard Hanslick]

42. William Sterndale-Bennett, born 1816 in Sheffield, died 1875 in London, went to Leipzig in 1837 and enjoyed friendly relations with Mendelssohn and Robert Schumann. [Eduard Hanslick]

43. Johann Nepomuk Vogl, prolific and esteemed ballad poet, born 1802 in Vienna, died there in 1866 as an elected civil servant. Carl Löwe set several of his ballads to music. [Eduard Hanslick]

44. The original letter is in the Library of Congress, Washington, D. C. [ed.]

45. Giovanni Pacini (1796–1867), Italian opera composer. [ed.]

46. Baron Friedrich von Kerstorf (1803–1880), Munich attorney. [ed.]

47. The original letter is in the Pierpont Morgan Library, New York. [ed.]

48. The Wittgenstein sketchbook, now in the Beethoven Haus, Bonn. See also note 5. [ed.]

49. The letter is likely from ca. 20 April 1832. Mendelssohn arrived in London on 23 April. See Ignaz Moscheles, *Recent Music and Musicians*, ed. C. Moscheles, trans. A. D. Coleridge (New York, 1873, reprint 1970), p. 178. [ed.]

50. The first version of Rossini's *Stabat mater* was finished in 1832, with the collaboration of Giovanni Tadolini. [ed.]

51. D.-F.-E. Auber (1782–1871). Reference is to his opera *La muette de Portici* (1828). [ed.]

52. Arnstein and Eskeles, Viennese banking firm. Two aunts of Mendelssohn's mother, Lea, were Fanny von Arnstein and Caecilie von Eskeles. Mendelssohn's sister Fanny was named after them. [ed.]

53. Abraham Mendelssohn had injured his leg in June in London; the two arrived in Düsseldorf in late August. Felix accompanied his father to Berlin in mid-September. [ed.]

54. Mendelssohn spent a few days in Frankfurt prior to his return to Düsseldorf on 25 September. [ed.]

55. Benjamin Mendelssohn (1794–1874). [ed.]

56. On Hauser's activities as a collector of Bach, see S. Grossmann-Vendrey, *Felix Mendelssohn-Bartholdy und die Musik der Vergangenheit* (Regensburg, 1969), pp. 206–14. [ed.]

57. Probably meant is the second volume of Moscheles' op. 70, *Studien für das Pianoforte zur höhern Vollendung bereits ausgebildeter Clavierspieler, bestehend aus 24 charakterischen Tonstücken*, which had appeared in 1825 and 1826. [ed.]

58. Righini, *Requiem for Queen Louise*. Daughter of Prince Charles of Mecklenburg-Strelitz; she married the crown prince Frederick William in 1793. In 1799 he acceded to the throne of Prussia as Frederick William III. She died in July 1810. [ed.]

59. String Quartet in E♭, op. 12, finished in London on 14 September 1829, and published in 1830. The autograph from Fuchs's collection is now in the Bibliothèque Nationale, Paris, Conservatoire ms. 191. [ed.]

60. Mendelssohn visited Cologne, Cassel, and Wittenberg in July, and Berlin in August, before arriving in Leipzig in September 1835. [ed.]

61. Probably the portrait by James Warren Childe (1780–1862). See the cover illustration of *Felix Mendelssohn Bartholdy: Der schöne Zwischenfall in der deutschen Musik* (Vienna, 1981). [ed.]

62. Mozart's arrangements of *Messiah* and *Alexander's Feast* are K. 575 (1789) and K. 591 (1790), respectively. [ed.]

63. Baron Gottfried van Swieten (1733–1803), Prussian emissary who introduced Mozart to the music of J. S. Bach and Handel in 1782 and 1783. [ed.]

64. The piano score of op. 138 in fact did not appear until 1838. See note 30. [ed.]

65. Mendelssohn directed the première of *St. Paul* in Düsseldorf in May, then visited Frankfurt before traveling to Holland in August. [ed.]

66. This letter later came into the autograph collection of Louis Koch. See Georg Kinsky, *Die Musikautographen-Sammlung Louis Kochs, Manuscripte, Briefe, Dokumente von Scarlatti bis Stravinsky* (Stuttgart, 1953), no. 198. [ed.]

67. Moritz Hauptmann (1792–1868), composer and theorist. [ed.]

68. J. A. André (1775–1842). In 1799 André bought the Mozart *Nachlass* from the composer's widow, Constanze. Mendelssohn had access to Mozart autographs from André, including the *Jupiter* Symphony. See his letter of 7 March 1845 to Moscheles in *Letters of Felix Mendelssohn to Ignaz and Charlotte Moscheles*, ed. F. Moscheles (Boston, 1888), p. 253. [ed.]

69. A portion of this letter was published in the *Musical Times* 41 (1900): 526. [ed.]

70. The original letter is in the Library of Congress, Washington, D.C. [ed.]

71. Samuel Arnold (1740–1802), composer and editor. His edition of Handel appeared between 1787 and 1797. [ed.]

72. Heinrich Konrad Schleinitz (1802–1881), Leipzig attorney. [ed.]

73. Friedrich Rochlitz (1769–1842), German critic. [ed.]

74. Anton Felix Schindler (1795–1864), biographer of Beethoven. [ed.]

75. The name Fuchs also means "fox." [trans.]

76. This, the last letter Fuchs received from Mendelssohn, was given by Fuchs in 1853 to the Stift Gottweig. For a facsimile, see *Musikalische Schätze aus neun Jahrhunderten*, ed. F. W. Riedel (Stift Gottweig, 1979), pp. 54–55. [ed.]

77. Johann Nepomuk Vogl (1802–1866). [ed.]

Mendelssohn as Teacher

With Previously Unpublished Letters from Mendelssohn to Wilhelm v. Boguslawski

BRUNO HAKE

TRANSLATED BY SUSAN GILLESPIE

As a teacher, Mendelssohn is chiefly remembered for his role in founding the Leipzig Conservatory, which admitted its first class of students in 1843. Throughout his career, however, he maintained an active correspondence with young composers seeking his advice. The little-known *Briefwechsel* with Wilhelm von Boguslawski, a civil servant in Breslau, offers an especially rewarding glimpse into Mendelssohn's critical approach to composition spanning the years from 1823 to 1842. At the center of Mendelssohn's interest are the scores of operas that Boguslawski submitted for his review. Mendelssohn's critiques, inevitably precise and to the point, shed light on his own views about opera, about the relation between music and text, and about the use of the orchestra to advance the dramatic thread. Of course, one of Mendelssohn's greatest frustrations as a composer was his own inability to discover and set successfully to music a suitable opera libretto, a task that intermittently engaged him throughout his career.

Bruno Hake (1883–1917) studied theology in Tübingen before attending the University of Berlin, where he completed his *Habilitationsschrift* on the poet Wilhelm Müller (*Wilhelm Müller: Sein Leben und Dichten*) in 1908. In 1914 he was appointed editor of the *Deutsche Rundschau*; three years later, he died in Flanders during the First World War. [ed.]

[Source: "Mendelssohn als Lehrer, mit bisher ungedruckten Briefen Mendelssohns an Wilhelm v. Boguslawski," in *Deutsche Rundschau* 140 (1909): 453–70.]

•

If, in the last century, Leipzig was for several generations the unrivaled musical capital of Germany, then it owes this prominence to the activity of Mendelssohn, who carried out in Leipzig what had failed in Berlin, as a result of the indecision of Friedrich Wilhelm IV, after endless negotiations and in spite of the best intentions. Mendelssohn founded a conservatory, the first modern institution of higher learning in music, which, by means of the strictest demands made on its students during their training, lifted them high above a craftsmanlike level of artistic performance. This helped the class of musicians to attain a position in polite society like that which Mendelssohn himself enjoyed as a result of his personality and his well-rounded humanistic education. His pedagogical principles, which he had already written down during the planning for the Berlin Music Academy, are sharp and clear and obviously influenced by reflection about the course of his own development. "Every genre in the arts is first elevated above the level of craft when it devotes itself by means of the greatest possible technical perfection to a purely spiritual purpose for the expression of a higher idea. Thus thoroughness, correctness, and discipline must be made the first rule of teaching and learning, so that—while not lacking in craftsmanship—the various subjects are taught and learned only as they relate to the ultimate idea they are meant to express, the higher purpose that governs every technical perfection in art."[1] Mendelssohn's idealistic view of art is expressed here in an unconcealed, almost polemical fashion. Even if the artist's technical capacity for expression is to be developed to its highest level, he must subject his ability to "purely spiritual purposes" and not use them merely for their own sake. That would be desecration. But what Mendelssohn understands by "craft" is not professional practice in the interest of earning one's daily bread, but rather the empty virtuosity and straining after effect that he always opposed in the most passionate way.

Although Mendelssohn applied his powers with particular zeal in the service of his fondest creation, which rapidly blossomed and served as an exemplar for all other institutions founded later, still he did not perceive within himself any special calling to be a teacher, someone who follows the now faster, now slower development of the student, and he therefore refused to accept the official leadership of the institute. Conscientiously he taught lessons in composition, piano, and ensemble playing, but found no deep satisfaction in it. "I have convinced myself through repeated experiences that I am quite lacking in the talent to be a proper teacher, to give regular, step-by-step, progressive lessons, either because I take too little pleasure in it or because I have too little patience. In short, I am a failure at it," he complained in a letter to Naumann (19 September 1839)[2] and expressed himself similarly in later conversations with Devrient.[3]

Only at the higher level that *follows* methodical training in technique did his productive nature express itself in a freer exchange of ideas with his students. Thus it is well known that he gave generous encouragement to up-and-coming talents like Gade, Taubert, Hille[r], and Joachim.[4] Von Wasielewski, who has made a name for himself with his Schumann biography, reports: "Every word that the master spoke, founded as it was on rich experience, deep insight, and vision, was worth its weight in gold. Mendelssohn possessed the rare gift of expressing himself briefly, clearly, and incisively, without mincing words, on every point that came up during the lessons."[5] Of greater significance are the comments of the great Leipzig master Carl Reinecke, who later took over Mendelssohn's position as director of the Gewandhaus concerts, regarding the experiences of his student years in his appealing book *Und manche liebe Schatten steigen auf: Gedenkblätter an berühmte Meister der Tonkunst*[6] [*And Many a Dear Departed Shade Appears: Memorials to Famous Musicians*]. Reinecke characterizes the contrast between Schumann and Mendelssohn as follows (where their educational impact is concerned, his opinion carries all the more weight because he was so much closer, both as a human being and as a musician, to the former): "While Felix Mendelssohn Bartholdy was very free with his comments and had the knack of giving clear expression to sharp but accurate criticism, so that in a quarter of an hour one could glean enough hints and musical rules of wisdom for an entire lifetime, Schumann proved, in general, to be rather uncommunicative. In his personal dealings with the eager disciples of his art, however, he was more confidential and encouraging than Mendelssohn, who, admittedly, may have been forced to adopt a certain reserve on account of the unbelievable crowd of people who sought him out. Robert Schumann expressed more friendly recognition and encouragement than criticism."[7] The contrast appears self-evident. Schumann—taciturn, brooding—was engaged in struggle throughout his entire life, and traveled down lonely roads. Mendelssohn, on the other hand, was a man of action and quick decisions, who, with his animated temperament, easily found the appropriate expression for his impressions and feelings. Since he was more attached to forms that had been handed down from the past, he had at his ready disposal a wealth of established concepts, while Schumann had to search for them.

The following letters to Boguslawski, written over the course of

Mendelssohn's whole life—the first few were written when he was a boy of fourteen, the last, two years before his death—bear reliable witness to the pedagogical effectiveness to which these individuals attest.

The recipient, Wilhelm von Boguslawski, came from an old aristocratic family that had been driven out of Poland in the eighteenth century. He was born in Berlin in 1803, and was the son of Major General Karl von Boguslawski, the first military director of the War College. He studied law, served as law clerk of the Supreme Court and as assessor in Kottbus and Wriezen, and was transferred in 1842 to the Appellate Court in Breslau, where he died in 1874 as privy counselor. Behind the forbidding, unworldly manner of this man, who had grown up in a lively social and court setting, lay a rich emotional life and a tireless pleasure in creating. He was a competent official and a fiery politician, composer and poet, but he neither made a career for himself corresponding to his talent and extraordinary connections, nor achieved his lofty goals in his artistic works. In Boguslawski, universal education and a proclivity toward diverse activities were not grounded in a will capable of drawing distinctions, setting limits, forcing his production to increased creativity. In spite of everything, he remained a dilettante in his life and his art. He wrote songs, sonatas, overtures, symphonies and no fewer than seven operas—most of them drawn from the historical novels of Scott and Bulwer.[8] He noted down his musical ideas, which were often very pleasing, spun them out, combined them into larger structures—and, in this way, around the dry, humdrum legal work that filled his days he wove a web of imaginative dreams. He turned the night into day, and his devotion certainly provided refreshment and oblivion; but what he created quickly shot upward into blossom and soon wilted. No success crowned his efforts. After he had been rejected by several of the major opera houses, he once arranged for one of his operas to be produced at his own expense in Würzburg; it failed, and another one, which would doubtless have suffered a similar fate, was rehearsed in Breslau. The only copy of the score burned up, and its performance was rendered impossible.

While still a student, Boguslawski became friends with Mendelssohn, who was six years younger. The two shared compositions with each other, played music together, and liked to play chess. When their personal contact was broken off by Boguslawski's graduation, no regular exchange of letters followed, but Mendelssohn, loyal and devoted, always followed his friend's work with interest, and found it worthy of usually detailed criticism. Otherwise the name Boguslawski, so far as I know, does not occur in Mendelssohn's correspondence or records.

In the summer of 1823, Boguslawski[9] went on a walking tour from Dresden, by way of Switzerland, to Florence. Shortly before his departure, he sent a symphony to Mendelssohn, who was fourteen at the time, to ask his opinion, and received the following response:

Berlin, 30 Sept. 1823

Your letter made me very happy, for I see that you have not yet forgotten me altogether. Don't be angry that the answer comes so late. You requested an exact opinion of your symphony; but it did not reach my hands until six weeks after your letter, because it had been delayed in the mail. Since you demanded an expert opinion from me, I guess I have to give it. Here it is:

Generally, first, I must say that I like all of the motives of the first[10] piece quite a lot; that the Adagio pleases me altogether, except for the *forte* motive in the middle, where the contrabass enters; and that I find the Minuet fun and pretty, except for an extension at the end that holds things up. I like the theme of the last movement and the first *forte* passage and the development up to the *piano* very much, but from there on, it seems to me, it gets a little weak, and the trumpetlike conclusion doesn't please me at all.

Second, in more detail:

You criticized the introduction with the violin by itself, which must, in other words, be a solo; I like it quite well,[11] and also the following entrances of the four instruments one after the other. But I find this Adagio much too long. It is supposed to be an introduction, after all; but you have made it into a self-sufficient piece with its own modulation and development, so that the listener is tired before he even gets to the Allegro. Nevertheless, I have not cut anything, but await your orders before I do so. The theme and the way it is spun out in the Allegro is very pretty, but long after that, when you should conclude in A major (dominant of D major), you make a conclusion in D major and then start again in G major. It is clear that as a result the modulation becomes very monotonous. Now you modulate, quite skillfully, through D and there you begin a good new motive, carry it through properly, and when one thinks the passage is going to come to an end, you go through F♯ major and several extensions through sevenths to A major, and from there, finally, back to D major. That is quite superfluous. The introduction of the theme, again, at the end of the first part, is melodious, pure, brief, and very well apportioned among the instruments. The beginning of the development section is good and to the point, but the conclusion does not please me at all, on account of the modulation into A♭ major and A♭ minor in a piece in G major! The conclusion is not too long, and pretty.

In the Adagio, the passage for two violins and viola is too long. The entrance of the cello is a relief. In the middle part some cuts are necessary.

My opinion about the Minuet and the last movement you know already.

All in all, however, the symphony gave me a lot of pleasure, for I can appreciate the fact that you have left the pandects and the *corpus juris* in order to set some points in opposition, in other words—counterpoints.

In August Father was with Paul and me in Silesia,[12] which I enjoyed very much. Soon we will have a chance to talk about it, I hope.

My time is so limited that I must close. Be well, I thank you for your letter and your symphony.

Your
Felix Mendelssohn

The details of this letter are quite technical and not immediately clear. The young Mendelssohn, who had just written his own first few symphonies for string quartet,[13] surveys the complicated structure of a symphony with admirable sureness, breaks it down and expresses his likes and dislikes without mincing words. But he says nothing about the content and character of the whole, and hardly a word about melody and instrumentation; he is still too much interested in the economy of its parts and the formal structure. After his apparently justified criticism of the overly long introduction—evidently written in a misguided imitation of Beethoven—he devotes more time to the first movement that follows. In symphonies, as in sonatas, this movement consists of two parts, the first containing the two themes, the musical material, as a kind of exposition, followed by the "development section" in which they are developed. One of the two themes is written in the principal key (here, G major); the second in the next-related key of the dominant (D major). Between the two, a connecting passage is inserted, which forms a bridge from the first key to the second. In this case it appears at first as if Boguslawski takes the path of least resistance, by ending on a half cadence in D major, so that the second theme can begin. When Mendelssohn expresses dissatisfaction with this approach, which is actually not an inadequate one, and argues for a stronger, more intensive one in the dominant key of D major, he is following the example of Haydn and Beethoven; in contrast, Mozart preferred the simpler transition. But Boguslawski disappoints his listeners, for he does not introduce the second theme at all; rather, he returns tiresomely to the principal key, already sufficiently explored, and from there moves into D major and thus traverses the same path twice, so that the tension that has been created is naturally dissipated. Similar digressions occur in the following sections. Instead of concluding the first movement with a short cadential turn after the second theme, he brings in bold harmonic sequences resulting in garishly mixed colors that only confuse the listener at this point and are only appropriate in the development section. Thus far, one would have to judge Mendelssohn's criticisms to be well founded. However, when he criticizes in principle the use of A♭ major and A♭ minor in the development, then we can see the schoolmaster in him raising his head, taking offense at this unusual boldness. Here he speaks like his formally strict, even pedantic teacher Zelter, from whose vocabulary certain adjectives such as "pure" and "to the point" are drawn—these enjoyed particular popularity among the devotees of the "Berlin School," which strove for simplicity and tidiness. The same may be said of such turns of phrase as "carried through properly" or "quite skillful."

During the ten years between this letter and the next, only a few notes relating to social meetings of the two men are preserved. On the first, undated note Mendelssohn has written the beginning of a canon, whose theme he probably invented while waiting in vain for Boguslawski, to whom he passed it on to discover the solution. The strict form of the canon permits very little free invention in its elaboration. Canons have always been used as little demonstrations of proficiency and as riddles to challenge members of the musical guild.

Dear sir,
I have betaken myself here in hopes of finding you present. I was disappointed. Great is my distress. I wanted to pay you my most devoted respects and announce to you that tomorrow there

will be no music at our house, and invite you to do me the honor in the near future, and beg you to play a game of chess with your devoted servant, and plead with you to bring along a fugue or a canon, and assure you that I remain, unwaveringly, your devoted servant

Felix Mendelssohn Bartholdy

To be solved: Canon a 3[14]

in perpetuum

.

Motto: Has no time; come again another day.

Unfortunately I forgot on Sunday that I am invited out on Wednesday afternoon as well as evening, and that at 5:30 I have to return home for an hour, but in no case will I be able to be contented, calm, or in a word comfortable enough to show you my drawings[15] *con gracia*, as I had so long desired do to. I might also lack the time (nothing else) to checkmate you. But if it were possible for you to visit me either Thursday or Friday between 4 and 7:30, or, if this does not suit you, to let me know at what time I can meet you, then you would give me great pleasure. But if neither of these alternatives meets with your approval, and if you have made definite plans for tomorrow, then you will find me in any case at home at the time we have set. I ask only that you send me a line in answer by return mail through the bearer of this letter, that is, the postman.

I remain your
Felix Mendelssohn Bartholdy

$\frac{9}{3}$ 30

.

$\frac{12}{3}$ 30.

No doubt you will swear that this note is my excuse for not being at home this evening and that the whole sheet is covered with nothing but excuses? On the contrary, I ask only that you stay for a long time, and be quite certain to come, but 1/2 hour later. Yesterday my father accepted a dinner invitation for me today, and so I will scarcely be done before 6. But if you are perhaps so kind as to come at 6:45, and if you would spend the time that you wanted to spend with me from 5:30 on with my family, who will be delighted to see you, and then stay with us all the longer, you will see something Scottish,[16] will be checkmated, and will receive orally the Bravo for your sonata, which I now shout out through the megaphone of the municipal postal service all the way to Market Street.

Until then
your devoted
Mendelssohn Bartholdy

The correspondence was interrupted by Boguslawski's transfer to Kottbus; from there he sent his friend a score, probably an overture. Here is Mendelssohn's response:

Berlin, 27 December 1832

Dear Herr v. Boguslawsky [sic],

If you recognize my handwriting, you will throw the remainder of the letter into the wastebasket unread, or at least regard it with displeasure comparable to that with which you looked at me the first time I beat you at chess. Do neither, and do not be angry with me; admittedly, since the date of your letter is lying next to me, I am horrified all over again by the two months I have dreamt away, but I wanted to send you, as we had agreed, the arrangement of the overture in the same package as your manuscripts, and that is what I have been waiting for. Now it is here, but the New Year will be too; forgive my sins of correspondence in the old year, and be so good as to wish me as much happiness and good cheer in the coming period as I wish you. Your composition has given me great pleasure, and I found much in it very successful and appealing. Since you permit me to express my opinion quite openly, I would prefer if some things had been done differently in the instrumentation, here and there; at least, according to my manner of interpreting the various instruments, there are some things that don't seem quite right. For example, if you want me to be in Genoa, on the ocean, in cool climes in the still of the night, then you shouldn't disturb me right off with your deep oboes; they will make a thick and compact rattling sound there and I won't feel nocturnal sentiments and peace until the entrance of the clarinets. No matter how much *piano* you write for the oboes in the low notes, they will stare back at you with a peculiarly sharp look. In the same way the two bassoons on the third page are not arranged prettily enough; they won't sound airy like that, and that is what your introduction is trying to do, which, by the way, I find unusually pleasing the way you have done it, and it seems to me to be by far the best in the piece overall. The instrumentation in the Allegro, on the other hand, I would like to see more compact, again, more massed together; the clarinets on page 16, for example, with the deep violas in the *forte*; and again on page 17 the clarinets and bassoons and the oboes that follow them seem to me to make too isolated an impression there and in several similar passages. As far as the instruments are concerned, I would wish, in general, that you would make them more the servants of your idea, instead of distributing them in the same manner throughout. They should sound happy in a happy passage, broad and massive in one that is grandiose, etc. The same comment would apply, in my judgment, to the Allegro; there is much in it that I find pleasing, but I don't like the fact that it doesn't really ever come to a proper theme. It plays on, and one has no real proper point of reference; thus the whole thing appears indistinct, because one doesn't know how the basic features are meant, and that, too, is why the conclusion comes as too much of a surprise, and as not necessary in its context, although it certainly is in its basic conception. You know and it surely goes without saying that you will not take all of this the wrong way, that I ask you in all seriousness to write soon and to do many other pieces along the same lines and with the same thoroughness, and that I hope you will share them with me again, if I should be in your neighborhood. You want to know my opinion of the newest music? I have not heard any for a long time. Auber's[17] things are anything but musical, only intriguing, full of effects, and lucrative; that indeed they are, so let the theater directors praise them; I don't like them. *Robert le diable*[18] is even less musical than all that; it is the weakest confection that ever emerged from a sickly soul, or rather from a sickly body, for the soul had nothing to do with it. The text, a mixture of *Freischütz*, *Crociato*, and every variety of dissipation, is not the worst of it.[19] Marschner has written a new opera *Hans Heiling*. The text is by our singer Devrient;[20] but there are charming pieces of music in it and I hope it will make a big impression here when it opens, which will be soon. At least there is life and movement in his things. As for me, I am feeling better than I used to; I can't write my oratorio[21] this winter after all, because first of all the text is not finished, and second I have a commission for a symphony for England,[22] which I am to deliver and direct myself in the spring (in April, I think). Until then I will be properly busy, but I hope that I will hear from you before I leave for my trip, perhaps not to return until much later. Farewell, and much happiness.

Your most devoted
Felix Mendelssohn Bartholdy

When he was still a student of Zelter, Mendelssohn criticized Boguslawski's form and harmonic logic; now it is the instrumentation. He wants a more individual treatment of the instruments and he spends a good deal of time looking in detail at the use of the two complementary, low- and high-pitched woodwinds—the bassoon and, above all, the oboe—which gives that earthy but nasal tone that sounds now rough and obstinate, now dry and almost chaste, naive, and certainly not—especially in the low register—dreamily soft and airy, as the mood of Boguslawski's piece would seem to have demanded. Mendelssohn does not specify how the oboes could have been used here, as he does on a similar occasion in one of the later letters. For this certainly would have been possible; Haydn, for instance, described a sunrise by means of an oboe solo.[23] Here too, Mendelssohn betrays the caution he still practiced in approaching this instrument: in the just-completed overtures *Meere[s]stille und glückliche Fahrt* [*Calm Sea and Prosperous Voyage*, op. 27, 1828] and *Sommernachtstraum* [*A Midsummer Night's Dream*, op. 21, 1826], with their masterful tone painting, oboes and bassoons take a very discreet back seat, especially in the *Meere[s]stille*, where the oboes are used only occasionally to strengthen the wind section. Not until the *Hebrides* Overture and [*Die erste*] *Walpurgisnacht* are they used independently to create distinct musical characters.

The remarks about contemporary opera composers have many parallels in Mendelssohn's other letters. He disdains Auber, and his distaste for Meyerbeer's *Robert der Teufel* swells almost into hatred, while his positive interest in Marschner's *Hans Heiling* is expressed even more vociferously elsewhere. The underlying irritation in his tone can be explained as a result of the many unsuccessful attempts he himself made during these very years to find suitable material for an opera with which to conquer the musical stage. The libretto of the Heiling opera had actually been written for Mendelssohn by his friend Devrient,[24] who passed it on to Marschner only after Mendelssohn had returned it. The opera was produced with great success, which has continued to this day.

Following his return from England, where he directed the *Italian Symphony* mentioned in the previous letter, Mendelssohn assumed his position at the Düsseldorf Theater, which Immermann[25] was ambitiously attempting to build into a German national theater. Since at the same time Mendelssohn directed the major concerts of the Musikverein, we can easily understand the excess of work that caused his delay in responding.

Düsseldorf, 16 Nov. 1833

Dear Herr v. Boguslawski,[26]

Excuse my long silence in response to your very friendly letter. As you had expected, it arrived here just as I had flown the coop and was wandering around in the Upper Rhine Valley, partly in order to get hold of some good old church music, of which we were in need here, and partly in order to take part in the wine harvest.[27] When I returned there were so many, varied tasks awaiting me, and I had so much to do, that I couldn't seem to get to letter-writing, and now, when I can actually see that over the winter things will get rather worse than better, I must send you in all haste my thanks and a sign of life from me; this will not be a proper letter after all. I am very pleased that you continue to occupy yourself with music right along, and I would be very glad if you would continue to send me something of your work. The overture and the third act, or the first, in addition, or all of it, if it is possible; you should certainly receive my frank opinion, and although I cannot guarantee that it would contain anything as extraordinary as the enclosed letter, still you would be spared the grand theories and high-flown tone, for both displease me mightily. Actually I regret that you sent it to me, for there is a brand of judgment in it that I don't like anywhere, least of all concerning music and by musicians. Preferably by carpenters, there the Master knows exactly how the joints must lie and how to clean up rough spots, but in that case he has to have been both journeyman and apprentice and cannot make himself into one all of a sudden all by himself; and if someone is a proper carpenter, then he must, I believe, regard every table with a certain affection. I loathe cold reasoning about music. And as a result I will perhaps criticize more and praise less, but both more honestly, and you must only promise me ahead of time that you will not show my letter to any musicians and not be offended or call me to account for it, like so many chess games won or lost.

And thank you for continuing to think of me in such a friendly way.

We have the first performance of our new Düsseldorf Music Society on St. Cecilia's Day; we are performing the overture to *Egmont*, a piano concerto of mine, and Handel's *Alexander's Feast*, which was written for this day (22 Nov).[28] Two general rehearsals have already come off very well, and since we have two dress rehearsals still ahead of us, I think it will sound good. But there is a great deal to do, so forgive me if I come to a close. Let me hear and see something from you again soon, even if it is ♩ ♪ ♪ ♪ rather than your person. Now I will even end like Reissiger: "Won't you come to see me sometime on the Rhine?"

Farewell, and give my regards to your wife, if she remembers me from the exhibition.

Your devoted
Felix Mendelssohn Bartholdy

Reissiger,[29] whose character Mendelssohn elsewhere ridicules as "distinguished," was the musical director of the Dresden Opera. He had reviewed Boguslawski's work with an eye to its effectiveness and had attempted to sweeten his apodictic judgment with a strong dose of flattery. He agrees with Mendelssohn on the main points; however, Mendelssohn's negative opinion of Reissiger seems well-founded, if only because of the latter's smug comments about Beethoven. A couple of examples may serve as illustrations:

Your themes are short, and thus they make short movements, cut-up fragments. Your themes are too numerous, and this leads to vagueness, unclarity; the ear never comes to rest, one doesn't know which are the principal ideas, which secondary. In other words, too many and too short themes! The themes, because of their very brevity, are not autonomous enough. But I must also praise you, for you deserve it. Your work is good work, you know how to develop a theme splendidly, your imagination is very fruitful—but you are not economical in using it. The fact that you have studied Beethoven's last symphony closely is clear to me from your valued work and I won't hold it against you.

(25 October 1830)

So far as a performance in Dresden is concerned, that is a very difficult proposition for works by unknown composers, since there are many people—if not regiments—involved in the management, and the selection of new operas depends heavily on the approval of the court. If only your subject had something in common with the tasteless new operatic productions that throw poetic refinement out the window and indulge in sensational fight scenes, agitation, military demarches, long brilliant arias that leave the soprano practically prostrate, then you would be accepted. But what real musician is knowledgeable in such matters? (6 July 1833)

The *Overture* [of the opera *Elfino*] should be only half so long. It would be desirable if the details were less timid and artificial (the imitations in smaller figures, especially, go by without making an impression). This is written more in the style of a symphony; an overture must be more compressed; it smacks of Beethoven's manner; this is a dangerous path. The themes will leave the public cold; they are not singable enough to make a lasting impression.—It has bold flights of imagination, sometimes too rapid modulations, but the way it is realized and the composition are often masterful. (n.d.)[30]

In response to Mendelssohn's friendly request, Boguslawski sent him the score of his first opera, *Elfino*, which had meanwhile been completed, with a libretto by no less a writer than Ludwig Tieck.[31] The latter had composed his "musical Märchen," entitled *The Monster and the Enchanted Forest* [*Das Ungeheuer und der verzauberte Wald*], at the suggestion of Reichardt,[32] who failed, however, to carry out its composition. Into a fairy-tale plot Tieck had woven elements of earthy comedy, parody, and satire of contemporary conditions. Prince Aldrovan liberates his father's kingdom from two terrible plagues: he conquers a dragon that "destroys the countryside, strangles people, makes the post roads unsafe, opens and intercepts letters . . . ," and lifts the enchantment from the forest that lures people with marvelous music, bewitches them, and never sets them free. Evil is represented by Ollalin, who is in league with the ambitious queen. She covets the crown and to that purpose she has had her eldest son turned into the dragon. Ollalin's opponent is Elfino, the good spirit; Aldrovan has fallen in love with his beautiful daughter Angelika. The king himself is a buffoon, sniveling and complacent. Just about to dispatch the dragon, Aldrovan recognizes that it is his own brother—"Scene change. Music." But then, after Aldrovan has resisted the charms of a seductive fairy and lifted the enchantment from the forest, the two evil spirits, not seen until now, appear on a cloud, and Elfino kills them with a shot from his bow.

Boguslawski had condensed the text of this witty libretto, with its "appealing foolishness," by cutting the entire fourth act, including the lifting of the enchantment, even though it was this final act that gave the fairy-tale qualities of the story their purest expression. He also included scenes of great theatricality, which he set entirely as a vehicle for the music. This may have caused Tieck, who received the opera through Reissiger's efforts, to speak against its production; as an excuse, he cited its length.

Here are Mendelssohn's views about *Elfino*:

Düsseldorf, 19 April 1834

Dear Herr Boguslawski,

I did not have a chance until today to send you my sincere thanks for the pleasure you have given me by sending your opera. Forgive me for keeping the score for such a prolonged period and for not replying for so long. You can imagine how busy I was in the first winter in a musical situation that is still so disorderly, and since, at the same time, I was completing several pressing projects of my own, I had almost no time left. But as soon as I could see daylight around Easter time, I played the work for myself at the piano and sang and acted it out, and would have been applauding as a member of the public too, at a great many points; but now I will get around to doing so in writing. You will receive your score by coach a few days after this letter; I will send it before the end of the day. By the way, you took my comment about the table that one should regard with affection in quite the opposite sense from that I intended, for it is precisely this love for every artistic product, which I *demand* of every artist and (as I wrote then) from every craftsman, too, which seems to be entirely *lacking* in Reissiger's letter. For the compliments don't do the trick, and there could have been many fewer compliments and more recognition in it. For that really is deserved in the greatest degree when someone refuses to be discouraged by circumstances and difficulties from continuing to develop his talent, and, in a word, is irrepressibly diligent. That is lacking in most of the professional artists nowadays, and it is all the more welcome when it occurs without external, but rather purely as a result of inner necessity. Precisely because you yourself know that "without your note writing you would now have a better position in life," you prove by that very fact that you "would not have done better to do so" and that you could not have acted differently, for, after all, what matters in the end is not whether someone has become a president or a minister, but whether he has achieved the greatest possible development. So don't let yourself be dissuaded by some distinguished silence, or some distinguished praise, or anything else, from continuing to work, and even if it were to have no other result, the work and the joy in it are already result and benefit enough. My opinion on this point is quite firm, and I don't believe that I am wrong; continue to work, and let me see something else soon, because it must always give me pleasure to recognize and pay tribute to your progress.

The question inevitably arises, if anyone considers the lack of success accorded Boguslawski's musical work, why Mendelssohn did not simply advise him to put away his pen, instead of encouraging him. It was not that Boguslawski's admirable formal achievements deceived him about the slightness of content from a purely musical standpoint; for he himself clearly expresses his apprehension: "even if it were to have no other result . . ." But his conviction is that the artist does not work for any purpose, but purely for himself—and so long as artistic creation affords him pleasure and freedom, he should continue. And because Mendelssohn believed in Boguslawski's inner drive and necessity, he spurred him on. This comment also speaks well for Mendelssohn himself, who did not allow himself to be dazzled by success and slack off in his development or his work.
Mendelssohn continues:

Now you want to know my opinion of the work, and I am going to set it right down, although it is not intended as a judgment and cannot be that even so far as I am concerned. I can only speak of the impression it made on me, and if there is something unfavorable in it from time to time, you mustn't be angry with me, for it may be my fault as much as yours that it seems that way to me. Two principal comments have occurred to me: in all the light, songful pieces, in the happy, lively situations your music pleased me almost without exception, for example the entire conclusion of the first act with the lovely French horn entry at the end of the oath scene; the chorus at the beginning of the third act, which ends especially gracefully; the duettino in F-ma-

jor $\frac{6}{8}$, "glückliche Stunde" [happy hour], even more when it recurs the second time; the cavatina in F, no. 18; and many individual passages in all of the pieces. On the other hand, all the more
somber, passionate pieces in sad, emotional, or romantic situations are less to my liking. Almost all your motives in these sections are too short, too small, too cut-off; and the orchestra in-
terrupts the musical idea too much, so that the progress of the
whole piece of music is not even, simple, and compelling enough.
And, again, these ideas themselves, if I gather them together
from the varied instrumental and vocal parts, are too simple;
that is, too conventional, too little suited to this particular situation and arising too little from it; and on account of this lack of
specific, simple, but fully compelling motives drawn from the
content and the words, your music seems to me in all these places
not dramatic. Take, for example, the aria no. 15 of Aldrovan, in
the third act, and you will find the singer's every word, practically even every measure, interrupted by a pause. The first two
times, when he calls out, it seems natural enough, but then the
music should come together, then a dramatic-musical motive
should appear, instead of the pauses in the 16th measure and
even more in the 22nd and so on and on at the words "denn
mich lockt—des Ruhmes Kranz" [for the wreath of victory—
beckons me onward]. Even an interruption like this could be justified, but then the connecting passages in the orchestra would
have to be in that spirit, not just a continuation of the same idea.
The theme that follows: "lebet wohl" [farewell] . . . , etc., is also
too short for me, too small for a great hero's farewell and an
important moment. A man doesn't let himself be interrupted so
soon there by the orchestra, stand quietly around on stage, or
play dumb; he must have more to say than that before the chorus, with its quiet observation "er trotzet" [he defies] can intervene. Since your instrumentation, at the same time, seems much
too heavy, too thick, almost everywhere, I could now sum it all
up as follows: I would like to see your ideas *expressed* more simply
and naturally, but *thought out* more complicatedly and specifically. And the only way to achieve this is to let the form and the
idea of the entire piece be suggested more—or rather exclusively—by the words and the situation, and then carry it out as
simply and clearly as possible. For example at the beginning of
the finale, no. 7, the actual idea is quite foreign to the words, for
"nun ist die Stunde da" [now the hour has come] is not something that can be expressed by the small figures in the orchestra,
and the entry of the vocal part is quite arbitrary, almost as if it

were an inner voice, and again the 32 instrumental parts are too small for it. The same error seems to me to occur throughout the piece; the vocal part follows the instruments back and forth, and I think it should be the other way around. "Höre, ich beschwöre" [listen, I invoke]—at that point those trills and dotted notes would never have occurred to me, and if this is to be repeated often the invocation would have to be dreadfully intensified, or else there's enough invoking. The passage "Die Stunde rückt" [the hour advances] starts out more to my liking, and the expression "Singe das bekannte Lied" [sing the familiar song] is beautiful, only again all the trombones, drums, etc., seem much too much for me, and do too much harm to the voice and the comprehension of the words; and precisely because it is supposed to be the old familiar (magical) song, what follows should be much less isolated and—supported by instrumental passages—cut off. The same in the third act, no. 17. There the theme is not the words of the parting lovers, but an instrumental motive, and the words just turn up somewhere in between; he waits three measures before he answers her; and the speeches are always interrupted by pauses; in the cavatina, no. 19 (the pause and repetition of "die zärtlichen Küssen" [the tender kisses]), which in keeping with the situation should probably be quite short and lively and go by quickly, without a brilliant conclusion; the same in the following aria, no. 20, where the entry of the vocal part does not seem *invented* enough to me, whereas the preceding parts, with the imitation by the viola, etc., are too invented. The same in no. 21, where the entire dialogue during the challenge and the fight seems much too freighted down with repetitions and interrupted by pauses. (For example, "dass meine Wohnung, meine Wohnung" [that my home, my home] or "Ich, ich bin es, ich" [I, it is I, I] and where, throughout, the voices accompany the instruments). Briefly, in my opinion, in your more solemn, emotional passages the movement is almost always carried by the instruments, or else they interrupt it severely, and that I think is an error. I would not say this so openly and directly to you if I didn't hope and wish that you should keep on occupying yourself with music, where you will then either agree with me and do it differently, or not, and do it alone,—but in both cases you will not be offended by my remarks.

Your changes in the text, to the extent that I could tell them from the score, seem very appropriate to me; the repetition of several motives is very apt and good, specifically at Angelika's last appearance; by the way, in my opinion there are serious offences against drama on Tieck's part; in particular the whole plot development seems so accidental, for Ollalin could just as well have shot Elfino dead, that as a result I would overlook many individual parts of great beauty, which, nevertheless, I find in abundance. Your overture is lively and flowing; I would like very much to hear it sometime, and, even more, to receive something soon from among your new compositions, in which your progress would once again be demonstrated so clearly.

For, as I said, I have made my criticisms only in order to express my opinion honestly, and in order to spare you the trouble, in case I am right in some cases, of having to notice it alone and by yourself. To continue in your work is what you must do, and since you are in perfect mastery of all technical means, a pure style, the proper use of the instruments, etc., and since you are driven to it, you will, too. But if you would like to give me a report from time to time, or send me one thing or another, you will give me heartfelt pleasure each time, and I will let you know my true gratitude. Farewell.

Always, your
Felix Mendelssohn Bartholdy

P.S. About me and the amusing life here more anon.

The letter critiques neither the entire work, nor the question, for example, of whether the peculiarly bizarre mood of the libretto also predominates in the music; Mendelssohn does not take up these most crucial points, since the elementary problems in Boguslawski's composition have a prior claim on his attention. But—even if no one will dispute the "offenses against drama" in Tieck's hastily composed libretto—his praise of the composer, who instead of overcoming these shortcomings only hurts his own cause by his cuts, betrays Mendelssohn's uncertainty in theatrical matters.

He prefers the evocative lyrics that describe the happiness of the lovers and the sunset in the forest, in which the French horns are used effectively, or some other cleanly and transparently constructed passages. But where there are strong emotions or quick changes of mood, the composer's gift of invention and ability to bring the orchestra and the vocal part into a successful interaction are deficient. Here Mendelssohn believed he had located the precise point he always tried to detect and expose in his criticism. He once expressed himself thus to Hiller:[33] "I wouldn't say this to you if I were not so completely convinced that this is the very point that is left to every man himself, that neither nature nor talent, even the greatest, can overcome, but only his own will. There is nothing more disagreeable to me than criticism of a person's nature or talent; it creates ill feelings and confusion and doesn't do any good; it doesn't add an inch to anyone's height—no striving or working will help there—so one can only keep silent on that score." He demands progress, life; so he urges onward, instead of holding himself up with theoretical considerations, and he seeks to influence his student by working with him on the inner development of his thoughts. In so doing, he proceeds from the exterior; he points out a number of passages where pauses divide two words that belong together, or even two syllables of the same word, in a way that runs counter to their meaning, or where the orchestra's behavior does not correspond to the situation, and he asks Boguslawski to dissect the entire scene psychologically before he puts anything on paper, and even before he invents it, so that from this "complicatedly and specifically thought-out" and thought-through imagining there will flow a confident musical form that is not arbitrary, but characteristic.

To his detriment, Boguslawski never took the suggestion of a revision; the score shows no corrections in the places that Mendelssohn criticized. Instead, he soon took on new large tasks, in which his friend, again and again, discovered the salient errors he had already criticized. Since he believed that Boguslawski's further development was dependent on their correction, he never tired of pointing them out to him emphatically.

Berlin, 22 February 1842

Dear Herr v. Boguslawski,

I received your friendly letter and very welcome package a few days ago and need not tell you how happy I was to hear from you again and then something so much hoped for. Now, however, I am about to travel to Leipzig (departure is tomorrow morning) and to remain there for two or three weeks, in order to present a new symphony and *Antigone*;[34] that gave me so much to do in the last few days that I had no peace with which to get acquainted with your score. There in Leipzig it will be impossible for me, too; I know that already, and I will therefore have to save it for the first free time after my return. Since several weeks will go by before then, I wanted to let you know the reason for the long silence, so you don't think anything is amiss with that, or with me, and are not angry with me if my proper answer to your letter and package takes longer than it otherwise would have. As soon after my return as I have come to myself, and to your score, I will write to you in detail.

Always your devoted
Felix Mendelssohn Bartholdy

.

Berlin, 11 March 1842
Dear Herr v. Boguslawski,

Since I returned from Leipzig three days ago I have used my first hours of leisure to become acquainted with the text and the score that you sent, and you receive both back, with gratitude, in the enclosure. It was with the most heartfelt interest that I made the acquaintance of your work; I hardly need tell you that, for you know what affection I have had since childhood for you and for everything that has to do with you, which I shall retain my whole life long. In the text, already, many highly successful passages delighted me, and in the music as well, and how often I harkened back to the old carefree times and felt happy that you have ceaselessly continued to develop and ennoble your talent. But you want to have a proper musician's judgment from me, you said so expressly; and so in addition to the things that please me I must not pass over in silence the things with which I might have to find fault. If, then, there is a criticism to be made, it is that I would wish that in the next acts (and, I hope, I can also say in the next operas) you would turn your attention more toward a certain simple *structure* for the pieces, to which then the details would be subordinated. First a rather musical, dramatic, and above all *vocal*[35] theme, which determines the piece's base, its foundation (its physiognomy, so to speak), right from the beginning, and from which everything else evolves, and which can then return or not return, be developed or not developed, but always remains the chief aspect of the whole, without which the impression, even with the best of details, must remain vague. Such a basic theme, in your work, is found all too often in the instruments, in the first violin, for example, and the most beautiful effects can result, it is true, as is often the case with exceptions to the rule; and the interplay of instruments with the quasi-conversational interruptions of the vocal parts can become a matter of necessity, for example in intrigues and the like; but the dominant form, the rule will always have to be that the singers are predominant and the instruments accompany them in expressing the decisive and deciding theme. And precisely that is what seems to me too seldom to be the case in your first act. Although it does occur at times, for example at the beginning of the Matins, still, in my opinion, you leave the theme and its character behind too quickly, and turn your attention back to the play of smaller figures, which you love, but which, considering the seriousness and elevated nature of the material, would not seem to me even on that account alone to be quite appropriate. The progress of your pieces, as a result, takes on a somewhat disjointed character, a turning back and forth, both in the whole, and even in the details of the accompaniment, etc., which I would rather see replaced by a calm, planned-out structure (the principal thought or the principal mood in the lead, then the details following in a subordinated way), so that in your music one could experience a progression in place of the changes of course; a peaceful flow in place of awkwardness and discontinuity. This seems to me to be the main thing that could perhaps give cause for a critical rebuke; but you are not angry with me now on account of my outspokenness? I hope not, for you did ask me expressly to speak to you as one musician to another, and that is what I have done, and if I am wrong about it, it is done, as Shak[e]speare said, with good intentions. Farewell for today, and think always with friendship of

Your truly devoted
Felix Mendelssohn Bartholdy

.

Leipzig, 2 May 1842

Dear Herr v. Boguslawski,

On the day before my departure I received your letter and package. In the tumult that a departure with wife and children etc. creates, you can imagine that it was not possible for me to get to know your score; but I brought it here with me, and hoped there would be a few quiet hours for it. Unfortunately, however, they have not been found here either. I had, in the few days, so many old friends to visit, such varied things to discuss, that evening arrived before I had been able to garner a minute alone for myself. Now I have to rush off to the Düsseldorf Musikfest, and then immediately to England,[36] and there I know in advance how little free time remains for me; and I don't know, either, how I would be able to return the score to you from there. Therefore I am sending it from here, without having been able to get to know it—I don't have to tell you that I feel sorry about that, or that the fault lies not in any lack of interest but in the complicated and hurried trip that I have ahead of me, and that robs me of free time and quiet thoughts. Don't be angry with me on that account; keep me in friendly remembrance, as I always and under all circumstances will remain, your

Felix Mendelssohn Bartholdy

.

Leipzig, 11 December 1845

Dear Herr v. Boguslawski,[37]

Forgive me that I am able to respond to your friendly letter and return the score only today. I received both a day before my departure for Berlin,[38] where I lived for six weeks among the press of all possible business and whence I returned only last week. Thus the delay in my answer; I need not reassure you that I take pleasure every time I see and hear something from you, and I hope you are now, as in times of old, and so on forever, firmly convinced of that. For, quite apart from our personal attachment, your loyal love of art, your continued noble striving for it, would be one of the most gratifying, welcome phenomena in any individual, even if he were completely unknown to me. How much more so in a childhood friend, when everything good seems twice as good, and everything bad hurts twice as much! So, above all, thank you for continuing to pursue music with such seriousness and such love! Certainly you are right when you say that the content of this opera, with its contemporary references, can have a more lively effect than the previous one. But I would like to warn you about two places that in my opinion could become problematic—which should doubtless bring you some objections from the side of the management: the first is the money matter . . . at the conclusion of the first act, then the poisoning with the nonpoison at the end of the last. The first, since it has already been composed, may be difficult to eliminate altogether, but it would still seem necessary to me to *soften* some things in it, so that the haggling and paying does not seem overly practical and petty; the latter I would prefer to delete entirely as a motive—it is one of the surprises that, I believe, do not work well on stage. Perhaps you could find another, less petty motive to put in its place. That is also the objection that I have against some passages of your music; I wish for *broader, less short,* less abrupt *motives.* This was quite striking to me in the songs (the

English and French ones; and the one sung by the Greek girls); none of them is to be criticized and yet not one of them gives decisive expression to a truly melodious motive. And here it is so important that I almost think you should try again—it is a matter only of the actual choice of the notes, the melody; for the English song could remain quite nicely in A minor $\frac{6}{8}$, the French one with four voices in D major, the one sung by the girls in the key it is in, F major. But the actual motive seems to me to be lacking in all three. At the beginning of the overture, too, for example, the material is too small and abrupt. But forgive my candor; things like this should be carried to their conclusion, or left unsaid, and I am never in a position to bring it to its conclusion in a letter. But at least you will see from it that I have taken a serious and truly sympathetic interest in your work, and that I consider it to be my duty to speak with you about it as openly and unreservedly as I would with myself. Now farewell and maintain a friendly and constant memory of

Your always devoted
Felix Mendelssohn Bartholdy

Mendelssohn's interest in Boguslawski's music, which, for all its skill, has no real physiognomy, weakens in his last letters. His rebukes grow sharper, and still he must refrain from going into detail, since he no longer believes in any progress on the points that seem the most important to him. Mendelssohn senses the contradiction to his once-encouraging letters and emphasizes all the more strongly the continuation of his comradely sentiments for his childhood friend.

In retrospect, Mendelssohn's criticism in these letters shows itself—as is the rule for creative artists—to be subjective. He does not judge according to well-defined norms and objectives; he is, as he himself felt, not a "proper teacher." Rather, there must first exist some inner sympathy, before he can pay closer attention to the work of another. On the other hand, he continues his brusque rejection of other composers—Meyerbeer, for example, for whose music (which was primarily aimed at creating sensual effects) he has no sympathy, not even deigning to enter into a discussion with him. In order to form his judgment, he imitates, he imagines himself faced with the task his pupil has attempted to solve, and from this contrast he derives his reflections and advice. This also explains why in each instance he looks at the compositions almost exclusively from whatever issue happens to be of greatest concern to him at the moment. The young pupil of Zelter dissects the structure, the successful composer of over-

tures the instrumentation; he demands an inner coherence between
the various arts and musical elements in dramatic works precisely
during the period when he himself is busy with plans for an opera;
finally, he gives advice about melody of a generic nature that applies
equally well to the opera and to the lied.

This subjectivity mirrors the stages of Mendelssohn's own development: he gradually rose above formal technique to the conscious
expression of spiritualized sentiment. Hence he himself represents
the highest fulfillment of those goals he sets forth for the education
of musicians.

A letter, touching in its simple sincerity, with which Mendelssohn's
widow answered Boguslawski's expressions of condolence after her
husband's early death, may provide a fitting conclusion to these lines:

Dear sir,
I beg you very sincerely for forgiveness that I have let your sympathetic note remain unanswered for so long. Do not believe that
I have therefore been insensitive to your kindness; only a rather
long-lasting indisposition, and the resulting debts in correspondence owed, could prevent me until now from expressing my
deeply felt thanks.

It is a very gratifying feeling for me to know that the interest and
the friendship of acquaintances and friends for my late husband
has to some degree been transferred to his children and me, and
I thank you heartily for this assurance. I hope that God will give
me the joy of bringing up the children of so much love and
friendship in a not unworthy manner, at least that is the only
object of this life now devoid of joy.

Recommending myself to your continued good will, I remain
with genuine respect

Your devoted
Cécile Mendelssohn Bartholdy

Leipzig, 24 Feb. [1848]

NOTES

1. Given in facsimile by Ernst Wolff in his splendid Mendelssohn biography (after p. 148). [Bruno Hake] The reference is to Ernst Wolff, *Felix Mendelssohn Bartholdy* (Berlin, 1906). In November 1840 Mendelssohn was ap-

proached by the new Prussian king, Friedrich Wilhelm IV, to assist in plans for a new conservatory of music in Berlin. [ed.]

2. Moritz Ernst Adolf Naumann, a professor at the University of Bonn. The letter appeared in the *Briefe aus den Jahren 1833 bis 1847*, ed. P. and C. Mendelssohn Bartholdy (Leipzig, 1863). [ed.]

3. Eduard Devrient (1801–1877), whose *Erinnerungen an Felix Mendelssohn-Bartholdy und seine Briefe an mich* appeared in Leipzig in 1869. [ed.]

4. Niels Gade (1817–1890), Danish composer of several symphonies and works based on Ossian, such as the concert overture *Nachklänge von Ossian* and the cantata *Comala*; Wilhelm Taubert (1811–1891), composer, pupil of Mendelssohn's piano teacher Ludwig Berger, and a conductor in Berlin; Ferdinand Hiller (1811–1885), pupil of Hummel and close friend of Mendelssohn, whose oratorio *Die Zerstörung Jerusalems* was performed in Leipzig in 1840; and Joseph Joachim (1831–1907), violinist and composer, friend of the Schumanns and of Brahms, who had his Leipzig debut under Mendelssohn in August 1843. [ed.]

5. Reference is to Wilhelm Joseph von Wasielewski, *Robert Schumann* (Dresden, 1858). Wasielewski was among the first class of the Leipzig Conservatory, where he matriculated in 1843. See also W. J. von Wasielewski, "Felix Mendelssohn Bartholdy und Robert Schumann: eine künstlerische Parallele mit Einflechtung persönlicher Erinnerungen," in *Deutsche Revue* 43/3 (1894): 332. [ed.]

6. The title derives from a line in Goethe's *Faust*. [trans.]

7. Carl Reinecke, *Und manche liebe Schatten steigen auf: Gedenkblätter an berühmte Meister der Tonkunst* (Berlin, 1900), pp. 45, 101. Reinecke arrived in Leipzig in 1843, where he studied with Mendelssohn but did not attend the conservatory. He set down further memoirs of Mendelssohn in "Mendelssohn und Schumann als Lehrer," which appeared after Reinecke's death in the *Neue Zeitschrift für Musik* 78/1 (1911): 2–4. [ed.]

8. I.e., the celebrated *Waverly* novels of Sir Walter Scott, whom Mendelssohn met at Abbotsford in 1829. The English writer Lord Edward Bulwer-Lytton (1803–1873) was also acclaimed for his historical novels; Richard Wagner's opera *Rienzi* (1842) is based on Lytton's novel *Rienzi—the Last of the Roman Tribunes* (London, 1848). [ed.]

9. See *Deutsche Rundschau* 96 (1898): 48. These letters later appeared in book form: *Aus der preussischen Hof- und diplomatischen Gesellschaft*, ed. A. von Boguslawski (Stuttgart, 1903), p. 52. [Bruno Hake]

10. As is evident from this letter, the symphony is in G major and has four movements: Adagio, Allegro; Adagio; Minuet; Finale. The score no longer survives. [Bruno Hake]

11. Mendelssohn's violin sonata composed in the same year (1823; op. 4, dedicated to Rietz) begins similarly with a long recitative for violin solo. [Bruno Hake]

12. In Breslau Mendelssohn was impressed by the musicianship of the organist F. W. Berner (1780–1827), who improvised on a theme provided by

Mendelssohn. In Reinerz Mendelssohn himself improvised on themes of Mozart and Carl Maria von Weber. [ed.]

13. Mendelssohn completed thirteen string *sinfonie* between 1821 and 1823; no. 8, finished in 1822, exists in an alternate version for full orchestra. Mendelssohn's first published symphony, op. 11 in C minor, was completed in 1824. [ed.]

14. Mendelssohn was a devoted practitioner of the canon throughout his career. The undated canon for Boguslawski may be solved by introducing the third voice at the seventh below (on D) in measure 3. [ed.]

15. Mendelssohn possibly means the drawings made during the Scottish sojourn in 1829, including a view of the Hebrides completed on the same day that he drafted the opening of the *Hebrides* Overture, on 7 August 1829. [ed.]

16. What is meant is probably one of the two great instrumental works on which Mendelssohn worked after his trip to Scotland in the summer of 1829: the *Hebrides* Overture (*Fingalshöhle*) and the *Scottish* Symphony (in A minor), which were completed in December 1830 and January 1842, respectively. [Bruno Hake] The full chronology of the *Scottish* Symphony has not yet been reconstructed; Mendelssohn dated his autograph 20 January 1842. The first version of the *Hebrides* Overture, entitled *Ouvertüre zur einsamen Insel*, was finished in Rome on 11 December 1830. Several versions followed, before Mendelssohn adopted the title *Fingalshöhle* (*Fingal's Cave*). See R. Larry Todd, "Of Sea Gulls and Counterpoint: The Early Versions of Mendelssohn's *Hebrides* Overture," in *19th-Century Music* 2 (1979): 197–312. Conceivably, Mendelssohn may have referred in this letter to an early version of one other work, the *Fantasy* in F♯ minor for piano, op. 28, originally known as the *Sonate écossaise*. [ed.]

17. D.-F.-E. Auber, French composer of *opéra comique*, whom Mendelssohn met in Paris in 1825. A letter to his family, dated 20 April and preserved in the New York Public Library, contains a harsh review of Auber's *Léocadie*. [ed.]

18. *Robert le diable*, grand opera by Giacomo Meyerbeer, premièred in Paris in 1831. [ed.]

19. *Der Freischütz*, romantic opera by Carl Maria von Weber (1821); *Il crociato in Egitto*, opera by Meyerbeer (1824). [ed.]

20. Heinrich August Marschner (1795–1861), German opera composer. Eduard Devrient, singer and actor and close friend of Mendelssohn; he describes the libretto in his *Erinnerungen an Felix Mendelssohn Bartholdy und seine Briefe an mich* (Leipzig, 1869). *Hans Heiling* was premièred in Berlin in 1833. [ed.]

21. Meant is *St. Paul*, which was finished only in 1836 and premièred in Düsseldorf. [Bruno Hake]

22. The *Italian* Symphony, op. 90, first performed in London on 13 May 1833 but published posthumously in 1851 as op. 90. [ed.]

23. Hake refers to the opening of Haydn's Symphony no. 6 (*Le matin*) of ca. 1761. [ed.]

24. See Devrient, *Erinnerungen*, p. 126. [ed.]

25. Karl Immermann (1796–1840), playwright and poet. [ed.]

26. This letter is printed from a hastily prepared copy, not from the original, which is lost. [Bruno Hake]

27. Mendelssohn left London in August 1833 and arrived in Düsseldorf by the end of the month to take up his position as city music director. In October he traveled to Elberfeld, Bonn, and Cologne, where he studied the sacred music of Orlando di Lasso, Palestrina, Allegri, Baini, Lotti, Leo, and Pergolesi. See the letter of 26 October 1833 to his sister Rebecka in Felix Mendelssohn Bartholdy, *Briefe aus den Jahren 1830 bis 1847*, ed. P. and C. Mendelssohn Bartholdy (Leipzig, 1878), vol. 2, pp. 6ff. [ed.]

28. For a discussion of the Düsseldorf Festival, see Susanna Grossmann-Vendrey, *Mendelssohn und die Musik der Vergangenheit* (Regensburg, 1969), pp. 67–75. [ed.]

29. Karl Gottlieb Reissiger (1798–1859). [ed.]

30. It is uncertain which of these three Reissiger letters was enclosed with the letter to Mendelssohn. [Bruno Hake]

31. Ludwig Tieck (1773–1853), poet, playwright, and writer of short stories and novellas. [ed.]

32. J. F. Reichardt (1752–1814), composer and music critic. [ed.]

33. See Mendelssohn's letter of 24 January 1837, in Ferdinand Hiller, *Felix Mendelssohn Bartholdy: Briefe und Erinnerungen* (Cologne, 1874), p. 74. [ed.]

34. The performance of the new *Scottish* Symphony, finished in January, took place on 3 March; and that of *Antigone* two days later in the theater at Leipzig. [Bruno Hake]

35. That is, a songlike theme. This expression is especially characteristic of Mendelssohn, whose music is always thoroughly based on melody, after the model of the classical masters Bach and Handel. Standing in contrast is the type of art beginning with Beethoven and brought to a triumph by Wagner, whose foundation is the recitative, the characteristic motive—an opposition in which the old schism between Italian and French music persists in a rejuvenated form. [Bruno Hake]

36. This letter places us in the middle of Mendelssohn's restless activities. On 25 April he conducted his *Lobgesang* in Berlin, then traveled a few days later to Leipzig, directed the music festival in Düsseldorf on 15, 16, and 17 May, and performed the *Scottish* Symphony in London on 18 June. [Bruno Hake]

37. In this letter, as well, I was unable to refer to the original, but had to content myself with a copy. [Bruno Hake]

38. Since August 1845 Mendelssohn was again living permanently in Leipzig. In Berlin he performed his incidental music to *Atalia* [on 1 December 1845] and *Oedipus* [*at Colonos* on 1 November 1845]. [Bruno Hake]

PART

·IV·

CRITICISM AND
RECEPTION

Robert Schumann with Reference to Mendelssohn-Bartholdy and the Development of Modern Music in General

FRANZ BRENDEL

TRANSLATED BY SUSAN GILLESPIE

In 1844 Robert Schumann retired as editor of the *Neue Zeitschrift für Musik*, the journal he had founded in 1834 and developed to promote high critical standards for German musical life. By the beginning of 1845 the journal's editorial mantle had passed to Franz Brendel (1811–1868), who gradually reoriented the journal into an organ for the newer aesthetic ideals of Wagner and Liszt and of their so-called *Zukunftsmusik* ("Music of the Future"). Brendel had studied Hegelian philosophy at the University of Leipzig, and, beginning in 1846, gave lectures in the history of music at the Leipzig Conservatory.

For Brendel the future of German music lay not in instrumental music, which Mendelssohn and Schumann had developed to a high degree, but in a national German opera, the art form that could best meet the political and cultural aspirations of a united Germany as it was envisioned in the *Vormärz* period leading up to the revolution of 1848. For Brendel, neither Mendelssohn nor Schumann had met this particular challenge, and in Brendel's view of music history both composers were therefore susceptible to substantive criticisms. Thus, in a major article that appeared in several installments in 1845, Brendel concluded that neither Mendelssohn nor Schumann could found a progressive school viable for the future of German music. In particular, Mendelssohn, who, as Brendel admitted, had mastered the traditional forms with remarkable facility, was regarded as a "representative of classicism in our time," a position not congruent with Brendel's "progressive" expectations. (For a study of Brendel's editorship of the *NZfM*, see Jürgen Thym, "Schumann in Brendel's *Neue Zeitschrift für Musik* from 1845 to 1856," in *Mendelssohn and Schumann: Essays on Their Music and Its Context*, ed. J. W. Finson and R. L. Todd [Durham, 1984], pp. 21–36.) [ed.]

[Source: Franz Brendel, "Robert Schumann mit Rücksicht auf Mendelssohn-Bartholdy und die Entwicklung der modernen Tonkunst überhaupt," in *NZfM* 22 (1845): 113–15, 146–47, 149–50.]

Along with Beethoven, the Mozartian school of music has had a decisive influence that has persisted well into the present time. In the introduction to this essay I described this tendency and its significance. Our present task is to show how Mendelssohn's artistic beginnings evolved from this tendency; then to examine the development of the two composers [Mendelssohn and Schumann] together; and to clarify that development by comparing the two.

If, for example, we focus on pianoforte music—a subject of immediate interest to us because Mendelssohn, too, had his musical beginnings on this instrument—then we see, beginning with Mozart, an increasingly greater attention paid to the technical aspects of the instrument. The wealth of figures becomes predominant, and spiritual expression recedes as the single determining force. As the Mozartian school continues to evolve, accommodation to the nature of the instrument, study of its peculiarities, and attention to its [technical] effects become principal concerns. In contrast, Beethoven always imposed the stamp of his originality on the instrument and made its treatment dependent on the musical content that was to be portrayed. In effect, the Mozartian school became the conservator of everything essentially academic in music (including theory and execution), the conservator of rule and measure, of the formal element in general; it remained aloof from Beethoven's broadening of the medium. In keeping with the above-mentioned balance between objective and subjective aspects in Mozart, the larger instrumental compositions of this school are dominated by a certain process of externalization, while the imaginative element and spiritual expressiveness recede.

This explains Mendelssohn's individual character in his earlier works.

Even Mendelssohn is not without originality in his artistic beginnings, not without the striving to form and develop preexisting material in an original way. He is by no means a student of Mozart's in the narrow sense, for he was equally receptive to Beethoven and to the latter's efforts oriented toward the future. But he did not take Beethoven's last period—where a composer dedicated to the new ideal would have found the point of departure for further development—as his starting point, nor, in general, did he follow any one specific master; rather, he tended to take the entire past, Sebastian Bach *and* Mozart, as his prerequisite, and not so much in order to seize upon a specific task or to set out straightaway in an entirely modern direction. Even the place where Mendelssohn received his earliest artistic training does not seem particularly favorable to the development of an ambitious artistic, musical talent; true, significant perceptions are to be found there [in Berlin], and the intellectual life is generally lively, but all this is suited more for reflection and less for the artistic—especially the youthful—imagination, and Mendelssohn was still very young when he began to compose.[1] Thus we see him from the beginning bound by the influences of his schooling and by the objectivity of the past, absorbing the influences of his surroundings, of L. Berger[2] and Zelter[3] with their distinctly unmodern artistic views. Further, we notice how, in agreement with the prevailing artistic tendency, Mendelssohn begins with the objective and the generally applicable, in contrast to Schumann, who limited himself to the narrow scope of his individuality at that time, and began with himself, with his personality, so closely related to the newest epoch in literature. Mendelssohn's earliest works are sometimes more in the nature of exercises in composition; he experimented quite early in all the forms and genres, without being able to make them come completely alive or give them an original shape. The inner drive to create brought forth these works, but did not bring them to complete fulfillment. On the other hand, Schumann, once he had taken up a particular genre, held fast to it longer and limited himself to what completely suited him. Such more formal compositions were but a transitional point for Mendelssohn, a means for him to understand himself. Everywhere his striving to achieve the highest is visible, but he does not storm boldly toward the peak. Rather, he wants to conquer it through docility, through loyal obedience; he does not yet dare to express himself. Schumann begins less clearly and consciously, more seeking and feeling his way, but with deep inner feeling; Mendelssohn begins clearly, surely, but more externally. In his case we find more conscious imitation of previous work, and conscious effort; Schumann's innovations, in contrast, are more an instinctive expression of his individuality as it actually happens to be. Both composers, partial from the start to the pianoforte, hold as one of their cardinal principles the modern, virtuosic treatment of the instrument. Schumann adopted this richness of performance, but immediately abandoned the empty formalism it contained, injected more spiritual meaning into this greater fullness, and formed his musical figures in an entirely original way. In Mendelssohn, at first, we find the same—the higher talent, still undeveloped, remaining in the background, the striving for intellectual expression; but from the beginning Mendelssohn tends to adhere to the older way of handling the instrument, and the musical figures only gradually take on an original character. In the *Charakterstücke* dedicated to L. Berger (op. 7),[4] for example, one is reminded of the latter as soon as one begins to leaf through the score; in other works we find Beethoven's influence.[5] Schumann begins in an original, but highly subjective, occasionally almost odd manner, so that it sometimes appears as if he has written only for himself and we are merely watching the artistic spirit playing with its own content, without regard for the external world. Mendelssohn begins objectively, but does not know how to infuse this element thoroughly with the spiritual; hence much is formal. In the one, therefore, what we see is an early mastery of form, along with the capability to represent things in plastic forms;[6] in the other, an inner life struggling for expression, a less clear formulation of ideas; *in the one, a comprehensive basis, with all past artistic development as background; in the other, no immediately recognizable background, no past, but a broad view toward the future—the future of art as its perspective.* The direction, the development of the two is diametrically opposed. *Mendelssohn strives from the external inward, trying by means of what is accepted and generally recognized to arrive at self-knowledge and poetry. Schumann strives from the internal outward, beginning with his original personality; hence the law of his development is to mold this originality into the accepted forms and genres and gradually take possession of them.* Schumann, to point out an analogy with literary personages that is, in my opinion, apt in several respects, shows in the first period of his artistry much similarity with N. Lenau and H. Heine; Mendelssohn, with Platen-Hallermünde.[7] On the one hand, in Schumann, there is the same imaginative dreaming as in Lenau, but also, especially earlier on, the same lopsidedly prominent intellect and the same tendency to wit and irony as in Heine—in general, the same modern element, the same modern moods. On the other hand, in Mendelssohn, one observes the same virtuosity of form, the same individuality [as in Platen-Hallermünde], original but rooted in the past, which builds bridges between it and the present.

In the overture to *A Midsummer Night's Dream*, the *Songs without Words*, and the works that followed, Mendelssohn first learned the extent of his originality, and to seize upon a specific task that corresponded to the modern ideal. The consequence was that he now gained decisive recognition from the public, although the earlier compositions, too, had won acclaim.

Now the modern principle made itself felt in Mendelssohn, as well; hence the two composers drew closer together and found themselves engaged in related tasks, but with a difference: in Mendelssohn the new and original breathes fresh life into older classical forms; the new portrays itself as if it has just struggled free of them; whereas Schumann seeks his own forms earlier and makes their creation completely dependent on his inner excitement. If Mendelssohn had produced purely instrumental compositions earlier on, works of music without specific expression, he now saw it as his task to imitate works of literature and to give musical rebirth to their content; he recognized in the striving for the greatest possible distinctness of expression the task of modern instrumental music, and thus he paid homage to the same principle that appeared in Berlioz, despite the fact that the two composers were very dissimilar in individual talent, artistic attitudes in general, and, especially, nationality.

Mendelssohn took up another task of the times when he elevated to an artistic form something that had manifested itself earlier (for example, in the Adagio of Beethoven's C#-minor fantasy,[8] or in the etudes of L. Berger,[9] to name an artist who affected Mendelssohn directly), but only sporadically and without a clearly expressed consciousness. Melody is the subjective element in music, the form in which the subject is able to express itself and its particular sentiment. Thus we see how, in the course of the historical development of music, melody, in conformity with the widespread general evolution of the spirit toward subjectivity, emerges more and more from polyphonic forms, how it reveals itself as ever more separate, free and independent, becoming more expressive and songlike. Thus [it is] with Mozart in comparison to Haydn, and thus with Beethoven in comparison to Mozart. When Mendelssohn, in the *Songs without Words*, placed the melody at the center of a work of art, he drew the historically necessary consequence and carried it to its ultimate conclusion and perfection.

.

Both artists named in the title of this essay have now been described in terms of their individualities, as expressed in the first period of their creativity, and the historical contexts have been developed; in the next and last installment I shall proceed to an overall summary. . . .

Mendelssohn, after he had worked himself free from the chains of the academy, seized first upon the fantastic, as the territory where he could recognize his mastery; and in the *Songs without Words* he expressed his consciousness of the task of the times. Expanding and intensifying his individuality in all directions, he then produced his great religious and dramatic works and his larger instrumental compositions. Mendelssohn is an eclectic, but in the noblest sense of the word; everything that the past offers for study and attention he used, and blended it with everything that was fundamentally his own and was characteristic of his original talent. All this, and especially his broad education, gives him the right to claim the title of a talent of the first order. While other great masters may have surrendered themselves with a more luxuriant imagination to an artistic instinct that was unconscious in its creation; while their works may make a deep impression through a freshness and immediacy of invention that Mendelssohn does not possess in the same degree; while they, at the same time, betray the weaknesses that are inevitably linked to such a creative standpoint—too much dependence on chance and the accidents of inspiration, something purely natural and untamed and not purified by artistic consciousness—in Mendelssohn the background everywhere evinces a thoroughly educated taste, careful consideration, and classical contemplation. At first, Mendelssohn's individuality, too, was more narrowly confined; but through his studies he expanded it, and nourished to the greatest possible perfection every seed that he bore within himself. The objective point of view that he naturally assumed made these efforts easy for him, in contrast to Schumann. Therefore, for all these reasons, we find in Mendelssohn the possibility of successfully achieving the goals of a bygone age in art, along with the polemic—expressed most particularly through his creations themselves—against purely romantic music in the narrower sense, and against artistic tendencies themselves when they serve as an expression of the progressive movements of history. If I am not mistaken, Mendelssohn would express the view that everything once beautiful remains so for all times *in the same way*, and must always awaken the same sympathetic emotions, without regard to the fact that the highest beauty, which unites and comprehends everything within itself, including all the elements of development, within itself, never appears in this world, but stands only as a historical ideal that is determined by the character of the times and by the progressive stages of history. Mendelssohn stands at the head of that tendency that makes art less an expression of the mood of the times, and prefers to pay homage to the beautiful per se. It cannot be denied that this point of view contains a great deal of justification, for attempts to reduce all poetry and art to the political, as the liberals have most recently desired to do, are entirely mistaken. But the task of art is just as much to portray the epoch in its struggle, and to give expression to the highest forces that propel it forward. Mendelssohn has the advantages of the older classical tendency; through this classicity he became the man of the times, but we are also justified in criticizing his lack of modern sensibilities.

Since our purpose here is not to examine Mendelssohn's creations, I will not mention individual works. I only wish to touch on the music of *Antigone*,[10] because it offers proof of what has been said in the preceding, and provides an opportunity for remarks about the art of the present day. We have already correctly observed that there is something contradictory in the attempt to reclothe an ancient play in modern garb, thus combining the most extreme antitheses, the inwardness of Christian music and the "externality" of the Greek-plastic principle. However, once the undeniably contradictory and actually impermissible nature of the task is admitted, we must admit that the composition deserves the highest praise, even though Mendelssohn, by the nature of his individuality, has little affinity with the heroic. But everything in *Antigone* is so superbly, so finely and cleverly imagined, that when it is performed the audience is carried away and does not become conscious of the contradiction at all. This is especially true because here, for once, the words that are sung are really sublimely poetic. It is beautiful to have an ancient piece restored to life in this way; only we must take care to avoid excess in imitating such attempts, and, as we thank the creator of this extraordinary first attempt, reject others. We have already suffered so much from classical antiquity; our nationality and language have been held back so severely by it, and by the excessive influence it has enjoyed right down to the present day, that we do not want to be inconvenienced in the field of music, as well. If we had a national theater, if we possessed a solid, educated taste in art, then this could only be greeted with joy as a sign of higher educational attainment. Under the present circumstances, however, everything foreign only distracts us from our development and limits its progress, quite apart from the fact that such attempts can easily lead to something artificial, as appears already to have happened in Berlin, where they have begun to set all antiquity to music, and have returned, by way of setting Horace's odes, to a stage of development that, though it was dominant in the sixteenth century,[11] was fortunately overcome by the subsequent improvement of our art.

Schumann began with the most pronounced inwardness; he was not immediately able to absorb the more objective forms and could shape them only along the lines of his own originality. He had to create everything from the inside out and therefore struggled with its expression until he was able to reproduce the adopted elements independently as his own. Hence, if we find the characteristic essence of Mendelssohn in his broad, commanding view, his strength in the control of [musical] quantities, then we see Schumann, far inferior to Mendelssohn in these regards, more concerned with the working out of particulars, easily losing his orientation over the richness of a detail, paying less attention to clear articulation. Mendelssohn pays attention externally to what will be successful; this fine knowledge of what is appropriate holds sway over him. Schumann follows only his inner drive, and what is new springs forth more unconsciously. Schumann tests; Mendelssohn knows his strength. Mendelssohn, turned backward toward the past, knows how to portray his thoughts in a plastic, visual way; Schumann struggles with expression, but he delves much more deeply and brings the undiscovered to the surface. In Schumann's less successful pieces, he does not achieve the final, greatest clarity; Mendelssohn, in his less successful works, falls into formalism and mannerism, and noticeably repeats certain favorite phrases and figures, for example in his works for pianoforte. Schumann writes quickly, at times probably too quickly; Mendelssohn polishes and considers, at times probably too much. Schumann awakens more immediate sympathy, Mendelssohn creates a stronger impression of the classical and the perfect, in somewhat the same way as has been observed in the cases of Goethe and Schiller. In Mendelssohn, nothing is ventured that does not succeed. Schumann often lacks this effectiveness; but, by the same token, Mendelssohn's thought occasionally seems to have been inspired by the knowledge of the effect it will have externally, while Schumann's thought has come from within. The originality of each composer, as I have outlined it here in its main features, is the consequence of a fundamental principle they each uphold; for each, this originality derives from that principle as a necessary consequence. . . .

In my preceding remarks I believe I have identified the crucial point regarding the development of art in the present day, and have offered an initial explanation of this program in nos. 1 and 2 of this journal. What remains is for me to add to these observations my sup-

positions about the future, to elaborate on some practical consequences, and to express a final judgment as my own subjective view.

I have characterized Schumann as subjectivity developed to its
highest degree, only gradually fulfilling itself by means of the objective element; and Mendelssohn, as the opposite. Therefore, from the
beginning, Mendelssohn's task was clearer and more firmly fixed; it
is the most beautiful fruit that has ripened in recent times on the old
tree, and this explains the reason for his far greater popularity in
comparison to Schumann. Within these more narrowly defined
boundaries, Mendelssohn achieved with certainty everything he attempted; it was this clearly expressed character that earned him the
royal scepter in the kingdom of the musical present; he is the representative of the classical in the present day, and thus not an expression of the character of the whole period, least of all its future striving. Schumann is forced to seek his ideal, the ideal of the younger
generation, and to struggle to give it form; he is by no means finished, and his direction does not lie before us, clear and developed.
Both artists, therefore, are poorly equipped to form a school, to form
close attachments with a circle of younger talents. Mendelssohn's pupils would work even less for the future than the master had, [and]
except for the benefit that they would gain in a purely musical, technical sense from their association with him, they would, in keeping
with the entire tendency, fall into a certain "externality" and formalism. Schumann's pupils would have to do without the most essential
thing gained from observing a greater predecessor—namely, firm
and clear leadership toward an already well defined goal. Schumann
has changed greatly in the course of his activity as a composer, and
has drawn closer to the objectivity of the opposing artistic tendency,
perhaps motivated, even unconsciously, by external influences and
his stay in classical Leipzig. But we must ask whether final perfection
is attainable for him in this way. Would it not have been possible for
Schumann to treat the orchestra in the same imaginatively humoristic
manner in which he had earlier written for the pianoforte, of course
with appropriate modifications, but in the same spirit; and would not
such a free outpouring of the soul have corresponded to the ideal of
the times, which lets technical treatment recede and places the greatest emphasis on the dramatically agitated life of the spirit, on humor
and imagination? Or are the newer larger compositions of Schumann
only a second great element of his development, through which the
latter is raised to a higher level in order to be able to reach a broad,
all-encompassing standpoint? I have a very high opinion of his earlier
works for pianoforte; they were the necessary next step following

Beethoven. Schumann did not have popular success with them, but the time will come when these works will receive more general recognition, and I therefore believe that this point of departure must not, as it seems, be denied and rejected by the composer.

Now I have followed the development of the two most significant musicians of the younger generation, emphasizing their historical significance and the rich talent they both possess; and the result, it would seem, is that neither one can serve as a model, and that not even the reference to the first talents of our time can free us from the doubts of our contemporary public life or provide a firm guarantee for the future of art.

As if in response to the predominance of Protestantism in Germany, which forces individuals to rely upon themselves and separates them more and more from communal life, our entire artistic development is less often characterized by the grouping of individuals around a strong center. This is particularly true in the present, when, in place of the earlier aristocracy of spirit, which had few members, a republic of intellects has begun to emerge. For these and the above-mentioned personal reasons, it is not possible for younger talents to follow the two artists closely or *immediately*. But if we inquire into the reasons why Mendelssohn and Schumann have attained such pre-eminence for the present, we find that an essential and influential factor, in addition to their individual talent, was their great cultivation—not only musical, but also literary, aesthetic, and, in Mendelssohn's case, biblical as well. That both of them filled their inner lives with the spiritual treasures of our people, with attention to what was occurring in their time, and with an open mind and susceptibility to other interests not necessarily of a musical nature, has been one of the principal reasons for their significance. In this sense—that is, indirectly—the two can have the most lively influence on struggling artists, not by encouraging narrow-minded imitation, but through their example, through attention to the excellent model that they have both provided for the present. Our more competent artists—I am not speaking of salon artists or *routiniers*—so often forget to familiarize themselves with the spirit of the immediate present; the education of musicians, up until now, has been far too much a purely musical one in the narrow sense, and thus it was possible to believe that we had acquired the content along with the form. Old masters were studied, with perfect justification, but we overlooked the fact that the purpose of this study is merely to acquire the formal skills with which to express a new spirit. The content of works of art of earlier periods has been passed on to our younger artists and has imprisoned their own sensibility; they move within the earlier, more limited *Weltanschauung*, and are, in part, still far removed from our new thinking and feeling. This explains the fact that nowadays we are so often presented with the spirit and, even more, the form, of the past. It is less a lack of musical productivity in general that prevents us from moving forward and makes the creations of the present appear insignificant when weighed against our contemporary public life; rather, it is a lack of independence and thorough education of the spirit, a lack of spiritual uplift and broadening of perspective, a lack of sympathy with the movements of history and of familiarity with the new content that has moved the world since 1830. If our musicians are really filled in a living way with the spirit of the present, then more original creations will result, new forms alongside the revival of the old ones, and I have written this essay in this sense and for this purpose: in order to make us aware of what we must strive for; to distinguish what is justified from what is untrue and becoming outdated; and to give voice to that point that we must mainly address on the question of progress—namely, to draw attention to the significance of content in art. The opera—its past, present, and future—will now give me an opportunity to explore the tendency suggested here in further detail.

NOTES

1. The earliest surviving composition by Mendelssohn is the "Lied zum Geburtstag meines guten Vaters," finished on 11 December 1819. [ed.]

2. Ludwig Berger (1777–1839), pupil of Muzio Clementi. [ed.]

3. Carl Friedrich Zelter (1758–1832), director of the Berlin Singakademie, confidant of Goethe. [ed.]

4. *Sieben Charakterstücke*, op. 7 (Berlin, 1827). [ed.]

5. E.g. the Piano Sonata in E major, op. 6 (Berlin, 1826). [ed.]

6. The borrowing of descriptive terms from the visual arts—here, sculpture—was a widespread tendency in nineteenth-century musical criticism. [trans.]

7. Nikolaus Lenau (1802–1850); Heinrich Heine (1797–1856); Count August von Platen-Hallermünde (1796–1835). [ed.]

8. The *Sonata quasi fantasia* in C♯ minor, op. 27, no. 2 ("Moonlight"). [ed.]

9. Ludwig Berger, *12 Etüden*, op. 12; and *15 Etüden*, op. 22. [ed.]

10. Incidental music to Sophocles' *Antigone*, op. 55, first performed at Potsdam on 28 October 1841. See also pp. 137–157. [ed.]

11. C.G.V. von Winterfeld, *Der evangelische Kirchengesang [und sein Verhältnis zur Kunst des Tonsatzes]* (Leipzig, 1843–1847), vol. 1, p. 169. [Franz Brendel]

Heinrich Heine on Mendelssohn

SELECTED AND INTRODUCED BY

LEON BOTSTEIN

TRANSLATED BY SUSAN GILLESPIE

Heinrich Heine (1797–1856) was among the most important literary figures of nineteenth-century Germany. Like Mendelssohn, Heine was born a Jew. He experienced much more of a Jewish education than Felix Mendelssohn, however, and his relationship to his Jewish identity was far more complex. Heine converted in 1825 as an adult, not as a child. In 1850 he characterized his ambivalent relationship to Judaism by declaring that he never made a secret of his Jewishness because he had never stopped being Jewish. Yet Heine penned some of the most severely self-critical and sarcastic prose about Jews and their predicaments at a time when assimilation and conversion seemed possible and yet always flawed. The measure of success, of course, was an exit from anti-Semitism and the exceptional conditions of Jewishness. Unlike Mendelssohn, Heine always considered himself an outsider—even an outcast.

After 1830 Heine lived in Paris. Like Mendelssohn, he was a beneficiary of family wealth. His uncle supported him for many years. Bedridden for the latter part of his life, he is remembered for both the lyric economy of his poetry and the ascetic elegance of his prose style. Later critics, including Karl Kraus, accused Heine of journalistic self-importance, of superficiality, and of distorting the German language and Frenchifying it.

Heine was neither a musician nor a music critic, but his writings are crucial documents on the integration of music with the other arts. From them one learns more about the function of music and culture in society than about the works of music.

These selections give the reader a characteristic sampling of Heine's wit and his keen eye. As a somewhat older contemporary of

Felix Mendelssohn, Heine felt certain he could see through the social agenda of the Mendelssohn family and Mendelssohn's claim to piety and Christian faith. One learns a bit more about Heine than about Mendelssohn in these selections, but a Mendelssohn-Heine comparison is important in order to place Mendelssohn in his proper context. Heine's influence and reputation, like those of Mendelssohn, suffered with the advent of modernism at the fin de siècle. Later, the Nazis banned Heine's work and sought to eradicate the memory of him. In the history of music, Heine's lyrics, particularly his early works written before 1830, served as texts to generations of lieder composers, from Schubert to Hugo Wolf. Heine's writings also influenced Wagner, not only as sources for the early music dramas—*The Flying Dutchman* and *Tannhäuser*—but also in the tone of Wagner's polemical articles.

[Sources: Heinrich Heine, *Deutschland. Ein Wintermärchen*, vol. 4, pp. 613–16; idem., Letter to Ferdinand Lassalle, in *Briefe*, ed. Friedrich Hirth (Mainz, 1950), vol. 3, pp. 50–51; idem., *Lutetia. Reports on Politics, Art, and Popular Life*, in *Sämtliche Schriften* (Munich, 1984), vol. 5, pp. 396–400, 528–30.]

.

From *Deutschland. Ein Wintermärchen* [*Germany. A Winter's Tale*] (1844)

Caput 16

The carriage's jolting shook me awake,
But my eyelids drooped through the tossing.
They closed again, and I fell asleep
And dreamed of Barbarossa.

I walked around shooting the breeze with him
Through all the echoing hallways.
He asked me this, he asked me that,
He asked me to tell him stories.

For as far the world above was concerned
For years and years he'd heard nothing,
Since around the time of the Seven Years' War—
Not a word from a soul up above him.

He asked about Moses Mendelssohn
And Lady Karschin,[1] with interest;
He asked about Countess Dubarry,
Who was Louis the Fifteenth's mistress.

O Kaiser, I cried, how backward you are!
Moses is long since deceased,
With his Rebecca, and their son Abraham
Is equally dead and defeated.

Abraham had begotten with Lea
A little boy, Felix. The youngster
Has made great strides in the Christian world—
Has already become *Kapellmeister*.

Old lady Karschin is likewise dead,
And the daughter is dead, name of Klenke;[2]
Helmine Chézy,[3] the granddaughter,
Still lives, if I'm right in my thinking.

Dubarry's life was lighthearted and gay,
As long as Louis held power,
The Fifteenth, that is; she was already aged
When they finally guillotined her.

The king himself, Louis the Fifteenth, died
Quite peacefully in his bed,
But the Sixteenth went to the guillotine
With the queen, Lady Antoinette.

The latter displayed a great deal of mum,
Quite suitable for a queen;
As for Dubarry, she howled and cried,
When she came to the guillotine.

The Kaiser suddenly stood quite still
And looked at me with a piercing
Gaze, and spoke: "For heaven's sake,
What is that—the guillotine?"

"The guillotine"—I explained to him—
"Is a newfangled invention
That tranports folk from all walks of life
From this world straight to heaven.

"In applying this method one makes good use
of an equally new machine
Invented by Mr. Guillotin
So we call it the guillotine.

"You're buckled onto a wooden board;
It is lowered; one clean swift motion

Inserts you between two posts—while above
A three-cornered blade's in position.

"A rope is pulled, and down it plunges
The blade, in all its glory;
On this occasion your head falls down
Into a bag readied for it."

The Kaiser interrupted my tale;
"Say no more about this appliance.
I don't want to know, and God forbid
I should ever have to apply it!

"What's that you said? Buckled fast to a plank
Of wood—the king and the queen!
That goes against every rule there is
And every bit of good breeding!

"And you, who are you, that you dare to speak
To me in the second person?
Just wait, you punk, you may be sure
I'll give you measure for measure.

"It fills my belly with deepest bile
To hear you talk in this fashion.
Your very breath is a treasonable crime
Against the monarchic system."

When I heard him waxing warm in this way,
The old man, with no compunction,
Snorting at me, I began to spout forth
My own innermost conviction.

"Mr. Barbarossa!"—I cried—"you are
Nothing but an old fable;
Go back to sleep, we will do without
Your help in our salvation.

"The Republican forces are laughing at us;
They have quite enough to mock.
If we follow a ghost with a scepter and crown
We'll be a laughing-stock!

"Your banner is not to my taste anymore,
It's defiled by the Old German fools.
They spoiled my taste, in our student days,
For the red and black and gold.

"The best thing would be if you stayed at home
Here in old Kyfhauser,
When I think about it quite clearly now—
We've no need at all for a Kaiser."

Letter to Ferdinand Lassalle

Paris, 11 February 1846

Dearest Lassalle!

You forgot in your last letter to communicate your direct address to me, and I am hesitant to express my unvarnished opinion to you on the most important point of your letter when the delivery is by third party—in any case I convey to you that everything you request will come to pass. With respect to Mendelssohn—how you can attach importance to this unimportant matter, I do not comprehend—respecting Felix Mendelssohn I am glad to submit to your wish, and not another harsh word shall be printed against him—I feel malice against him because of the way he pretends to Christianity.[4] I cannot forgive this man, whose independence is assured by financial circumstances, for serving the Pietists with his great, enormous talent. The more acutely I become aware of the significance of the latter, the angrier I become at its vile misuse. If I had the good fortune to be a grandson of Moses Mendelssohn, I would truly not devote my talent to setting the piss of the Lamb of God to music! Between us, the immediate reason that I sometimes goaded him had to do with some of his local followers—enthusiasts to the core—whom I wanted to annoy, for example your countryman Frank, and Heller,[5] and who were ignoble enough to ascribe to those attacks the motive that I wanted to curry favor with Meyerbeer.

I write all this to you with premeditation and in detail, so that later you can understand the grounds for my quarrel with Mendelssohn better than the common pack, among whom deformed versions will be insinuated. I will write to you in detail as soon as I have your direct address. Until then it remains between us. I am still suffering a lot, can almost not see at all, and my lips are so numb that it spoils my pleasure in kissing, which is even more indispensable than talking, which I could probably do without. I look forward a great deal to the arrival of your brother-in-law and your sister. Here everything is quiet; masked balls and opera; for a week no one has talked of anything except Halévy's *Mousquetaires*,[6] about which my wife raves. The latter is well and quarrels as little this year as one could desire from any virtuous woman. Farewell and be convinced that I love you inexpressibly. How happy I am that I have not been mistaken in you— I, who [am] so suspicious by experience, not by nature. Since I received letters from you, my courage swells and I feel better.

Your friend
H. Heine

Lutetia

Reports on Politics, Art, and Popular Life

PART 2, REPORT NO. 43

Paris, mid-April 1842

When I arrived in Cette last summer on a lovely afternoon, I saw that along the quay, with the Mediterranean Sea stretching out before it, the procession was passing by, and I will never forget the sight. Up front were the brotherhoods in their red, white, or black robes, the penitents with hoods pulled down over their heads, two holes with eyes peering out like phantoms; in their hands burning candles or crusaders' banners. Then came the various monks' orders. And a crowd of lay people, women and men, ghastly broken figures that swayed devotedly back and forth in a touchingly sorrowful singsong. I had often come across such sights in my childhood on the Rhine, and I cannot deny that those tones awakened in me a certain nostalgia, a kind of homesickness. But what I had never seen before and what appeared to be a neighboring Spanish custom was the troupe of children that portrayed the Passion. A little boy, costumed the way one is accustomed to portray the Savior, the crown of thorns on his head, whose sad golden hair flowed down his back, gasped all bent over under the burden of a great wooden cross, on his forehead garishly painted drops of blood, and stigmata on his hands and naked feet. At his side walked a little girl dressed entirely in black, who, as the *Mater dolorosa*, bore on her breast several swords with gilded handles and almost dissolved in tears—an image of deepest sadness. Other little boys, who followed her, represented the Apostles, among them Judas, with red hair and a purse in his hand. A couple of other tiny youngsters were helmeted and armed as Roman soldiers and swung their sabers. Several children wore monastic habits and church regalia: little Capuchins, miniature Jesuits, tiny bishops with infula and crosier, adorable little nuns—none, surely, more than six years of age. And strange, among them were also children dressed up as Cupids, with silken wings and golden quivers, and in the immediate vicinity of the little Savior, waddled two even smaller, at most four-year-old figures in old Germanic shepherds' costume, with berib-boned hats and crooks, pretty enough to kiss, like marzipan puppets: they probably represented the shepherds who watched over Christ's cradle. Believe it or not, this sight aroused in the soul of the observer the most earnestly sorrowful emotions, and the fact that it was inno-cent little children who were acting out the greatest, most colossal martyrdom made it all the more moving! This was no imitation in the grand historical manner, no two-faced sanctimoniousness, no false faith in the Berlin style; it was the most naive expression of the pro-foundest thoughts, and the condescendingly miniature form of it prevented the content from having a devastating effect upon our emotions, or from devastating itself. This subject has such monstrous power to arouse sorrow; it is so sublime that it overreaches and bursts the bonds of even the most heroic-grandiose and passionately exag-gerated portrayal. For this reason the greatest artists, in both painting and music, have prettified the overpowering horrors of the Passion with as much ornament as possible and softened its bloody earnest with playful tenderness—and this is also what Rossini did when he composed his *Stabat Mater*.[7]

The latter, Rossini's *Stabat*, was the most outstanding event of the recently departed season. The review of this piece is still the order of the day, and the very criticisms that are heard from North German quarters against the great master are irrefutable proof of the origi-nality and depth of his genius. The treatment is too worldly, too sen-sual, too playful for the spiritual content; it is too light, too pleasant, too entertaining—so the groans of a few ponderous, boring pedants, who, if they are not intentionally feigning a falsely exaggerated spir-ituality, have at least forced themselves to adopt very limited, very mistaken ideas about sacred music. Among musicians, as among painters, an entirely false view of the treatment of Christian subjects is in vogue. The former believe that whatever is truly Christian must be portrayed in subtle, gaunt contours, as haggard and colorless as may be; in this regard, Overbeck's drawings are their ideal. To counter this perceptual error with fact, I would merely like to draw attention to the images of the saints painted by the Spanish school; here, fullness of contours and colors predominates, and yet no one will deny that these Spanish paintings breathe with the most unattenuated Christianity and that their creators must have been as intoxicated with faith as the famous masters in Rome[8] who converted to Catholicism in order to paint with more perfect fervor. The true signs of what is truly Christian in art are not external aridity and pallor, but a certain inner excess of enthusiasm, which—and this applies to music as to painting—can neither be baptized into a person nor accomplished by study. And so I also find the *Stabat* of Rossini more truly Christian than *St. Paul*, the oratorio of Felix Mendelssohn-Bartholdy, which is held up by the opponents of Rossini as an exemplar of Christian genuineness.

Heaven help me if, in saying this, I should express any criticism of such a worthy master as the composer of *St. Paul*, and the last thing that would ever occur to the author of these pages would be to find fault with the Christianness of the above-mentioned oratorio on account of the fact that Felix Mendelssohn-Bartholdy is by birth a Jew. But I cannot forbear to point out that at the age when Herr Mendelssohn was taking up Christianity in Berlin (for he was not baptized until the age of thirteen), Rossini had already forsaken it and plunged himself wholly into the profane world of opera. Now, as he took leave of that world again and dreamed himself back into the Catholic memories of his boyhood, into the times when he sang as a choirboy in the cathedral at Pesaro or served as an acolyte at mass— now, as the sounds of the old organ roared back into his memory and he seized his pen to write a *Stabat*: at that moment, verily, he did not need to construct systematically the spirit of Christianity, still less to make slavish copies of Handel or Sebastian Bach; he needed only to call up the earliest sounds of childhood from his heart, and, O wonder! however solemnly, profoundly painfully these sounds may reverberate, however strongly, sighing and bleeding, they express the most powerful content, they still retain a quality reminiscent of childhood that reminded me of the portrayal of the Passion by children, which I had seen in Cette. Yes, I was reminded of this pious little mummery when I first attended a performance of the *Stabat* of Rossini: the tremendous, sublime martyrdom was portrayed here, but in the most naive tones of youth; the terrible laments of the *Mater dolorosa* rang out, but as if from the innocent small throat of a girl; next to the buntings of the blackest grief the wings of all the Cupids of gracefulness were rustling; the horrors of death on the cross were ameliorated as if by a playful pastorale; and a feeling of eternity billowed and flowed around the whole, enfolding it like the blue sky that looked down on the procession of Cette, and the blue sea along whose shores it passed singing and resounding! That is the eternal loveliness of Rossini, his indestructible mildness, which no impresario and no *marchand de musique* could worry to death or even tarnish. However meanly, shamelessly, and perfidiously he may often have been dealt with in life, in his musical creations we find not a trace of bitterness. Like that spring Arethusa, which retained its sweetness even though the salt waters of the ocean flowed through it, so Rossini's heart retained its melodic charm and sweetness, although it had drunk its fill of all the cups of gall this world offers.

As I said, the *Stabat* of the great master was the foremost musical event of this year. I need not report about the first, trendsetting performance; the Italians sang—that says it all. The hall of the Italian Opera seemed to be the antechamber of heaven; holy nightingales wept and the most fashionable tears flowed. Even *France musicale* included the greatest part of the *Stabat* in its concerts, which were met, I need hardly emphasize, with enormous applause. In these concerts we also heard *St. Paul* by Herr Felix Mendelssohn-Bartholdy, who laid claim to our attention precisely by this contiguity, and himself occasioned the comparison with Rossini. For the general public, this comparison was hardly to the advantage of our young compatriot. It is as if one were to compare the Apennines of Italy with the Kreuzberg in Berlin. But this does not diminish the virtues of the Kreuzberg; to earn the respect of the great mass of humanity, it is sufficient that it bears a cross on its top. "Under this sign you shall be victorious."[9] Admittedly not in France, where Herr Mendelssohn has had nothing but fiascoes. He was the sacrificial lamb of the *saison*, while Rossini was the musical lion, whose sweet roar can still be heard. It is said here that Herr Mendelssohn will come to Paris personally one of these days. This much is certain—that high influence and diplomatic efforts have so far brought things to the point at which Herr Leon Pillet[10] has had Scribe prepare a libretto that Herr Mendelssohn is to set to music for the Opéra.[11] Will our young compatriot stand this test successfully? I do not know. His artistic ability is great; but it has very grave limits and gaps. I find in respect to talent a great similarity between Herr Felix Mendelssohn and Mademoiselle Rachel Felix, the tragic actress. They are both characterized by a great, strict, very serious seriousness, a determined, almost importunate tendency to follow classical models, the finest, cleverest calculation, sharp intelligence, and finally complete lack of naiveté. But is there in art any originality of genius without naiveté? Until now there has been no such case.

Musical Season of the Year 1844

REPORT NO. 1

Paris, 25 April 1844

A tout seigneur tout honneur.[12] We begin today with Berlioz, whose first concert opened the musical season and could be regarded as a kind of overture to the same. The more-or-less new pieces that were here presented to the public found the applause they deserved, and even the most sluggish spirits were swept away by the power of the genius that is revealed in all the great master's creations. Here is a wing beat that betrays no ordinary songbird, but a colossal nightingale, a thrush the size of an eagle, like those that are supposed to have existed in prehistoric times. Yes, in general Berlioz's music has for me something primordial, if not antediluvian, and it reminds me of extinct species of animals, fabled kingdoms and transgressions, heaped-up impossibilities; of Babylon, of the hanging gardens of Semiramis, of Ninevah, of the miracles of Misraim,[13] similar to those we can observe in the works of the English painter Martin. In fact, if we look for an analogy from the art of painting, we find the most elective affinity[14] and resemblance between Berlioz and the mad Briton: the same appreciation for the monstrous, for the gigantic, for material immensity.[15] In the one, harsh effects of light and shadow; in the other, screeching instrumentation; in the one, little melody, in the other, little color; in both, little beauty and no feeling at all. Their works are neither ancient nor romantic, they remind us neither of Greece nor of the Catholic Middle Ages, but call us to the much higher things of the Assyrian-Babylonian-Egyptian period of architecture and the massive passion that finds expression in them.

What a properly modern man our Felix Mendelssohn-Bartholdy is in comparison. We mention our highly acclaimed compatriot today first of all on account of the symphony[16] of his that was presented in the concert hall of the Conservatoire. We have the active zeal of his friends and supporters to thank for this pleasure. Although this symphony of Mendelssohn's was received very frostily in the Conservatoire, it nevertheless deserves the recognition of all those who are truly knowledgeable about art. It is of genuine beauty and belongs among Mendelssohn's best works. But how is it that no laurel wreath seems to want to grow on French soil for this so deserving and highly talented artist, since the performance of *St. Paul* was forced upon the public? How is it that all attempts here fail, and that even the last desperate stratagem of the Odeon Théatre—the performance of the choruses from *Antigone*—has brought forth only a pitiful result? Mendelssohn always offers us an opportunity to reflect on the most elevated problems of aesthetics. We are always reminded, in his case, of the great question: What is the difference between art and lies? We ordinarily admire this master's talent for form and stylistic matters, his skill in assimilating what is most extraordinary, his charmingly beautiful construction, his fine saurian ear, his sensitive feelers, and his serious—I might almost say passionate—indifference. If we look for a comparable phenomenon in a related art form, we will find it this time in poetry, and its name is Ludwig Tieck. This master, too, whether writing or reciting, always knew how to reproduce what was most outstanding; he even knew how to make something naive, and he never wrote anything that gripped the great mass of humanity and lived on in its heart. The talented Mendelssohn would have a greater chance of creating something lasting, but not in the arena where truth and passion are the first requirement—that is, on the stage; Ludwig Tieck, though he lusted after it hotly, did not have what it took for a dramatic achievement, either.

At the Conservatoire, besides the Mendelssohn symphony, we heard with the greatest interest a symphony by the sainted Mozart, and a no-less-talented composition by Handel. Both were received with great applause. . . .

NOTES

1. Anna Luise Karschin (1722–1791), lyric poet. [trans.]

2. Karoline Luise von Klenke (1754–1812), author of plays and poems. [trans.]

3. Wilhelmine Christiane von Chézy (1783–1856) was known to Heine from the period when he frequented Berlin salons in the early 1820s. She wrote romantic poems of orientalizing posture. [trans.]

4. Heine uses the disdainful term "Christeln," which has gone out of common use, along with its pendant "Jüdeln." [trans.]

5. Stephen Heller (1813–1888), composer-pianist of Hungarian birth active in Paris. [ed.]

6. Fromental Halévy's opéra comique *Les mousquetaires de la reine*, premièred in Paris on 3 February 1846. [ed.]

7. The work originally appeared in 1832; an expanded version was premièred in 1841. [trans.]

8. The Nazarenes, among them Friedrich Overbeck, Peter Cornelius, Julius Schnorr von Carolsfeld, and Philipp Veit, were Catholic romantics who based their work on medieval and Renaissance models of art. Their most

important works—for the most part, figural studies with biblical themes—were painted in Rome. After their return to Germany they became supporters of artistic and political reaction. [trans.]

9. These words appeared in a vision on a flaming cross to Constantine the Great before his decisive victory over Maxentius in 312 B.C. After the victory, Constantine converted to Christianity. [trans.]

10. Director of the Opéra. [trans.]

11. The project never came to fruition. [trans.]

12. Every honor to every lord. [trans.]

13. Egypt. [trans.]

14. Reference to Goethe's novel *Die Wahlverwandtschaften* [*Elective Affinities*], in which the fatal attraction of the main characters is likened to a chemical reaction. [trans.]

15. Reference is to John Martin (1789–1854), eccentric English painter known as "Mad Martin." [ed.]

16. The Symphony no. 3 in A minor, op. 56. [trans.]

On F. Mendelssohn-Bartholdy's
Oratorio *Elijah*

OTTO JAHN

TRANSLATED BY SUSAN GILLESPIE

The remarkably versatile classicist-philologist-archaeologist Otto Jahn (1813–1869) is chiefly remembered today as the author of the first full-scale critical biography of Mozart (*W. A. Mozart* [Leipzig, 1856–1859]), the idea for which was conceived during a conversation Jahn had with Professor Gustav Hartenstein at Mendelssohn's funeral in November 1847. Mendelssohn himself had corresponded with Jahn concerning the composer's ongoing search for a suitable opera libretto (see S. Grossman-Vendrey, *Felix Mendelssohn Bartholdy und die Musik der Vergangenheit* [Regensburg, 1969], pp. 215–16). For his part, Jahn had published a study of Mendelssohn's first oratorio, *St. Paul* (*Über F. Mendelssohn Bartholdy's Oratorium Paulus* [Kiel, 1842]). Early in 1848 Jahn released a companion study of *Elijah*, translated here. [ed.]

[Source: Otto Jahn, "Über F. Mendelssohn's Bartholdy's Oratorium *Elias*," in *Allgemeine musikalische Zeitung* 50 (1848): cols. 113–22, 137–43.]

·

It is never an easy matter to appreciate a major work by a great artist immediately in its whole significance, and in the case of *Elijah* this task is rendered especially difficult. The grave that covers the precocious master is still too fresh for our pure pleasure in his work not to be dampened by our grief at his loss. That is no state of mind for an impartial judgment, if the memory of his true, tireless striving after the noblest in art did not obligate us to look at his work in just this way. One may lay a laurel wreath on the coffin of a young man as a token of what he promised to accomplish; but a mature master can be honored only by the respect and seriousness with which we honestly strive to understand his creations; for in this understanding alone lies the capacity to judge what he strove for and achieved.

What makes a critical examination [of *Elijah*] even more difficult is the inevitable comparison of it to *St. Paul*. In several respects, *Elijah* immediately assumes all the disadvantages of a latecomer. In both conception and treatment, *St. Paul* laid the foundation for an essential advance in sacred music; it exerted a decisive influence on all subsequent efforts. If one comes to *Elijah* with the expectation that it, too, breaks new ground, the result is disappointment. But we have no right to expect this; and if we ask whether, in this work, we find the master striding forward with fresh vigor along the path that he has laid out, with the same fine sense of the noble and true, then I answer with complete conviction: yes. I am able, when I look at the oratorio as a whole, to discern no falling-off; it expresses Mendelssohn's individuality clearly and strongly, in conception and invention as well as in treatment and execution; it reflects the original beauty of his style as well as the little weaknesses of his manner.

Again, the new piece would seem to be at a disadvantage on account of its choice of subject matter: Elijah compared to Paul; how much less is the interest with which we approach Elijah! There is some truth in this, but in the interest of art we should not overemphasize it. The greater interest lies principally in the Christian standpoint which we ourselves occupy, and which no one, no matter what his religious viewpoint may be, can gainsay. It is certainly advantageous to the artist when the subject he is treating partakes, so to speak, of the soil and atmosphere of popular sentiment, so that the general interest meets him halfway, as it does here in regard to religion; but this is actually not the main focus of artistic appreciation. Every work of art wants, first of all, to have its effect *as* a work of art, not merely as a result of the subject it treats, but through the artistic form that is given to that subject. The artwork addresses itself directly and principally to the [viewer's] artistic sensibility and cultivation. Its goal is no more to arouse an interest that is restricted to the subject matter, even if it is religion, than it is to pander to mere sensual pleasure, which remains superficial. The only thing to consider, therefore, when we make a judgment about the subject matter of an artwork, is whether it is capable of engaging and holding our interest, from a purely human point of view, and, above all, whether it is suitable for artistic representation, in such a fashion that its significant elements can be conceived of and presented in a manner appropriate to one art form or another. The task of the artist is to develop the general interest that we feel for the subject into the specific interest that is created according to the nature of each individual artistic genre. Unless his material contains a kernel and seed of general significance, the artist labors in vain and is only able to involve us externally in his subject matter. But this subject matter need not be restricted at all to the content of our current education. For example, the true artist, in treating a Jewish or heathen subject, does not require us to deny our own instincts by becoming Jews or heathens; instead he grasps what is purely human in that material, and by recreating it, as a child of his own times, through free spiritual activity, and by giving it form according to the eternal laws of his art, he makes it the property of all eras that are responsive to art. This is true of all the arts, including music.

The oratorio, by its nature, is not necessarily either Christian or churchlike. Subjects from the Old Testament have actually provided the prime material for oratorios from Handel on down to the present day, and one can surely not say of them, in general, that they are foreign to us. We find ourselves in a territory that, from the standpoint of Christian education, is not only well known but, more significantly, is rendered symbolic by its preparation for Christianity, and offers the artist the advantage of a firm foundation on which to build. This symbolic element in the Old Testament, as a subject for Christian contemplation, is found throughout *Elijah*, too, in the passages throughout that not only advance the action, but also draw together into a general outlook the ideal content of elements that would otherwise appear as merely external events, especially at the conclusion, where the reference to Him who will come is given verbal expression. Along with *Elijah*, Mendelssohn had begun an additional oratorio *Christus*, which he never completed.[1] Possibly the two were meant to form parts of a certain complementary whole, so that in a certain sense the prophet of the Old Covenant [Testament] was to precede Christ, assuredly not in the sense that *Elijah* was not conceived and not to be understood as an autonomous work.

The libretto is composed of the words of the Holy Scripture, specifically of the Old Testament, but they are treated more freely than in *St. Paul*. Not only are they shortened and presented in a different order whenever necessary, but the words of the Bible are changed to such an extent that they provide only the basis for the text that is created from them. This results in part from an essential difference in the composition of the two librettos. Namely, in *Elijah*, the epic element that provided the continuing narrative thread of the oratorio

St. Paul has fallen away entirely, and the characters are introduced directly as speakers. As a result, *Elijah* more nearly approaches the form we find in Handel's oratorios, from which they are clearly distinguished, however, by the above-mentioned symbolic element in many choruses and solo passages. This change would seem to stem partly from the fact that in *Elijah* it did not seem necessary to retain the biblical narrative, which would have led to difficulties from time to time; and partly from the insight that, in this way, the oratorio would achieve greater unity and be shaped in a more purely dramatic way.

I am convinced that this is based on an error, that the epic element is peculiar to the essence of the oratorio, and that, in abandoning it, one relinquishes a true advantage in the creation of the artistic form, for the sake of an imaginary one. The oratorio is incapable of truly dramatic form. What is generally referred to as dramatic presentation is in the actual and true sense of the word not that at all, but only characteristic representation. That the characters in the action appear as speakers is not actually an element of drama, but only a means of lively presentation that portrays the situation as one that is immediately present, a means inevitably used in epics, as well. The same is true of all other devices of vivid characterization, which lead us so directly into the midst of the subject matter being portrayed that we believe we are taking part in it, and which may lead to the misconception that all that is lacking for true drama is the scenery—the same misconception that makes poor dramas of excellent narratives. For, on closer inspection, it is evident that in cases like these the artist achieves his purpose only by making masterful use of the means that are specific to his genre, and that precisely those things that appear to be dramatic, if transplanted into drama, would be ineffective. But what is lacking is the main element in drama—action. For the essence of drama consists in the continuously advancing action, in which one moment necessarily leads to the next, motivated by the specific character of the characters who are the bearers of the main plot. Like the epic, the oratorio limits itself to depicting the action in characteristic situations. This is precisely the reason why this genre is so well suited for musical treatment, for here it coincides with an essential and fundamental characteristic of music. Constant forward movement of the action does not belong to the essence of music, which, rather, expresses the mood, the inner basis of the action. Music has, by its nature, a tendency to dwell on things, and it necessarily seeks a firm point from which it can expand its theme in a certain breadth and in all directions. But here it possesses a depth and fullness, an inexhaustible wealth of the finest nuances unmatched by any other art form. One can demonstrate that, in all the musical forms developed independently, this principle proves to be the creative one.

The most appropriate poetic treatment of a subject to be portrayed musically is, therefore, one that relates the progress of the action more externally, using the situations it creates as occasions to portray the mood and sentiments of the actors. This is precisely the manner of the oratorio. But as soon as the oratorio attempts to adopt the outer forms of drama, it evidently lacks the most essential prerequisite. Since the oratorio cannot achieve true action, but cannot do without the continuing thread of a plot, avoiding the natural form of the narrative must inevitably lead to artificialities and make it difficult to achieve complete clarity and definition. The calmer sort of narrative, for which the recitative offers such an outstanding format, because its simple, almost typical character enables it to follow the finest nuances of expression with the greatest flexibility, forms a background from which characteristically developed situations can emerge clearly. If, on the other hand, everything must be put into the mouths of the actors as their freestanding speech, then this forces the piece into a constantly intensified characterization that can easily conflict with the subject matter or dissolve into its constituent details, becoming tiresome. To what extent the narrative element must take precedence depends, it is true, on the subject matter, and it almost appears as if the true observation that very little narrative is required in *Elijah* led to an attempt to do away with it altogether. This, however, was not without its negative consequences.

What we find in *Elijah* is not true action, which develops steadily, but rather a series of situations in which Elijah is the focus, and which show his originality from various points of view. This is the source of the work's unity. But these individual scenes must also be externally connected; since the simplest means for this—namely narrative—has been discarded, the result is a certain disjointedness, sometimes even indistinctness, as one is introduced unexpectedly into the midst of a situation that only gradually becomes comprehensible, as it develops. Music, furthermore, can only express individual characterization up to a certain point, and it is, within its limitations, completely incapable of historical characterization. Whatever means it employs—and here everything has been done with a great deal of refinement and cleverness—alternation of voices, of instruments, or whatever, does not suffice to identify a certain character in advance; this is one of the conditions upon which all musical characterization rests. This applies, above all, to all the secondary characters, who do not have independent roles, but who act as levers to keep the action moving forward. They do not achieve individual form and are therefore recognizable only in the context of the event. This is true of the king, the queen, and Obadiah, as well; only the widow, with her sharper outlines, stands out in the context of the work. This is a weakness, since these characters are presented as independent entities who must be recognized in their individuality if the situation is to unfold clearly. In a continuous narrative they would certainly stand out recognizably within a short time.

In order to avoid narrative, the main expedient that has been devised is to have the events of the plot put into the mouths of angels, either as decrees of the Lord to Elijah, or as prophecy. Undoubtedly this immediate presence of God, whose voice issues forth to Elijah, belongs to the essential character of the piece, and the angels' voices are exceedingly well utilized in several passages, such as the "Heilig" [Holy] when the Lord appears, or the song above Elijah as he slumbers in the wilderness. For here, with the most complete clarity and energy, these voices give corporeal vividness to a significant aspect of the situation that could only be suggested by narrative. But when they merely recast the narrator's speech in another form, then they bring about a monotony that is all the worse because it is artificially induced. From this defect a second necessarily follows: that their characterization cannot be maintained throughout at the level we expect from the appearance of angels. This is true, for example, in the first part, where the intent is to show how Elijah is miraculously rescued from the general famine. The angel orders him: "Get thee hence, Elijah, depart and turn thee eastward; thither hide thee by Cherith's brook. There shalt thou drink its waters; and the Lord thy God hath commanded the ravens to feed thee there, so do unto his word." This is followed by the double quartet [no. 7]: "For he shall give His angels charge over thee, that they shall protect thee in all the ways thou goest, that their hands shall uphold and guide thee, lest thou dash thy foot against a stone." And then the angel immediately continues: "Now Cherith's brook is dried up, Elijah, arise and depart, and get thee to Zarepath, thither abide, . . ." Here nothing has really happened; one has only been informed about a fact for the sake of the context. The appearance of the angels is a theatrical machine. As one would expect, this has not failed to have its effect on the musical form, as well; one senses the lack of musical impetus here. Obviously, simple narrative would have been the right thing.

Following these general observations, I shall now proceed to a more detailed characterization.

The oratorio opens immediately with the prophesy of Elijah, who, in a recitative accompanied by wind instruments, predicts years of drought, with an eminently successful expression of the most earnest solemnity. The overture follows, which thus serves as the introduction not to the whole work, but rather to the following situation—the carrying out of the curse. The basses introduce the theme, which expresses a heavy muffled gloominess, along with the lament of a few wind instruments. This thought is the foundation of the masterfully composed movement. It never vanishes, but introduces the most varied phrasing and continual intensification through the entire gamut of emotions from the most dreadful extremity, laments, and complaints to despair and indignation. The overture forms the transition to the following chorus: "Help, Lord! Wilt thou quite destroy us!" in which the misery of the languishing populace cries out for help [no. 1]. While two female voices lament, "Zion spreadeth her hands for aid and there is neither help nor comfort," the chorus, alternating male and female voices, sings in unison, "Lord, bow thine ear to our prayer!" in an unvarying repetition, so that this sentence takes on a gloomy, but also strangely liturgical character [no. 2]. Then Obadiah (tenor) cries out to the people, "Ye people, rend your hearts, and not your garments" [no. 3], and in a simple, very heartfelt aria, " 'If, with all your hearts, ye truly seek me, ye shall ever surely find me,' thus saith our God" [no. 4]. Quite effective is the chorus, which then breaks in stormily, "Yet doth the Lord see it not; he mocketh at us!" and with the same tones in which Elijah spoke his curse, "His curse hath fallen down upon us, his wrath will pursue us till he destroy us" [no. 5].[2] The furious passion turns to weighty solemnity at the thought of the vengeful God: "For he, the Lord our God, he is a jealous God, and he visiteth all the fathers' sins on the children to the third and the fourth generation of them that hate him." With the words "his mercies on thousands fall, on all them that love him, and keep his commandments," this solemnity then tears itself loose from the sad burden and grows upward, higher and stronger, to joyful trust.

The entire scene must be called masterful, as a whole and in its details. It is all of a piece and a single mood, sketched in different nuances, in the most perfect balance of individual motives, with a growing intensification founded on deepest truth; it is finely laid out and executed in grand style. We hear the curse being spoken; we see it come to pass. In the misery of the people we feel its guilt, as well, and that the Lord who has sent this suffering will also remove it from them. In this way, one is prepared that Elijah, who has appeared mysteriously like a dark storm cloud, will appear again to lift the curse.

But first we are led with Elijah into the desert and then to the widow whose child he raises from the dead. An aria expresses the anguished fear of the widow for her son, who is dying before her eyes; she begs Elijah for help, despairing of any possibility of it. His prayer gives life to the boy again, and she recognizes in him the prophet of the Lord, and cries out with him, "O blessed are they who fear him!" which the chorus takes up and continues.

One is not mistaken if one explains the insertion of this episode here primarily as an attempt to achieve a contrast to the massive, broad treatment of the first scene, a contrast that also assures a fresh impact for what follows, where a similar type of presentation is required. But here loftier principles should have taken precedence over this consideration. The episode of the widow weakens the impression of the preceding scene, and it is detrimental to what follows. The general suffering is made real to us in such powerful strokes that the extended description of the suffering of one individual must necessarily pale by comparison. The intensification of the emotions has already brought us to the stage where a turning point must occur; when something else intervenes, the flow of our feelings is interrupted—we become cold. Afterward, when the turning point really occurs, our feelings no longer perceive it as being motivated by necessity; it seems rather like a new beginning. After his splendid prophecy, Elijah should not make his next appearance in this manner; he should reappear as equally mighty and sublime. The miracle that he works here is too insignificant compared to the other, nor can it be seen as preparation. In addition, there are other misgivings about the nature of the episode itself. It is too long, both in the description of the widow's suffering and in the portrayal of the miracle itself. This length was based on the composer's desire, justified in itself, to secure a broad foundation for variations in nuance and contrast so as to achieve a full and rich expression of the mood, and a continuous intensification. But this is not the place for broad development, and the entire passage might better have been omitted. In addition, the long, drawn-out complaint of the mother is somehow emotionally awkward. The power of the miracle is weakened by Elijah's threefold repetition of his prayer before it is answered. The musical intensification, heightened by interruptions of the unbelieving widow, is superb, but in the context of the whole it is not appropriate here; all the less so when one considers that the same intensification of the thrice-repeated prayer recurs when Elijah later causes rainfall.

There the repetition is suggested by the particular situation, so that it has the greatest effect, as a means of expressing the general, enormous tension; but it should not be prefigured in the widow scene for the sake of a lesser effect. These weaknesses are also evident in the musical treatment, and I must admit that this section appears to me the least successful. Individual moments are fine and beautiful, but on the whole I find here more external representation of a restless passion than inner depth and warmth. The motives are not large and meaningful, and the entire depiction is somewhat hastily drawn. Because similar criticisms are not infrequently appropriate for operas, one is perhaps inclined to call this method dramatic, as the word is often used apologetically or critically; with the same justification one might call decorative painting "dramatic." The noble quality does not return until the chorus reappears [no. 9]; the agitation of the preceding scene reverberates only in the emotional figure of the string instruments, which is dominated and conciliated by a beautiful feeling of devout joyfulness.

Now Elijah announces for the first time that he wishes to present himself to the king, and that the Lord will make it rain on earth [no. 10]. The recitative corresponds to this statement; very beautiful is the phrase that expresses that the curse, too, will be lifted. Elijah appears before the king and in a highly emotional speech, in which the populace participates with short sentences, he challenges the priests of Baal: "And the God, who by fire shall answer, let him be God." And now there follows a scene full of force and life that continues in unbroken forward motion until the conclusion of the first part.

In a passionate prayer, at first sung by a double chorus accompanied only by wind instruments, then with a roaring accompaniment of strings, the priests of Baal, mostly singing in unison, call to their god for fire. In response to Elijah's mocking challenge, they repeat their cry, impatiently and with increased vigor, and as Elijah again mocks their cry, because it remains ineffective, the music grows into a real storm [nos. 12 and 13]. But when the repeated cry "Hear and answer!" interrupted by general pauses, has no effect, then Elijah speaks: "Draw near, all ye people, come to me!" These choruses are characterized by great freshness and liveliness, and are generally handled in a manner similar to the choruses of the heathen in *St. Paul* and some in *Antigone*, but without any actual imitation of these. In all of them an original expression of passionate, excited sensuality holds sway, which, however, remains far from weakness or voluptuousness; rather, it is earnest—at times even austere. Distinguished is the gradually intensified progression in the three choruses from the faith certain of victory, even arrogant, calling on the gods with joyful serenity; to the wild, passionate challenge; and finally all the way to despair, which in its rage turns against the gods themselves. The mocking speeches of Elijah, and finally the simple dignity with which he calls the people to himself, form an excellent contrast. Now he turns in prayer to God, asking, with a consummate expression of the most intense piety and firm faith, that he reveal himself to him and the people. A solo quartet, sung almost without accompaniment—"Cast thy burden upon the Lord, and he shall sustain thee"—objectifies this mood of Elijah's spirit, as it were, and gives it a higher certitude; extremely simple and clear, and equally deeply felt, it is treated like a chorale [no. 15]. Even for observations of a general nature, Mendelssohn refrained from using chorales in *Elijah*, and only appeared to refer to the form of the chorale in a few places. This was doubtless in order to avoid inserting into the Old Testament material an element that, by its very form, was foreign to it; and in fact the whole concept of the oratorio would have to have been more decisively symbolic in order to permit such a thing. A ruthlessly strict criticism might even speak against this movement, if it were not disarmed by its simple beautiful effect, which has something truly purifying about it.

At Elijah's bidding, which takes on a solemn expression corresponding to the anxious mood, the fire falls from heaven [no. 16]. With the thunderclap that accompanies it, the people cry out, "The fire descends from heav'n! The flames consume his off'ring!" and bow before the Lord, the sole God. The chorus is extremely agitated at first, and the figures of the vocal parts recall Handel's manner; the chorus closes with a solemn Grave. At Elijah's command, the priests of Baal are slain, and now he reveals himself with the vehemence of a burning zealot: "Is not his word like a fire, and like a hammer that breaketh the rock?" [no. 17]. The aria is full of passionate excitement and anger, in a wild, restless movement; it demands a singer whose voice is equally vigorous and well trained. This angry zeal is then moderated quite beautifully in an alto solo in which suffering on behalf of the faithless is expressed with touching simplicity: "Woe unto them who forsake him! destruction shall fall upon them." The aria refers to the mercy of him who forgives those who repent [no. 18].

Now Obadiah addresses Elijah, asking him to beg God for rain, and Elijah prays to him with the people. Then he sends the boy out to look for rain. "There is nothing. The heavens are as brass above me" [no. 19]. And again Elijah prays with the people to the Lord; the answer is the same. Then Elijah cries out in the highest enthusiasm of fervent prayer, "thy great mercies remember, Lord!" and the boy replies, "Behold, a little cloud ariseth now from the waters: it is like a man's hand. The heavens are black with clouds and with wind; the storm rusheth louder and louder!" Then the people shout in jubilation toward the streaming rain: "Thanks be to God for all his mercies." The musical representation of this scene is eminently successful and has the greatest effect. The tension, caused by the recurring, monotonous answer of the boy with the stubborn C of the oboe; the intensification in the pleading prayer, rising to violent crests; the approaching rain; and finally the sudden, forceful cry of gratitude of the chorus are all of a piece, and through a wise choice of means an extraordinary effectiveness is created in a very simple manner.

This spirited mood is maintained and increased in the final chorus, which follows immediately upon Elijah's words: "Thanks be to God, for he is gracious, and his mercy endureth for evermore!" [no. 20]. Although nondescript, it takes on an original coloration from the circumstance from which it emerges, and this is expressed in the rich and full accompaniment. To the simple "thanks be to God, he laveth the thirsty land!" which resounds powerfully again and again, is added the roaring movement of "the waters gather, they rush along! They are lifting their voices," and this reaches its peak in the words "but the Lord is above them, and Almighty." The surprising harmony built up here and intensified in triple repetition is of truly awesome enthusiasm and lifts this chorus to more than ordinary heights. . . .

The second part begins with a soprano aria. The softly warning lament "hear ye, Israel, hear what the Lord speaketh: 'Oh, hadst thou heeded my commandments!' " becomes the fiery cry, "I, I am he that comforteth. Be not afraid, for I am thy God, I will strengthen thee!" [no. 21]. A vigorous chorus, fresh and powerful, sets in immediately, and sustains the mood: "Be not afraid, saith God the Lord, Be not afraid, thy help is near" [no. 22]. There is a beautiful intensification in these passages, which come together in a splendid unity; as the mood becomes more vigorous and spirited, the movement grows, the motives become larger, the treatment broader, more massive, and this applies particularly to the instrumentation, which is fine and sensitive at first and grows to a brilliant splendor. These passages have a specifically Mendelssohnian character, by the way—especially the choruses, in their reminiscences of elements from earlier works. The trumpet entries, for example, are closely related to the way these instruments are used in *St. Paul* in the chorus: "Mache dich auf, werde Licht" ["Be gone, let there be light' "],[3] although there is no exact correspondence.

This introduction establishes the mood for the following scene, a recitative of Elijah, who comes before the king without fear of any man, trusting in God, and proclaims the punishment that will overtake him and his people [no. 23]. The proclamation is presented as original, solemn, and firm, and at the same time mysterious: "And the Lord shall smite all Israel, as a reed is shaken in the water, and he shall give Israel up, and thou shalt know he is the Lord." Immediately after that, there follows a spirited scene in which the queen incites the people against Elijah, and, after several exchanges of dialogue, the populace, in a stormy chorus, demands the death of Elijah. In its manner, the chorus recalls similar dialogues in *St. Paul*. This is one of the scenes that are ostensibly dramatic, but in fact quite undramatic. True, the characterization of these scenes is quite lively and is based primarily on the clever use of certain moments of the scene that can hardly fail to have their effect: for example, the quick alternation of brief speeches between the queen and the people, the varying emphasis of the exclamations in the various voices, and other elements that encourage the expression of passionate excitement. It is therefore understandable that the artist took advantage of these auspicious situations, all the more so since only a vivid description of imminent danger can motivate the following scene, in which Elijah flees into the wilderness.

And, yet, I believe that within the whole conception of the oratorio this scene is not developed proportionately. Elijah's opposing position to the king, who has turned to idolatry mainly under the influence of the queen—the cause of all the continual struggles and persecutions that define Elijah's whole life and maintain the strength of his character—is not the basis of the oratorio. One can see that the outlines of a truly dramatic development have been left unused; hence the root of the action, the conflict of various characters, each stamped with his own originality, is cut off. In itself, this is perfectly well justified, but when their relationship is taken for granted and is introduced as a separate element at various points in the development of the oratorio, then this has something disturbing and upsetting about it; one does not know what to do with it. Naturally, one can no more object that we bring with us the historical knowledge of these relationships, which quickly put everything into perspective, than point to the libretto, which informs about everything—the work of art must be comprehensible in and of itself. But we can see that here, too, because of the form that was chosen, something that was necessary to establish the external framework has been expanded unnecessarily; a simple narrative would have transmitted the purely factual material with an appropriate brevity and would thus have prepared the ground for the extensive depiction of what is essential. Equally evident is that, in those passages not inevitably emanating from the fundamental idea of the whole, the musical treatment is less profound and significant, but is restricted to a more external characterization.

On the other hand, the scene that follows, with its noble simplicity, is one of the most beautiful in the entire oratorio, and among the most beautiful things Mendelssohn wrote. At Obadiah's warning to escape from the threatening danger, Elijah flees into the wilderness; in deep pain because his efforts have been in vain, he longs for death in a simple beautiful cantilena with obbligato cello: "It is enough, O Lord, now take away my life"[4] [no. 26]. Then, in more vivid distress: "I have been very jealous for the Lord God of Hosts, for the children of Israel have . . . slain all thy prophets with the sword." The aria moderates through painful earnestness—"And I, even I, only am left"—to wistful resignation—"It is enough, O Lord, now take away my life." The pain and burden weighing upon the soul of this strong man who sees no end to his vain struggle is expressed beautifully and nobly, without any admixture of weakness. And for him who is exhausted unto death, heavenly comfort is near; while he sleeps under the juniper tree in the wilderness, the angels of the Lord take their places around him, and a trio of female voices rings out, without accompaniment, "Lift thine eyes to the mountains, whence cometh help!"—a number of unusually lovely melodiousness, so tender and strong, so simple and clear, as if it could not be otherwise, an expression of the purest, most serene peace [no. 28]. The last words of this trio are followed by the chorus "he, watching over Israel, slumbers not nor sleeps. Shouldst thou, walking in grief, languish, he will quicken thee" [no. 29]. Here, too, the same serene mood is retained and expressed in the most graceful manner; the contrast, "Shoudst thou, walking in grief, languish," casts only a slight shadow that emphasizes the tone of deeply felt trust. The chorus flows clearly and with a transparence that brings the entire movement to a benevolent conclusion.

Now the decree goes out to Elijah to proceed to the mountain; however, distressed and tired by his futile striving, he no longer hopes to accomplish anything with his strength: "O, that thou wouldst rend the heavens, that thou wouldst come down! . . . O Lord, why hast thou made them to err from thy ways? and hardened their hearts, that they do not fear thee? O, that I now might die!" [no. 30]. Then the warning voice resounds to the despondent man: "O rest in the Lord, wait patiently for him, then he shall give thee thy heart's desires. Commit thy way unto him and trust in him, and fret not thy-self because of evil doers" [no. 31]. These words are spoken like a heartfelt, soft warning, simply and with feeling in an alto solo, and they are underscored by the following chorus: "He that shall endure to the end shall be saved" [no. 32]. The peace of a soul that has be-come calm and clear through firm trust in the Lord is expressed truly and with intimate feeling in this chorus. Perhaps only a few can por-tray successfully a mood devoid of all passion and incapable of every external characterization, and can portray it so deeply and truly that in its very peacefulness it takes on an artistic expression warmed by inner life. Thus the impression is a truly purifying and in the noblest sense a moving one. The musical form corresponds perfectly to the mood; from the simple basic thought, expressed clearly and com-pletely at the very beginning, the movement develops organically into a solid unity, and without any extraneous decoration.

These two scenes clearly demonstrate the advantages of free, sym-bolic composition. Here one cannot speak of any particular action; there is only portrayal of the inner emotional state of Elijah. He, him-self, however, does not merely express this to us. Rather, that which holds sway in the inner depths of the human being, unbeknownst to him, finds objective expression here, thus assuming the character of a higher truth that transcends the individual. Because this expression of the general is occasioned by the portrayal of an individual, and refers to and transfigures that individual, it appears not as something abstract but as integrally necessary and truly living, and in this way perfects the artistic portrayal.

We sense that Elijah is deserving of being lifted up from his de-spondency by the appearance of the Lord, and so the angel bids him hide his face before the approach of God.

The appearance of the Lord himself was without a doubt one of the greatest and most difficult tasks, although the poetic description in the Holy Scriptures afforded excellent motives for a musical depic-tion. A form of presentation other than the narrative was not at all feasible here, and so a type of narration was chosen, but the form in which the narrative appears—namely, from the mouths of the cho-rus—already demonstrates that what is intended is more than a sim-ple narrative. Here the imposing powers of the natural phenomena and the deepest excitement of the human heart should find a com-mon, unified expression in the presence of the most holy and greatest things. To this end, all the forces of the vocal parts and the orchestra are assembled; but here, where the most unusual things were to be depicted, one is rather surprised by the strictness of form observed both in the general conception and in the details. This betrays the sure hand of the master, who even here did not overstep the proper measure, and it lends the whole piece, as stirring and unusual as it is, a great firmness and clarity. The twice-repeated "Behold, God the Lord passed by!" and the phrase, also repeated yet so different in its expression, "But yet the Lord was not in the tempest (earthquake, fire)" create completely distinct rhythmic divisions and hold the stirring descriptions of the tempest, earthquake, and fire within a frame, as it were [no. 34]. For these descriptions themselves, the extremely felicitous choice of the canonic form has been made—which, while held in check as if by a strong force or a law of nature, simultaneously has something driving and pressing about it that keeps the hearer in a state of the most suspenseful attention. This is intensified by the accompaniment, which, in part, drives forward in quick movement, and, in part, hits home with its solid mass; and especially by the original treatment of the basses, which, for the most part, remain for a long time on one tone. But since the harmonies above change rapidly, this dwelling on one tone, which only occasionally appears as a fundamental bass tone, does not create a sense of calm, but drives forward all the more. After the greatest force is concentrated in the words "But yet the Lord was not in the fire," a pacifying element emerges—"And after the fire there came a still, small voice." Here the harmony becomes simple and clear and moves quickly toward the pure triad, on which it rests for a long time without moving. Then a gentle motion begins with the words "And in that still voice, onward came the Lord," melodically and harmonically quite moderate, and it leads in its breadth to the very salutary calm that follows after so much intense excitement. There is no tone painting here; the composer has not, for example, tried to imitate natural phenomena or represent them directly. Still, where a musical element appears in the real world, he has taken the freedom to elevate and develop that element into an artistic motive, with real tact. The poet takes advantage of this right both in language and in rhythm; in music, the technique extends much farther, because many musical elements are scattered throughout nature. This may lead to the misunderstanding that the natural sound is carried over into music as imitation, which can only be permitted in rare cases, where it serves as a witty device. However, it is an entirely different matter, and should not be called painting at all, when a musician's creativity has been excited by a natural phenomenon and when, in the representation of all that this has awakened inside him, the relationship between this phenomenon and certain elements of music exercise a necessary influence on the form. And this applies to the case in question.

A true feeling led Mendelssohn not to end the appearance here, but to hold fast to the impression of the presence of the Lord. The angels that sing the "Heilig" are very well suited for this [no. 35]. This movement, a solo quartet for female voices with chorus, very simple in its invention and with a decided liturgical character, gives the impression of a solemn brightness, through the dexterous and original way in which all the vocal and instrumental means are employed, and it makes a magnificent conclusion for the preceding chorus.

Undoubtedly, to create a climax after this appearance was difficult; and, above all, to give the oratorio a worthy conclusion was no mean task. For Elijah does not appear again as a figure of the action; his ascension remains an isolated phenomenon, offering no particulars that divulge a more explicit portrayal, and his transfiguration actually pales in comparison. This is apparent in the artistic treatment, as well; the conclusion is not entirely even and rather too extended.

Elijah is ordered to go down again into Israel [no. 36]; but when this command is placed in the mouth of the same angels who have just sung the "Heilig," then this seems to me to be an inappropriate use of means—all the more so since no result of this order ever becomes evident to us. Though Elijah may express his joyful obedience, we do not see him act. His aria is rhythmically and harmonically distinctive, and expresses the calm serenity of the old man who awaits death with joyful trust, but it does not bear the stamp of a powerful nature, capable to the last of powerful deeds [no. 37]. For that reason the words of the next chorus, "Then did Elijah the prophet break forth like a fire," follow less appropriately [no. 38]. Everything that occurs immediately preceding them has given us the impression of an old man weary of life.

The above-mentioned chorus reports the ascension of Elijah in brief intimations. To have the chorus that described the appearance of God followed so soon by a second one with a content that is, after all, so closely related was a bold stroke. But the second chorus is conceived in an entirely different spirit from that of the first one. In the former, the thrill of the unearthly had set its distinctive stamp on the whole; here it is not the miracle of the ascension that determines the mood. On the contrary, the mood reflects the necessary conclusion of such an extraordinary life; its basic tone is one of admiration for the powerful and strong nature revealed in Elijah. Thus the entire posture of this chorus is unusually strong and energetic, more powerful, one might almost say, than Elijah's own.

If we call to mind the individual traits of Elijah, who is depicted with such partiality, and bring them together into a portrait, we find that he is not the man of iron who, with unwavering courage, challenges the king and, with flaming words, knowing no danger, the people who have fallen away from God; not the prophet of the Lord who visits the crimes of the fathers upon the children; not the harsh man who himself slaughters the priests of Baal. Mendelssohn's Elijah is above all the pious man who is firm in his faith that God hears him when he prays to him; in this trust, which turns into deeply felt enthusiasm, he performs miracles and warns with solemnity and dignity. For a moment passionate anger wells up in him, too, but zeal and harshness are not the fundamental traits of his character. He is soft and full of pity; deep sorrow grips him because his warning is not heeded, and only the appearance of God lifts him up again. Thus all the traits of warm and deep feeling, of a sincere and powerful heart, are given preferential emphasis and are especially effective in their treatment; Elijah nowhere appears weak and sentimental, but always possessed of a noble and strong dignity. The Elijah whom the chorus describes, "His words appeared like burning torches, mighty kings by him were overthrown, he stood on the Mount of Sinai, and heard the judgments of the future, and in Horeb, its vengeance" [no. 38] is not the Elijah of the oratorio.

After the ascension, a general conclusion follows that points to the One who will come after Elijah. This conclusion is completely appropriate to the basic idea, but it seems to me too broadly developed. The immediately following tenor solo, "Then shall the righteous shine forth as the sun," does not quite follow consistently in its content, and in its invention and treatment—not just in comparison to the preceding chorus—it is somewhat flat and weak [no. 39]. On the other hand, the following recitative and chorus, "But the Lord, from the north hath raised one," are serious and great, and have a certain solemnity that suits their symbolic character excellently [nos. 40 and 41]. Unfortunately this impression is somewhat attenuated by the quartet "O come, ev'ry one that thirsteth, O come to the waters, O come unto him," which does not correspond to the climax that is called for, particularly at the conclusion. The last chorus then leads, after a broad introduction, into a lively fugue: "Lord our creator, how excellent thy name is," which, in the usual manner, brings the oratorio to a powerful and brilliant conclusion [no. 42].

In these observations, I have attempted to set forth the oratorio as I believe it must be understood. I have not permitted myself a close examination of details, specifically an analysis of so many beautiful and fine features. Not much is generally achieved through mere description, and it is better for me to leave the purely technical to the specialists. What was important to me was the general aesthetic appreciation. Therefore, where I could not agree with the intentions of the master, I have attempted to give reasons for my divergent opinion, as I would have given them to him himself, if this joy had been vouchsafed to me. As it is, I have considered it a duty of piety to strive with all the honest effort I can muster to help make the work that he has left behind truly beneficial for us.

NOTES

1. *Christus*, posthumously published as op. 97 in 1852. [ed.]

2. A reference to the curse motive, announced in no. 1 as a series of interlocking descending tritones, C–F♯–G–C♯–D–G♯. [ed.]

3. Reference is to *St. Paul*, no. 14, "Denn siehe, Finsterniss bedeckt das Erdreich" ("For see, darkness covers the kingdom of earth"). [ed.]

4. For a study of this aria, see Martin Staehelin's article, pp. 121–36. [ed.]

On Mendelssohn and

Some of His Contemporary Critics

FRIEDRICH NIECKS

One sign of the shifting attitudes toward Mendelssohn in the closing decades of the nineteenth century was the appearance in 1875 of Friedrich Niecks's "On Mendelssohn and Some of His Contemporary Critics," an attempt to reassess Mendelssohn's sphere of influence and to defend his music against the charge that it was superficial and derivative. If, in Niecks's view, Mendelssohn did not compete well against the "gladiators of modern times," he nevertheless excelled in capturing the fanciful in music.

Trained as a violinist in Düsseldorf, Niecks arrived in Scotland in 1868; from 1891 he served as Reid Professor of Music at the University of Edinburgh. He contributed regularly to the *Monthly Musical Record* and produced biographies of Robert Schumann and Frédéric Chopin. His magnum opus, *Programme Music in the Last Four Centuries: A Contribution to the History of Musical Expression* (London, 1907), included a sympathetic treatment of Mendelssohn's orchestral works, which, according to Niecks, were "regarded by opponents of programme music as an extremely inconvenient fact." [ed.]

[Source: "On Mendelssohn and Some of His Contemporary Critics," in *Monthly Musical Record* 5 (1875): 162–64.]

·

The cause of the diversity of opinion with respect to Mendelssohn's merits and rank as a composer must be looked for not in his works, which are pre-eminently crystal-like in their intelligibility, but in the widely differing notions of critics and public, musicians and amateurs, concerning the musical art. It is with art as with religion: people think too often that all truth, all perfection, is confined to one sect, to one school, and that beyond it there is nothing but error and imperfection. Nature and the spirit that pervades her is too great a theme to be exhausted by one man or school—a theme to which not even the united schools of all arts and all ages can do justice; it is inexhaustible, infinite. Let us be careful that by disregarding any branch of art, however slight, or by disparaging any style, however uncongenial to our individual taste, we may not lose part of the interpretation of that glorious mystery.

Musical criticism and criticism generally is, with rare exceptions, so more than the expression of a liking or disliking which has its origin in temperament, habit and education; a truly aesthetical judgement, on the other hand, is as much a matter of the head as of the heart, the one serving to correct and ratify the other; or in other words it is objective as well as subjective.

These are the truths often enunciated, all but universally accepted, and yet so frequently lost sight of. Most of Mendelssohn's critics are guilty of the latter offence.

In the following remarks an attempt is made to give an impartial account of the subject indicated in the heading. The present writer does not pretend to be in possession of ideas or material which throw new light on the subject, though he hopes to contribute something towards the settlement of the question by placing side by side and comparing the opinions of three of the greatest contemporaries of Mendelssohn. To speak of them as contemporary critics, is not quite correct, as only one of them wrote in Mendelssohn's lifetime, the other two several years after his death; but all were born nearly about the same time. More of this by-and-by.

Mendelssohn's most characteristic work and most successful achievement, in fact "the result of his existence," is the music to Shakespeare's *A Midsummer Night's Dream*. Schumann, who called it "the most beautiful of Mendelssohn's dreams," says of the overture, "The bloom of youth lies suffused over it as over scarcely any other work of the composer; the finished master took in his happiest minute his first and highest flight."[1] Mendelssohn opened a new world to the musician. Fairyland had not been a part of his domain—Mendelssohn conquered it for him. With the knavish sprite Puck, Peasblossom, Mustard-seed, Cobweb, and the lightsome throng of their nameless compatriots, we meet again and again in his works. The frolics of these merry sprites take in Mendelssohn's music the place which the purely human contents of Beethoven's scherzi hold in the latter composer's works. What is humour in Beethoven becomes fancy in Mendelssohn. This may serve as a key to Mendelssohn's position.

Three elements may be distinguished in music, the emotional, the imaginative, and the fanciful. The first is pre-eminently human, the second is descriptive, yet not of things—*i.e.*, objects of nature and art—but of the impression we receive from them; the last of the three is best characterized by the definition which Leigh Hunt gives of Fancy, it is "the youngest sister of Imagination without the other's weight of thought and feeling."[2]

The peculiar virtue of music lies in its emotional power. It is this which distinguishes it from and raises it, in this respect, above all other arts. Words, paint, and marble, are of too gross a nature to render the fine gradations of mysterious light and shade and colour, that constitute the picture of man's emotional life. Music, as the language of feeling, is as far above the poetical language, as the latter is above everyday prose. Where words fail, music speaks.

If an artist, a painter who imitates visible objects, could say—"Passion and expression is beauty itself; the face that is incapable of passion and expression is deformity itself. Let it be painted, and patched, and praised, and advertised for ever, it will only be admired by fools"—how much more ought the musician, whose theme is the invisible, to hold views like these?[3] Blake's observation, looked at from the standpoint of an artist, is very likely wrong, certainly it contains much that is exaggerated; but a musician, I venture to say, could not do better than take these words for his motto—"Passion and expression is beauty itself." Not because they contain the truth and nothing but the truth, that they do not—indeed, what aphorism does so?— but because they point out to the musician the cardinal virtue of his art; because they oppose *expression* to *non-expression*, *life* to *death*, and in this sense the word "beauty" cannot be judged as being misapplied.

If it be granted that the strength of music consists in us being the exponent of our feelings, we cannot but conclude that musical compositions must be ranked according to the truth and depth of their emotional contents. Fancy is the lowest of the three art-producing faculties. "It plays," says Ruskin, "like a squirrel in its circular prison, and is happy."[4] Imagination is Fancy set at liberty—it sees, it feels, though vaguely; these feelings are, indeed, like shadows compared with those we experience in our intercourse with men, and in those moments when we feel ourselves nearer the All-creator. Now let us ask ourselves, which of these three elements predominate in Mendelssohn. I think the answer must be the fanciful and the imaginative, though the emotional is far from being absent. Mendelssohn was a man of feeling, but his feelings were rather refined than deep. His temper pointed rather to the tender than the pathetic. When he depicts the deeper passions he seems to speak from hearsay—not from experience, not instinctively. His pathos is hollow, it is borrowed. Bach's deep-toned feeling of a simple, trusting faith, Beethoven's daring aspiration and ardent yearning towards the Incomprehensible, Handel's heroic grandeur and noble popularity, were equally foreign to his nature. Thus also, his religious feeling is sincere, as far as it goes, but it does not go far. He is too happy a man to fathom the deep ocean of human passions, to penetrate the boundless infinity of speculation. He sees so many lovely shapes on the surface, hears so many sweet voices around him, awaking in him pictures of beauty and delight that feels not the want of a beyond. He is no prophet, who in words like thunder flashes upon us new truths, recalls old ones, leads us nearer the solution of a problem of existence, reproves us and urges us onward; he is rather a companion whose gentle beauty of thought manner, and feeling, whose harmonious completeness refines, gladdens, and comforts us.

The harmonious inner life of Mendelssohn, of which his works are the reflex, is to a great extent attributable to the favourable circumstances in which he was placed from his cradle onward. These, like the warm rays of the sun, brought forth the precious seed that lay within him. The inner harmony must have also done much to preserve him from many of those adversities that embitter the life of so many artists. For are we not, to some extent at least, as well the shapers of the circumstances in which we live, as they of our character and actions. But although as an artist Mendelssohn cannot but have gained in some respects by these advantages, in other respects he must have lost. If he gained in perspicuity, roundness of form, and serenity of aspect, he lost in depth, height, intensity.

Of Mendelssohn's performances, his overtures are the centre of gravity. Here he had a canvas allowing him full scope to display the luxuriance of his fancy and excellence of his workmanship, give expression to his exquisite sympathy with nature, and yet not so large as to let the absence of the greater passions be too much felt. They represent most distinctly the imaginative element of his music. *Die Hebriden* is perhaps the best specimen of this kind of writing. In the overture to *A Midsummer Night's Dream*, the fanciful predominates.

There is hardly any composer of Mendelssohn's reputation who has written so many pieces from which the emotional element is so wholly absent. Schumann remarks that Mendelssohn often seems to break single bars and even chords from his *Midsummer Night's Dream*, and enlarge upon them and work them out.[5] These pieces have much to remind one of Arab ornament. In both there is the same pleasing lightness, pure elegance, and wonderful ingenuity. These arabesques, whether they lull or gently stimulate our senses, gratify them, but here their influence ceases.

Schumann's criticism of Mendelssohn's sonata, op. 6, is a capital characterization of Mendelssohn's emotional music, his songs with and without words, and those emotional parts of his larger works where he is true to himself and not led by ambition to stretch himself above his natural height. Let me add, to avoid misunderstanding, that his ambition was noble, and combined with such earnestness, mastery of his art, and general culture as to preserve him from complete failure even where he attempted the highest—examples are his oratorios and symphonies. But to return to Schumann's criticism, he writes, "So green, so morning-like, everything as in a spring landscape. What here touches and attracts us is not the strange, the new, but even the dear, the accustomed. Nothing places itself above us, nothing will surprise us, only the right words are lent to our feelings, so that we imagine we have found them ourselves."[6] I do not remember that Schumann on any occasion used stronger expressions in speaking of Mendelssohn's emotional music, unless it be the following: "This song is impassioned, if one may say so of the rarer emotions of a beautiful heart."[7]

It must be confessed that the serene beauty of Mendelssohn's music has to most of us not the same charm as the rugged energy, the subtle thoughtfulness and morbid world-weariness of other composers. As the Romans of old took delight in the struggle and writhing agony of the gladiator, so we of the present day enjoy watching the beats and throes of the human heart as exhibited by our tone and word poets, the gladiators of modern times.

In the closing part of these remarks, I wish to draw your attention to the three critics before alluded to, and to show that their estimate, apparently wide apart, is in reality the same on all principal points. These men are Schumann (in "Gesammelte Schriften"),[8] Wagner ("Le Judaïsme dans la musique"),[9] and Liszt ("Des Bohémiens et de leur musique").[10] In comparing these critiques we must take into account the individuality of the writers, their different standpoints and aims, as well as the circumstances under which these works were written. Schumann welcomes Mendelssohn as an ally against those unprincipled composers who infested the musical literature of the time, men to whom art was but "the good cow that provides them with butter," whilst Mendelssohn had shown himself a true artist to whom she is "the divine goddess." Although Schumann never censures him, the absence of praise and sometimes even the very words of praise, show that he also felt that a something was wanting. Schumann has been already quoted so often that very little need be added. He is very warm in his expressions of praise, but, no doubt, also sincere. If proof were wanted, his later works and the marks they bear of Mendelssohn's influence would be a satisfactory one. He calls Mendelssohn "the most cultivated artist-nature of our time," and speaks of him as "the Mozart of the 19th century, the brightest musician who penetrates the contradictions of our time."[11] Query: Did he not rather evade these contradictions? He also mentions Mendelssohn's struggles, but I fail to perceive any sign of them.

In reading Wagner, we must keep in mind that he was no personal friend of Mendelssohn's—Schumann was—that he wrote five years after Mendelssohn's death, and lastly, that having revolutionized a great province of his art, he met with a strong opposition, which made the name of Mendelssohn one of its battle-cries. His language is, like that of all reformers, bold, unsparing, and at times exaggerated. "In Mendelssohn," he writes, "we recognise that a Jew may be endowed with the greatest and most beautiful talent; that he may have received the most careful and extensive education, that he may have the greatest and noblest ambition, without being able, with the help of all these advantages, to succeed a single time in producing on our mind and heart that deep impression which we expect in music; of which we know it to be capable, having so often experienced it, as soon as a hero of our art lets a single of his accents be heard." In another place we read:—"This series of the choicest, subtlest, and most artistically executed forms amused us, as the combination of colours of a kaleidoscope, but our higher musical feeling was never satisfied when these forms were to express the deep and strong feelings of the human heart."[12]

Liszt stands, as it were, between these two, and may be expected to be more impartial, as he was not under the immediate influence of Mendelssohn, and on the other hand is of a more tolerant and catholic nature. But let it be understood that Liszt speaks of the Jews in general, not of Mendelssohn in particular, though there is little doubt he had Mendelssohn in his mind. "Faire de l'art, et même en bien faire, n'est cependant pas encore posséder le don suprême de créer" [To make art, and even to make it well, is, nevertheless, still not to possess the supreme gift to create]. He thinks that the Jews do not possess this creative faculty, but that nevertheless they served the art well, and adds—"Who knows where the musical art would still be in our day? Who knows whether the genius of the great masters would be better understood now than in their lifetime, without the insinuating, enterprising, bold and persevering spirit of the members of that nation?" Again, "They have known always to do well, and often better, what others have done before them."[13]

These extracts speak for themselves, and will afford some aid in forming an opinion of Mendelssohn. By pointing out his weakness they caution us not *to be blinded by* his brilliant qualities, by extolling his strength not *to be blind* to them.

To the disparager of Mendelssohn let me say this—shall a man forego his due share of our esteem and praise, because he has trodden ground over which others have passed more heroically? Shall we ignore his many excellencies, because he does not possess all? Need we be blind to the grace of Correggio, because we think Raphael and Michael Angelo artists of greater power and higher aims? Correggio is said to have exclaimed on looking at a picture of Raphael's—"Anch' io sono pittore" [I too am a painter]. He was right. Mendelssohn might have used the words of a similar purport, on hearing a symphony of Beethoven's. Art is wide, there is room for all that are true to her, for all that serve her, not themselves. Such an artist was Mendelssohn. Therefore—honour to him!

NOTES

1. *Neue Zeitschrift für Musik* 20 (1844): 7. [ed.]

2. Leigh Hunt, "In Answer to the Question: What is Poetry?" Introduction to *Imagination and Fancy* (London, 1844). [ed.]

3. William Blake, Annotations to Sir Joshua Reynolds, *Discourses on Art*, 5. I am indebted to Professor Robert Gleckner of Duke University for this identification. [ed.]

4. John Ruskin, *The Works*, ed. E. T. Cook and A.D.O. Wedderburn (London, 1902–1912), vol. 4, p. 288. *Modern Painters* (1846), vol. 2. [ed.]

5. *NZfM* 20 (1844): 7. [ed.]

6. *NZfM* 3 (1835): 208. [ed.]

7. *NZfM* 7 (1837): 58. [ed.]

8. Robert Schumann, *Gesammelte Schriften über Musik und Musiker* (Leipzig, 1854). [ed.]

9. Freigedank [Richard Wagner], "Das Judenthum in der Musik," in *NZfM* 33 (1850): 101–7, 109–12. [ed.]

10. Franz Liszt, *Des Bohémiens et de leur musique en Hongrie* (Paris, 1859; Leipzig, 1881). [ed.]

11. *NZfM* 13 (1840): 198. [ed.]

12. Wagner, p. 107. [ed.]

13. Liszt, pp. 57, 63. On the question of Liszt's authorship, see Emile Haraszti, "Liszt—Author Despite Himself," in *Musical Quarterly* 33 (1947): 490–516; and Edward N. Waters, "Chopin by Liszt," in ibid., 47 (1961): 170–94. [ed.]

Felix Mendelssohn

HANS VON BÜLOW

TRANSLATED BY SUSAN GILLESPIE

Perhaps more than any other major musical figure from the second half of the nineteenth century, the pianist-conductor Hans von Bülow (1830–1894) found himself at the center of debate about German music and aesthetics. His early musical training included the study of piano with Friedrich Wieck and of counterpoint with Moritz Hauptmann in Leipzig, where he had opportunities to attend Mendelssohn's concerts. But by 1851, von Bülow was a devoted disciple of Liszt in Weimar, and in 1857, he married Liszt's daughter Cosima. In 1864 von Bülow was established as the court orchestra conductor in Munich, where he premièred Wagner's *Tristan und Isolde* and *Die Meistersinger von Nürnberg*. In 1869, Cosima left him for Wagner; after a series of concert tours (including an American tour in 1875 and 1876, during which he gave the première of Tchaikovsky's First Piano Concerto in Boston), von Bülow assumed the position of music director for the duke of Meiningen (1880–1885). During the Meiningen period, von Bülow turned his attention to the music of Johannes Brahms. The following article appeared in 1880 as a preface to von Bülow's edition of Mendelssohn's *Rondo capriccioso*, op. 14. [ed.]

[Source: Hans von Bülow, *Briefe und Schriften* (Leipzig, 1896), vol. 5, pp. 206–9.]

·

Only a very few works for piano in the *stilo galante* have managed to remain so fresh and blooming, so reliably not "out of fashion" despite the passage of more than half a century, as Mendelssohn's *Rondo capriccioso* (composed in 1824[1]). With the possible exception of Weber's *Invitation*,[2] with which it shares comparable charm and originality of

invention while betraying a much greater—as it were, an absolute—
mastery of form, style, and appropriateness for the piano, there is—
and this is completely justified—no other nearly so beloved, ubiquitous possession of the educated dilettante. There is scarcely a piano
teacher alive who would dare to strike it from the program of his
teaching material—a fate to which the favorites of the previous generation, Dussek's *Consolation*[3] and even Hummel's *Bella capricciosa*,[4]
are, for most part, gradually beginning to succumb. The inner value
of the composition (stemming from that youthful period of the master, in which—so characteristic of his individuality and its regressive
development—the most genuine productivity was paired with the
most conscious maturity), its general usefulness for the formation of
taste and technique, justify conservative desires in this regard, a view
that in our opinion must be supported by every objectively thinking
musician, inclusive of all teaching *sufferers* for whom the more-or-less
tortuous tinkling on the part of their students has transformed "Mendelssohn op. 14" into a *bête noire*. Our task is a dual one: first, to fa-
cilitate performance study for the teacher or autodidact; and then to
protect the content of .this valuable composition from the threat of
untimely aging.

As a boy in the years 1844–1846, the editor frequently had the
good fortune to hear the master play the piano (and organ) in private
circles, and also to hear him direct rehearsals of the Gewandhaus
concerts. Finally he enjoyed the greater honor that the master con-
descended, with rare patience, to offer him a lesson of several hours'
duration on the performance of opp. 14 and 22 (Capriccio in B minor with orchestral accompaniment)[5]—two works that despite their
great diversity of invention are closely related in form and style. The
impressions gained in this wise—the force of the master's enchanting
personality helped counteract the relative immaturity of the accidental student—have understandably continued to stick in his mind:
most vividly those negative prohibitions that, by clearing out misunderstandings, open the way for the true understanding that can only
come from within, and will ultimately prove to be the most productive. Before we come to recount the most essential of these, an explanation is required as to what we mean by the threat of untimely aging
of Mendelssohn's music.

His music was faced with a similar threat once before. It was at one
time thoroughly "out of fashion," for example in Germany and its
musical metropolis Vienna (the German Reich does not have anything comparable). In the 1860s Schumann-mania had completely replaced the Felix-fanaticism that had flourished just as exclusively ten

years previously, before local patriotism enthroned Schubert as Beethoven II—for how long is a matter that need not concern us here.
This fact has a deeper significance only insofar as it indicates—as may
be substantiated elsewhere—that the "romanticizing" of the musical
public by the muse of Schumann (a fair portion of Chopin, and not
exactly the best part, was also involved here) rendered it ill-disposed
to and estranged from the muse of Mendelssohn. This came about in
a very straightforward way. Whoever plays Schumann tolerably well
will play Mendelssohn rather intolerably; the matter goes somewhat
better in reverse. S. is a sentimental poet; M. a naive one: one could,
cum grano salis, go on in an aestheticizing vein to explore in the two
composers the contradiction between Nazarenes and Greeks from
various points of view.

Now, "sentimentality" in the field of poetry is admittedly no vice:
after all, Schiller recognized this characteristic as belonging to the Roman in contrast to the Greek poets.[6] But an all-too-diligent occupation with the "sentimental" masters does not merely cloud one's understanding of the "naive" ones, it makes them quite unpalatable.
The whole gamut of feelings that are generated and nourished by
enthusiasm for the "sentimental" artists mentioned above will, if
transferred to the works of the "naive" ones, make them shallow, boring, sober, contentless—in short, insufferable. Mendelssohn, played
in the same style (if in view of the preponderance of arbitrary subjectivity one is still justified in speaking of style) as one not only may but
sometimes must play Schumann (there are exceptions, such as the
Schumann Piano Concerto, absolutely his most perfect work), produces a distortion that is all the more disagreeable because nothing
that comes of it can even approximate the appreciation of his greatest
virtues, namely purity and beauty of form. One plays into Mendelssohn things that are completely foreign to him; and plays out of him
the things that constitute his greatest virtue.

If one wants to play Mendelssohn correctly, one should first play
Mozart, for example. Above all, one should renounce all *Empfind-
samkeit*[7] of conception, despite the temptations that are provided by
certain frequently recurring melismas peculiar to Mendelssohn. One
should try, for example, to play passages of this apparent character
simply and naturally in rhythm, with a beautiful and regular attack,
and one will surely find that they will sound, in this fashion, much
nobler and more graceful than in a passionately excited rubato. The
master was committed, above all, to the strict observance of meter.
He categorically denied himself every ritardando that was not prescribed and wanted to see the prescribed ritards restricted to their

least possible extent. He despised, furthermore, all arbitrary arpeggiation (chords that could not be played without breaking them, à la Schumann, he did not write, or only when he wanted successive chords—see the introduction to op. 22).[8] In op. 14 there is not a single arpeggio mark, despite the "brilliant" style. He permitted the use of the pedal only for certain tonal effects. What subtle caution was to be exercised in this matter can be gleaned from his specification of the appropriate symbols throughout. Finally, he also protested against that "thrilling" haste, against the rushing and forcing of his pieces by players who believed that the best way they could meet the charge of "sentimental" interpretation was through this kind of speeded-up, summary behavior. Here we must nonetheless observe very decisively that his most frequent comments while teaching were "lively, briskly, keep going . . ." and that the tempi of these pieces are usually taken much too slowly by today's conductors. The correct tradition for the tempo of the *Scottish* Symphony, which in northern Germany is usually dragged out, exists since David's[9] death in Leipzig only in Vienna, where it was planted through the influence of Mendelssohn's student Carl Eckert, also recently deceased.[10]

The study of Mendelssohn's piano music will prove more productive for utmost refinement of attack and movement, to the degree that the limits of purity in his markings are strictly observed; and if it is scarcely possible that a pianist should appear among us who would be capable in the case of the all too well known *Frühlingslied*[11] without words of producing a showpiece of such grace, unaffected naturalness, and artistic refinement as the master himself in performance, still this study will always lead to a more "musical" music making than tinkling away at Schumann, which significantly encourages melancholy and pathological effusiveness.

NOTES

1. The *Rondo capriccioso* originally consisted of the E-minor portion, which was conceived as an étude in 1828 (not 1824). Mendelssohn's first autograph, dated 4 January 1828, survives in the Pierpont Morgan Library, New York. For a facsimile, see R. Larry Todd, "Piano Music Reformed: The Case of Felix Mendelssohn Bartholdy," in *Nineteenth-Century Piano Music*, ed. R. L. Todd (New York, 1990), p. 211. In 1830 Mendelssohn reworked the étude and added the lyrical Andante in E major. This second autograph, in the Bibliothèque Nationale, Paris, was dated in Munich on 13 June. The work then appeared as op. 14 in 1830. [ed.]

2. The famous *Invitation to the Dance* (*Aufforderung zum Tanze*) of 1819. Berlioz later made an orchestral arrangement of Weber's piano work. [ed.]

3. J. L. Dussek, *La Consolation* in B♭ major, op. 62 (1807). [ed.]

4. J. N. Hummel, *Polonaise la bella capricciosa* in B♭ major, op. 55 (ca. 1811–1815). [ed.]

5. *Capriccio brillant* for piano and orchestra, op. 22 (1832). [ed.]

6. Von Bülow refers to Friedrich Schiller's famous distinction between "naive" and "sentimental" poetry in his essay "Über naive und sentimentalische Dichtung" (1795-1796). The essential difference is in the self-reflexive character of the sentimental poet and his works. [trans.]

7. A style and movement emphasizing sentimentalized feelings that became prevalent in the early eighteenth-century literature of Pietism. [trans.]

8. In the opening measures of the *Capriccio brillant* the piano presents a sustained treble melody accompanied by rolled, punctuated chords, an effect similar to the piano entrance in Carl Maria von Weber's *Konzertstück* for piano and orchestra in F minor (1821). [ed.]

9. Ferdinand David (1810–1873), violinist and composer, concertmaster of the Gewandhaus orchestra in Leipzig. [ed.]

10. Carl Eckert (1820–1879), violinist and pianist. [ed.]

11. Op. 62, no. 6. [ed.]

Index of
Names and Compositions

List of Contributors

Leon Botstein, President of Bard College, is the author of *Music and Its Public: Habits of Listening and the Crisis of Modernism in Vienna, 1870–1914*, forthcoming from the University of Chicago Press. He has contributed to the *New Republic*, *19th-Century Music*, and the *Musical Quarterly*, and is the conductor of the Hudson Valley Philharmonic Chamber Orchestra and the American Symphony.

David Brodbeck is Assistant Professor of Music at the University of Pittsburgh. He has served as Vice President of the American Brahms Society since 1985 and is the author of numerous articles on the works of Brahms and Schubert.

Susan Gillespie is Vice President for Public Affairs and Development at Bard College, where she has also taught German poetry. Her published translations of German works include several that appeared in *Brahms and His World*, edited by Walter Frisch (Princeton, 1990).

Wm. A. Little is Professor of German at the University of Virginia. He is the author of *Gottfried August Bürger* (New York, 1974); the editor of the historical-critical edition of Felix Mendelssohn-Bartholdy's complete works for organ (London, 1987–1990); and the former editor of the *German Quarterly*.

Nancy B. Reich has written and lectured extensively on music and musicians of the nineteenth century. She is the author of *Clara Schumann: The Artist and the Woman* (Ithaca, 1985). She will join the faculty of Bard College as Visiting Professor in 1991–1992.

Claudio Spies is a composer and Professor of Music at Princeton University. He is the author of numerous articles on the works of Stravinsky. His compositions are published primarily by Boosey and Hawkes, Elkan Vogel, and Presser.

Martin Staehelin, Professor of Musicology at the University of Göttingen, has served as director of the Beethoven-Archiv and the Beethoven-Haus in Bonn. He is the editor of *H. Issac: Messen* (Mainz, 1970–) and in 1976 he won the Edward J. Dent medal for musicology.

Michael P. Steinberg is Assistant Professor of History at Cornell University. He is the author of *The Meaning of the Salzburg Festival: Austria as Theater and Ideology, 1890–1938* (Ithaca, 1990).

R. Larry Todd, Professor and Director of Graduate Studies in Music at Duke University, is the author of *Mendelssohn's Musical Education* (Cambridge, 1983); the editor of *Nineteenth-Century Piano Music* (New York, 1990); and the co-editor of *Mendelssohn and Schumann: Essays on Their Music and Its Context* (Durham, N.C., 1984) and *Perspectives on Mozart Performance* (Cambridge, 1991).